Colonial Cinema in Africa

Colonial Cinema in Africa

Origins, Images, Audiences

GLENN REYNOLDS

McFarland & Company, Inc., Publishers
Jefferson, North Carolina

LIBRARY OF CONGRESS CATALOGUING-IN-PUBLICATION DATA

Reynolds, Glenn.
Colonial cinema in Africa : origins, images, audiences / Glenn Reynolds.
      p.   cm.
Includes bibliographical references and index.
Includes filmography.

ISBN 978-0-7864-7985-6 (softcover : acid free paper) ∞
ISBN 978-1-4766-2054-1 (ebook)

1. Foreign films—Africa—History.   2. Motion pictures—Africa—History and criticism.   3. Motion picture industry—Africa—History—20th century.   4. Africa—In motion pictures.   5. Africans in motion pictures.   6. Imperialism in motion pictures.   7. Colonies in motion pictures.   I. Title.

PN1993.5.A35R49 2015   791.43096—dc23   2015016756

BRITISH LIBRARY CATALOGUING DATA ARE AVAILABLE

© 2015 Glenn Reynolds. All rights reserved

No part of this book may be reproduced or transmitted in any form or by any means, electronic or mechanical, including photocopying or recording, or by any information storage and retrieval system, without permission in writing from the publisher.

On the cover: Meru porters in the employ of Martin and Osa Johnson, on expedition in Kenya, 1921 (courtesy of the American Museum of Natural History); *background* Mount Kilimanjaro; savanna in Amboseli, Kenya (iStock/Thinkstock)

Printed in the United States of America

McFarland & Company, Inc., Publishers
Box 611, Jefferson, North Carolina 28640
www.mcfarlandpub.com

This book is dedicated to Kent Berkeley Reynolds.
He always drummed to a different beat.

Acknowledgments

In the long and arduous process of bringing a book to fruition, authors invariably receive critical assistance from a long list of people who contributed in one way or another. Although the following acknowledgments are incomplete, I would be remiss if I failed to extend my gratitude to some of these individuals and institutions. Numerous staff members at libraries and archives have been enormously helpful, including private and public institutions in the United States, Britain, South Africa, Zambia and Kenya. I would like to extend special thanks to those who assisted me at the Human Studies Film Archives and the American Museum of Natural History, as well as to Mount Saint Mary College, which provided me with a research grant. This project began some years ago at SUNY Stony Brook, and thus my dissertation advisors—Wilbur Miller, John Williams and Nancy Tomes—were important players as it evolved in the early stages. I have profited from the advice and collegiality of a number of scholars, including, among others, James Burns, Guido Convents, Charles Ambler, Rosaleen Smyth, Neil Parsons, and Tali Keren.

I gratefully acknowledge permission granted by Taylor & Francis (www.tandfonline.com) to draw significantly from my previously published articles: Chapter 3 appeared in modified form as "Image and Empire: Anglo-American Cinematic Interventions in Sub-Saharan Africa, 1921–1937," *South African Historical Journal* 48, 1 (2003), 90–108; Chapter 4 derives from "'Playing Cowboys and Africans': Hollywood and the Cultural Politics of African Identity," *Historical Journal of Film, Radio and Television* (August 2005), 399–426; Chapter 5 originally appeared as "'From Red Blanket to Civilization': Propaganda-Recruitment Films for South Africa's Gold Mines, 1920–1940," *Journal of Southern African Studies* (March 2007), 133–152; and Chapter 7 was first published as "The Bantu Educational Kinema Experiment and the Struggle for Hegemony in British East and Southern Africa, 1937–39," *Historical Journal of Film, Radio and Television* (March 2009), 57–78.

I am deeply appreciative of the long-term support of my parents, Charles and Berkeley Reynolds, who always humored me and my siblings in our childhood as we produced "Grade C" horror movies, built haunted houses, constructed elaborate tree forts, and even became magicians and private eyes. In the final analysis, though, this project was only possible through the infinite patience of my immediate family, and I would like to send out a loving "thank you" to my wonderful daughters, Amelia and Miranda, and my dear wife, Melissa. More than anyone, they were on the frontlines as I struggled in my "office" (dining table) at home to finally realize this book project. While I thank all of the above, I should note that any mistakes in the text are those of the author alone.

Table of Contents

Acknowledgments	vi
Preface	1
Introduction: Flash Forward: A Century of Cinema in Africa	3
1. In Search of Origins: Screening Motion Pictures in Africa	17
2. The Scramble for Images: Strange Savages, Paid Primitives, Negotiating Natives	39
3. Silver Screens and Cities of Gold and Copper: The Mines' Compound Cinema Circuit	86
4. You Don't Know Jack: Hollywood, Hybridity and the African Cowboy	115
5. From Red Blanket to Civilization: Movies and Migration in South Africa	131
6. Image Imperium: The Origins of British Film Policy in Africa	153
7. Films of Africans, Made in Africa, for Africans, Under Effective Control: The Bantu Educational Kinema Experiment	171
Conclusion: From Reel to Real: New Horizons	197
Chapter Notes	203
Bibliography	227
Index	231

Preface

In 2002 I boarded a bus in Lusaka, the capital of Zambia, and headed north toward the Copperbelt. Surprisingly, this stretch of copper-rich land on Zambia's border adjoining the Democratic Republic of the Congo played an important role in the early evolution of cinema in Africa. Equally surprising, perhaps, was that this bus defied the usual horrific stereotypes of Third World travel. Rather than some antiquated, rusty rattletrap hurtling along the highway, skirting Lusaka's seemingly endless corrugated shanties, the bus was a smooth-running, pristine vehicle catering to the Zambian middle class. The bus service provided twice-daily trips along the only two-lane expressway leading north out of Lusaka to Ndola, stopping at small, rural rest areas along the way.

As a scholar tracing the origins of cinema in Africa, I was intrigued when, several minutes into the trip, a generous number of overhead flip-down video monitors suddenly appeared. What visual fare, I wondered, would be served up for passenger consumption as the bus made its way along the sparsely settled rural landscape of what four decades earlier was still the British colony of Northern Rhodesia? Ironically, I soon found myself confronted not by the shock of the "exotic" but rather the shock of the familiar. For the first film screened was *Home Alone 2: Lost in New York* (1992), starring Macauley Culkin. Vertigo-inducing, the film's setting ripped me out of Africa's embrace and temporarily escorted me back to the familiar streets of my home base. The second film was equally unnerving, with its plotline of a mysterious über-criminal determined to wreak havoc on the world with a home-bred army of Ninjas who killed without remorse. To see a movie in Central Africa as vacuous as *American Ninja 2: The Confrontation* (1987), starring Michael Dudikoff, so soon after the global game-changer known as 9/11, left me in a state of stunned disbelief.

On a different level, though, the fact that these particular films were being shown on the Zambian bus line—or the fact that any films at all were being shown—spoke volumes. For rather than viewing the fruit of independent African filmmakers already blossoming in Senegal, Nigeria, Mali and elsewhere, what bus passengers were in fact experiencing was the terminal point of global film distribution—what businessmen refer to as the "channels of allocation," bringing the often-dubious products of the Hollywood fantasy factory right into the heart of Africa.

In some ways, the institutionalization and routinization of these film showings on the bus line constituted a clear departure from the first half of the 20th century, when mobile cinema vans with generators only occasionally snaked their way through the African bush, and excited villagers flocked for miles to view films under starry skies. Passengers on the bus in Zambia, in contrast, displayed little anticipation and mostly watched with a bemused and detached interest. This poignant cultural shift from the colonial to the post-colonial era points to other problems for the modern researcher: while some scholars have conducted interviews with aging Africans to secure their reminiscences about film showings in the colonial period, this is made more difficult by the fact that Africa has the lowest median age, by far, of any continent in the world. Moreover, memories fade and stories change for those few who actually helped to swell colonial-era audiences before the 1960s.

If my experience on the bus, casually watching Hollywood productions deep in the heart of Africa, mostly contrasted with the past, in one important way it echoed what has always been the case—that Western interests, with key exceptions (such as the recent Nollywood explosion in Nigeria), have generally controlled most of the levers of motion picture production and distribution.[1] Ultimately, what became apparent in Zambia was that Africans approximately a half century after independence still lacked the political and economic muscle to assume control over the transnational flow of images, even in the deep recesses of the continent. Indeed, it was deeply telling to me on the bus in Zambia that the titles of the two films I was viewing referenced New York and America explicitly. And it is precisely for this reason that the evolution of the independent cinema sector in Africa has been inflected with a heightened political dimension unique to its colonial legacy. For earlier colonial governments, and later transnational interests as well, it had always been imperative to retain hegemony over both image-making and distribution, just as it became equally pressing for African filmmakers to "decolonize the image" after independence and produce indigenous films that would belatedly present sympathetic portrayals of African life.

In recent decades, African historians have begun to unpack the deeper underpinnings of colonial rule, moving beyond an earlier focus on the structures of political and military occupation, to more subtle investigations into the deeper tentacles of imperial power that undergirded the fields of medicine, religion, and culture. Yet despite this fact, due to the sheer size of the continent, the number of European interests involved, and the difficulty in securing information, to date no single text has appeared to provide an overview of the introduction of cinema into Africa as a whole. A daunting task, this book thus begins as something of a synthesis building upon a number of regional studies of the early years of cinema in the continent, both in terms of exhibition and production. Yet through research at numerous archives on three continents, and tapping an array of previously unexamined material, I expand upon these able studies to trace the impact of film and filmmaking in the African interior, and explore the evolution of black spectatorship from its earliest manifestations before World War I to several interwar projects that targeted Africans as cinema consumers for a variety of purposes. As such, this book constitutes the first broad study of the origins of cinema in Africa, looking at how images and audiences were interwoven into the broader tapestry of colonial power in Africa in the many decades before independence.

Introduction

Flash-Forward: A Century of Cinema in Africa

Flash-Forward: The Politics and Promise of Post-Colonial African Cinema

An important trend in African cinema studies is the exploration of the maturing indigenous film industry and the effort to chart its future—especially given the dynamics of the relatively new commercial video format so popular in the streets of Nigerian cities—in a world where global film distribution is still largely controlled by the West. Consequently, both postcolonial filmmaking and scholarship on the nascent industry have decidedly political overtones, as producers, directors and academics challenge the celluloid stereotypes of African life that were so pervasive and pernicious during the colonial era between the Scramble for Africa (roughly 1880–1914) and the independence era (roughly 1957–1966).

The origins of this phenomenon were not unique, but were, rather, part of a rethinking of global power relations that included efforts elsewhere to wrest control over the technologies of cultural representation. To this end, Argentinian filmmakers Fernando Solanas and Octavio Getino threw down the gauntlet in 1969 with their essay "Towards a Third Cinema," which called for a cultural revolution to complement the revolutionary ardor sweeping developing areas around the world.[1] Far from critiquing the medium as such, in their ringing manifesto cinema was (re)conceived as a critical technology in need of liberation from "bourgeois mystification." In an African context, James Genova has recently reminded us that contemporary African critiques of colonial cinema were similarly restricted to content, for in terms of form, "The first filmmakers in postcolonial West Africa did not attach inherent moral attributes to the tools associated with film but instead viewed them as the patrimony of mankind."[2] Thus, in a conscious attempt to distance their films from the products imported from the West, the filmmakers put these tools to use in a variety of ways, developing plotlines that included, 1) critiques of European colonialism; 2) examinations of the African diaspora; 3) the interplay between traditional African culture and modernity; and 4) lyrical treatments of time-honored African themes and rich oral history. Collectively, these thematic templates exemplified the desire to move from in front of the camera, where "Africans were being filmed and being told what to do and how to do it," to a new position behind the camera in their search for what one scholar referred to as "a useable identity."[3]

Given the potency of visual representation—both in its visceral appeal and its function as a handmaiden to colonial forms of power and knowledge—it was no accident that fearful European colonial administrators in the first half of the 20th century had intentionally restricted the development of a class of African directors. What Matthew Stanard has recently claimed for the Democratic Republic of the Congo at mid-century could equally be said of other colonial regimes of the time: "The administration's control over motion pictures and other information was a way in which they could conceal conflicts and project an image of stability."[4] Although a few Africans were, in fact, sporadically handling cameras or otherwise assisting film crews before independence—an important phenomenon often overlooked today and an issue to which I return—these individuals were never given the chance to fully develop their own film stories and were never in complete control of the medium until the push for independence.

Thus, the earliest cohort of indigenous filmmakers on the continent did not truly appear until after World War II, when a new Congolese Ciné Club in Leopoldville bore fruit with student films by Albert Mongita and Emmanuel Lubalu, entitled *La Leçon de cinéma* (*The Cinema Lesson*, 1951), and *Les Pneus gonflés* (*Inflated Tires*, 1953), respectively. The Guinean Mamadou Touré also produced a film in 1953, entitled *Mouramani*, detailing the relationship between a dog and his owner.

In 1955, African filmmaking went transnational when the diasporic African experience became the subject of the ground-breaking film *Afrique-sur-Seine* (*Africa on the Seine*) by Paulin Vieyra. Born in the small West African country of Benin, Vieyra had been sent abroad by his family to attend a boarding school in France as a young man. In the movie houses of Paris he was introduced to the ubiquitous Western genre and the comedies of Charlie Chaplin. By the early 1950s Vieyra's interests had shifted from Biology to Film Studies, and he enrolled at *L'Institut des hautes études cinématographiques* (Institute for Advanced Cinematographic Studies), the leading state-run film school in Paris, established in 1943 by Marcel L'Herbier. With funding from the Musée de l'Homme's Committee of Ethnographic Film, Vieyra detailed in his short 21-minute film the cultural alienation experienced by African workers, artists and students living in Paris, a theme that contrasted with more popular films that stereotypically portrayed Africans as exotic Others in impenetrable jungles.[5]

Another remarkable figure in the African filmmaking diaspora during this period was Lionel Ngakane, who had worked on (and acted in) Zoltan Korda's *Cry the Beloved Country* (1952), a cinematic adaptation of the Alan Paton novel that follows a black Anglican priest as he searches for his son. Ngakane was born in Pretoria and spent decades outside of South Africa, yet directed *Vukani* (*Awake*, 1962), a ringing critique of the apartheid system and the first film by a black South African to be made on a South African subject. In 1977, Ngakane moved to Senegal, where he accepted the position of director of Golden Baobab Entertainment, and soon became a regional secretary for the Pan-African Federation of Filmmakers (FEPACI).[6] Following the dismantling of South Africa's apartheid regime in the 1990s, he returned to his ancestral home, promoted new township cinemas and served on the Council of the National Film and Video Foundation before his death in 2003.[7]

In a cross-racial phenomenon that speaks even more directly to the revolutionary potential of motion pictures during African struggles for independence, an alliance of Algerian rebels and French sympathizers formed an independent film unit known as *Groupe Farid* during the Algerian anti-colonial war that commenced in 1954. Young French filmmaker René Vautier was a founding member and had traveled to Niger several years before on assignment to tout the work of *La Ligue de l'Enseignement* (the League of Schooling).

What he saw repelled him. As a result, instead of lauding the thin veneer of French civilizing efforts he filmed exactly what he saw—a deplorable physical infrastructure coupled with brutal counterinsurgency measures implemented by the French military against a burgeoning African resistance movement. This brilliant exposé, one of the first truly anti-colonial films made in Africa, would eventually be released as *Afrique 50* (*Africa 50*), although it was promptly suppressed at the time and Vautier was even imprisoned for a short period for violating the 1934 Laval Decree, which restricted unauthorized filmmaking in French-held territories. *Afrique 50* opens with predictable, picturesque scenes of quotidian African life, and then almost imperceptibly pulls the unwitting spectator deeper into the sordid reality of colonial life and a denunciation of the inadequacy of French medical and educational services. The film continues with images of bullet casings littering the ground, African blood splattered on a wall, and concludes with a ringing call to arms. Strident and uncompromising, if one looks closely, even the opening scenes of the film deviate from common ethnographic chronicles of the time. Rather than formulaic celluloid natives dancing on the screen seemingly oblivious to the presence of the camera, the countergaze is fully operational as a voice-over referring to the "curiosity" of Africans accompanies shots of a young African boy staring confidently into the camera, followed by African children similarly huddled around and looking directly at the aperture, and by extension the viewer himself. Vautier's deconstruction of the normal subject position—in these scenes the observer becomes perilously close to becoming the observed—parallels the film's exposure not so much of the "African Other," but rather the entire edifice of the French colonial system. Certainly ethnographic film scholar Alison Griffith's claim that the "return gaze breaks the circuit of power" between spectator and subject is merited, to the extent that the relative positions of observer and observed are disrupted (but not inverted), and that the engagement of the subjects' eyes with the camera's eye compels an acknowledgment of shared humanity.[8]

The emerging Algerian crisis inspired an undaunted Vautier to film the short *Une Nation, l'Algérie* (*One Nation, Algeria*, 1955), and Cécile Cujis to produce *Les Réfugies* (*The Refugees*, 1956), a film that earned Cujis a two-year detention in France. Under the sponsorship of Abbane Ramdane, who helped spearhead the anti-colonial struggle, the FLN supported *Groupe Farid* with the goal of propagandizing for the independence movement by tapping into an indigenous revolutionary ardor augmented by European activist sympathy.[9] The unit proceeded to send Lakhdar-Hamina to train at a film school in Prague, and oversaw the production of a number of documentaries, including Vautier's *L'Algérie en flammes* (*Algeria in Flames*, 1958), and Pierre Clément's *Sakiet Sidi Youssef* (1958), named for the Tunisian town bombed by French forces in 1958 for reputedly harboring FLN officials.

The medium of motion pictures was similarly deployed for explicitly revolutionary purposes in Rhodesia (now Zimbabwe) with the production of *Rhodesia Countdown* in 1968–69. Born to parents of British and Egyptian ancestry, young filmmaker Michael Raeburn had become increasingly disenchanted with the white minority government that had declared its independence from Britain in 1965. Raeburn confesses that his 35-minute film was a cry to arms utilizing every trick he learned in film school, and was fully intended as a "satire of [Prime Minister] Ian Smith, making him look completely ridiculous." As such, Raeburn quickly became *persona non grata* and Rhodesian authorities tried to prevent distribution of the film. Nevertheless, *Rhodesia Countdown* was spirited out of the country and shown at Cannes, among other film festivals, while within Rhodesia itself prints circulated the guerrilla camps of the Zambian African People's Union (ZAPU) during the height of the Bush War.[10]

As many African nations gained control over the instruments of governance in the 1960s, so, too, did Africans begin to exert increasing control over the technologies of representation. This shift was facilitated in part by French filmmaker Jean Rouch, who had both revolutionized and institutionalized ethnographic filmmaking after serving as a civil engineer in Niger in the 1940s. Rouch began filming the spirit-possession rituals and other social practices of the Sorko, Zarma and Songhay peoples who lived in proximity to the Niger River, and eventually formed the Institut de la Recherche en Sciences Humaines (IRSH) to archive the traditions of West African cultures. His role in launching a film institute in Niamey cemented his place in African film history as a key transitional figure nestled uneasily between the colonial period and independence. Through Rouch's encouragement, Oumarou Ganda, Safi Faye, Inoussa Ousseini, and Africa's first animator, Moustapha Alassane, began their pioneering careers in indigenous West African cinema.

In 1963, a forty-year-old Senegalese author named Ousmane Sembène, from the southern commercial hub of Casamance, produced *Borom Sarret (The Wagoner)*, an 18-minute film that has since been rightly crowned an early masterpiece of African cinema. In part, Sembène's shift from written forms of expression to a visual medium was due to the high illiteracy rate in Senegal, coupled with his appreciation for the strong appeal of popular cinema among the local population. After a brief period of film training in the Soviet Union in 1962, Sembène returned to Senegal, started his own production company and began work on his film. Produced in Wolof and French with English subtitles, *Borom Sarret* was important in that it targeted African audiences primarily, yet could also lay claim as the first truly African film distributed outside the continent. Through deft editing and subtle narrative, this short black-and-white film chronicled a day in the life of a simple African cart driver in Dakar struggling to earn his keep in the modern world. Eschewing "exotic" Africa in favor of confronting head-on the social realities of post-colonial Senegal, the film provides stark visual contrasts of life in the early independence period between the impoverished masses—including a crawling street beggar—and the sophisticated urban elite. A griot's contemplations in the film powerfully evoke the African ancestral past while expressing Sembène's deep ambivalence about the trappings of modernity thrust upon his people: "Even if this new life enslaves me, I am still noble."[11]

Sembène's later film *Emitaï* (1971) spoke even more directly to the theme of European-African relations through its forceful critique of French colonialism. In contrast to earlier pre-independence era films made by Europeans that glorified the civilizing mission in Africa, *Emitaï* instead re-enacted the brutality of a 1942 massacre of Africans in the village of Effok by Vichy-era French troops.[12] In the film, we see young villagers forced into military service, followed by women who later hide the local rice crop from French forces intent on impounding it. Despite an intervention by African religious elites, soldiers eventually open fire to suppress native resistance, fatally wounding dozens of men, women and children in the process. The artistry and political engagement of Vieyra, Ngakane, Faye, Alassane, Sembène and others helped generate a politically engaged African film industry both on the continent and beyond. The Mauritanian filmmaker Med Hondo (Mohamed Abid Hondo), for instance, released *Soleil Ô (Oh, Sun)* in 1967, eight years after migrating to France. The winner of the Golden Leopard award at the 1970 Locarno Film Festival, the film resonates with Vieyra's earlier *Afrique-sur-Seine* in its depiction of the discrimination and marginalization experienced by West African immigrants in Paris. And Flora Gomes from Guinea-Bissau in his 1988 film, *Mortu Nega (Death Denied)*, portrayed graphically the armed struggle for liberation in the colony a decade and a half earlier.[13] The uncompromising stance and the willingness to tackle the uncomfortable realities of the African experience, both in the colonial period and beyond, has thus characterized much of African cinema.

The push to promote an African corps of filmmakers during the independence era was a key catalyst in the creation of FESPACO (Festival Panafricain du Cinéma et de la Télévision de Ouagadougou) in Burkina Faso in 1969. Now Africa's largest film festival, FESPACO was founded in part through the efforts of Alimata Salambare, and has stimulated significant international interest and is rightly a source of pride for those in the industry. Yet, even here, we can see the heavily politicized nature of this putatively cultural enterprise, for the organizing committee eventually began promoting a unifying theme for each festival, with the first slogan in 1985 establishing a link between "The Cinema, People and Liberation."

While FESPACO cultivated a mostly continental focus, some countries after independence took the initiative to jump-start their own domestic film industries, with Nigeria as a case in point. Following years of relative inaction, in October 1982 the government realized the Nigerian Film Corporation, authorized by Decree No. 61 three years earlier. Among other goals, the NFC sought to "produce films for domestic use and export; establish and maintain facilities for film production; and acquire and distribute films."[14] Accordingly, the NFC nurtured a nationalist vision for Nigerian cinema, encouraging the projection of noble themes to help move the nation beyond earlier crude colonial stereotypes. Yet the subtle cultural elitism guiding the NFC met with stiff resistance through the eruption of the "guerrilla" cinema sector now known as Nollywood. If the mainstream cinema world conjures up visions of red carpet premieres, Nollywood invokes the energy of the street as films go straight to video at Lagos's Alaba International Market, a bustling place "where few laws restrain profiteers, piracy is rampant and all creative calculations yield to the lowest common denominator."[15] And yet the irony of the video revolution in Nigeria is that it was in its earliest manifestation not a grassroots movement, but rather an indirect result of the rampant violence and general sense of insecurity pervasive in both the streets of Lagos and the city's dilapidated, darkened theaters. For this reason, as early as the late 1970s, families with means were increasingly inclined to purchase videocassette players to watch (usually pirated) foreign films in the comfort and relative safety of their homes.[16]

While Nigeria experienced a lull between independence in 1960 and the launch of the government-directed film sector, such was not the case in Mozambique. The country had only recently won its independence in 1975 after an ugly decade of armed struggle against its Portuguese overlords, when the Instituto Nacional de Cinema (INC) was founded the next year by Ruy Guerra. Born a Portuguese citizen in Mozambique, Guerra studied film in Paris in the 1950s and worked as an assistant director in France before migrating to Brazil. Following a successful career there, directing several critically acclaimed Cinema Novo productions, in 1980 he returned to Mozambique, where he shot the country's first feature, *Mueda, Memória e Massacre* (*Mueda, Memory and Massacre*, 1980), recalling the 1960 massacre of roughly 600 Makonde protesters.

More recently, Uganda has moved incrementally toward the establishment of a cinematic culture through Kinna-Uganda (K-U). The year before *The Last King of Scotland* (2006) was filmed in the country to international acclaim, Hajji Ashraf Ssemwogerere directed *Feelings Struggle* (2005) in an attempt to forge an industry and audience united behind a national program for cultural regeneration. Unfortunately, the capital city of Kampala hosts the country's sole major Cineplex, so K-U film showings are often hosted in local bars, theaters, and most notably, numerous small video halls known as Bibandas.[17]

As the broader African film industry matures, established filmmakers have increasingly drawn their inspiration from the rich reservoir of African oral culture and treasured mythologies for their themes. A case in point is the Malian director and screenwriter Souleymane Cissé, who, like Sembène before him, trained in the Soviet Union in the 1960s. After making a number of films in the 1970s and early 1980s, he emerged as a major force in African cinema with the release of *Yeelen (Brightness)* in 1987, which received acclaim at the Cannes Film Festival that year. Loosely set in the great West African Mali Empire of the 13th century, the film was made in both Fula and Bambara with English sub-titles, and, through dreamlike sequences, chronicles the story of a man tracking down his son, who is in possession of remarkable magical powers.[18] In a similar vein, Dani Kouyaté's *Keïta! Le Heritage du griot (Keita! The Heritage of the Griot*, 1995) evokes the grandeur and dignity of the West African past in its adaptation of the classic Sunjiata Keita epoch.

The expansion of the indigenous film industry in Africa, which we have just touched upon here, has led to increasing interest among scholars. Following on the heels of Francoise Pfaff, who provided an early analysis of the work of Sembene and other pioneers during the formative period,[19] more recent texts on African cinema often debate the goals of indigenous filmmaking: "Should filmmakers attempt to resurrect the African past?"

"Is there a distinct Afro-essence?"

"How will funding be secured to institutionalize industry growth?"

"Who will distribute the films?"

"What film format is best suited for African audiences given budgetary restrictions?" And most importantly, "Will supply fuel demand?"[20]

Invariably, these authors promoting a politically engaged and culturally sensitive cinema include a few paragraphs on the embarrassing shortcomings of early commercial films with African-related themes, briefly reminding us of the humorous defects of *Tarzan of the Apes* (1918), filmed "on location" in the Louisiana "jungle"; or *Sanders of the River* (1935), starring Paul Robeson, which romanticized British rule in Nigeria and, in so doing, led its star to publicly disown the film upon release. In these studies, cinema's arrival on the continent is often viewed through the prism of the cultural imperialist perspective: "Cinema came to Africa as a potent organ of colonialism. Because film is a powerful visual medium with an extraordinary ability to inordinately influence the thinking and behavior of its audience ... films proved to be a powerful tool for indoctrinating Africans into foreign cultures."[21] Thus, African spectators (and the so-called primitives who "starred" in early ethnographic films) in the colonial era are generally marginalized as a voiceless mass victimized by an international cabal of western cultural brokers and film trusts: "Film," we are told, "now destroyed the previous art forms and colonized ... cultural space" in Africa.[22] Indeed, according to a 1991 article by Hyginus Ekwuazi, cinema functioned like a new Trans-Atlantic Slave Trade, with a twist: "The more foreign films pumped into the African landscape, the more the cultural enslavement and the more dire the consequences."[23]

Although these texts sometimes discuss briefly the interplay between imported images and the colonized, generally the nuances of the early cinema experience, when many Africans willingly flocked to see Wild West thrillers or other films, is merely apologized for or explained away. The irony here is that, however unpalatable for some, the growth of a thriving African film industry in the 21st century actually stems from the very expansion of black spectatorship that first came into being in the colonial era. Even for Thelma Gutsche, who first traced the outlines of South African film culture, African spectatorship garners only scattered references. Not until the 1970–80s did the relationship between colonial rule and moving pictures become a legitimate topic of inquiry, as scholars like Rex Stevenson, Rosaleen Smyth, Guido Convents and others began to chart the post–World

War I push to establish colonial hegemony, and to uncover the ways in which the West justified imperial ambitions through movie-making and exhibition.[24] Some years later, Manthia Diawara, James Burns, Charles Ambler and others expanded the inquiry to include modes of resistance to the spectacle. Additionally, research on the colonial era has merged with the broader field of film studies, in which scholars often analyze the racist cinematic stereotypes of blacks both in Africa and the diaspora perpetuated by the industry.[25]

Most scholars have assumed that the representations propagated by Hollywood and apartheid South Africa's smaller film sector, have been at least partly responsible for the pervasive intolerance of racially divided societies. Recent research into the social impact of images, though, is becoming more nuanced through the examination of audience demographics (race/ethnicity/class/gender/nationality), especially within the U.S., and a focus on theaters themselves as sites of negotiation and contestation.[26] The once monolithic audience passively imbibing the ideological thrust of a film *in toto*, has now been reconstructed as micro-nodes of political engagement, variable response, and conflicting interpretations.[27] But while black film audiences in America have been highlighted in the last decade, the exploration of the origins of film in Africa, including the demographics of early African film spectatorship, is still in its infancy. Although the discipline is developing at a rapid pace, it was possible only several years ago for Paul Landau to state that "historians have hardly begun to consider the practical involvement of visual images in the structures of power that compose imperialism."[28]

Bringing Africa's Audience Back In

If one takes a common stereotype of Africa at face value, especially given the increasing proliferation of the ethnographic genre in the years following World War II, cinema as late as the mid–20th century was a strange, new importation from outside—an incomprehensible tool of the West's visual culture machine that exposed the "otherness" of Africans and the limits of indigenous cinematic comprehension. We know the stereotypes: confused natives huddle together and look askance at the movie camera; villagers believe midgets inhabit the projector's aperture, while others believe the strange contraption of the whites is stealing their souls. But does this "shock of the new" tell the whole story? It is one of the goals of this study to show that, by World War II, cinema had come to key areas of Africa in many guises, and many Africans, in fact, already had some familiarity with the medium, either as spectators of pre-war government-run mobile cinema shows, educational film showings in schools or missions, labor recruitment films shown in local villages, municipal township exhibitions, or commercial cinemas catering to black viewers in urban areas. In rare instances, they even made films themselves. Indeed, it appears that in some areas locals after World War II were already experiencing "film fatigue"—especially when they believed filmmaking crews were perpetuating antiquated stereotypes of African social life.

Given this crucial transformation in the cultural landscape of the subcontinent that was already manifest by the mid–1930s, the earliest years of the spectacle in Africa has drawn surprisingly little scholarly interest; in fact, while post-colonial African filmmakers and Nigerian video producers have received significant attention, there are few parallel studies on the early importation of film and/or film technology into the continent between the late 1890s and World War I, and fewer still on the more vexing issue of their impact on, and interaction with, the African social fabric. Despite the rich and contentious literature on ethnographic film, for instance, many studies content themselves with deconstructive readings of the genre with surprisingly little attention paid to the actual conditions of their production.

More remarkably, there are few broad-based studies to facilitate our understanding of the intersection of colonial policy, racial ideology and moving pictures south of the Sahara during the interwar years, despite the fact that it was during this pivotal period that many Africans first encountered moving images, giving birth to mass black spectatorship. Hence, more than half a century after South African film historian Thelma Gutsche declared that "the astounding activities of mobile cinemas in Central and East Africa will one day be written into the chronicle of the continent's development," the subject is only now attracting the serious attention of historians seeking to uncover the hidden traces of political consciousness embedded in the emerging cultural practice of film spectatorship.[29]

More broadly, the global proliferation of the cinema in the early 20th century, while sometimes criticized as a crucial factor in the broader machinations of cultural imperialism working hand in glove with Western capital, has not, in fact, been explored in detail for many parts of the world. From Herbert Schiller's ground-breaking *Communication and Cultural Domination* (1976), to John Tomlinson's *Cultural Imperialism: A Critical Introduction* (1991), much of the literature on what has sometimes been called "neo-colonialism" or "cultural dependency" has contented itself to reframing the debate and refining the broad theoretical models of analysis. What they tend to hold in common is the assumption that American culture is dominating the fields of media and popular culture around the globe, particularly in highly developed regions like Europe. Yet all too often the entire African continent (its rural environs in particular) is overlooked as merely an underdeveloped mass on the margins where little infusion of American culture has occurred. Even more remarkably, one has to fast-forward to 2007, with the publication of Melvyn Stokes and Richard Maltby's edited volume *Hollywood Abroad: Audiences and Cultural Exchange* to find what the publishers bill as "the first book to examine the reception of Hollywood movies by non–American audiences."[30]

By largely dismissing entire portions of the globe, like Africa, which on the surface seems to have avoided many of the tentacles of capital diffusion, many studies miss the opportunity to chart, for one, the dramatic effects of the American cowboy film on local populations. Indeed, it would not be far-fetched to claim that while the Wild West motif was certainly a part of the European landscape, as evidenced in the well-attended 19th-century Buffalo Bill shows, it may actually have had a deeper and more sustained cultural impact in Africa. In Europe, the cowboy theme was popular, but not transformative. In Africa, the Wild West motif had deeper social repercussions and led to forms of imitative behavior that were lacking elsewhere. This phenomenon, however, was belatedly addressed in a flurry of three essays in 2001 alone: Charles Ambler, Andrew Burton and Marissa Moorman blazed the trail for understanding the impact of the frontier genre in Africa in particular locales.[31] These efforts, coupled with James Burns's "John Wayne on the Zambezi: Cinema, Empire, and the American Western in British Central Africa," and his later investigations into the demographics of Cape Town audiences, provide new perspectives on the agency of the spectator.[32] African audiences, we now know, must be taken into account.

The point here is not just the cultural imperialist school's failure to extend its model to seemingly peripheral areas of the globe, but rather, the lack of effort invested in disaggregating the effects of Western culture on different regions based on their unique cultural specificities. In other words, rather than assuming a universal model of cultural imperialism that applies equally to passive consumers in, say, London, Lahore, or Luanda, one goal of this book is to fill a lacuna in the field of African colonial film studies and global cinema studies, by examining how cinema was first introduced into Africa, and providing a theoretical framework for the emergence of mass black film spectatorship, particularly in Southern Africa, following World War I. Every continent, country, and colony had unique political and social dynamics in play that ultimately must be studied in more detail before we can move to more expansive claims about the impact of film on the global village of the early 20th century. This also becomes evident in the discussion of the periodization of the evolution of cinema. As Marcus Power rightly stresses in his discussion of the origins of African cinema, when it comes to areas beyond the so-called "First World," we must treat with caution the "histories of fearless pioneers of firsts."[33] In Africa, conditions were such that in some areas cinema made an early appearance, and in others late. Moreover, it must be remembered that in colonized regions, including the internally colonized South Africa, there were specific politics of race, space and imperial power at play that were lacking elsewhere. Therefore, in referring to the earliest years of the spectacle in the colonies that would soon comprise South Africa (1895–1910) as the "novelty phase" before the institutionalization of remodeled buildings specifically designed for cinema exhibition, one obviously cannot apply that same periodization to those areas where cinema had yet to arrive. At the other end of the timeline, while many African nations were already enjoying independence celebrations and working to build viable domestic film sectors free of European control in the 1970s, apartheid South Africa was busy cranking out what one scholar recently dismissed as "shoddy films in Zulu, Sotho, Xhosa and other South African languages … screened in churches, schools and community and beer halls."[34]

Thus, this book is, in part, a prolegomenon to future research into the introduction of film into colonial milieus worldwide—to explore the link between the global flow of images, colonial governments, and community and individual desires. But more immediately, it seeks to answer a host of questions about the evolution of cinema in Africa: how did Africa's colonized status shape the introduction of cinema into the continent? What sorts of African stereotypes undergirded the ideological narratives being constructed in films made in Africa? Furthermore, it explores the origins of film-going as a cultural pursuit, with special reference to South Africa and the British-held territories of Tanganyika, Nyasaland, Uganda, Kenya and the Rhodesias: when and why did mass black film spectatorship in Africa emerge? Under what conditions were many of the colonized first allowed to view films? How did indigenes respond to filmmaking crews, and the crude colonial cinema campaigns designed for their consumption?

Images and Audiences in Africa

By the middle of the 20th century, European powers were tapping into the potential of motion pictures to help consolidate their African empires. Following World War II the Belgians, recognizing they were lagging egregiously behind Britain in producing propaganda films for the colonized, commissioned no fewer than 15 cinema vans to navigate the terrain of Central Africa to exhibit educational and instructional films in the Belgian Congo.[35] Similarly, the French Overseas Ministry supplied films to a French Equatorial Africa film unit for mobile vans to foster colonial integration.[36] By the late 1950s, in Belgian, French, British, and Portuguese possessions, colonial film units had begun producing and/or exhibiting movies for indigenous audiences with the improbable goal of instantaneously transforming African behavior and building consensus for postwar development schemes.[37]

Film also filled a niche in the private sector of an increasingly globalized industry.

Films from the West, of course, had traveled the circuits of worldwide trade networks since the earliest days of the spectacle. But competing with colonial film units, transnational corporations in areas like Nigeria and South Africa chartered their own mobile cinemas to access the countryside advertising their wares—tea was a perennial favorite—through privately produced industry films. Film was thus not only a new commodity itself; rather, it could serve double duty in conceivably opening up virgin markets in the darkest recesses of Africa, thus realizing at long last the lofty goals of earlier European explorers.

Not to be outdone, religious bodies and non-profits like UNESCO tapped into the seemingly universal potential of the medium to magically save souls or dramatically transform African communities, a process still very much alive today with organizations like FilmAid that provide "community-based films on critical public health and safety issues," shown in Kenya by mobile cinema units using inflatable screens.[38] These examples give a sense of the wide range of films collected under the banner "cinema in Africa." Yet film scholars were always painfully aware that Africa was deplorably behind the rest of the globe when it came to an indigenous film industry and a viable consumer base. For instance, in Clyde Taylor's 1985 country-by-country analysis of the state of the art around the globe, the first country for which there is an entry is Africa. Taylor's assessment was bleak: "Those who set out to frame authentic African images after the flag-lowering ceremonies soon found that the necessary material resources were almost entirely out of African hands."[39] This arrested development was traceable to various factors, including European/American domination of international distribution, weak markets, an underdeveloped technological base, and earlier colonial restrictions.

As Chapter 1 of this study makes clear, however, by the mid–20th-century, cinema had arrived in Africa in a variety of guises. While many of the earliest film showings targeted whites primarily, the demographics of audiences began to broaden due both to the pressures of the private sector, and as colonial governments increasingly sought to harness the medium to buttress white authority and promote development along Western lines.

Chapter 2, like the previous chapter, takes a bird's-eye approach as it explores the veritable scramble in the early–20th century to secure images of Africa for export to the metropoles. In cinema's first decade or so, non-fiction actualities played a key role in advertising the empire abroad for audiences at home. During this early period, images actually traveled both ways: while European shorts were offloaded in African ports, "foreign views" were being produced primarily in the southernmost and northernmost tips of Africa and exported to Europe for commercial distribution. In other cases, African films were produced outside the continent itself, with filming conducted on the River Thames, or the negro villages at the colonial fairgrounds in Tervuren.

Technological improvements eventually led to the obsolescence of the actuality, but another key non-fiction genre—the newsreel—introduced longer narratives focusing less on the static landscape or images of the everyday, and more on the exceptional and the newsworthy. Increasingly sophisticated and well funded, newsreels were a revolutionary visual substitute (audio-visual by the 1930s) for the newspaper, instilling in Euro-American spectators the sense of being witnesses to history, especially to the transformative events around the globe with long-lasting cultural and political impact. While both museums and individual scholars engaged in high-profile scientific expeditions with camera in tow—in the interwar period especially—various adventurers, explorers and even advertisers tried to accomplish by motor vehicle what a few years before required herculean effort by foot. Related to endurance expedition films which documented those efforts was the wildlife genre, serving an important function in the West as a putatively depoliticized trope that ignored the political realities of colonization while highlighting Africa's "untamed savagery."

If Africans had been excluded as spectators in cinema's early years, they were nevertheless the witting or unwitting stars of ethnographic filmmaking, which became a major preoccupation with Euro-American scholars and adventurers traveling to Africa. Although the use of motion pictures within the emerging field of anthropology was controversial from its inception, the medium was touted as an important tool for capturing on celluloid the culture of vanishing primitives—a form of two-dimensional taxidermy—during a period of rapid social transition due to the Scramble for Africa. Because of the long-standing presence of missionaries in Africa, and because their use of film evolved out of the earlier deployment of still images in the 19th century in the form of photography, lantern slides and stereographs, it is important also to emphasize their pivotal role in the early evolution of cinema in Africa. Indeed, Christian missionaries of all faiths, Protestant and Catholic alike, made significant cinematic inroads into the interior.

Chapter 3 addresses the origins of mass black spectatorship in Africa. In cinema's first three decades, there was a key characteristic of Africa that set it apart from the formation of a film culture elsewhere: unlike Europe and America, where much of the general population was fairly quickly tapped as consumers,[40] in Africa black colonial subjects themselves were often prohibited from viewing films. The reason for this was two-fold. In part it was because Africans were just being introduced (often forced) into the cash nexus and thus did not constitute a consumer base worth targeting, but even more it was due to the powerful myth of African primitivity that many believed hindered their ability to properly "read" both still images and motion pictures. Thus, in the early colonial period cinema and civilization were parallel terms—perceived as accouterments of white culture—an ideological framework that underwent a major transformation with the inauguration of mass black spectatorship around 1920.

Missionary Ray Phillips in South Africa designed the Mines Compound Cinema Circuit in Johannesburg soon after the conclusion of World War I. As the largest program of its kind prior to World War II, the circuit sought primarily to introduce wholesome forms of leisure to the expanding black proletariat laboring in the gold mining sector, and soon mushroomed to include dozens of exhibition sites as far north as the Rhodesias. While many spectators on the Mines' circuit were seeing films for the first time in the early 1920s, Phillips was painfully aware that he was competing with the commercial cinema market which had begun incrementally to target the African as consumer. In fact, as Chapter 4 makes clear, the Hollywood cowboy genre reverberated throughout Africa, and seemed to fuel imitative behavior that white settlers and colonial officials found troublesome. Africans, many feared, were becoming too quickly seduced by questionable thrillers from Hollywood, and were constructing new identities through the cultural practice of film spectatorship that, at times, seemingly threatened colonial stability.

Chapter 5 reflects the rapidly changing ideological stance toward African spectatorship by the early 1920s. Following the perceived success of Phillips's film circuit, the mining sector decided to join the field and produce a spate of recruiting films like *From Red Blanket to Civilization* (along with Safety-First films) to satisfy demand for contract laborers to service the South African gold mining sector. It is not clear whether recruiting films paid dividends for the mines, but what had become clear by 1930 or so was that black spectatorship was a *fait accompli*.

Chapter 6 explores the search within British colonial circles for a responsible and realistic film policy for its African possessions. With increasing instability in India blamed, in part, on a poorly regulated film industry, officials hoped lessons would be learned for Africa, and motion pictures somehow harnessed to their grand civilizing project before the clock ran out. Chapter 7 explores the fruits of these discussions and the proposed solutions designed by missionaries and British officials who took the lead among European nations with a colonial cinema program targeting African audiences. The propaganda-educational-instructional films that comprised the Bantu Educational Kinema Experiment generally eschewed fast tempos, cross-cutting, close-ups, and bird's-eye shots to conform to the perceived limits of African visual comprehension. Although some critics denied the claim that Africans lacked the ability to comprehend sophisticated film angles and advanced editing techniques, this genre, with its attendant ideological baggage, guaranteed that most colonial cinema projects targeting indigenous audiences would similarly restrict themselves to simplistic shots and slow-moving plots.

Movies, Men and Migration

A crucial part of the story of evolving mass black spectatorship is the relationship between the three large-scale film projects designed specifically for Africans by missionaries, colonial administrators and industry officials between 1920 and 1937. Not coincidentally, I argue, all three were related in crucial ways to the mining sector as transnational corporations and European powers sought to enrich themselves through the extraction of Africa's precious resources. To maximize profits, these industries required a large pool of unskilled workers from which ready recruits could be drawn. It was this mass movement of bodies, the steady march of displaced African recruits from country kraals to mining meccas, which led to the rapid expansion of film-viewing opportunities for indigenous spectators after World War I.

The growth of mass black spectatorship was thus inextricably linked to the migration of labor recruits to urban-industrial centers. Missionaries showed films in company compounds on the Witwatersrand, and areas beyond; the South African mining industry itself produced recruiting films to satisfy the need for new workers; and in response to rural degradation in Central Africa due to labor migration to Northern Rhodesian copper mines, British colonial officials and missionaries made over 30 experimental instructional-propaganda films for widespread African consumption to promote rural development along Western lines.

Uncovering and mapping the nexus between these programs, and deciphering their relationship to colonial ideology and policy, is crucial to understanding how whites sought to transform Africans through projected images in subtly different ways. Most white elites (and later proponents of the cultural imperialist school) subscribed to the "magic bullet" theory of mass culture and audience reception, arguing for a causal link between projected images and induced behavior.[41] The perceived power of the image, capable of either seduction or incitement, was therefore reflected in the opposing and often contradictory agendas of those in power: just as some officials and missionaries bemoaned the new African pastime of movie-going and focused on censorship, others appreciated the propagandistic appeal of the medium and struggled to incorporate film into the colonial imperative. Ironically, then, mass black spectatorship in Africa paralleled the rise of stricter censorship measures, in part due to the fact that the regulatory net was often prone to inevitable loopholes and leakages.

In addition to the obvious racial dynamic at play in cinema exhibition in Africa, the relationship between the mining sector and film viewing displayed a gender component. During the interwar years, film programs displayed a bias toward African males, who were targeted by gold-mining labor recruiters. This is not to deny that women were consumers of moving pictures. While not present at the Witwatersrand mining compound bioscopes (cinemas), women sometimes attended municipal township showings. And Ian Phimister and Charles van Onselen have also shown that in Bulawayo, Southern Rhodesia, women attending a bioscope were, in fact, the cause of an ethnic conflict between the Shona and Ndebele in 1929. The trigger effect for this street battle was that "MaShona" males were attending screenings with "Matabele" women as their dates, thereby exacerbating ethnic animosities dating back a century to the massacres and social disruptions known in southern Africa as the *mfecane*.[42] In another case in this same time period on Northern Rhodesia's Copperbelt, where African women were originally prohibited from attending motion picture shows, a boycott of the programs by sympathetic males actually prompted colonial officials to reverse colonial cinema policy.

Ethnic differences, especially in South Africa, constituted another fault-line in African reception, forcing the Chamber of Mines to produce separate recruiting films for the major tribal groupings in the Eastern Cape to stimulate the flow of migrant labor. Those groups, underrepresented on the screen in earlier films, in fact, often treated the showings with derision. The time and expense required in making new propaganda films acceptable to diverse ethnicities reflected two important facts: industry officials were forced to come to terms with African opinion; and Africans, despite many reports to the contrary, were capable not only of comprehending moving images on the screen, but more importantly, articulating those very experiences. Through personal interviews, British Colonial Office memos, colonial archives in Africa, museum archives, missionary archives and diaries, mining industry reports, screenplays, explorers' memoirs, newspaper accounts, and films themselves, this book charts white colonizers' desires to expand colonial power during the era of consolidation. Antonio Gramsci's analysis of ideology and culture, and his focus on the structure of class hegemony in Western nation-states, can be extended if only partially to this period of colonial rule, and more narrowly, this study. The exhibition of films in the peripheries, and especially the production of cinematic forms of visual propaganda in the colonies using indigenous actors, reflects the attempt to reconfigure and extend prevalent forms of normalizing power to imperial strategies of political and economic dominance in the peripheries. Ultimately, though, while apprehending the hegemonic intentions of those responsible for African film exhibition is necessary for understanding the workings of colonial power, hegemony theory fails to account for the competing agendas of those seeking dominance, as well as the voices of the "historically inarticulate" as the colonized absorbed, negotiated or contested the film crews moving through their villages, and the moving images projected to them on the screen.

1

In Search of Origins

Screening Motion Pictures in Africa

Screening in Africa: The First Decade

Due to the rapidly improving transportation and distribution networks of the late 1800s, motion pictures were quickly introduced into many areas of the globe by the end of the century. Yet in Africa, due to regional differences based on European affiliation, imprecise record-keeping and the lack of a continent-wide blueprint for cinematic intervention, the earliest years of the spectacle have an uneven history and have been difficult to chart. "It is not quite clear," African film historian Nwachukwu Ukadike admitted as late as the 1990s, "when cinema came to black Africa." This was an astonishing (if revealing) admission by a leading African cinema scholar, and reflected the generalizations that framed early investigations into cinema's origins in the continent. Broad assertions by Elizabeth Heath and Edward Horatio-Jones, respectively, for instance, that Africans in British colonies and the Belgian Congo prior to World War II "were forbidden to watch European and American movies," and that in the "African countries [south of the Sahara] cinema never arrived until 1925," are gradually being subtly revised through further research.[1]

When were motion pictures first screened in Africa? This is a difficult question to answer definitively, but in the earliest stages, concurrent with the partitioning of Africa by European superpowers, it was primarily European and American enterprises and entrepreneurs that pushed to open new markets for commercial exhibition while simultaneously securing footage of "foreign views" of the continent. Almost certainly, the first motion picture exhibition can be dated to Edison's Kinetoscope, which came early to the mining center of Johannesburg, in what is now the Transvaal, South Africa. At the time, a unified South Africa was still an unrealized dream of British imperialists who struggled with recalcitrant Boers determined to carve out their own destiny in the region. Geopolitical considerations had first steered the British to the Cape Colony by the late 18th century, and they soon followed in the path of fleeing Boers heading into the interior. The eventual discovery of gold on the Witwatersrand, a phenomenon important both for the British and for this study, led to the rapid industrialization of Johannesburg in the late–19th century as the British moved to cement their control in the region.

Subsequently, in large part due to the mushrooming white population, this city at the heart of the new global gold rush played a pivotal role in the introduction of cinema to Africa. In the United States, Thomas Edison and his employees had been experimenting as early as 1889 with a strip of flexible, perforated film with sequential still images offering the illusion of movement when viewed through a single peephole of a large box, soon marketed as the Kinetoscope. Thus, while the Holland Bros. opened the first commercially viable Kinetoscope parlor near New York's Herald Square on April 14, 1894, with ten Edison machines,[2] only one year later on April 4, 1895, a "group of literary and scientific men" gathered at Johannesburg's Grand National Hotel to enjoy "a specimen of Edison's perhaps most wonderful invention, the kinetoscope," including shots of a cockfight and Buffalo Bill giving a quick-firing exhibition.[3] Two weeks later, at nearby Henwood's arcade, the Kinetoscope debuted for urban Boers with the abovementioned films, complemented by *Carmencita's Skirt Dance*. Touted as the "Greatest Scientific Marvel of the Age," this moving picture arcade succeeded in attracting thousands of customers.

The Kinetoscope may have arrived early in the Transvaal, but by 1895 technological improvements in projection by the Skladanowsky brothers, the Lumière brothers, William Dickson and others were already making it obsolete. Based on the emerging technology of throwing images on a wall with a beam of light, the first publicly projected film showing for which admission was charged is generally credited to Max and Emil Skladanowky's November 1895 Bioskop spectacle at the Wintergarten theater in Berlin,[4] although by that time fellow German inventor Ottomar Anschutz had already debuted his Projecting Electrotachyscope—a rotating wooden disc with sequenced still images projected onto a large screen to simulate movement. These early exhibitions would soon be followed by the famous December 1895 premiere of the "Cinématographe Lumière" in Paris, and scattered film screenings with similar devices by Thomas Armat in the U.S., and Robert W. Paul and Birt Acres in England. In America, Thomas Edison's April 1896 Vitascope premiere also cemented its place in the pioneering era of film projection. But as Thomas Prasch and others have stressed, these "seminal" dates are, in reality, more convenient than precise, as a number of these visionaries had already been showing their films privately for months prior to their official premieres.[5]

In terms of exploiting the new technology of projecting moving images, once again Johannesburg was not far behind. In fact, only 18 days after Edison's American Vitascope premiere, enterprising showman Carl Hertz had already begun showing moving pictures in Africa. Hertz also attended London's Alhambra Theatre, where Robert Paul's Theatrograph was being promoted, and imported one of Paul's two projectors into the Transvaal.[6] A famous "prestidigitateur," Hertz was contracted to perform at Johannesburg's Empire Palace of Varieties, managed by Edgar Hyman, and eager to incorporate "animated photographs" into his show; thus, according to Hertz, he virtually forced Paul to sell him one of the Alhambra projectors for £100. The result was southern Africa's first projected cinema show on May 11, 1896, advertised as "the photo-electric sensation of the day," with five Robert Paul "filmlets" comprising the visual entertainment.

Later that year, cinema continued its march into another center of British imperial power on the other end of the continent. Despite British hegemony in Egypt, French representatives of Lumière first unveiled the magic of their Cinématographe at Café Zawani in Alexandria's Tousson stock exchange on November 5, 1896, causing much discussion among the excited locals. Here cinema undoubtedly functioned as a poignant expression of the technological and cultural prowess of the West; for, unlike Johannesburg, the showing was not restricted to white elites as an amusing curiosity, and thus its impact was more quickly felt by the Egyptian rank and file. An article in *El Mou'ayed* entitled "When Will We Catch Up with Them?" captured the exhilaration:

> What has happened is that a few days ago some foreigners came to Alexandria with a camera capable of capturing motion pictures, which they call a "cinematographe." They presented it in a spacious hall in the Toussoun Pasha Bourse. An incredible number of people gathered round to watch it, and I among them. I left intoxicated by the wonders I had seen.[7]

This riveting spectacle was soon followed by showings in the European Quarter of Cairo and the Khedival Palace. Of course, Egypt could boast of visual attractions of its own, and soon the grandeur of its ancient civilization provided a wealth of material captured on celluloid and brought back to Europe to thrill European audiences. Following the shows in Alexandria and Cairo, screenings of these Lumière shorts were given by the end of the year in the coastal cities of Algiers and Oran; simultaneously, in Morocco, film showings were organized at the Royal Palace in the capital city of Fez.[8] In contrast to Egypt and most areas of the Maghreb, where foreign firms provided the impetus, in Tunisia it was the native-born Jew Albert Samama Chikly who spearheaded the first cinema exhibitions. Chikly was an avid advocate for technological diffusion, and, in addition to the cinema, was pivotal in the introduction of bicycle, X-ray, radio, and photographic technologies into Tunis. In 1897 his interests led him to organize several 10–12 minute Lumière film showings, including *L'Arrivée d'un Train en gare de La Ciotat* (*The Arrival of a Train at La Ciotat*, 1895), which proved so popular among the city's spectators that, upon completion, many stayed for the next show.[9]

In 1903, coinciding with British pacification campaigns in West Africa that would soon unify disparate regions into Nigeria under the Union Jack, Herbert Macaulay became the first African to organize a cinema showing in the sub–Sahara when he introduced the seventh art to Lagos. Macaulay was a remarkable figure: his grandfather was Samuel Crowther, Niger Territory's first African bishop. Macaulay worked for the British civil service in Nigeria, but had resigned in 1898 with his new interest in Nigerian independence—eventually inspiring future President Nnamdi Azikiwe—and by 1903 had made a name for himself as a prominent critic of British colonialism. That year, though, he rented Glover Memorial Hall—constructed in commemoration of colonial Governor John Glover as a venue for indigenous theater—and contracted with the Spanish firm Balboa and Co. to put on a series of cinema shows that proved quite popular.

The dating for the introduction of cinema into French West Africa is a bit murkier, with existing scholarship providing more confusion than clarity. It seems that in either 1900 or 1905, representatives of Lumière screened *L'Arrivée d'un train en gare de la Ciotat* and *L'Arroseur arrosé* (*The Sprinkler Sprinkled*, 1895) in the coastal city of Dakar. Even more unclear is the allusion in many texts to "animated cartoons" being shown in the city in 1905, with subsequent showings by mobile cinemas in surrounding rural villages. The origin for these references is a 1962 article by ethnographic filmmaker Jean Rouch published in *The UNESCO Courier*,[10] but the fact that cartoons as a recognizable genre only begin after the appearance of Winsor McCay's *Gertie the Dinosaur* (1914) make this assertion problematic unless they refer to Georges Méliès's experimental animations like *Le Voyage dans la lune* (*A Trip to the Moon*, 1902). On that note, other claims that Georges Mèliès himself traveled to Dakar and produced two shorts are also spurious.[11]

Bioscopes and Cinema Houses

In Egypt and the British colonies in southern Africa cinema came early and venues soon expanded in the interior. Residents of large cities and even smaller towns enjoyed the new "living pictures" of Trafalgar Square, Queen Victoria's Diamond Jubilee and other spectaculars projected by an array of machines with tongue-twisting names like the Heliochromoscope, Zenomettoscope, Projectoscope, and most famously, the Bioscope. Although there were actually a few projectors which went by the latter name, the most successful was the model designed by Charles Urban. The impetus for this machine was the perceived problems with Edison's projectors, including electrical current issues and the fact that the Vitascope could hold only 50-foot reels and had no take-up spool.[12]

The Bioscope was practical, effective, and was destined to have such lasting appeal in southern Africa that cinema itself there would be given the generic term "the bioscope," with slight variations (bioskop, bioskopo) in Afrikaans, Setswana, Zulu and so on. Not surprisingly, Edison recognized its value and by 1897 a "Mrs. James" was presenting "Edison's American Bioscope" at Cape Town's Good Hope Hall. Within a decade new bioscopes opened throughout the colonies that would soon comprise South Africa (in 1910), with distribution monopolized by the Warwick Trading Company. Warwick also supplied vaudeville houses and music halls with lightweight bioscopes developed by Skladanowsky.

In its early novelty phase, motion pictures were thus harnessed to existing forms of entertainment in southern Africa. Yet the quality of motion pictures continually improved and the spectacle soon equaled or surpassed in popularity other attractions like vaudeville acts or music hall performances, as in the case of Johannesburg's Empire Palace of Varieties, which incorporated "Edison's Life-Size Pictures" into all performances by 1900. Another venue out of which early cinema in the Cape Colony, Natal, and the Transvaal evolved was the circus, because, unlike some attractions, it traveled on a circuit and played to audiences in more remote areas. Frank Fillis had taken over W.H. Bell's circus and quickly added novelties like cinema to his innovative programs. In addition to his traveling show that incorporated film into his repertoire, Fillis's newly opened Amphitheatre in Johannesburg and Cape Town began advertising The Cinématographe to expand the customer base.[13] The exhibitions of Fillis and other itinerant showmen replicated to some extent the evolution of cinema elsewhere. As historian Charles Musser has shown, traveling circuits were the primary means by which cinema in the United States worked its way into small towns,[14] and in France, while early films were shown in vaudeville houses or music halls, they also appeared in traveling fairs.[15] Similarly, in Germany, the Skladanowsky's were, at heart, itinerant showmen showing macabre magic lantern "fog-images" throughout Europe.

By the early–20th century, bioscopes were replacing the grab-bag of venues that had first sponsored the motion picture revolution. For a brief period early bioscopes, in what were sometimes advertised as "animated picture saloons," were sometimes an appendage to urban tea houses and cafés. Campbell's Model Tea Room in Durban was a prominent example, offering six daily showings by "Chronos—King of Bioscopes."[16] Frederick Mouillot, who had already launched Electric Theatres in England, was responsible for institutionalizing the industry in South Africa in the second decade of the century. His Natal Electric Theatre was the region's first full-time bioscope, opening in Durban on July 29, 1909. Mouillot and others soon opened more bioscopes with small seating capacities, although Cape Town's Wolfram's and Johannesburg's Tivoli could accommodate 500–600 spectators. The new venues—initially retro-fitted storefronts, church halls and recreational buildings—were important because they were venues tailored specifically for film audiences. Their growth was nothing short of spectacular. No scholar has provided an accurate figure for their number in the early–20th century, in part due to poor record-keeping and because they were so numerous, and often so short-lived, that providing precise figures becomes difficult. However, the list below, while incomplete, is a testament to the popularity of the cinema as the Boers took over effective control of the newly named Union of South Africa:

Early South African Bioscopes, with launch dates:
<u>Durban</u>: Electric Theatre (1909)
　　　　　Electric Theatre (1909: "Coloured Only"—Indian)
<u>Cape Town</u>: Theatre de Luxe (1909)
　　　　　Wolfram's Bioscope (1909)
　　　　　Empire Bioscope Theatre (1909)
　　　　　Ridout's Bioscope (1909)
　　　　　Alhambra's Bioscope Theatre (1910)
　　　　　American Bioscope (1910)
　　　　　Union Bioscope (1910)
　　　　　Royal Bioscope (1910)
　　　　　Fisher's Elite Bioscope (1910)
<u>Muizenberg</u>: Electric Theatre (1910)
<u>Port Elizabeth</u>: Electric Theatre (1910)
<u>Germiston</u>: Electric Theatre (1910)
<u>Johannesburg</u>: Bijou (1909)
　　　　　Fordsburg Bijou #2 (1909)
　　　　　Vaudette (1909 or 1910)
　　　　　American Bioscope (1909 or 1910)
　　　　　Tivoli (1910)
<u>Pretoria</u>: Bijou Bioscope (1910)
<u>Krugersdorp</u>: Lyric Theatre (1909)

　　Just as intriguing as the question of the number of bioscopes, is the question of the demographic makeup of early audiences. In the late 1890s, audiences comprised primarily males, but as films were introduced to spice up other amusements, and later with the proliferation of bioscopes, women began attending shows in greater numbers. Moreover, the racial makeup of early audiences was almost entirely white, although a few Durban and Cape Town bioscopes began to cater to Indian and Coloured populations.

　　In other areas, the bioscope often trailed along the migrating white population. Within a year of a dramatic diamond discovery in 1924, over 150,000 Afrikaner fortune hunters converged on Lichtenburg, in South Africa's North West Province. In nearby Bakers (now Bakerville), thousands of shotgun shacks were quickly erected, with cafés, restaurants, and a local bioscope to service the diamond boom. The Lichtenburg yield was huge, but it eventually petered out and all but the poorest residents closed up shop and departed. The bioscope, too, fell victim to the times, leaving one observer a decade later to comment on the dreary "tin cinema plastered with torn and ancient bills."[17] The short life span of the Lichtenburg cinema reflected a common fate for early bioscopes, as many were small, poorly capitalized fly-by-nights that opened and closed with regularity.

　　Interestingly, the Lichtenburg rush actually affected a film showing as far away as Bloemfontein. Captain Wetherell and Aloha Baker were presenting a film lecture there to raise revenue for their "Model T" Cape to Cairo film expedition, when a rumor circulating through the theater about the impending ground release led the audience to stand up *en masse* and suddenly vacate the hall. But the enterprising Wetherell and Baker simply packed up their gear and followed the wagon trains to Lichtenburg, where they proceeded to set up the short-lived *Diggers' Biograph* to sold-out audiences for five nights. Unfortunately, on the final evening a gunfight erupted inside the theater and the projectionist was killed, putting a damper on the proceedings.[18]

　　Egypt had also developed a significant cinematic culture by the end of the 20th century's first decade. In the towns of Tanta and Port Said, the Egyptians Maqar and Mohamed

Osman opened cinema halls early on, but in Alexandria the market was initially dominated by enterprising Greeks and Italians. By 1910, the city had multiple theaters competing for largely middle- and upper-class audiences: Lumière Cinematograph, Teatro Abbas, Asiz & Dorés Cinephone, Urbanora Cinematograph, Salle le Fonte, Casino San Stefano, Cinema Isis and the Casino Eden.[19]

In French West Africa, in Dakar in particular, some of the first fledgling cinemas were opened by members of the small expatriate Lebanese community in the 1920s. As elsewhere, these venues catered initially to the French population and screened popular French or American films, thereby reinforcing the cultural divide between white and black, "civilized" and "savage."[20] Incrementally, despite originating as a form of white leisure, cinemas in some areas of Africa increasingly serviced non–European populations, although before World War I opportunities for Africans to attend were severely circumscribed. Johannesburg had implemented racial segregation in urban bioscopes as early as 1910, no doubt due to the fact that the African population was expanding, putting pressure on officials to establish urban amenities catering to "whites only." Cape Town, in contrast, where the number of bioscopes probably hovered somewhere around an astonishing 150–300, resisted some of the formal mechanisms of racial separation. Yet this was due in part to political pressure from the Coloured population, and because "the city's ethnic diversity also made it difficult for theatres with a Europeans-only policy to prosper."[21] No doubt the elevated status of the Coloured population vis-à-vis the black African population was a factor as well. It should be noted that Cape Town bioscopes were defined more by their quantity than quality. The American explorer Paul Hoefler, who stopped off in Cape Town in 1925 on his way to the Kalahari to film the "Bushmen" (San), was distressed to find "no movie theatres," although he did attend a showing at a bioscope, which he found sorely lacking in comparison to America's sumptuous movie palaces:

> No uniformed doorman, no neatly attired usherettes, no cool air in summer or warmed air on chilly days, no orchestra, or novelties between pictures, no upholstered chairs. You enter the mostly barnlike hall, and sit on a hard chair, while a piano pounder or phonograph manages to hide the sound of dropping peanut shells, and then comes the picture. It is the same one you saw years ago in Hollywood.[22]

Despite Hoefler's criticism, where the film-going experience was introduced into other colonized regions in southern Africa, it clearly emerged as a form of leisure for European businessmen, settlers and colonial officials. Distributors in South Africa began sending animated and educational films to the bustling diamond-mining town of Luderitz, in German Southwest Africa, where, by 1910, cinema had become an attraction in local hotels. Following South Africa's occupation of the colony after World War I, full-time bioscopes opened in larger towns, leaving smaller communities to enjoy traveling "Wanderkinos" like Prinsenschaums Kino and Ohlmanns Kinematograph, both of which provided shows in Windhoek and Swakopmund.[23]

If film was initially a marker of white civilization in Southwest Africa, black spectatorship was further circumscribed by racialized urban curfews and other restrictions, phenomena present in other areas as well. In Angola, cinema mostly appeared in the form of newsreels some years after the turn of the century, initially targeting urban whites. In Mozambique, the first motion picture exhibition dates to the late 1890s, when Portuguese civil engineer José Onofre incorporated Pathé films into his theater and concert performances in Lourenço Marques, leading to the opening of the Cinematographo. By 1907, Manuel Rodrigues had opened the Salão Edison, followed by the Teatro Gil Vicente six years later.

Lourenço Marques, like Luderitz on the opposite coast, was an active port city and served as a conduit for black laborers bound for South Africa's mineral mines. But early Mozambican cinemas were never intended to serve the recreational needs of the black population. On the contrary, as Marcus Power notes, the "Teatro Gil Vicente occupied a prominent role in the formation of Portuguese colonial identities, particularly in the construction of Portugalidade as 'civilized.'" The naming of Rodrigues's theater is revealing in this regard. In 1913, two months before the premiere, Portuguese colonists penned an open letter to Rodrigues pushing for a "genuinely Portuguese" name that would not find offense among white settlers. He thus suggested Teatro Gil Vicente to pay obeisance to the great 16th-century Portuguese poet.[24] Needless to say, black mining migrants, dock stevedores, and rural chibalo laborers were not expected to attend. In 1920, authorities sought to reinforce the racial firewall by updating a decree of ten years before, specifically prohibiting indigenous spectators from cinema performances which might expose them to themes of murder, theft, robbery and arson.[25]

Early cinema exhibitions in German East Africa were mostly restricted to "civilized" white and Indian residents, first dating to a traveling showman by the name of Wexelsen, who organized a screening in April 1908 in Tanga. By World War I cinema was being increasingly incorporated into the leisure life of urban residents, with small makeshift tents in Zanzibar Town and Dar es Salaam offering the spectacle to a curious public. In the 1920s, now under British administration, the first permanent but modest theaters, Bharat Cinema and Krishna Cinema, opened in warehouses in the Indian district. The first substantial cinematograph, The Empire, opened in 1929 and enjoyed a brief monopoly with audiences numbering up to 600. However, as film-going became further ingrained in Dar es Salaam, newly opened theaters like the Globe, Chox, Avalon, Empress, Cameo, and Odeon offered significant competition. One characteristic worthy of note is that almost all of these theaters were owned by Indian elites who imported European, American, and early Bollywood films.

In Tanganyika (formerly part of German East Africa), as elsewhere, Africans initially experienced the spectacle only in small numbers due to pervasive discrimination.[26] Concerns raised in the *Tanganyika Times* in 1929 echoed both white and Indian "civilized" opinion: "The amusing exploits of an urchin picking pockets in a Charles Dickens film may be a bad guide for the African mind. He may just miss the point that villainy is nearly always punished in the end, and only remember the easiness with which the incipient rogue 'got away with it.'"[27] Hence, according to James Brennan, "In the early 1930s, Africans were simply denied access to cinema except for those films specially designated for 'general exhibition.'"[28] Gradually, though, Africans secured greater access to discretionary income at the same time that more modest theaters in Dar es Salaam began to admit blacks regularly. The changing demographics of film-going thus paralleled the massive influx of blacks from rural villages into the city, a pattern we return to in this study. It should be noted that the expansion of black spectatorship occurred despite the best efforts of the emerging black bourgeoisie to stop it. Fearing that young African hooligans, influenced by celluloid scenes of wanton criminality, jeopardized their tenuous class position, Rufiji elders in 1931 actually requested that "a cinema catering for an African audience be closed."[29]

In Zanzibar, film was introduced by 1916, and within a few years a cinematic culture was fairly well established as the population increasingly bought into this new social marker of urban sophistication. The first cinematograph was apparently organized for a Zanzibar War Society function in May 1916, at which "a large and varied programme of films was enjoyed by a large audience." Later that year, silk merchant Hassanali Adamji Jariwalla put cinema on a firmer footing with the launch of White Tent (a.k.a. Zanzibar Cinema), soon expanding his operations with the Merry Theatre (renamed Alexandre Cinema). Advertised as the "Pioneer Cinema of Zanzibar and Mombasa," the White Tent showed primarily European shorts along with the "Famous Charlie Chaplin." By the 1930s, however, Egyptian films were in greater demand and distribution companies began ordering films from Cairo.[30]

By 1921, Jariwalla had opened Royal Cinema in Zanzibar Town but was also experiencing competition. As early as 1917, Hassanali Nazarai had launched Excelsior Cinema, which offered showings in an old building near the wharf before it closed in 1930. In contrast, soon the beautiful Royal Cinema had opened in the town center, reflecting the expanding appeal of the spectacle among the upper classes. The theater was increasingly important for the socializing needs of the urban aristocracy, where one could see plays, music and lectures—indeed, as a place where one could be seen by others. By the 1920s, enterprising Indians were even showing films on the nearby island of Pemba. These venues, originally urban in nature, had begun to attract rural native workers on clove plantations by the 1930s, leading anxious colonial officials to fret about the drain on workers' finances and the impact of commercial cinema on the "primitive" mind. As a result, in 1941 the Pemba Film Licensing Board voted to oppose "the showing of films in country districts at the present time."[31]

In the Belgian Congo, cinemas were first introduced as part of an expanding array of European leisure pursuits for Belgian expatriates, especially in Leopoldville, where soccer, bicycling and other recreations were already commonplace. Scenes from World War I—imported from Allied nations—figured prominently on the big screen when Henri Legaert opened one of the colony's first cinemas in 1916. Over the next few decades, film-going became routinized in Leopoldville and Elizabethville with the opening of larger cinemas, most notably the Cinéma Apollo Palace, Ciné Central, and Cinéma Hennion. For one newly arriving missionary cinema was a key accouterment of civilization, with Elizabethville applauded for being a "well laid out European town, with good streets, electric lighted stores, [and a] high grade moving picture cinematograph."[32] Competing with commercial cinemas, the Brothers of St. Francis de Sales incorporated cinema showings into their missions to blend educational work with popular entertainment.[33] And by the 1930s, even in smaller cities cinema was increasingly institutionalized in hotels as an amusement for (white) guests. In Buta, for instance, hotel proprietor Monsieur Sissel provided cinema showings regularly to a packed house, despite one guest noting that the films were "ancient" and the projectors suffered frequent breakdowns.[34] The popularity of the cinema was not lost on other colonies, and some soon began entertaining the idea of the African as consumer. In fact, as early as World War I the British Colonial Office and some colonial governments were beginning to consider applications from enterprising businessmen hoping to open bioscopes for blacks in West Africa. These solicitations were mostly unsuccessful, or, like the Anglo-African Cinema Company, quickly became insolvent and collapsed; yet soon other private concerns began using cinema vans and started touring cocoa-producing regions. The 1920s and 1930s saw mostly white-owned bioscopes being opened in the Gold Coast, Nigeria and elsewhere to service the increasing African demand for films. In other areas, like French Equatorial Africa and Bechuanaland, some businesses and cafés used films to attract potential African customers, a strategy first used in South Africa years before to entice white passersby.[35] In Brazzaville, for instance, a Portuguese storeowner used films "to increase the sale of his coffee."[36] The changing demographic of cinema-going as a leisure pursuit in Africa leads to important questions. How, for instance, did early African audiences respond to the films? What impact did the white man's "magic" have on local communities?

First Contact: "The Machine That Spits Out Shadows"

The injection of cinema into the cultural landscapes of the Western world, followed by rumors of spectators fleeing the theaters in terror, quickly became thematic fodder for films themselves. Robert Paul's *A Countryman's First Sight of the Animated Pictures* (1901) and Edison's *Uncle Josh at the Moving Picture Show* (1902) capitalized on the supposed gullibility of first-time spectators, although this genre failed to retain much traction beyond the novelty stage. In contrast, in Africa the theme became the overriding trope of cultural difference, the bluntest expression of what was perceived to be the yawning cultural chasm separating the civilized from the savage. From the introduction of photography in the mid-1800s and continuing with moving images well into the next century, one finds a barrage of references from photographers, filmmakers, explorers, officials, and settlers concerning the African's putative inability to comprehend both the evolving technologies of mimetic representation and the images they produced. In grappling with this theme, Robert Gordon, James Burns and Megan Vaughan have largely dismissed these reports either as self-serving expressions of assumed cultural superiority, or an inability to recognize African irony. In a similar vein, Michael Taussig and Ruth Mayer have commented on the ongoing fascination that whites exhibited with the so-called fascination of the primitive when confronted with the camera or the image.[37] But what strikes one immediately about the supposedly uniform African reception to European technology is how many human emotions are thereby reduced to mere "fascination," distorting or conflating in the process a wide array of possible sensations, including confusion, loathing, dread and sometimes even excitement. In this vein, Brian Larkin has rightly urged us not to overlook the potentially very real "destabilizing, [and] terrifying effects of technology" as the tools of cinema were first carted into remote areas.[38]

In fact, many of these interpretations are compatible, for we should remember that the technologies of visual representation (still cameras, movie cameras, tripods and projectors) were being introduced into the interior concurrently with modern technologies of war, and thus the very diffusion of the white man's "magic" clearly buttressed colonial control even as it sometimes led to apprehension among local populations. It is thus useful to reconfigure the varied forms of initial reception to "magical" technologies within the more specific context of European power over life and death in the colonial setting, rather than simply some hypothetical control over the supernatural. Indeed, the rhetoric of warfare often suffuses first contact folklore, with the related tropes of capture and slaughter figuring prominently. Through this prism, the declining influence of the Church Missionary Society (CMS) in Uganda in the early years of the 20th century was hardly surprising: revealingly, not long before missionaries showed films that "frightened the Acholi audience half to death" based on the notion that the missionaries had captured the *tipu* (souls) of those depicted on the screen, missionary Albert Pleydell had accidentally shot and killed a native woman.[39]

British travel writer Rosita Forbes and her small film crew experienced similar problems during her 1926 Ethiopian expedition when they stopped to film near the village of Burra:

> Jones set up the camera, knee-deep in the grain, but the result was surprising, for the whole concourse [of nearby Africans] threw themselves on their knees and bowed repeatedly, their eyes screwed up, their heads burrowing into the earth.
> "They think it is magic," said Hassen, and addressed them in halting Amharic.
> "If that thing looks at me I shall die," wailed a woman, tearing at her very scanty covering.[40]

And on another occasion when Forbes attempted to photograph two girls in a remote district, they quickly sprang away, "uttering shrill, far-carrying calls that were obviously the battle-cry of their people." Not sure exactly how to interpret the response, Forbes nevertheless drew the telling parallel between "magic" and weapons of war: "Whether they thought the Kodak was a manifestation of devildom, or a new form of firearm, I don't know."[41]

Two years after Forbes traveled through Ethiopia, famed glaciologist William O. Field was in the Sudan, working his way up the Bahr el Zeraf (an arm of the White Nile) taking footage for a travelogue entitled *Up the Nile to Central Africa* (1928). Spotting "a group of Dinkas" beside the river, he decided on a whim to film them. "On seeing me turn the telephoto lens toward them they all put up their hands and one woman grabbed a kid and thrust him behind a tree. I quickly took the camera away again and took no pictures, as one of the shikaris came up and said they [thought] I was going to shoot them."

More surprising than mistaking a rotating telephoto lens for a weapon was Field's interpretation of what had just transpired: "This seemed a primitive touch," he mused, "which in a way is nice to see, for it makes you realize how little some of these people come in contact with the outside world."[42] An alternative interpretation might be that the response was due less to a lack of familiarity with modern technology than it was to repeated exposure to the machinery of colonial subjugation. Indeed, the Dinka and the nearby Nuer were reticent to submit to British rule in the region, and had launched several resistance campaigns between 1919 and 1927 that were summarily suppressed (during a period of turmoil in which Britain allowed for nominal Egyptian independence but re-affirmed its imperial interests in the Sudan). Moreover, the fact that only a year before the anthropologist Frederick Wulsin was traveling up the Nile and filming a Dinka forced labor party being escorted by armed colonial authorities, may have cemented the uncomfortable parallel between "shooting" the Dinka and shooting the Dinka.[43] To round out the theme, Ruth Ben-Ghiat has shown that a similar correlation was purposely cultivated in North Africa, where the film projector was intentionally deployed by Italian officials as a veritable "'battleship on wheels,' creating images that would 'trample' and disarm the credulous native spectator" as a way to solidify colonial authority.[44]

As the colonial period proceeded it becomes clear that first contact folklore, functioning originally as a cultural corollary to colonial conquest, was increasingly bound up with what Mary Louis Pratt famously referred to as the "anti-conquest," with Europeans establishing hegemony while yet asserting their innocence: *the natives think we're here to kill them, but our intentions are noble—we only want to film them, and show them pictures.* During this era of consolidation, with many wars of conquest a bitter memory, "first contact" as a cultural trope became more formulaic, and indeed, seems to have entered its decadent stage. In the 1930s, a Cape Town newspaper smugly provided this headline for its British and Boer readers: "Bushmen Rush Screen to See Where Talkie Comes From. They like Mickey Mouse but Dancing Zulus Scared Them."[45] And by the 1950s John Brom, who was filming extensively in Africa on several expeditions, was repeating the refrain but with a twist: at this late date, argued Brom, the superstition of some Africans had begun to break down due to the scientific mindset imported by Western powers. As a reward to one dedicated African actor, Brom allowed him to look through the viewfinder: "I see, missiè, you catch images in the magic box, so that you can take them back with you into the white country."[46]

Due to different contexts and the richness of human experience there were, in fact, a number of possible first responses to the medium—according to some reports audience response even varied during a single showing. This was apparently the case in 1929 when director W.S. Van Dyke was securing footage for *Trader Horn* (1931), Hollywood's first feature shot on location in Africa. Van Dyke and his crew were entertaining visiting British officials in Uganda with production footage and safari films they had taken in the Congo. The audience also included some "native boys" and "native seamen" seeing motion pictures for the first time:

> I was absorbed during the course of the evening in studying the effect of the pictures on the natives. They appeared awe-struck during the first few minutes of the program; the thing was new to them and it took a little time to digest it and work out a satisfactory explanation. Then, gradually, it became an amusement and, as such, was a subject of merriment. For with the African there is no such thing as mute and inward enjoyment.[47]

In other cases, film showings generated a very different response, sometimes even constituting a forum for resistance when local communities recognized their possible political overtones. In Bandiagara (in present-day Mali) for instance, colonial officials first exposed locals in 1908 to moving pictures during an exhibition which reflected the underlying struggle between the two forms of authority in the region—Muslim and European. African Oralist Hampaté Ba provided a fascinating glimpse into the ensuing power struggle when local marabouts tried to sabotage the proceedings by framing the event as an evil seduction. Why would it take place in the darkness, they asked? Clearly there must be wicked intentions. On exhibition night, officials arrived with projector and films but were surprised to learn that the only spectators present were a few African noteworthies. As Hampaté Ba remembers it, the senior officer "began to shout like a dog: 'So, Alfa Maki! Why haven't more people shown up as I ordered? Are they making a mockery of me, or what? What are these manners here?'" The chief of the Sofa responded that Bandiagara residents were frightened to death, and even those few spectators who showed up felt like condemned men about to die, and might run away when the show began. The audience then initiated a subtle form of resistance by attending the screenings without actually watching them: "We attended the event ... but to ease our consciences, we closed our eyes and saw nothing."[48]

Because of Muslim taboos regarding religious imagery, this issue became even more pronounced in situations when whites tried to photograph local Muslims. Dorothy Pond was accompanying her husband on a Beloit College scientific (and filmmaking) expedition in Algeria in 1930 when her husband spotted some boys in a Muslim school playing outside. "That looks like a picture," said Alonzo, and they asked permission from the teacher to snap a photograph. Although the teacher gave his consent, when Alonzo focused his lens on the boys and prepared to snap the shutter, suddenly "the teacher gave a command. All the boys turned their backs to the camera just as it clicked."[49]

If these examples of resistance—an analytic framework developed by Manthia Diawara in the context of black spectatorship[50]—constituted one discernible response, it was equally true that many spectators embraced image-making technologies. In 1913, German explorer and filmmaker Hans Schomburgk was in central Togo filming *The White Goddess of the Wangora* (1913), one of the first feature films to be produced on the continent. According to actress Meg Gehrts, the crew initially experienced difficulty getting villagers to face the camera. "Like most savages," she commented, "these Togo natives have an inherent rooted aversion to being photographed." But Schomburgk, it turned out, had actually filmed some of the locals on a previous safari. Thus, in one of the very first examples of what would subsequently serve as the *raison d'être* of British colonial cinema, he set up a crude screen "and showed them themselves, their wives and their little ones, going about their avocations in their own homes. The effect was instantaneous. They had, of course, seen ordinary photographs before, but none of them had ever beheld any moving pictures," and the audience was ecstatic.[51] The film screening quickly succeeded in securing the needed extras for the shoot.

Stories proliferating in the white press, when not highlighting first contact fear, suggested that many African spectators quickly developed an irrational euphoria for the medium. In Leopoldville, for instance, one report following World War II claimed that a virtual riot broke out in a "native location" when regular film shows for Africans were temporarily interrupted. And British Medical Officer William Sellers, who pioneered experimental instructional and propaganda films in the 1920s, delighted "in recounting how, when a long procession of Native mourners approached an open air show in Nigeria, the bearers solemnly deposited the corpse at the edge of the audience whom the entire courtege contentedly joined, laughing heartily before resuming their macabre journey."[52] Yet whether reports issued from the white world were describing fear or euphoria, they collectively cast Africans as primitive neophytes reacting irrationally when confronted with new visual technologies, reinforcing claims of racial superiority that were continually invoked in the colonial setting.

Thus, inscribed upon the racialized African landscape was the notion of bewildered natives confronted by all-knowing Europeans bearing the priceless gifts of civilization. There were a few opposing opinions, however, about Africans' supposed inability to read images correctly: roughly half a century before Robert Gordon argued that "stories of Bushmen rushing movie screens should be read as morality plays that served the settlers' needs,"[53] Anthony Sampson, liberal white editor of South Africa's *Drum* magazine in the 1950s, made a similar point involving the introduction of other "magical" technologies imported from the West:

> I doubt if the white man's magic had ever really surprised them; the story of the blanket-boy gazing in astonishment at the Golden City is, I suspect, a white man's folktale, a kind of projected admiration for himself. I remember a doctor telling me how disappointed he was by primitive Zulus seeing an X-ray. They looked at it, understood it, nodded and walked away.[54]

As we will see later in this study, the vexing issue of audience reception increasingly absorbed British officials as they developed the ideological framework for a colonial cinema project targeting African spectators. J. Koyinde Vaughan, providing a Nigerian perspective in 1960 on the relationship between didactic cinema and European power, has spoken critically of British colonial film units "faithfully reflecting [only] the psychology of the colonial power anxious to appear enlightened and able to guide her subjects along prescribed paths to 'progress.'"[55] This was clearly the guiding principle of the several units operating both before and after World War II. However, while most white settlers and officials argued for years that African viewers were incapable of understanding basic storylines and plot development, many missionaries and mining officials as early as the 1920s assumed that "sophistication" was only a matter of time. Just as important, regular exposure to moving pictures over a short period, they believed, would lead not only to basic comprehension but also increasing demand. It was true that, in the 1920s, the majority of African spectators were seeing moving pictures for the first time. But there was a small minority that had had some exposure in the very earliest period. Besides the examples mentioned above, where did the first indigenous spectators south of the Sahara find opportunities for viewing movies? The archives are scattered, the records are sparse, yet slowly the picture of early African spectatorship is coming into focus.

Around the turn of the century, French West Africa provided some of the first venues for African spectatorship when Lumière shorts were screened publicly by a French circus group. Film screenings in Dakar were most likely intermittent in the early years, but by the mid–1920s had become institutionalized as a form of urban entertainment. The city had played a key role in French colonizing efforts in the late–19th century, and had been made the capital of French West Africa in 1902. Despite its prominence, it was notorious for its uneven development and dreary African quarters. Yet in a nod perhaps to French associationist rhetoric, authorities eventually initiated open-air film screenings on a side street in an African residential area, with rows of seats set up for adult spectators, an African stationed in the back to read the subtitles to the European films, and children "lying on the ground behind the screen at the foot of a gigantic tree."[56]

If Francophone Africa set the stage early but incrementally, other areas were not far behind. In German East Africa, although Africans were given few opportunities for viewing films, in 1909 traveling showman Wexelsen returned a year after his successful cinema exhibition for whites, this time organizing a show for both black and white spectators.

In the Belgian Congo, Catholic missionaries began showing films to the colonized as early as 1910, only two years after Leopold II sold his private fiefdom to the Belgian state.[57] Yet fearful of the unknown consequences that might result from film spectatorship, the Belgian Congo before World War II restricted African access to commercial films, and during the conflict, Africans were restricted from viewing any films other than war propaganda films demonizing the Nazis. Yet after the war an enterprising ex–Army sergeant from Belgium named Jean Hourdebise opened the first cinema to cater to an African clientele in Leopoldville, and later opened two cinemas—Albertum Cinema and the Roxy.

In Anglophone Africa, as we have seen, indigenes first encountered motion pictures at Glover Memorial Hall in 1903 at screenings of what were presumably early actualities deemed significant enough to bring out the Prince of Lagos. Surprisingly, these daily showings originally scheduled to run between the 12th and 22nd of August have been little explored in the literature, presumably because of the overarching model of cultural imperialism that guides the field. However, while recognizing that the films were of foreign import, and shown by the Spanish firm Balboa and Company, it was in fact Nigerian nationalist Herbert Macaulay who instigated the events, which were frequented by residents of Lagos. Thus, the showings were an arena wherein Africans enjoyed a spectacle organized by a highly respected Nigerian who was already issuing critiques of British rule.

In an interesting case revealing that trade does not always follow the flag, the *Lagos Weekly Record* reported that "a somewhat curious incident [occurred at Glover Memorial] when His Majesty King Alphonso of Spain was exhibited" at the showing. Apparently the audience was surprised that images of the Spanish monarch were not followed up by images of Britain's own King Edward. In any event, this shows the lack of governmental oversight during the anarchic first years of cinema's introduction into Africa. Yet this confusion did not detract from the popularity of the screenings. On the contrary, the showings were "the talk of the town," and even on the sixth night, Saturday, the hall was so crowded that a representative of Balboa struggled for a quarter of an hour just to get from the vestibule to the seating area.[58] In fact, even though one newspaper suggested that admission prices be lowered, the crowds kept coming and Balboa agreed to extend their dates, and even introduce new films on the following Saturday. Perhaps because of their popularity, the next weekend, on August 22, Prince Eleko arrived along with a number of White Cap Chiefs. The celebrity status they brought to the proceedings, along with the new slate of films, guaranteed that crowds would continue to surge to the hall throughout the following week, until the show finally closed to great fanfare and a large ball on Friday, August 28, after an impressive run of 19 nights.[59] Following the success in Lagos, Balboa apparently took its spectacle on the road, giving shows along the West African coast which have yet to be charted.

One of the earliest records of a film showing for indigenous spectators in British East Africa dates to September 1909, as William Boyce prepared the launch of his massive "African Balloonograph Expedition" (see next chapter). In addition to the spectacle of the largest expedition to date organized in Nairobi, Boyce offered three motion picture shows at a local club to raise money for St. Andrew's Church. The first was an afternoon show for white children, the second an evening show for adult white settlers, and the third a showing for "natives" the following night.[60]

In general, Africans had limited exposure to motion pictures in the first decade or so, but this pattern began to change in the 1910s. In Southern Rhodesia, for instance, a detective from the Rhodesian Criminal Investigations Department visited Salisbury's segregated Empire Theatre in 1914 to study the demographics of the audience. His report expressed concern that cinema "has a tendency to create a certain amount of lewdness in the minds of the younger persons and natives." The dual concerns over black male sexuality and white female purity, expressed in colonial milieus in Africa, soon led to calls within the colonies and the metropoles for a differential censorship for blacks and whites. In fact, during this transitional period, as Africans were given more opportunities to see films, venues became increasingly segregated and film exhibitions explicitly targeting black spectators were often subjected to an additional level of censorship over and above that for whites.

In 1910, the showman Wexelsen (whom we encountered before showing films in German East Africa), expanded his activities in West Africa. He was one of the pioneer cinema exhibitors on the Gold Coast, returning again two years later to "entertain the public" as well as taking his show on the road to Southern Nigeria, presumably Lagos.[61] According to a report in the *Lagos Standard*, in 1914 Glover Memorial Hall hosted another cinema screening, with Empire Cinema Company now providing the entertainment. Curiously, editors seemed not to have heard of the famous film showings of 11 years before, as they erroneously claimed that "this is the first time we believe such an entertainment was held in West Africa."[62] Glover Memorial Hall, it should be noted, was a leading multi-use venue for aspiring African thespians to perform European plays, and in later decades became a venue for film classics like *Gone with the Wind* (1939). By 1925, another enterprising independent operator (Wexelsen again?) had logged in an impressive 30,000 miles along the West African coast carrying a stash of films and projector in an old Ford, and even making forays deep into the forested interior where many Africans had their first glimpse of both a white man and motion pictures. Not only did the condition of the roads make this enterprise impressive, but the films themselves, even when stored carefully in film tins, tended to erode very quickly in the warm and humid equatorial climate. Yet the exhibitions were conducted successfully outdoors, some shown on a sheet outstretched between oil cans in a cocoa shed.[63]

Up until the independence era, film showings for Africans, whether within British Africa or beyond, were frequently held outdoors, although during the Mau Mau Emergency in Kenya some venues were discontinued over security concerns. According to one African account in 1953: "All but one of the fifty-odd cinemas in the Gold Coast and Nigeria are open-air, ranging from well-built concrete amphitheatres with canvas chairs of the type favored by film directors on the set to a few square yards of sand, enclosed by a cane fence and holding half a dozen benches." Yet the exception was impressive: Accra's Opera had a seating capacity of 2,000, and offered three shows a day (with different films) and new programs presented daily. The most popular films included Westerns like *Tomahawk* (1951) about a gold strike, and *Mark of the Renegade* (1951) starring Ricardo Montalban; but the surprise hit was *The Boy Kumasenu* (1952), a documentary about West African life produced by the postwar Gold Coast Film Unit with an all–African cast.[64] The Opera showings reflect how routinized film-going had become in Accra and other urban areas by 1950, although it was not the first cinema house in the city catering to an African clientele. In the early 1920s, in fact, the Accra Picture Palace was already pulling in the crowds. Despite its name, this salmon-painted theater with four "crooked pillars" in the front was a fairly small venue, but served as a melting pot for Fanti, Ga, Hausa and Kru men congregating in close proximity as they cheered their heroes on the screen.[65]

In discussing the general reaction of Africans to moving images, Onookome Okome has asserted that "the initial response from the indigenous population was understandably euphoric. The people loved the magic of the moving image." Yet he suggests that such exhilaration was partly a by-product of colonization: cinema for a people largely severed from their traditional culture served as an exciting new diversion and was simply a cathartic release from the drudgery of colonial life.[66] As we have seen, there were, in reality, a variety of first-contact responses, depending partly on context and location. What does emerge from the historical record is that Europeans were frequently mystified by unanticipated African responses. In 1940, members of Nigeria's Health Propaganda Unit brought health and hygiene films to the remote city of Daura, whose residents had never witnessed motion pictures. The film unit pulled into the marketplace, where a makeshift screen was stretched across the back of the propaganda lorry. After a preliminary short showing "twelve tiny, black boys" marching, the main program began. The object of the film was "to demonstrate in a village, such as they would recognize, the evils of carelessness and the virtues of cleanliness":

> There flashed on the screen a village with tumbledown huts and rubbish strewn alleys. In the untidy compounds broken pots held puddles of dirty water, ideal breeding places for the mosquito. Bits of refuse and food, swarming with flies, lay about in the sand, where dirty-nosed children sprawled naked. At the well stood an old man, his unbandaged feet suppurating with guinea worm sores.... The men were weak and ridden with disease, so their farms were neglected and bore poor crops; the women were undernourished and bore sickly children. It was indeed a most pitiful sight.[67]

The object of the presentation—"to impress upon the people the tragedy which results from death and disease"—apparently failed. Rather than taking the moral to bear, the Hausa spectators "on the contrary found it highly amusing! The sight of an old man, wielding his pick so feebly that he merely scratched the surface of his farm, was the object of unsympathetic laughter and ribald remarks." Responses like these reverberated throughout the colonies as moving images began to circulate the subcontinent. Were Africans contesting the depiction of crude stereotypes of village life? Were they amused at "seeing their own kind" on the screen, or was the medium itself unsettling to neophytes? In this particular case, officials initially argued that the response was due to the "fatalist" orientation of the Muslim Hausa: "He does not view sickness and death with our eyes. He considers them as inevitable and natural events. Allah wills it. There is no more to be said." But this in itself was not sufficient to elicit laughter. In fact, the film unit finally conceded that the propaganda message was ineffective primarily because of the film's narrative deficiencies, and therefore Hausa spectators had "rejected the authenticity of the picture. Where had anyone ever seen a village so utterly miserable, so utterly destitute? It was exaggerated; and, like the antics of the court fool at sala time, an object for mirth." Based on this conclusion, they suggested that future films should contain more nuanced storylines with a single village containing "some rich men and some poor, some good some bad, some clean, some dirty." What is noteworthy here is that the film unit's own conclusions concerning African reception, and the colonizers' subsequent call for revised plots, belies the claims of most white observers that Africans were incapable of decoding moving images.

During World War I, newsreels about the conflict increasingly permeated colonies such as Nigeria, where *The Time of Lagos* and similar documentaries were shown in August 1916. Furthermore, within several years of the successful 1903 Glover Memorial Hall showings, Europeans like Stanley D. Jones had begun to show films twice a week at the Empire Hall and four other Lagos locations. By 1921, cinema was becoming entrenched as a popular recreational pastime among young and old residents alike, who often waited in long lines for the doors to open. Enthusiasm for motion pictures extended to smaller areas like Ebute Meta and Oshodi as new cinemas opened throughout the colony.[68]

By the end of the war Africans elsewhere were also seeing films in increasing numbers. Returning soldiers of the Rhodesia Native Regiment, for example, were invited to a screening at Salisbury's Palace Theatre and walked down First Street in two single-file columns, entering the theater through the main concrete arch while white elites looked on.[69] And in the 1920–30s, mission stations and schools, including Makerere and Lovedale, sporadically showed movies to their charges,[70] while in Uganda, Provincial Commissioner Arthur Weatherhead even tried his hand at cinematography and produced some amateurish shorts to be shown to the local population. Those deemed most successful in "making natives laugh," he discovered, included "(1) a bull pawing the ground, (2) the greasy pole, (3) two men stirring up locusts to make them fly."[71]

In Togoland, part of which had been parceled out to France after World War I, a few Africans by the end of the 1920s were finding enough disposable income to purchase films and show them privately in homes or short-lived cinema houses. In one example in Lomé, the proprietor of the Tonyeviadji café was regularly entertaining up to 30 patrons with motion pictures, a fact that did not go unnoticed by colonial commissioner Robert de Guise, despite the absence of any legal restrictions in the *indigénat* prohibiting the showings.[72] Similarly, white guests staying at the nearby Hotel du Golfe around midcentury could hardly have failed to notice the boisterous open-air cinema adjacent to the hotel which might be showing a Lex Barker *Tarzan* film or similar fare to rowdy native audiences.[73]

In many areas, however, venues for blacks were slow to materialize. We have seen that officials in Lusophone Africa seem to have looked askance at the idea of cultivating a black film-going culture. Yet even in Mozambique and Angola, where cinema was originally considered a white diversion, newsreels were increasingly projected for black audiences for propaganda purposes. In British-controlled Nyasaland, too, colonial officials looked upon the cinema with some trepidation. It is unclear when Africans there were first exposed to the medium, but a mid–1930s memo to Colonial Secretary Cunliffe-Lister stated "during the past four years not more than ten films have been exhibited to natives at the Blantyre Cinema." Of these, approximately eight were categorized as "educational or instructional," while the remaining two were comedies. In 1934, four local Europeans tried to fill the void with Traveling Cinemas, Ltd. to show films in Zomba, Cholo, Mlanje and Lilongwe. Unfortunately, the first batch of films procured from African Consolidated Films (formed in South Africa in 1931 through the merger of Kinemas Ltd. and African Theatres and Films) in January 1935 was deemed "entirely unsuitable" for the prospective audience:

1. In Search of Origins: Screening Motion Pictures in Africa 33

Some of the films sent were old and broken, one depicted minute mechanical and scientific curiosities, and others appeared again to represent such strange forms of American humour ... that they were scarcely understandable even to the Europeans present at the trial exhibition, whereas the few natives watching appeared entirely perplexed.[74]

Opportunities for African spectatorship remained circumscribed in other areas as well. Southwest Africa was a case in point, despite the fact that motion pictures had been introduced by the Germans as early as the 1910s. In 1915, during the Southwest Africa Campaign, Allied forces from South Africa successfully occupied the colony. After the war, two colonial NCO's saw their proposal to provide an open-air "educational cinema for natives" in the Windhoek African Township rejected by an administrator who argued that "the time was not yet ripe for such an experiment." Another proposal in 1925 met with a similar fate when U.E. Ludwig attempted to provide movies for Ovambo workers at the copper, lead

Explorer John Brom helped construct this crude cinema, the first in Kasongo, Belgian Congo. African spectators gather here to witness their first film, 1955 (courtesy Olga Brom Spencer).

and zinc Tsumeb Mine. Initially securing management assent, Ludwig purchased a projector and was preparing to show *Die Schwarze Katze* (*The Black Cat*) when mine director Herr Regel back-pedaled and canceled the experiment.[75] In fact, one has to fast-forward another 20 years before a "Coloured" was able to secure a license to exhibit films in Luderitz.[76]

While in some colonies officials were restricting African access to motion pictures, in others they were the first to introduce them. Cinema had become an integral part of urban life in the Belgian Congo by the 1950s, but in many towns and rural areas the medium had made little to no impact. When filmmaker John Brom visited the town of Kasongo, home to the Catholic Mission of White Sisters who ministered to thousands of Africans, he found a local official there eager to incorporate film into community life. Fortunately for Brom, not only had "Mr. Jacques" been given instructions by the colonial government to provide Brom assistance for his film *On the Footsteps of Stanley* (1955) that traced the route of the 19th-century explorer, but he was already in possession of both a collection of 16mm films and a projector. Thus, when Brom arrived, Jacques solicited his help and together they erected a bamboo structure that served as the town's first movie theater. It may have been crude, but it was nevertheless the pioneering venue in the vicinity, bringing cinema to the local population.[77]

These anecdotes of early African spectatorship share several features: the showings were intermittent, local in scope, and, with a few exceptions, were controlled by whites. Moreover, many regions increasingly restricted or regulated opportunities for both film production and exhibition. Francophone Africa is particularly instructive in this regard. Despite a benign neglect in the early years, there was increasing concern by the 1930s, leading Pierre Laval, Minister of the Colonies, to issue *Le Décret Laval* (the Laval Decree) in 1934: "The cinema is becoming more and more an instrument of propaganda," he declared, urging that the time was right for "colonial administrators to use the screen for their profit." The decree, though, also showed the extent to which France was concerned about unrestricted filmmaking undermining the positive image of its civilizing mission. According to Phyllis Martin, officials were to maintain "strict vigilance" over "stray Europeans with photographic equipment ... wandering in remote corners of a colony,"[78] while Africans were to be restricted from producing films altogether, a policy that Diawara has denounced as a way "to keep cinema from playing a revolutionary and/or evolutionary role in Africa."[79] In addition, a censorship board would review imported talkies and issue licenses for film exhibition. In reality, though, this policy (even with its draconian implications) had mixed success due to pressure from above and below. Not only did the French film industry ensure that most films would pass the censorship test, but young film-goers who occasionally boycotted shows or rioted when a given film seemed to lack "action," apparently led to an attenuation of the government's censorship zeal.[80] Another simple but effective strategy for bypassing racial restrictions of the decree, one exploited by a young Ousmane Sembène in the late 1930s,[81] involved creating a diversion outside theaters, thus enabling one's friends to enter surreptitiously.

Cinema restrictions also had mixed results elsewhere. When the Empire opened in Dar es Salaam in 1929, the colonial government established a Cinematograph Licensing Board made up of Europeans and Indians to oversee censorship. Pointedly, even with the growing number of imports following the talkie revolution and the growth in black spectatorship, the board was empowered to restrict Africans from viewing certain objectionable films. And yet within three years the censorship laws had been significantly revised. The new Cinematograph Ordinance of 1935 retained the right of the board to censor films, but now all films passed for circulation could be viewed by all races.[82]

First Contact Reframed

With the notable exceptions of Samama Chikly, Herbert Macauley, and scattered screenings elsewhere, records of first contact suggest that non–Europeans had little control over the medium. While this is largely true, scholarship on colonial-era cinema is uncovering previously obscured traces of African agency. Indeed, the first bioscope in the Gold Coast was actually the realized dream of an African businessman granted a license by the colonial government. And in Nigeria, colonial authorities granted the Lagosian S.H. Pearse a license to form the (presumably short-lived) Kelvin Traveling Cinema Company as early as 1918. Similarly, another enterprising African, S.O. Dawodu, put together a film showing at the African Tennis Club in Lagos in October 1927.[83] Other non–Europeans also played a role in Nigerian cinema history. In 1937, the West African Pictures Company was formed by S. Kahlil—a Syrian expatriate in Lagos—and his company was granted the use of Glover Hall for three nights a week to host cinematograph shows. Kahlil soon established Regal Cinema and Royal Cinema in the city, and Rex Cinema in nearby Ebute Metta.

The most remarkable attempt to inaugurate a cinema exhibition circuit under African control was Solomon Plaatje's Travelogue and Coloured American Bioscope. During a visit to America in 1920, Plaatje secured a projector in Philadelphia and films from Henry Ford and Tuskegee President Robert Russa Moton. He then organized his own circuit for indigenous audiences throughout South Africa and the Bechaunaland towns of Serowe and Kanye to promote black uplift and education along Bookerite lines. His shows opened with talks in Sesotho, Zulu and other African tongues, with one report of a showing at the West Fort Leper Asylum in Pretoria noting the patients' enthusiasm:

> The programme started with the Islands of the St Lawrence..., it finished with an interesting display of the city and people of Havana, Cuba. None of the pictures, however, evoked so much enthusiasm as the work and drills of the famous Tuskegee, Booker Washington's great institution in Alabama. At the close, the visitors were loudly cheered, and asked to "come again with the pictures."[84]

Plaatje's Bioscope, popular in rural environs, seems to have elicited less interest among industrial workers and township residents, no doubt due to the popularity of new bioscopes in places like Johannesburg serving up the usual dose of Western thrillers in the mining compounds. While Plaatje's Bioscope was an extraordinary attempt by a lone African to bring cinema to the black masses in southern Africa, ultimately it failed to blossom into a sufficiently remunerative operation and the circuit was soon abandoned.

During the colonial period, as Africans were increasingly reconceived as cinema spectators, many began working as crewmembers of filmmaking expeditions (commercial or otherwise), but generally served as lowly porters, interpreters and cooks, hauling supplies and vehicles over rough terrain, and performing domestic duties required by film crews. Occasionally, however, they were pulled into the inner circle and given opportunities to work the camera. The expeditions of wildlife filmmakers Martin and Osa Johnson are instructive in this regard. Originally traveling with small teams, by the mid–1920s the technological requirements for making good films required larger expeditions and a broader distribution of duties. During the filming of *Simba* in East Africa in 1927, African crewmembers (and Osa as well) began handling the Akeley cameras mounted on cars, although, not surprisingly, film credits fail to name them. Indeed, Martin sometimes spoke disparagingly of the African's ability to operate a camera. Trying to capture footage of a sleeping rhinoceros, for instance, he allowed his cook Phisie to try

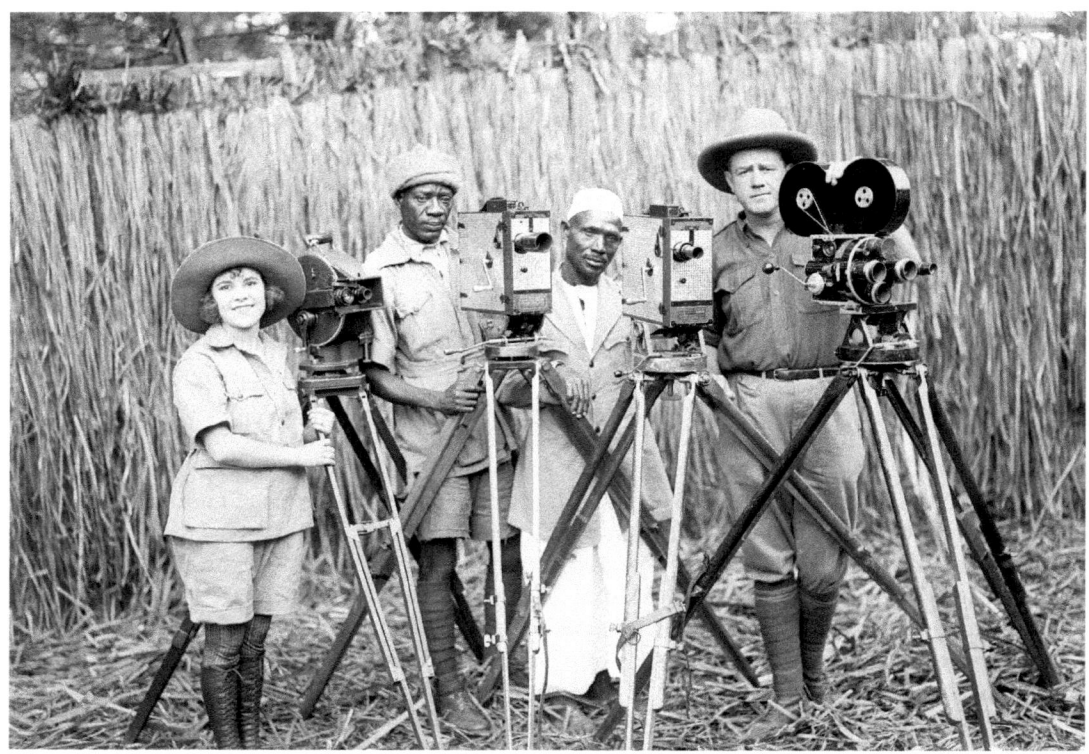

Martin (far right) and Osa Johnson (far left) posing with African assistants and cameras, 1921 (Image #129104 American Museum of Natural History Library).

his hand at filming despite Martin's complaints that "it is difficult to teach natives how to handle the crank of a camera evenly. They have a tendency to pull sharply on the downward stroke and push slowly as the crank ascends." Although Phisie had apparently performed well during a test take, Martin discovered later that during the filming of the rhino, Phisie was operating another crank simultaneously that opened the panoramic lens. The result was that when developed, the footage "showed nothing but a view of the clear sky above." While for Martin this mistake was due to native ignorance, we should note that not only was Phisie new to the task, but during the filming the crew had moved dangerously close to the rhino and intentionally wakened him. According to the report, the dangerous animal suddenly "jumped to its feet, startled, [and] charged within eighteen feet of us, snorting and pawing the ground" before retreating. One's suspicion that Africans played an increasingly pivotal role in the Johnsons' film projects is largely borne out by both cutaways and photographs of their expeditions showing indigenous crewmembers handling the cameras with regularity.[85]

Another overlooked example of an early African cinematographer was a remarkable Barotse named Mudalla, who at 70 years old worked with American wildlife filmmakers Wynant and Margaret Hubbard in Northern Rhodesia and Portuguese East Africa in the 1920s. During much of the shooting, Mudalla, who himself suffered from a "crumpled shoulder, where a lion had bitten him," was tasked with filming solo in lion country, a phenomenon rare in the colonial era. Mudalla filmed at considerable risk to himself (despite herd depopulation), although on occasion the Hubbards expressed frustration when he

1. In Search of Origins: Screening Motion Pictures in Africa 37

Mohamed Bayoumi, a pioneer of independent African Cinema, 1920s (courtesy Alexandria and Mediterranean Research Center at the Bibliotheca Alexandria, Egypt).

failed to secure needed footage of buffalo, while at other times it was simply too hot to handle the camera effectively.[86]

While Phisie and Mudalla were working in the employ of Americans, there were a few cases of Africans filming independently of external control. Indeed, Kgosi Molefhi of Bechuanaland seems to have transgressed a few racial norms: in the 1930s he emerged as a pioneering amateur African cinematographer, shooting home movies in the protectorate and exhibiting them to African audiences in Mochudi.[87] While British authorities seem to have had little objection, the same was not true a few years later when he publicly whipped a white man during a personal dispute. In another example in the same decade, when Geoffrey Chitty Latham and Leslie Alan Notcutt were showing the products of their colonial film unit (see Chapter 7) to African locals in the Ugandan Administrative Headquarters at Iganga, they were intrigued when the Saza Chief of Kamuli, William Wilberforce Kajumbula Nadiope, showed up with a number of his own films. Interestingly, Notcutt and Latham actually agreed to include some of his short productions in their own program.[88] In many ways, though, the real pioneer of indigenous cinema in Africa was Mohamed Bayoumi, born in Tanta in 1894, in the Egyptian Delta. Due to his strong nationalist leanings, Bayoumi had taken part in the 1919 Revolution, and in the 1920s traveled to Berlin, where he was mentored by the German filmmaker Boehringer, who encouraged him (through his expertise and funding) to form his own production company back home. Therefore, after relocating to Cairo, Bayoumi founded Amon Film in 1923, and released the landmark short fiction film *Barsoum Looks for Employment* that same year. An interesting precursor to *Barom Sarret* (Ousmane Sembène's social commentary on postcolonial Dakar produced 40 years later), Bayoumi's film critiqued the disparity of wealth in Egyptian culture through the sad struggles of protagonist Barsoum as he seeks employment. Bayoumi was also notable in that he developed his own newsreel series to counter British imperialism and champion Egyptian heroes and traditional culture. Notably, upon the return of popular indigenous leader Saad Zaghlul after his exile in the Seychelles, Bayoumi positioned himself to take riveting newsreel footage of the boisterous parade in Cairo.[89]

While important, these isolated stories of African agency should not detract from the lived reality of most Africans in the colonial period—that the power to control the world of images was, for the most part, lodged firmly in the white world. It was true that in the tense years leading up to independence in the Ivory Coast, an African named Gogro (described by filmmaker Hassoldt Davis as an "RDA Communist man") actually tried to turn the tables on Davis and his wife, who were scrambling to secure footage of "the customs of ... primitives before they completely disappear through their own evolution." Because the Davises were especially interested in capturing "sorcery, cannibalism, [and] ritual murder" wherever they could find it, Gogro had apparently secretly trailed behind them to expose their efforts.[90] During the filming of a series of bloody animal sacrifices for *Jungle Terror* (1949), Hassoldt reported that he suddenly "saw the flash of another camera lens, pointed straight at us":

> And that, my dear, is our favorite Communist dwarf, Gogro, the one who will travel ahead of us to ruin our chances with the villages. Do you see what he wants? To show photographs of us filming this ceremony of a backward tribe, claiming that we will exploit it for our vile capitalist ends.[91]

Hassoldt Davis was apparently unperturbed by the distraction, and would continue the theme of *Jungle Terror* in his 1959 film *Sorcerer's Village*. But while Davis may have thought of himself as swimming against the tide, he was not alone as he struggled to salvage on celluloid the alleged primeval backwardness of Africa. Indeed, as the next chapter reveals, Africans throughout the colonial period were largely relegated to satisfying Western stereotypes of primitive Others as motion picture cameras began to roll at the dawn of the 20th century.

2

The Scramble for Images

Strange Savages, Paid Primitives, Negotiating Natives

A glance at the manifests of trade goods before the modern age reveals one product conspicuously lacking: images. But during the trans–Atlantic slave trade and the subsequent "era of legitimate commerce," European printers mass-produced elaborate maps of Africa reflecting an expanding culture of visuality in the West and the deep associations forged between images, empires and cartography. As Thomas Bennett has noted, it was the "color, cartouches, vignettes, boundary lines and blank spaces" that helped facilitate a European colonial presence on the African continent.[1] These maps, so critical to the expanding imperial mindset of Europeans, were supplemented by a brisk trade in black-and-white etchings of coastal Africans in their "natural habitat" that circulated among cosmopolitan European society.

In the 1800s, with the slave trade in steep decline, Africans themselves were still occasionally pulled from their surroundings and displayed in the western world, individually as circus or zoo freaks in the case of Saartjie Baartman (the "Hottentot Venus") and later, Ota Benga; or collectively, in the case of 250 Congolese on ethnographic display at the *villages nègres* built for Tervuren's 1897 world's fair. Expositions functioned as revealing celebrations of a new imperial splendor as scientific inquiries and leisure pursuits coalesced with Europe's rise to global pre-eminence. Accordingly, the African as (often naked) performer exposed a shift in how Africans were perceived through the West's racialized cultural prisms. Formerly a hewer-of-wood and drawer-of-water, the black body—whether exhibited in the flesh or in emerging media—was reconfigured through ideologically charged visual constructs that denoted its still disempowered status: Physical Curiosity / Cultural Other / Vanquished Enemy / Noble Savage / Last Primitive.

These stereotypes were hard at work in the 19th century, as David Livingstone, Henry Morton Stanley and others popularized the exploration genre with hefty tomes describing their harrowing adventures among the natives. Etchings to complement travel accounts became a veritable *sine qua non* as printing presses went into overdrive. By the turn of the century, images of Primeval Africa were having a profound effect in Europe—indeed, in many ways European notions of what it was to be "civilized" were crafted in contradistinction to the images of the Dark Continent in these accounts.

If etchings provided Europeans with some sense of the radically different cultures of Africa, photography brought those differences into stark relief, yet at the same time generated a profound sense of closeness, a tactile immediacy hitherto lacking in other, more vaguely articulated forms of representation. Following Joseph Niepce's grainy 1827 black-and-white image, photography revolutionized how the Western world looked at itself, and in the case of Africa, how it viewed indigenous peoples. It was, thus, no surprise that Livingstone's brother Charles joined him as official photographer for his famous 1858 Zambezi expedition.[2] By the end of the New Imperialism period it was clear that images would play a role in the cultural mapping of Africa, given the potpourri of lantern slides, stereographs and *cartes postales* bringing Africa increasingly within the purview of the "civilized" West.[3] But while cinema might be expected to play a similar role, it was unclear initially if European imperial powers would themselves seize the initiative. Whereas large-scale monuments and huge colonial expositions were public ventures that could be justified as integral to colonial state–building projects, motion pictures constituted a new medium developed, as was photography, through individual initiative in the private sector. Therefore, while there was, in the first instance, no carefully designed master plan for cinema in Africa, no premeditated conspiracy to interweave film into the fabric of imperialism, there was nevertheless a pre-existing ideological loom capitalizing on the power of the visual to capture far-off peoples and incorporate them into new discursive tapestries. When European explorers, then, discovered that "the Tswana of southern Africa [made] reluctant subjects because of the belief that the photograph separated a person from his image and hence could capture the self," they were perhaps more right than they knew.[4]

These varied uses of the visual to delineate cultural superiority, however, do not a coherent colonial policy make. In his study of German colonial culture, John Short has rightly stressed the ambiguous rather than airtight relationship between recreational colonial amusements and actual colonial policies. In fact, the many ideological variants of exoticism in the over-determined images of Africans at the dawn of the 20th century were not tied exclusively to a single colonizing project but rather had a broader pan–European pedigree.[5] Because of this, colonial policies for European powers ultimately required a more carefully articulated notion of the function that moving images might serve in colonial bureaucracies. Beginning with a discussion of the intersection of empires, images and ideologies, this chapter continues with a rough taxonomy of the many documentary cinema projects in Africa that comprised colonial cinema, although a full compilation of the thousands of films produced during this era is beyond the scope of this study. Moreover, the genres were never discrete, but rather blurred significantly at the boundaries: some safari films sensationalized African wildlife, while others sought scientific validation; some ethnographic films enlarged the scope of anthropological enquiry, yet others served as little more than colonial propaganda aids; and some missionary films advertised their religious calling exclusively, even as others peddled ethnographic themes, and so on.

Boundaries, in fact, were blurred in a second sense. As this study makes clear, mass black spectatorship appeared in tandem with concern over African migration patterns from rural areas to industrial centers. Yet the determination by colonial officials to regulate that movement was often absent when it came to European and American filmmaking endeavors, excepting those cases where internal security was deemed an issue. Film crews presumed the right to move unencumbered through pacified African communities across the broad continental mass. As a result, with the onset of the Scramble for Africa and the resulting continental partitioning, commercial interests, missionaries, scientists, adventurers and colonial officials engaged in a veritable Scramble for Images that continued unabated up to decolonization.

Empires and Images

Just as Germany jump-started the Scramble for Africa by hosting the 1884–1885 Berlin Conference, so did its influential colonial lobby jump-start campaigns to sell German expansion into Africa, New Guinea and the Marshall Islands. Strands of the colonial movement coalesced in 1887 as did the Deutsche Kolonialgesellschaft (DKG) to generate colonial enthusiasm through lectures, colonial exhibitions, chromolithographs and lantern slides. Although a proposal by a Dr. Stuhlmann to incorporate motion pictures was rejected in 1898, cinema's increasing popularity put pressure on the DKG, which acquiesced by sponsoring a 1905 tour of German Southwest Africa and German East Africa by amateur filmmaker Carl Müller, the owner of an Altenburg café. Scenes of dancing natives contrasted with images highlighting the weighty colonial presence, including a German ocean liner, colonial administration buildings, and Askari soldiers engaged in military exercises. Müller's films were important because they appeared just as German officials were eager to portray the supposedly benign features of colonial rule, especially given the fallout following suppression of the Herero and Maji Maji revolts.

Müller's films played only a minor role in the larger world of colonial-themed marketing in Germany, given that "caricatured images of exotic peoples in exotic places smiled down from posters or peeked out from pantries advertising all manner of products," by the turn of the century.[6] Furthermore, rising in tandem with this expanding commodified exoticism, British, French and Italian films still inundated the German market in the early 20th century, making it difficult for domestic filmmakers to enter the fray.[7] Müller did return to Africa the following year, though, traveling through Togoland, Cameroun and German Southwest Africa, securing images applauded by the *Deutsche Kolonialzeitung* for "their great freshness and liveliness [and] insight into the life and activity of Africa."

Similarly, pioneering cinematographer Georg Furkel traveled to Southwest Africa and filmed the Herero Revolt, while the firm Deutsche-Bioscop Gesellschaft and its competitors succeeded in producing a number of colonial films on location, including the Ernst Schlüsser Company's *Bilder aus unseren deutschen Kolonien* (*Images from Our German Colonies*, 1913). But as Wolfgang Furhmann notes, in terms of government sponsorship the Reichskolonialamt (German Imperial Office) generally resisted offering filmmakers direct support in the colonies until World War I, a conflict that "made any supply of films from the colonies impossible and marked the end of film production in the colonies" due to Allied blockades.[8] The newly formed Deutsche Kolonial-Filmgesellschaft refused to let this annoyance hinder it, however, continuing to produce colonial films in Berlin during the hostilities.

Italy, during the pre-fascist period, saw the private film sector harnessing cinema to the country's empire-building aspirations, often championing Ancient Rome's imperialist adventures in the littoral. Director Giovanni Pastrone took advantage of recent gains from the Turko-Italian War for his ground-breaking epic *Cabiria* (1914). Filmed largely in Turin and using lavish backdrops, but complemented by location shooting in Tunisia, Gabriele D'Annunzio's screenplay featured a tale of kidnapping, slavery and rescue set in Rome and Carthage during the Second Punic War. The film's popularity among Italian audiences justified its later use as a template for films on Ancient Rome that glorified Italy's North African presence. Yet in the short term, *Cabiria* was released concurrently with European hostilities which led to social destabilization and a crisis within the film industry, resulting in the heavy importation of films from Hollywood's "Big Four."[9] Mussolini later countered American influence by promoting the Educational Cinematographic Union (*Istituto Luce*), which served fascist newsreel propaganda needs during the Ethiopian occupation and World War

II. Indeed, one scholar asserts that because of its perceived value as a tool for mass education and persuasion, cinema was "the regime's strongest weapon" in the interwar period.[10]

Based on the 1923 novel *Kif Tebbi: Romanzo Africano* by Luciano Zuccoli, *Kif Tebbi*, a film directed by Mario Camerini in 1928, glorified the 1911 Italo-Turkish War in North Africa, and by implication, the interwar imperial aspirations of Mussolini.[11] Italian dramatic features of the 1930s continued to exude nationalistic sentiments, but Cecilia Boggio notes that they displayed as much concern as confidence given Italy's often tenuous colonial position. This anxiety is on display in *Lo squadrone bianco* (*The White Squadron*, 1936), a film shot in Libya about a missing Italian squadron, and in *Luciano Serra, pilota* (*Luciano Serra, Pilot*, 1938) about a World War I pilot returning to fight in Ethiopia.[12]

France was a major victor in the Scramble, and, like Germany, developed a colonial lobby promoting cinema to yoke national pride to colonial expansion. According to David Slavin, this led initially to "short ethnographic travelogues [that] wedded film to empire and stimulated interest in the colonies" at home.[13] But by the 1920s, administrative protocols in Francophone Africa reflected the shift from an earlier rapacious exploitation to a "managed" exploitation requiring sustained development and the growth of a collaborationist class of native elites.[14] By extension this necessitated an overriding film policy for the colonies, which often entailed showing French films to Africans to construct loyal Francophone subjectivities within the orbit of Greater France. Moreover, there were increasing calls for a heightened colonial humanism to integrate metropole and empire,[15] facilitated in part by greater attention paid to health and education. Peter Bloom has explained how this vision fueled the development of the 1928 Comité de Propagande Colonial par le Film (Colonial Film Committee) to "expand, edit, and supplement representative imagery that was first developed as part of a system of lending archives for educational, industrial, and fairground exhibitors."[16]

The Film Committee also requested 7 million francs to highlight development initiatives, resulting in director J.K. Raymond-Millet's *Promenade en AEF* (*A Stroll Through French Equatorial Africa*, 1931) which championed improved transportation, education and health measures in Gabon, Cameroun and the Congo. But if French officials touted the medium to invigorate their interwar imperial interests, so too did they fear its potential abuse by Communist agitators. Hence, as we have seen in 1934, the Minister of the Colonies prohibited filmmaking in French possessions without explicit consent. For Dominic Thomas, the Laval Decree was important in that it "announced the concern of the colonial authorities for the potential of film as an insurrectionary tool,"[17] a policy that served to impede the growth of an indigenous cinema sector. Yet it should be noted that the Laval Decree was the outgrowth of concerns that were rippling through French colonial circles as early as the 1920s. Paulin Vieyra has argued that the introduction of cinema soundtracks in 1928 led to the new regulatory oversight, although technological developments were surely supplemented by apprehension over trenchant exposés of French abuses in the colonies. In 1921, the black Martinique René Maran, who began his career in the colonial service in Ubangi-Shari, published his novel *Batouala*, critiquing colonial tax policies and the use of forced labor in the rubber and ivory industries.[18] The fact that the book won the coveted Prix-Goncourt created a national furor which was exacerbated by Andre Gide's two trips to Equatorial Africa in the mid–1920s, confirming Maran's accusations. Gide's tours resulted in a book and a film (produced with filmmaker Marc Allégret) sharing the title *Voyage au Congo* (*Travels in the Congo*, 1927) which criticized the failure of French colonization efforts to meet the empire's stated humanistic goals in Africa.

Thus, despite the fact that Africa was all the rage in the metropole—witness Josephine Baker's appeal and modern art's "primitive" turn—within Africa itself, conditions were quite different. In 1933, Englishman Alan Gilg was in Columb-Béchar, Algeria, taking a short break from a grueling trans–Saharan automobile expedition, when he learned that some restrictions against unlicensed filming predated passage of the Laval Decree: "Discovering a squad of soldiers working under guard we thought that we might be looking at a part of the notorious [Foreign Legion] penal battalion. This, I thought, would make good film material." But aware that the guards were unlikely to look favorably at foreigners filming colonial forced labor practices, Gilg and his driver Walter Kay retreated to a nearby tennis court and feigned interest in a game. Meanwhile, with cameras tucked under their arms, they surreptitiously filmed a French official whipping the "poor fellows ... slaving away digging and breaking huge rocks in ... 120 degrees Fahrenheit." Unfortunately for Gilg, the French noticed the subterfuge and promptly confiscated the footage. The two Englishmen were quickly ushered in for questioning by the Legion commandant, who informed them while gleefully burning the offending footage that all activities of the Foreign Legion were secret.[19]

World War II created a unique situation in Francophone Africa, with both "Vichy supporters and Gaullists call[ing] on Africans for their support."[20] In part this involved an aggressive Vichy propaganda campaign, including songs, posters, and statues reflecting the importance of an overseas empire for Marshal Pétain. Yet the intense discrimination of the period exposed the underbelly of colonial occupation, leading the postwar Fourth Republic to rethink strategies to restore consensus among its subject populations. Emphasizing the importance of cinema as a cultural tool—indeed, recognizing its potential to legitimize a French presence even as African colonies were pushing toward greater autonomy—recommendations from the Academy of Colonial Sciences to the Ministry for Overseas France included expanding the use of the documentary, as it could prove "more expansive and more effective than the book or newspaper."[21] Meanwhile, the new Overseas Cinema Commission promoted a fuller articulation of colonial cinema policy and infrastructure. James Genova has shown that the Ministry for Overseas France responded by promoting the "French spirit" through a quota system (difficult to uphold given the fractured postwar French film industry), and expanding regulations concerning film content for Africans due to destabilizing influences emanating from Communist, Arabic, and even American arenas.

Production was a bit slower to launch in Lusophone Africa. When it did, though, it was clear that the needs of the state were paramount. In 1909–10, Portuguese officials turned to the medium to dampen international outrage over its use of forced labor on the cocoa islands of São Tomé and Príncipe. Whether these films actually had any meaningful international impact is not known, but it is likely that they were produced in part for Portuguese audiences to deflect concern at home. In Angola, although there were scattered earlier examples, sustained filmmaking dates to 1912, when shorts were produced emphasizing either the effectiveness of Portuguese military operations in the colony or trumpeting the ongoing construction of the Benguala railway which, in 1929, would connect Lobito to the Belgian Congo's mineral-rich Katanga region.[22]

The Congo Free State, under the rule of Leopold II, was unique, as officials were made aware early on of the power of propaganda—both positive and negative—in framing the public's perception of colonial rule. Even as photographic evidence of Red Rubber atrocities circulated at the turn of the century, so too did Leopold mount campaigns to promote his fiefdom through museums, public monumentation and colonial expositions. *Optique belge*, formed in 1897, experimented with cinematic propaganda by sending Antwerp cameraman Weber to secure footage of the Congo for the Brussels' International Exposition. Weber was, thus, one of the first filmmakers in equatorial Africa, but because of problems in the developing process, the footage was deemed unacceptable and the company resorted to taking footage of the Congolese on exhibition at the native "villages" constructed at the fairgrounds itself.[23]

Optique belge may have foundered, but colonial cinema was temporarily re-energized in the private sector with the formation of Le Cinématographe des Colonies following Belgium's purchase of the Congo Free State in 1908. François Evenpoel and Léon Reinelt subsequently produced glowing documentaries about the newly named Belgian Congo that were shown at Congo Cinema in Brussels. The films, some released with Dutch titles, addressed two critical issues of the new King Albert I's agenda: bridging domestic cultural divisions between Dutch and French speakers, and repairing Belgium's colonial reputation following Leopoldian abuses. *Matadi* (1909) and *Banana* (1909) supplemented films showcasing Albert's trip to the colony: *Prins Albert in het Centrum van Kongo* (*Prince Albert in Central Congo*, 1910) and *De Reis van Prins Albert in Kongo* (*Prince Albert's Journey to the Congo*, 1910).

In the World War I era, Belgium experimented with state-produced propaganda, sending photographer Ernest Gourdinne to Ruanda-Urundi and the Congo to promote the war effort and to paint a positive image of Belgian imperialism. Gourdinne produced 20 short documentaries, including *L'Industrie du diamant au Kasaï* (*The Diamond Industry in Kasai*, 1919), *Plantations cacaoyères du Mayumbe* (*Cocoa Plantations of Mayumbe*, 1919) and most tellingly, *La Conquête belge de l'Afrique* (*The Belgian Conquest of Africa*, 1919), all of which were given extensive screen time in Belgium.

When colonial cinema was revived, it was again under the auspices of private enterprise when Ernest Genval formed Essor Cinégraphique in 1925. Genval and cameraman Victor Morin toured the Belgian Congo together, shooting educational, agricultural, industrial and travel films promoting further investment and white settlement. On another filmmaking venture, in 1928–29, Genval produced *De Stanleyville à Bukama par la voie des eaux* (*A River Journey from Stanleyville to Bukama*, 1929) showing the Congo River and the living conditions of Europeans and Africans. After a hiatus, Genval made his last Congo trip in 1936. Now working with the Fonds colonial de propagande économique et sociale (Colonial Economic and Social Propaganda Fund), he produced *L'Art Nègre* (*Black Art*, 1938[?]) and *Quand le nègre danse* (*When the African Dances*, 1938[?]), reflecting the increasing interest in Belgium in African art and the salvaging of traditional cultures. Genval continued to make promotional films for industrial interests, including *L'Or* (*Gold*, 1938), which opens with maps of the Belgian Congo and a narrator describing the Aruwimi River Basin's ore-producing regions. Subsequent scenes reveal the nature of the "partnership" between white and black as Genval recreated the search in remote forests for auriferous ore a few years earlier. According to the subtitles: "That was the job of the prospector, who, aided by a small group of indigenous workers, cleared a path through the African woods and mountains." In the film Africans are prominent, yet generally displayed in work teams digging, hauling supplies, or operating pneumatic drills. The prospector, in contrast, is individualized as director of operations and as the subject of a smiling close-up when gold is discovered.[24]

While Genval produced dozens of films, he was only one of the triumvirate of Belgian colonial filmmaking. His contemporary Gerard De Boe was a health official in the colony who spent time in rural villages with a staff of Africans. His early film *La Maladie du sommeil* (*Sleeping Sickness*, 1937) garnered little interest from the Belgian Colonial Office. In contrast, his next endeavor, *Le Lèpre* (*Leprosy*, 1938) caught the attention of the colonial governor general, who sent De Boe on assignment to produce films on native health, colonial development, and the Allied war effort. Following the conflict, De Boe became a force in colonial cinema, working for the Centre d'Information et de Documentation du Congo Belge, and forming his own production unit. His oeuvre was multi-faceted: health and hygiene films, Unilever films, and industrial documentaries about precious minerals complemented others with an ethnographic slant, including *Visages du Congo Belge* (*Faces of the Belgian Congo*, 1950[?]) and *Pêcheurs Wagenia* (*Wagenia Fishermen*, 1952).

The third Belgian filmmaker of note was Andre Cauvin, who produced a film about life along the Congo River and another on the Force Publique in 1939. During the war, the minister of foreign affairs tasked Cauvin with documenting the Congolese war effort and the positive effects of Belgium's civilizing mission. Covering 8,000 miles by car, he produced a vast amount of footage, resulting in *Congo*. This documentary featured living standards in the colony both before and after the introduction of colonial rule. Following the war, Cauvin released films under the auspices of the Fonds colonial de propagande économique et sociale and the Marshall Fund. *L'Équateur Aux Cent Visages* (released in the U.S. as *Black Shadows*, with color posters depicting an oversized gorilla preparing to swallow up a group of bare-breasted African women) provided extensive footage of indigenous cultures, including a reconstruction of secret leopard men rituals. Colonial authorities in Leopoldville actually censored the film intended for indigenous audiences on the grounds that it might be perceived as belittling African customs.

Perhaps for this reason, *Bwana Kitoko* (1955), covering King Baudouin's visit to the colony, appeared in two versions: one for Europeans and the other for Congolese, who were now seeing films in greater numbers. The film was a masterpiece of pro-empire propaganda championing the impact of Belgian culture, with scenes of an African family preparing for the royal visit: the husband "models his dress on the white man" by putting on a bowtie for the occasion while his wife wears a "traditional," colorful wraparound dress adorned in the middle with an image of the Belgian king. The narrator continually evokes the "dancing, shouting and singing" natives greeting the king's motorcade in Leopoldville. In Cauvin's *Bongolo*, entered into Cannes in 1952 upon its release, a young African man working as a nurse in a small jungle medicinal center courts a local king's daughter. Convincing her to abandon traditional African folkways, his plans for marriage are stymied when local village elites respond by burning down the hospital.

World War II constituted a watershed for Belgian filmmaking, with the Ministry of Information set up in exile and the release of the war propaganda film *Little Belgium* (1942). In 1947, propaganda efforts in the Belgian Congo intensified with the newly established Film and Photo Bureau, led by L. Van Bever, tasked with producing films targeting the native population and newsreels targeting Belgian audiences. Although the overriding ideological thrust of the films for Africans was based on their perceived inability to comprehend filmic language, Africans ironically served as production assistants for the films, which were distributed throughout the colony by way of mobile cinema vans.[25]

In general, European powers contemplated colonial cinema campaigns but frequently left the initiative to the private sector. Yet the heavy imperial slant of these films should not be underestimated. The British South Africa Company (BSAC), for instance, tapped cinematographers Alfred Kaye and R.C.E. Nissen for *Rhodesia To-Day* (1912), a film championing company-sponsored construction projects beyond the Zambezi, to visualize empire for company shareholders. Nissen was a pivotal figure in South African cinema. Not only did he have prior experience filming local scenes shown as filler in bioscopes, he directed Springbok Film Company's *The Great Kimberley Diamond Robbery* (1911), South Africa's first dramatic feature. Following the BSAC project, Nissen followed up with another long filmmaking expedition, turning his itinerary into a film title: *From Rhodesia via Katanga to Angola, Bulawayo to Elizabethville and Kambove to Lobito Bay* (1913). Because Britain would probe the possibilities of colonial cinema most deeply, its promotion of cinema from the 1899 Boer War to the 1935 Bantu Educational Kinema Experiment will be explored below and in later chapters.

Showing and Telling: Actualities, Newsreels and Travelogues

Many of the earliest products of what Tom Gunning calls the "cinema of attractions" were imported into the northernmost and southernmost periphery of the continent. In part because of their time limitations, ranging from several seconds to roughly a minute, narrative development was largely eschewed in favor of quick vignettes or moving snapshots which magnified the magic of movement and the moment. The Lumière brothers coined these films "actualities" and standardized their length (for Lumière) with 50-second filmstrips.

As the hazy outlines of an international industry began to form, film production in Africa was often harnessed to exhibition routes (Lumière projectors doubled as cameras). Following the success of its Egyptian Cinématographe showings, and as part of its effort to canvass the globe for the exotic, Lumière sent its chief globetrotting booster, filmmaker Jean Alexandre Promio, to capture the wonders of Egypt. *Place des Consuls, à Alexandrie*, shot on March 10, 1897, was Promio's first African production, and was one of the first produced by anyone on the continent.[26] Promio soon made his way to the Giza Plateau to secure footage of the Sphinx and the pyramids,[27] after which he shifted from Lumière to Pathè. Following World War I he moved out of the private sector to work directly for the French colonial government in Algeria as official filmmaker/photographer.

Lumière agents made quick inroads into Tunisia and Algeria, evidenced in an early catalog listing 34 actualities from Egypt, and 21 from Tunis and Algiers. Lumière also commissioned French filmmaker Felix Mesguich, who had already shot footage of a caravan near Timbuktu.[28] Mesguich had actually been born in Algeria, and would later work for Warwick Trading Company in 1905 on a trip marred by two events reflecting the dangers of shooting on location: first, disgruntled locals fired upon his vehicle, and, later, when he asked Algerian soldiers to discharge their rifles during an equestrian race to heighten the excitement, two riders unseated by their horses suffered fatal injuries.

Generally exported out of the continent for Western audiences, the African actuality served ideological functions that, despite the existence of a few Egyptian investors before World War I, rarely allowed for the meaningful contribution of indigenous peoples. Many actualities lauded the military might of colonizing powers, while others turned African "savages" into harmless performers and visual fodder for Western constructions of the Dark Continent. Two actualities reflecting the latter themes were given impetus by the Earls Court Exhibition in London, which, by the mid–1890s, was a veritable propaganda machine for British imperial prowess. The Anglo-Zulu War of 1879 had recently solidified British control in southern Africa, after British troops countered an embarrassing loss at Isandlwana and crushed indigenous resistance. The success of pacification campaigns prompted circus owner Frank Fillis to bring a troupe of 200 Zulu "performers" recruited from Boer farms to perform at Earls Court, an event noted by the *Western Mail*: "An unlikely scene was witnessed at Southampton Dock on Wednesday morning on the arrival of the Union liner *Goth* from South Africa. The vessel had on board the whole of the stock-in-trade "Savage South Africa," which is to be produced at Earls Court this summer."[29] In addition to daily stage shows, the troupe became the subject of *Landing of Savage South Africa at Southampton* (1899), a British Mutoscope and Biograph short showing Zulus in full native regalia incongruously performing what vaguely seems to be a war dance on the Southampton docks. De-territorialized and de-clawed, but dressed to kill, the "Savage South Africa" troupe stomps around looking menacingly at the camera until a white man with a top hat appears and leads them off.

The second "Savage South Africa" short was produced in London by Charles Urban's Warwick Trading Company, which had established itself as Britain's leading production company specializing in travelogues and war reportage. Warwick's *Savage South Africa—Savage Attack and Repulse* (1899) encapsulated the British victory over the Zulus in a brief recreation of actual events. For this actuality, Warwick filmed a "Savage South Africa" Earls Court performance, showing "a mixed group of [British] infantry and cavalry standing in array. Suddenly a scattered group of savages appear gesticulating in the foreground. The infantry fire; the cavalry pursue the natives from the scene. In a few moments the cavalry reappear and take up their former position, and all the men raise their hats and cheer."[30]

This theme of out-of-place Zulus for audience amusement would extend far beyond the actuality's demise; in 1906 alone, they became the subject of two shorts filmed in KwaZulu Natal. Although largely subjugated by this time, Chief Bambatha kaMancinza was vehemently protesting onerous taxation rates. Promptly deposed, he launched guerrilla attacks against the British, who, in turn, deployed machine guns against insurgents armed with knobkerries and assegais. The British victory was filmed by H.D. Roberts, one of southern Africa's first itinerant cinema exhibitors. A few months later a Charles Urban cameraman filmed the Zulus yet again under different circumstances for the 1906–08 Urban-Africa expedition travelogue *From Cape to Cairo*, which, according to *Optical Lantern and Kinematograph Journal*, had "as its object the securing of a comprehensive series of living pictures of the continent."[31] Although the title suggested a single, grand continental crossing, *From Cape to Cairo* was actually produced by four different camera operators working simultaneously: one on the Cape Town to Victoria Falls railway, a second on the Gold Coast, a third on the Uganda railway, and a fourth on the Nile. The expedition also resulted in several shorter films, with *A Trip on the Rhodesian Railway*, *Amongst the Central African Natives*, and *Life on the Zambezi River* showing stunning shots of Victoria Falls. A few years later, a Salvation Army film of a Royal Albert Hall performance offered yet another spectacle of Zulus holding fearsome weapons and dancing for the public. An organization newsletter made a revealing comparison between these "Zulus garbed in horns, wild-cat tails, rawhide and red blankets—bearing in their hands the implements of primitive savagery," and the high level of civilization attained by New Zealanders who were sharing the stage.[32] In 1927 and 1930, respectively, the Zulus were called upon again to grace the screen, first in the form of Attilio Gatti's *Siliva Zulu*—the first film shot in South Africa with an all-black cast—followed by *In the Land of the Zulus*, the first sound film produced on African "traditional" life.

Officials often complained about the indifference of the Crown to the promises and perils of cinema in the colonies, yet the history of British filmmaking shows that the private sector willingly took up the mantle by touting the empire's martial readiness. In one early example, John Montague Benett-Stanford (nicknamed "Mad Jack") produced *Alarming the Queen's Company of Grenadier Guards at Omdurman* in 1898, with shots of Lord Kitchener's invasion force preparing to engage Abdullah al–Taashi in the Sudan. It was the Boer War of 1899–1902, though, that spurred British firms to yoke the new medium to the imperial pursuits of the Colonial Office. Notably, while Afrikaners had no representatives filming the conflict, eight British cinematographers provided a strongly pro-empire perspective, with "Mad Jack" Benett-Stanford first in line. Warwick Trading Company released a few of his films in 1900, and subsequently sent Edward Hyman and Joseph Rosenthal to document war scenes near, but not on, the frontlines. Some of these actualities portray regiments of highly disciplined British soldiers marching, while *5-inch Siege Guns Crossing the Vaal River* (1900) shows African drivers and British soldiers directing oxen pulling heavy weaponry. Others are even more ideologically loaded, highlighting the Boers surrendering at Kroonstad and the Union Jack being raised triumphantly over Johannesburg and Pretoria.

Warwick prided itself on depicting only "real" scenes, especially because in some instances, rival production companies were concocting African actualities outside the continent. A prominent example of the latter was *A Sneaky Boer* (1901) by Lancashire firm Mitchell and Kenyon. Shot near Blackburn, England, the storyline involves a British soldier stabbed in the back by two Boers, who rob him of his cartridge and personal belongings. Fortunately, a British soldier heroically fights off the ambushers and conveys the injured man to safety. The film's narrative thrust is revealing: a brutal military conflict in which thousands of Boers died from British scorched earth policies and concentration camps, is reduced to a personal outrage committed by two "sneaky" enemy soldiers. William Dickson, who had left Edison a few years before to form the British Mutoscope and Biograph Company, also played a role in bringing the Boer War to the big screen. With an unwieldy 70mm camera, he traveled with the British Naval Brigade to secure footage of the campaign to relieve Ladysmith, for a film that would later be shown to sympathetic audiences in both London and Cape Town.[33]

Many of the earliest African actualities were thus shot in British colonies in Southern Africa, or along the North African coast. In other cases, some were produced in Europe by European firms. But while actualities were the mainstay of the industry during cinema's formative period, the genre was soon abandoned as longer films were introduced and the spectacle more fully integrated into Western culture. Lumière, initially leading the industry in producing actualities, abandoned them by 1905. American Biograph and Edison soon followed suit. Yet it is Pathé Frères that has been credited for initiating the ensuing newsreel revolution in 1908—soon expanding the genre with Pathé News (British Pathé) in London—a transition that might be characterized as the shift from "showing" to "telling." Newsreels, which spurred the growth of Charles Urban's Kinora Company and the Topical Film Company, were more expensive and longer than earlier actualities, allowed for greater narrative development, and served to institutionalize motion pictures as an important propaganda tool for colonial consolidation.

While newsreels about British Africa were soon being produced in relative abundance, Francophone Africa experienced an increase in filmmaking activity; in fact, by World War I at least three newsreel firms were active in French West Africa, including Gaumont Actualités. *Dakar and the Bay of Gorée* and *In French Guinea, West Africa*, for instance, were two shorts produced in 1911 and 1914, respectively. In addition, Pathé Frères produced *En Afrique Occidentale* (*In West Africa*, 1907), *Dakar, principal port de commerce de l'Afrique occidentale française* (*Dakar, Principal Commercial Port of French West Africa*, 1914), and *Le Ville de Saint Louis de Sénégal* (*The City of Saint Louis, Senegal*, 1914). These films showcased French culture and development, and lauded the incorporation of the West African coast into international trade routes.

Newsreels played an increasingly important role in promoting the European presence and empire-building projects in Africa, frequently demonstrating infrastructural projects and military expertise. Although newsreels provided a sense of immediacy and gave the appearance of cameramen being lucky to be in the right place at the right time to catch events "on the ground" as they occurred, in fact production companies invested significant time and money in long-range planning to move crews into position. This was nowhere truer than in Africa, where location shooting could be difficult given the size of crews and the bulk of early camera equipment. Nevertheless, companies rose to the occasion by sometimes redesigning cameras for African conditions, and newsreel production became commonplace in Africa by the 1930s.

British Pathé, launched in June 1910, was a major force in newsreel production and helped to institutionalize the genre in English culture with two "issues" a week. With early "Animated Gazette" shorts like *Outposts of Empire: British East African Troops Entraining on an Expedition Against German Territory* (1915), British Pathé played a key propagandistic function emphasizing African contributions to the Allied war effort. The newsreel's popularity opened the door to competitors, many of whom decided to try their hand filming in Africa despite the expense. In expectation of the impending Italian invasion of Ethiopia, for instance, Paramount blanketed North Africa with studios in Libya, Somaliland, Sudan, Djibouti and Ethiopia, while Movietone constructed ten specially built silent and sound cameras to be transported by "side-car equipped motorcycles" and "motor-trucks with protection compartments."[34]

During World War II, with longer running times and now augmented by sound, newsreels became increasingly integrated into the ideological arsenal of both Axis and Allied powers, despite newsreel production in Britain initially tapering off due to "newsreel editors ... [becoming] bored with 'six months of ruins and wrecks,'" and the early dissolution of the U.S. Film Service.[35] The British Armed Forces Film Unit hired Sergeant John Wernham to produce films of Allied engineering and African life in Kenya. One such film, *An East African Army Field Bakery* (1944), shows a wartime bakery staffed by Africans chopping wood, pouring flour, and cleaning a mud-brick oven. And despite lacking a direct imperial stake on the continent, the United States was determined to counter the outpouring of Axis propaganda newsreels like *Azioni su Sidi Barrani* (*Operations in Sidi Barrani*, 1940), extolling Italian Marshal Graziani's temporary capture of the Egyptian town, and *Tobruk* (1941), showing German Field Marshal Rommel speaking with captured British officers. Hollywood wonder-boy Darryl F. Zanuck was sent to Tunisia, where he was met by the head of the OSS's photographic unit, the famous director John Ford. Using Kodachrome cameras, Zanuck's "combat camera crews" comprised 20th Century–Fox personnel wading into battle, shooting both footage and firearms. On one occasion, Zanuck found himself trapped in a building coming under withering fire from the Luftwäffe: "Plaster flew off the walls. Machine-gun bullets splattered on all sides." Finally, during a lull he made his escape but kept his camera rolling as he ran: "The moment they turned away I grabbed my camera and headed for the airport, which was by now a mass of flames and billowing smoke. Wounded and dead lay in the roadside. I photographed right and left, stopping only to help where I could with the wounded."[36]

The film lecture was no less steeped in the twin practices of showing and telling, and was used widely in both educational and commercial contexts. The world's foremost practitioner—Burton Holmes—developed early a lifelong passion for images and positioned himself at the forefront of what became known in the early 20th century as the "travelogue." For years, Holmes crisscrossed the world in search of new and revealing imagery to accompany his popular lectures. Beginning with still images taken in Morocco in 1894, he was incorporating moving pictures into his programs by 1900, with his 1906 lecture series featuring footage from Cairo and the Upper Nile. Signing with Paramount, Holmes's output averaged one short every week between 1915 and 1921, producing four Africa films in 1916 from recycled footage: *The Upper Nile*, *The Lower Nile*, *The Real Streets of Cairo*, and *British Egypt*.

Holmes's five 1921 African productions *Alexandria*, *Bazaars of Cairo*, *Road to the Pyramids*, *Calling on the Sphinx* and *The City of Algiers* were followed in 1930 by *Into Morocco* and *Abyssinia*. For the latter, Holmes captured the only known footage of the historic coronation of Regent Ras Tafari as Emperor Haile Selassie, who himself promoted cinema as a tool for modernization. *Abyssinia* includes shots of the film crew positioning cameras on location, medium close-up shots of Selassie seated on the throne looking confidently at the camera, and Holmes dressed in his characteristic three-piece suit and top hat. More Africa-themed films were to follow, including *A Century of Progress: Darkest Africa* (1933), culled from footage taken at Chicago's Century of Progress International Exposition featuring Angolan firewalkers, and Ugandan and Nigerian dancers. In 1936, during the Italian invasion/occupation of Ethiopia, Holmes defended Selassie in his lecture "What I Saw in Ethiopia."

We have seen that the Italian invasion led to significant newsreel activity. In one case the conflict even breathed new life into a feature-length travelogue project that otherwise might have foundered. Director Lazar Wechsler and cameraman Emil Berna traveled from Switzerland to Ethiopia "by plane, automobile and mule" in 1934, producing a film which was released the following year by Paramount. The *New York Times* summed up best the added appeal of *Wings Over Ethiopia* (1935) following the onset of the Second Italo-Ethiopia War: "What, in an ordinary travel film, would be merely stock shots of mountain ranges, craggy roads, muddy plains and high plateaus are of dramatic interest here as indicating the terrain over which the Italian armies must advance." But the paper also noted the film's dramatic footage of "savage tribesmen in the hills" to fascinate "civilized" Western audiences: "Tall, Arabic-type women are shown anointing their hair with rancid butter; an infant has his face slashed for purposes of identification; debtors are chained to their creditors until payment is made; five murderers face a firing squad made up of relatives of the victims."[37]

Holmes might have been the world's most prominent travel film lecturer, but he had competition in the 1910s in Clarence Lyon Chester, who had served as Edison's chief travel cameraman. As head of C.L. Chester Inc., in 1916 he hired three cinematographers to execute a business plan for a "really high class series" of educational travelogues. In part because of rising expenses, one observer noted that instead of "taking scenery haphazardly, every scene is being planned in the office before the cameraman goes out."[38] Chester's success was largely due to his collaboration with the sporting magazine *Outing*, which facilitated production of weekly travelogues known as "Chester-Outing Scenics." With ponderous titles like *Cameraing Through Africa I* (1919), and *Cameraing Through Africa II* (1919), Chester's African travelogues reflected the new interwar emphasis on capturing images rather than killing animals. Originally based in New York, Chester moved to Hollywood and distributed Chester-Outing Scenics to commercial and non-commercial venues before *Outing* folded in 1923.[39] Chester's Africa footage was most likely purchased from Charles Cottar, an Oklahoma expatriate who founded Cottars' Safaris in Kenya. Following the termination of Chester-Outing Scenics, Cottar continued to send footage to Chester and actually traveled to California in 1939 to present his own film program *African Wild Life*.[40]

Although Burton Holmes traveled incessantly, his busy schedule often necessitated sending out camera crews to capture footage on location. His point man Andre de la Varre, who began working for Holmes in 1924, struck out on his own several years later as yet another competitor, calling himself "The Screen Traveler." In an example of the endurance expeditions explored below, in 1938–39 Varre drove (with cameras rolling) through the Atlas and Aurès mountains, logging in 10,000 miles in Morocco, Algeria and Tunisia.

The success of the educational film travelogue was assured both by the excitement of foreign views and by the popular persona of the speaker himself. Occasionally, to increase that star quality, travelers bundled their lectures. In 1931, famed *New York Times* critic Mordaunt Hall reviewed one such lecture at New York's Criterion Theater entitled, "Explorers of the World," featuring "six explorers, the most famous now living, giving a lucid and interesting account of the high lights of their expeditions."[41] The six "pictorial logs" were prefaced by a film sequence showing the worldly travelers and Harold Noice boasting of having "captured six explorers in the skyscraper jungles of Gotham," including James Lippitt Clark serving as the Africanist. Clark, a taxidermist-sculptor for the American Museum of Natural History, spent years in Africa with Carl Akeley, and had just returned from the O'Donnell-Clark African Expedition to secure eland specimens for Akeley Hall. As with so many other films, the resulting motion picture, *Adventures on the Upper Nile* (1931), blurred the lines between travelogue, scientific expedition film, and ethnographic study.[42] At the Criterion, Clark apparently showed only select clips from the film, providing glimpses of, by Hall's account, "all sorts of wild animals and birds," including "a fight between a lioness and an eland, in which the latter succumbs to the claws and teeth of the jungle empress." While Clark did include a few shots of Dinka cultural rituals, Hall simply shrugged them off as "voodoo dances."

Crossing Borders: The Endurance Expedition Film

The most geographically far-reaching cinema campaigns were the long-range expeditions with cameras in tow. Expeditionary filmmaking took several forms, loosely broken down into three genres which, in practice, often overlapped: Endurance / Safari / Scientific. One of the most commercialized was the safari film that sensationalized the hunt for wildlife roaming the African countryside. In the Western world where large game had been virtually exterminated, Africa became a highly romanticized repository of jungles and savannas inhabited by wild animals and savage peoples, a place where the primitive past could magically be resuscitated, commodified and brought to the big screen to thrill rapt audiences. The scientific expedition pursued the goal of indexing the flora, fauna and faces of Africa. In the interwar period especially, the Musée d'Ethnographie du Trocadéro, the Field Museum, the American Natural History Museum and other institutions sponsored scientific expeditions to fill in the blank spots on the maps of imperial cartographers. Ultimately, the twin processes of artifactual and image extraction allowed European colonial powers to embed themselves more deeply in the continent's soil.

Equally prominent at the time was the endurance expedition, sometimes accomplished on foot but more often enabled by automobiles or similar conveyances provided by manufacturers eager to promote fleet durability. Following the Scramble for Africa, which institutionalized colonial borders with little regard for traditional boundaries, 20th century endurance expeditions displayed a self-assumed authority over pacified local populations to travel virtually unimpeded across the continental mass. A distinguishing feature of many endurance expedition films was that vehicles themselves served as leading protagonists—

synecdochic substitutes for Western technological superiority carving up the rough African terrain.

This genre evolved from broader cultural characteristics of the 20th century West—the mass marketing of the automobile; the expanding global tourist sector; the popular travelogue; endurance travel; and the desire to "map the world." In Africa these cinematic excursions characteristically took one of three forms, or variants thereof: (1) the trans-Saharan journey: even with the benefit of the internal combustion engine, these films underscored the treacherous journey across the world's largest subtropical desert. Modern travelers used a variety of conveyances to trace ancient Saharan trading routes from the North African littoral to the Niger; (2) the trans-African expedition: these tours moved east to west, or west to east, with terminal points generally being the Horn of Africa or the Gulf of Guinea; (3) the Cape-to-Cairo journey: the longest of the three, these expeditions attempted to accomplish by motorcar what Cecil Rhodes had failed to complete by rail—the fabled Cape-to-Cairo corridor cutting right through equatorial Africa.

Although endurance expeditions mostly relied upon (and advertised) modern conveyances, occasionally travelers preferred more traditional means of locomotion. A case in point was Carl von Hoffman, a Russian émigré to the United States in the early 20th century. Originally working as a photojournalist for the *New York Globe*, he was hired by the Mutual Film Company and tasked with filming the launch of Teddy Roosevelt's River of Doubt expedition. Hoffman began working for Universal Newsreels during the war and later independently produced a successful ethnographic film in Morocco. In December 1924 he was hired as explorer/photographer by four Detroit businessmen, who subsequently headed out on "the longest walking trek in history": an 11-month excursion from Cairo to Cape Town.[43] Although Hoffman made a few more trips to Africa from which he culled material, it was primarily this long expedition that supplied the basis for two exploration books—*Jungle Gods* and *Jerry on Safari*—as well as the film *Jungle Gods* (1927).[44] Premiering at New York's Fifth Avenue Playhouse, one reviewer applauded the film for including "amazing hunt dances, where the natives become so hysterical that killing is but a mere formality. In these scenes the hunters trail the 'lions,' and the savages who play the beasts wear lions' heads over their own. When they are caught these 'lions' quickly snatch off their disguise."[45]

As Hoffman slogged his way to Cape Town, British travel writer Rosita Forbes resorted to mule caravan in Ethiopia, traveling a painful 1,090 miles "on gradients only suited to the centipede," an expedition that produced a film and book sharing the title *From Red Sea to Blue Nile* (1926).[46] When Forbes and her cinematographer reached Ethiopia, she informed her agent that they had fortuitously arrived "at the psychological moment when Ras Tafari, having visited Europe, is anxious for publicity & desirous of showing his country at his best. He sent us a warm message of welcome to Harrar & promises to facilitate our journey in every possible way."[47] With pack mules and native guards, she traveled in remote areas where few Europeans had ever set foot. The fact that Forbes was a woman was notable, but surprisingly, not unique. In fact, a particular allure of many endurance expeditions was the inclusion of women competing for various "firsts" in Africa. Beginning in 1924, for instance, Stella Court Treatt and her husband, Major Chaplin Court Treatt, traveled, according to a Crossley Motors promotional brochure, 12,732 miles from Cape Town to Cairo with Canadian cinematographer T.A. Glover on an expedition with "imperial value," as Stella revealingly phrased it.[48] Indeed, Chaplin had earlier been instrumental in constructing aerodromes on a British Air Ministry Cape-to-Cairo Air Route. Yet other expedition members were not unacquainted with Africa: Stella had been born in South Africa, while Glover had served as cinematographer on Captain Angus Buchanan's 1922–23 Nigeria-to-Algeria camel expedition, resulting in Buchanan's film *Crossing the Great Sahara* (1924) and travel book *Sahara*.[49] Glover would later return to West Africa with his wife to produce *Cities of the Desert* (1934).

In keeping with similar African endurance films, promotional materials for the Treatt expedition include photographs of the Crossley vehicles receiving assistance from the brawn of the African multitudes. One telling caption accompanies an image of approximately 50 men and boys "dragging a Crossley, with the help of natives, across a river in Uganda."[50] The film *Cape to Cairo* (1926) was the result of their 17-month journey, an arduous trip that would have proved impossible without the assistance of numerous African villagers all along the route. On one occasion, according to Stella, no fewer than 250 Dinkas dragged the vehicles across the Bahr el Arab despite the local chief's initial reluctance to offer aid.[51] But it was the presence of Stella on such a difficult journey that provided fodder for media accounts. *The Brisbane Courier*, for instance, reporting briefly on the expedition, made a point of mentioning that "Mrs. Treatt, who is a small, slight woman, is accompanying the journey."[52]

The Treatt expedition was newsworthy, and therefore caused consternation on the part of travel film lecturer Arthur Wanderwell. A few years earlier, in 1922, the globe-trotting Wanderwell had advertised in the *Paris Herald* for "Brains, Beauty and Breeches— World Tour Offer for Lucky Young Woman." Answering the call was 16-year-old Aloha Baker (born Idris Hall, in Winnepeg), then living in a French convent school. Aloha was quickly hired and joined Wanderwell's world endurance tour. Billed as the first woman to drive around the globe, Aloha was marketed as "the world's most widely travelled girl," a title coveted throughout her life until her passing in 1996.[53] As they prepared to leave China for Africa during their visit to over 40 countries, Wanderwell (who would soon marry young Aloha) fretted that he was in danger of being scooped by the traveling Treatt duo. Thus, while Stella might have been the first woman to travel the Cape to Cairo route, Wanderwell made sure the public was aware that "she did not drive herself," as did Aloha.[54]

In keeping with the travel lecture format common at the time, Wanderwell and Baker simultaneously produced and exhibited films as they worked their way around the world; in fact, Wanderwell hired Baker specifically because he desired an attractive face to narrate the films. The Africa segment of *Car and Camera Around the World* (1929) highlights their Cape to Cairo escapades, although their expedition was, in fact, stymied by the 1927 Dinka Uprising, which forced the crew to abandon the overland route in favor of a steamer at Mombasa. This disruption led to Aloha's observation that "the Dinkas are changeable in mood as Africa herself, sometimes smiling with good will and at other times snarling with hostility."[55] *Car and Camera Around the World*, in keeping with other films in the genre, begins with a typically crude continental map featuring a dotted line of the intended Cape to Cairo route. But even by the loose standards of the travelogue, the film is surprisingly weak, composed of random shots along the expedition with little narrative coherence. The selling point, of course, was the beautiful Baker herself, who not only narrated the films in person but who also appears in virtually every scene, holding African babies, drinking from gourds, and posing with Maasai women.[56]

In terms of prominent white females taking part in African endurance expeditions, the Treatt and Wanderwell excursions were followed by the 2nd Leila Roosevelt Expedition (a.k.a. Armand Denis Belgian Congo Expedition) of 1934–35. This power couple married in Oyster Bay, New York, in 1926,[57] with both achieving prominence before their African trip: Armand Denis produced *Goona-Goona* (1932) in Bali with Andrè Roosevelt (Leila's father) and Hassoldt Davis,[58] inspiring a number of films whose generous financial returns

Vehicles preparing for departure on the 2nd Leila Roosevelt Expedition, 1934 (courtesy Chrysler Group, LLC).

were guaranteed through the visualization of partly naked women of color. Denis achieved more fame with his work on *Wild Cargo* (1934), a jungle-adventure film produced in Singapore by Frank Buck that while financially remunerative proved controversial because of Buck's use of caged animals and fighting pits. For her part, Leila and mechanic Edna Olmstead had undertaken an impressive "10,000 mile overland automobile trip from Antwerp to Singapore" in 1933 that garnered attention due to Leila's familial connections to Teddy Roosevelt, and because both adventurers were female.[59]

The 2nd Leila Roosevelt Expedition was sponsored by the Dodge Division of Chrysler, which had opened its own film bureau—Dodge Motion Pictures—to produce "educational and informative" films to "serve both sponsor and audiences." Two specially designed Dodge trucks and one sedan carried the couple's tons of photographic equipment and doubled as sleeping quarters, on their quest to "make a film starring Mr. Gorilla," as one account put it.[60] *Life* magazine similarly sensationalized the trip, emphasizing the incredible stature of "the Watusi, aristocrats of Africa, who tower up to 8 ft. in height."[61] After traveling across the Sahara and circling Central Africa, Roosevelt and Denis released the 1936 promotional-educational film *Wheels Across Africa* (re-released commercially as *Dark Rapture*, 1938), and later, *Dangerous Safari* (1944). Because Dodge films were always a form of advertising, auto dealers around the United States stocked both projectors and the Dodge film library that would be loaned *gratis* to "responsible groups." According to Dodge, "Every one of the subjects is an 'advertising' film, [although] some of them present a factual product story."

2. *The Scramble for Images: Strange Savages, Paid Primitives, Negotiating Natives* 55

Map of second Leila Roosevelt Expedition, 1934–35 (courtesy Chrysler Group, LLC).

Lending to schools, church groups and other organizations, *Wheels Across Africa* was promoted by its sponsors as a way for the American public to "view pages from the dim past in this thrilling action film" while providing a "deeper impression of the importance of the entire automobile industry to our national existence."[62] The film opens with a rough map of the 42,000-mile route that would take the couple from Antwerp, Belgium, across the Strait of Gibraltar to Spanish Morocco, through the city of Fez and south to Timbuktu. From there the expedition would make its way through Central Africa to the Indian Ocean, and back again. The first scenes show the Dodge vehicles being inspected by King Leopold III, and the expedition making its way to North Africa, where viewers are quickly confronted with a world of radical otherness, including one street performer eating glass shards and another breaking glass bottles with his bare feet to make a "bed" for his naked torso.

By the time Dodge had entered the fray, European car manufacturers had already confirmed the importance of Africa in their global marketing schemes, with Crossley, Peugeot, Citroën and Renault all promoting by way of motion pictures the durability of their fleets in rough African conditions. Louis Renault, who had a long-standing relationship with the film industry (dating back to his appearance in an 1899 Lumière film seated in a Renault Voiturette), sensed earlier than most industrialists cinema's advertising potential. By the mid–1920s, the company was sponsoring long-range endurance expeditions, most notably the seven-day, 1,242-mile Gradis-Estienne excursion across burning sands, from Colomb-Bechar to Bourema (and back to Algiers) in 1924, with specially designed vehicles (12 wheels on three axles),[63] as well as the Columb-Bechar to Cape Town expedition of 1925–26, billed as the first automobile north-south crossing of Africa. The Renault jaunts served also to promote Francophone African tourism, with one 1929 advertisement touting the civilizing side-effects of the automobile: "You've done everything? Not unless you've pushed off in a 12-wheeled Renault into the sun and silence of that sea of sand…. North Africa is yours today … the playground of the international set who camp in the desert [and] motor along the perfect roads."[64] Renault produced *La Première Traverse rapide du desert (329 heures)* (*The First Rapid Crossing of the Sahara [329 hours]*, 1924)—indeed, crewmembers actually caught up to the Citroën Centrafrique (Citroën Central African) expedition on the "race" to Cape Town—but ultimately it would be the famous films of Citroën that would retain traction in the annals of colonial cinema.[65]

Like Renault, André Citroën was a marketing genius and had masterminded the idea of a Citroën expedition from Touggourt, Algeria, to Timbuktu, and back. Led by Georges-Marie Haardt and Louis Audouin-Dubreuil in 1922–23, the stated aim of the expedition—to assist in "establishing rapid communications between Algeria and western Africa"—reflected the dual focus on tourism and empire-building in Francophone Africa.[66] The resulting film, *La Traversée du Sahara* (*Crossing the Sahara*, 1923), released in different versions to international markets and public libraries, capitalized on the desert's mysterious allure recently evoked by Jacques Feyder's popular African epic *L'Atlantide* (1921) and helped inaugurate the 20th-century conquest of the Sahara through the aid of the automobile.[67]

In 1924, Citroën organized the Citroën Centrafrique expedition, again under the leadership of Haardt and Audouin-Dubreuil, and accompanied by film director Léon Poirier and photographer Georges Specht. The expedition—or "suicide mission," as many called it—was an extraordinary one, departing from Columb-Bechar in Citroën caterpillars (half-track vehicles), traveling across the Sahara, through Central Africa, to Cape Town, and even by ship to Madagascar. The impressive scope of the journey required five auxiliary missions to stock supplies, including film reels, along the route. According to the expedition account, "One of the most valuable means of keeping records was the cinematograph.

2. *The Scramble for Images: Strange Savages, Paid Primitives, Negotiating Natives* 57

Through it the incidents of the journey could be preserved." And preserved they were, with *La Croisière Noire* (*The Black Journey*, 1926) proving a commercial success in France. There were detractors in the scientific world, though; Wilfred Hambly, an unimpressed Chicago Field Museum curator, expressed concerns about "Citroen cars [that] have under the leadership of Haardt committed the sacrilege of ploughing across the Sahara, for centuries sacred to salt caravans and nomadic Tuaregs."[68]

Peter Bloom has explored brilliantly the intimate relationship between the Citroën "crossing" films and French imperial designs following earlier failed attempts to construct enduring rail and road networks throughout the region. But while he argues that Citroën vehicles "charted human difference through the hypnotic regularity of the caterpillar tread in motion,"[69] we know from interviews in the recent documentary *Half Track Heroes: The Crusades of André Citroën* (2006) that the unforgiving landscape and heat of the sand

John Brom's D.K.W. and camera straddling the equator in Uganda (courtesy Olga Brom Spencer).

required treads to be replaced with regularity. Moreover, like other endurance expedition films, a key ideological driver of *La Croisière Noire* was the arduous nature of the journey, emphasizing the perceived willingness of the African masses who physically assisted the crews. From the prominent expeditions of Treatt, Wanderwell and Citroën, to the filmed excursions of lesser-known amateurs (*Austrian Motorcycle Expedition Capetown to Cairo, 1935–36*), human difference was consistently charted through the pervasive trope of colonial "partnership," with Europeans supplying the technology and the brains, and Africans the brawn, the latter dragging vehicles through the muck and, in so doing, facilitating the very tools deployed for their subjugation.

Of course there were other endurance "firsts" in Africa chronicled by the cinematic Third Eye. Alan Gilg and co-driver Walter Kay became the first to drive a simple lightweight automobile (8hp Morris) the length of Africa, conquering the hazards of the Tanezrouft, the Ruwenzori, and the equator on their way to Cape Town in 1933. The vehicle, with "Alan Gilg Expedition 1933, Liverpool, Nairobi, Cape Town" painted on its doors, negotiated a multitude of obstacles as Gilg secured thousands of feet of raw footage with his 16mm camera—footage that remained undisturbed for a half century until edited by ITV documentary filmmaker Barry Cockcroft and released as *Turn Left—The Riffs Have Risen* (1933/1981). By the end of the 1930s, with many "firsts" already accomplished, many adventurers focused on speed records. Humphrey Symons, for example, set out in 1938 with friend Bertie Browning on the first high-speed London-to-Cape Town run, using a simple Wolseley touring automobile. Although the two mostly drove non-stop, they brought along the obligatory film camera to document their journey, eventually driving off the side of a bridge into crocodile-infested waters in the Belgian Congo. Fortunately, in keeping with so many other expeditions, 150 local African convicts were able to dredge out the car, and with repairs made the next day the daring duo continued southward.[70]

The endurance expedition continued to enjoy currency in the post–World War II era, even though new "firsts" were harder to come by. But that failed to deter cantankerous World War II hero Richard Pape, an Englishman described in his 1995 obituary as an alcoholic who was "neither an officer nor a gentleman." In 1955, he concocted yet another endurance feat to which the African landscape would be subjected: to drive from Norway's North Cape to Cape Town, an astonishing achievement later immortalized in his book *From Cape Cold to Cape Hot*.[71] Pape took film footage all along the way, which he apparently stashed away in his attic until the day he (intentionally?) burned his house down. In 1952, filmmaker and explorer John Brom secured the backing of automaker DKW and logged in an astonishing 20,000 miles, driving solo in the car he named *Soucoup Volante* (Flying Saucer) through the Belgian Congo, the Rhodesias, Tanganyika, Uganda and Kenya.[72] Inspired by Livingstone and Stanley, and intent upon procuring images of animals and Africans, Brom sought the vestiges of fading traditions in a continent veering quickly toward independence. His prominence in a field that included other well-known postwar African explorers—Louis Cotlow and Armand Denis, in particular—is confirmed through the honorific bestowed upon Brom by Germany in the 1950s: Explorer of the Decade.

Unlike many explorers/filmmakers, Brom developed enduring personal relationships with Africans. In fact, following Patrice Lumumba's 1961 assassination in newly independent Congo-Leopoldville, officials in Kasavubu's administration pleaded with him to serve as an advisor as the country sought to build economic and political ties with foreign nations. Brom reluctantly agreed, although he generally tried to remain unaligned because of shifting political winds. His dream of opening a film studio in Africa never matured, but he produced a number of documentaries and books about the continent, including his most successful film, *On the Footsteps of Stanley* (1955), and *African Odyssey* (1967), which premiered in Montreal as a six-part television series "about an Africa which we will never see again."[73] Brom passed away suddenly in 1969, leaving incomplete a second television series entitled, *The Changing Face of Africa*.

Untamed Africa: The Safari and Wildlife Expedition Film

The word "safari" was still an exotic term in the Western world at the turn of the 20th century, deriving originally from the Arabic word *safarīyah* and evolving into its current Swahili version, meaning "long journey." Safari films were an outgrowth of the popular sport of big-game hunting which had denuded the African landscape of much of its large game, with hunters in East Africa in particular after about 1910 now filming the thrill of the hunt. There were two developments discernible in the new practice of taking pictures of Africa's wildlife: (1) many hunters fueled the conservation movement by touting the transition from shooting firearms to shooting images; (2) Africa's diverse peoples increasingly came into the purview of these safari enthusiasts, allowing film producers to advertise the inclusion of "exotic tribes" like the "Pygmies" or the Maasai to draw spectators to "jungle safari" films.

The Edenic Myth is the overarching ideological theme framing the genre—the notion that Africa constituted the last, unspoiled continent ripe for European cinematic exploration. Roderick Neumann, though, has shown how evocations of the putatively empty expanses of African game country served to obscure histories of long African occupancy in these regions.[74] Moreover, romantic visions of a pristine natural world occluded discussion of the inevitable conflicts over resources that divided many pre-colonial African groups, and led to tensions between European powers during the Scramble for Africa, and between new colonial overlords and African communities.

The genre began early, perhaps with a short actuality entitled *Africa* (1898) that Palle Petterson attributes to Sir Philip Lancaster Brocklehurst.[75] Little is known about this film, but one of Brocklehurst's two sons would go on to achieve his own endurance milestone in Africa: traveling in two Chevrolet trucks in 1930, Philip (Jr.), his wife and a mechanic became the first to cross the Sahara in fewer than three vehicles (another African first!), in an expedition that generated photographs but no motion pictures. By the early 20th century, filmmakers touting Africa's unique flora and fauna were increasingly exporting their filmic records out of the continent. The allure of wildlife filmmaking in Africa was, in part, generated by the early photography of brothers Richard and Cherry Kearton (the latter later serving as expeditionary cinematographer for Theodore Roosevelt, Frederick Selous, and Colonel C.J. Buffalo Jones) and German photographer-author Carl George Schillings, who captured still images of animals on safari in East Africa in 1903–04.[76] Schillings may have expressed misgivings at the scale of slaughter by the early 20th century, but was criticized for provoking animals by wounding them and for using tethered donkeys as bait for predators.[77]

Pathé was eager to expand and hired French cinematographer Alfred Machin to travel to Africa with Swiss zoologist Adam David in 1907. Traveling up the Nile from Egypt to Sudan, Machin and David produced some of the earliest African wildlife footage, although they struggled with humidity, heat and insects and subsequently lost significant material. Yet Pathé sent Machin back to Africa, and because the reels were stored in wooden boxes insulated with ash, his footage was salvaged. Machin's shorts, including *Chasse à l'hip-*

popotame sur le Nil bleu (*Hippopotamus Hunting on the Blue Nile*, 1908), *La Chasse à la panthère* (*Hunting Panther*, 1909) and *La Chasse à la giraffe en Ouganda* (*Hunting Giraffe in Uganda*, 1910) spawned enthusiasm for the wildlife genre in France.[78]

Wildlife films could be promoted as a way to experience the dangerous recesses of the Dark Continent from the safety of darkened movie theaters. David's and Machin's films, though, had little impact in the United States. Instead, it was *Roosevelt in Africa* (1910), with the appeal of the charismatic ex-president taking part in the slaughter of hundreds of large animals that helped to institutionalize this genre across the Atlantic. The carnage associated with Roosevelt's safari was not unique, but sadly reflected the practice of massive herd depopulation that transformed the African veldt between 1910 and 1930—a phenomenon lamented by James Lippitt Clark, Carl Akeley, Mary Jobe Akeley and others. As Clark put it, "In 1909, when I first entered that animal Eden, the plains were literally swarming with herds of wildebeest and zebra, gazelle, impala, eland, and scores of other animals."[79] This was in marked contrast to his endurance drive of 1,100 miles from Nairobi to the Upper Nile in 1928, an excursion almost completely devoid of large game. The fact that many species experienced catastrophic decline during such a brief period led to calls for national animal reserves in Africa, the first being Albert National Park. Ironically, it was the semi-controlled environment of this new game preserve that provided the cinematic backdrop for East Africa's "wild savagery." But before the emphasis on preservation prevailed, the early 1910s witnessed a slew of big-game hunting films championing the killing prowess of safari enthusiasts.

A prominent example was wealthy playboy Paul Rainey, heir to a coal-mining fortune in Mississippi. Competing with Teddy Roosevelt, Rainey purchased an estate near Nairobi

Carl Akeley trying unsuccessfully to film Nandi lion-spearing sequence, East African Expedition, 1910–11 (Image #211912, American Museum of Natural History Library).

named Falcon Glen,[80] and received an invitation from British East Africa Governor Lord Delamere to help thin out the colony's lion population. After the "man-eating lions of Tsavo" impacted construction of the Kenya-Uganda Railway, officials encouraged hunters and settlers to take aim at the species. Using hunting hounds, Rainey cornered and killed a record number of lions on an expedition immortalized as *Paul J. Rainey's African Hunt*, released in 1912 to great fanfare.[81] As Palle Petterson notes, "The mixture of dramatic entertainment, the natural behavior of the animals and a light informative style made [the film] a box office hit. The film not only attracted audiences but also created an enormous interest in the African continent, resulting in *Paul J. Rainey's African Hunt* becoming the best-selling nature film of the entire decade," and serving as the template for other Rainey films.[82]

Roosevelt's famous safari inspired George Lawrence, a Chicago newspaper photographer, to attempt the first aerial footage of thundering herds on the savanna by mounting cameras on hot air balloons. Working with William Boyce, the two used "captive airships" designed by Lawrence for the "W.D. Boyce African Balloonograph Expedition," the largest to date setting out from Nairobi. Ultimately, though, equipment failure and other problems (including a lion chewing a camera) deflated the much-vaunted expedition. Other aerial experiments enjoyed more success; in 1917, Lowell Thomas ascended in a small aeroplane for a unique vantage point of the Nile and the Giza Pyramids (*Lowell Thomas' Film of Lawrence of Arabia*), and British Pathé released *Pyramids from the Air* (1923) highlighting the "stupendous engineering achievement" of British aviators who conquered Egypt from the sky. The commercial potential for nature aerial footage was realized by Martin and Osa Johnson in *Baboona* (1934) and *Wings Over Africa* (1934).[83] *Baboona* also laid claim to being the first sound film shown in the air (on Eastern Airlines), but it was not the first film to capture aerial footage of East African mountain ranges, as some have claimed.[84] Because the British government recognized early the imperial value of mapping the continent from above, cinematographer B.W.G. Emmott accompanied aviator Alan Cobham on his 1925–26 London-Cape Town-London Airways Survey. And in 1931, South African pilot F. Roy Tuckett flew solo in a Gypsy Moth above Kilimanjaro and Mount Kenya to attain footage shown at the Reading and Berkshire Flying Club.[85] Tuckett's success led him to launch British Air Travel Features, specializing in aerial films.[86]

Back on the ground, the successes of Lady Grace Mackenzie reflected the increasing prominence of white women on hunting safaris and camera expeditions. Capitalizing on Nairobi's emerging safari industry, Mackenzie traveled with Ernest Shelley to film East African wildlife for *Heart of Africa* (a.k.a. *Lady Mackenzie's Big Game Pictures*, 1915). In the film she shoots a rhino and two lions, and in later safaris cemented her sharp-shooting reputation by acquiring wildlife specimens sold to various zoos and museums.[87] Nairobi replaced Mombasa as capital of British East Africa in 1905, emerging as the hub for big-game enthusiasts by the 1910s, following the interest generated by Roosevelt's safari. Starting out as essentially a supply depot for the Uganda Railway, the city quickly blossomed into a British administrative center and a magnet for big-game sportsmen from Europe and the United States served by the new luxurious tent safaris offered by Newland, Tarlton & Co. In addition to head guide R.J. Cunninghame, indigenous Maasai, Lumbwa and Nandi were recruited as trackers, porters, cameramen and actors for wildlife safaris. The fact that movie theaters were also opening in the city center during the interwar years helped propel the medium into prominence in Kenya and surrounding colonies.

In German safari filmmaking circles, it was Hans Schomburgk and Paul Charles Lieberenz who were pivotal in popularizing Africa's wildlife during the Weimar years and beyond. Schomburgk, as noted above, had filmed features and ethno-dramas in Togoland before the war, and soon earned his stripes as a wildlife filmmaker with *Mensch und Tier im Urwald* (*Man and Animal in the Jungle*, 1924), made in Liberia with cinematographer Lieberenz. When Opel entered the truck market with their durable "Lastwagen" model in 1931, Schomburgk purchased a few and adorned them with a black silhouette of Africa and "Schomburgk Expedition" on the sides. Returning to Liberia, and then traveling widely through the continent, Schomburgk and Lieberenz produced *Das letzte Paradies* (*The Last Paradise*, 1932) and *Die Wildnis Stirbt* (*The Wildlife Is Dying*, 1933). The two enjoyed long careers in Africa. In 1956, accompanied by his niece, the indefatigable Schomburgk departed for Africa on his tenth expedition. And Lieberenz, while primarily interested in wildlife filming as attested to by *Auf Tierfang in Abessinien* (*Animal Trapping in Abyssinia*, 1926) and *Auf Tierfang in Afrika* (*Animal Trapping in Africa*, 1926), also produced *Unser Kamerun* (*Our Cameroon*, 1937) and later through his own company Lieberenz Filmproduktion, *Der Weg in die Welt* (*Stroll Around the World*, 1947), and a script for an unrealized film, "Der Ranger," on diamonds in Kruger National Park, to be produced by the Associated British Picture Corporation.[88]

Schomburgk and Lieberenz built solid careers in Africa, but competition for riveting wildlife footage was as fierce as the animals themselves during the interwar period. While the 1910s witnessed the shift from films highlighting the carnage of the kill to those promoting the thrill of capturing animals on celluloid, some filmmakers still intentionally blurred the lines. One prominent example was Professor H.A. Snow, sponsored by the Oakland Museum, who traveled throughout South Africa with Sidney Snow (his son and cinematographer) between 1919 and 1922. *Hunting Big Game in Africa with Gun and Camera* (1923), with scenes of Kimberley diamond mines, dancing natives and a complement of rhinoceroses, elephants, giraffes and other animals, proved financially remunerative with 250 first-run bookings.[89] Despite the fact that Universal Pictures pre-publicized the film through movie cards marketed in sets of 12, emphasizing its educational utility—one displays a baboon, with an explanation of the differences between tailed and non-tailed baboons on the back[90]—the film was bitterly attacked by Carl Akeley, who was busy promoting the simultaneous release of Martin and Osa Johnson's *Trailing African Wild Animals* (1923), for misrepresenting the continent.[91]

Akeley was a leading figure in African safari circles: among other accomplishments, he had traveled with his first wife, Delia, to Africa in 1905, accompanied Teddy Roosevelt on his 1909 expedition, and worked for the American Museum of Natural History, where he revamped the modern museum diorama. In 1917 he was named president of the prestigious Explorers Club in New York, and by the release of the Snows' film had explored gorilla habitats in the Virunga Mountains. Moreover, by 1918 he had completed the design for his Akeley Camera (which was more nimble than other models, included dual lenses for easier focus, and allowed for reel changes without a darkroom), which became a mainstay for wildlife filmmakers and which Akeley himself used for *Meanderings in Africa* (1922).

Martin Johnson joined the Explorers Club in 1921 and quickly became acquainted with Akeley. By this time, Akeley had moved into the animal conservation camp (yet justified killing animals for scientific research), and began pulling the Johnsons into his inner circle and pushing the museum to support their filmmaking endeavors. Equaling his distaste for large-scale slaughter for sport was his opposition to "nature-faking," and Akeley promoted the perceived ability of the Johnsons to deliver more faithful representations of what he was now calling "Brightest Africa." Although they struggled initially in their competition with Snow, ultimately the two globe-trotters from Kansas, Martin and Osa Johnson, set the standard for future safari-adventurers. Martin had achieved acclaim serving with Jack Lon-

2. The Scramble for Images: Strange Savages, Paid Primitives, Negotiating Natives 63

Carl Akeley and an African assistant, in camp with cameras and gorilla skins, Belgian Congo, 1922 (Image #260061, American Museum of Natural History Library).

don on board the *Snark*, and, after marrying Osa in 1910, the couple traveled to New Hebrides and the Solomon Islands, where they reportedly barely escaped from the cannibalistic Big Nambas. *Trailing African Wild Animals* was the fruit of their first African expedition, and over the next decade they released the African jungle-adventure films *Simba, the King of Beasts* (1928), *Wonders of the Congo* (1931), and *Congorilla* (1932), as well as authoring numerous articles and books. Akeley's intent was to tout the commercial films of the Johnsons to promote the American Museum of Natural History, yet the museum's trustees expressed concerns about the institution's non-profit status. As a result, museum supporter Daniel Pomeroy launched the Martin Johnson African Expedition Corporation, naming himself president and Akeley vice-president. The company sold stock publicly to finance the Johnsons' upcoming African expedition, but entered into an agreement allowing the museum to oversee, edit and even help market the corporation's films.[92]

Another key development during this period that led to a rethinking of the safari film was the appearance of the "talkie" in the mid-to-late 1920s, whose prospects for success were initially debated by the film industry. The Johnsons responded by releasing two versions of *Simba*: a silent version, and a partial-sound version with musical accompaniment that relied heavily on the use of intertitles. If at times the Johnsons were guilty of shamelessly exploiting the supposed alterity of Africans, it is clear that the Johnsons' popularity was reinforced by their ability to tap into Americans' nostalgia for their own pre-industrial

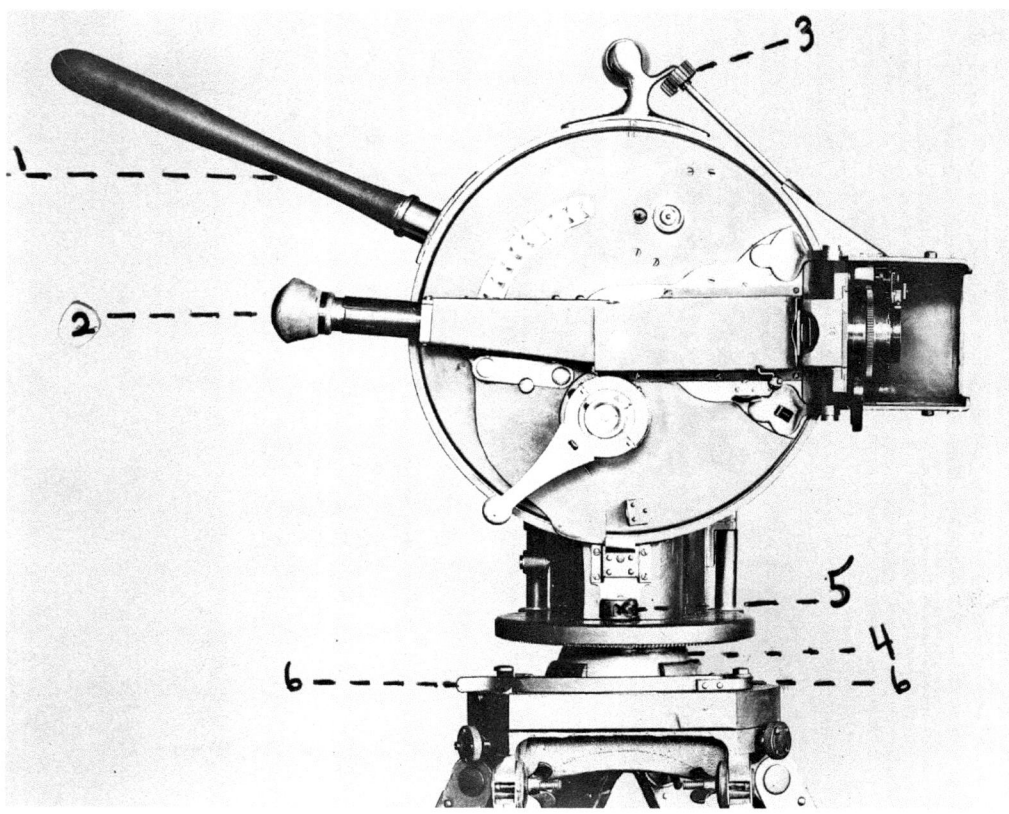

Close-up of Akeley camera that revolutionized location shooting in Africa (Image #337629, American Museum of Natural History Library).

past. We see this sentiment in *Simba*, which, in addition to sweeping panoramic shots of the African savanna, recalls the days of old: "On the plains of Tanganyika—Wildebeeste, by the thousands, countless as the Buffalo were in the American West."

Riveting lion footage constituted the holy grail of safari filmmaking due to physical risks, the species' nocturnal tendencies and rapid population decline. In 1914, lions were still relatively plentiful in British East Africa, as Cherry Kearton discovered. On safari in January, he enlisted the assistance of hunter Fritz Schindler to film a hunt. The targeted lion, not pleased with being cornered and taunted, proceeded to fatally disembowel Schindler.[93] The lion population soon noticeably decreased, leaving the Johnsons struggling during the filming of *Simba* to locate a single specimen, much less a pride. For this reason, in order to please moviegoers, they purchased footage taken by Alfred Klein years before, when he enlisted Nandi hunters to track and kill a lion for the camera.

By the interwar years, the struggle to get riveting footage of the elusive or "non-compliant" lion extended to lion country in southern Africa, where Wynant and Margaret Carson Hubbard spent three years (1922–25) trapping animals for zoos and later (1927–28) capturing images for the screen.[94] Wynant and Margaret had begun married life near Quebec in an asbestos mining town that closed during the 1921–22 depression. After their hope of finding asbestos work in Johannesburg fell through, they were offered a partnership in Northern Rhodesia's Mali Farm to capture wild game for resale. Eventually selling their stake, on their second

2. *The Scramble for Images: Strange Savages, Paid Primitives, Negotiating Natives* 65

Top: (Left to right) Martin Johnson, Carl Akeley, an African assistant and Osa Johnson filming *Trailing African Wild Animals* in Kenya, 1921 (Image #128559, American Museum of Natural History Library). *Above:* Martin and Osa Johnson filming in East Africa (Image #124549, American Museum of Natural History Library).

Akeley-Eastman-Pomeroy Expedition party posing for a photograph, Northern Frontier in Kenya, 1926–7 (Image #412213, American Museum of Natural History Library).

African trip they employed cameramen George Noble and Earle Frank and obtained thousands of feet of footage that was purchased by First National Pictures. This footage was edited and released commercially as a series of twelve shorts entitled *Adventures in Africa* (1931), with episodes including *Beasts of the Wilderness*, *Flaming Jungles*, and *The Witch Doctor's Magic*. Warner Bros. eventually repackaged the footage for a longer six-reel feature released as *Untamed Africa* (1933), which Margaret used to jump-start her lecturing career.[95]

Most footage was obtained after animals were successfully interned in a compound. While their leopard complied, taking "a flying, roaring leap toward the cameras," the lion proved less accommodating even after pitting him against a crocodile for a night scene:

> Action? Nothing moved but the maddening mosquitoes. The precious flares from our limited supply burned on. The crocodile refused to budge. He lay in one spot, playing possum.... The lion squatted under a small tree and stayed there. We poked them, we shouted, we coaxed, we teased. No. They would not budge.[96]

Because of the difficulty of finding lions even in Rhodesia, the Hubbards decided it would be prudent to purchase specimens from Pagel's Circus in South Africa, and take them north via rail. Margaret was keenly aware of the double ironies of animal trappers purchasing animals to facilitate the filming of "wildest" Africa:

> As insurance against the possibility that we might fail to catch a lion when we got to Rhodesia, the leader of the expedition had decided that we should buy lions in Johannesburg and

2. *The Scramble for Images: Strange Savages, Paid Primitives, Negotiating Natives*   67

take them with us to Rhodesia. Go to Africa and *buy* a lion? What kind of *Alice in Wonderland* trip were we on, anyway? Buy a circus lion? Why leave Hollywood?⁹⁷

Margaret Hubbard, as previously noted, allowed the African Mudalla to handle cameras and even travel alone on the savanna in search of footage. Yet her relationship with, and perceptions of, Africans remained firmly couched within the paternalist mindset of the colonial world. In the 1950s she watched with dismay as "agitators" like Tom Mboya called for independence, with the "misguided" support of activists like Ralph Bunche. And as late as 1958 she was still sounding warnings about African cannibalism—"once a person of any age has eaten human flesh they crave it"—and repeating old refrains—"What I'm stressing is that AFRICA IS NOT CIVILIZED and we shouldn't encourage ideas that it is."⁹⁸ For Hubbard, the mining sector played a key civilizing role in Africa, as well as providing subject matter for her earlier film *Gold*. In 1935, returning to Africa following her divorce, she became fascinated by Johannesburg's mining sector and filmed African boys descending into the shafts, a dance in a compound, and, in the words of her screenplay: "Pay day—the big day for boys, cut to gold bars, the big day for whites." Hubbard contracted with Paramount Pictures, and *Gold* was subsequently released in 1938 as Paramount Paragraphic #8.⁹⁹

Hubbard was not alone in highlighting Africans' perceived primitivity. Louis Cotlow, perhaps the 20th century's most prolific global explorer-filmmaker, made this his entire leitmotif. A successful insurance agent, Cotlow self-financed dozens of trips around the world "in search of the primitive" (the title of one of his books). In 1937 the Lewis N. Cotlow Belgian Congo Photographic Expedition explored Central Africa in part to search out gorilla habitats, sometimes employing Mbuti guides: "Interesting native tribes, awe-inspiring mountains and forest scenery and intimate views of wild animals are combining to make my trip through the 'Dark Continent' a memorable experience."¹⁰⁰ The result of his Cape to Cairo expedition was the now-lost *Through Africa Unarmed* (1937), followed by *Savage Splendor* (co-produced with Armand Denis, 1949), and later, *Zanzabuku: Dangerous Safari* (1956). Amy Staples notes that Cotlow touted his personal relationships with Africans: "I never treated them like an anthropologist. I never measured their ears or their calf joints," a phenomenon sometimes found in the ethnographic genre.¹⁰¹ It should be noted that while Cotlow touted *Savage Splendor* as Africa's first color film, earlier color footage of a South African water pipeline project is held at the Smithsonian Institution.

Artifactual Collection: The Scientific Expedition Film

The Scramble for Images in the early 20th century was complemented by a Scramble for Artifacts, as the scientific world and the international art community conceptualized the "Dark Continent" as a ready storehouse of plunder to adorn museum cases and gallery walls. Perhaps most famous in this regard was Marcel Griaule's 1931–33 Mission Dakar-Djibouti. Griaule recruited Claude Pignault from a photography company as cinematographer who assisted in collecting thousands of images and artifacts to bolster the Africa holdings of the Musée d'Ethnographie du Trocadéro.¹⁰² Fueled by public enthusiasm for the 1931 Colonial Exhibition, support came from a variety of sources, including the French parliament. While Mission Dakar-Djibouti has rightly garnered attention, in part for what Ruth Larson calls the large-scale cultural theft that was the cornerstone of the expedition's collecting strategy, the deployment of cinema as an adjunct to scientific research and specimen collection began years earlier.¹⁰³ In fact, Griaule himself making preparations for a previous trip to Ethiopia had contacted several motion picture firms, but after encountering obstacles concluded that "cinematographic preparation is a lot less simple than I imagined."[104] Yet while Griaule struggled in 1928 to find backing, other museum-sponsored expeditions armed with cameras were busy making inroads into the continent.

A number of scientific investigations gravitated to the Nile River corridor. Indeed, no waterway has captured the European imagination more than this powerful river in North Africa (Nero commissioning an exploratory journey two millennia ago). Steamship travel dates to the 1869 opening of the Suez Canal, leading British entrepreneur Thomas Cook to exploit its tourist potential with a fleet servicing historic sites in Upper Nubia. The two decades following the Egyptian Revolution of 1919 constituted the Golden Age of Nile River tourism, despite ongoing "pacification" campaigns, before World War II foreclosed opportunities for further travel. Not coincidentally, it was during this period that Britain reaffirmed its presence in the Anglo-Egyptian Sudan. What this meant was that for many in the interwar period business was booming, as archaeologists, tourists, diplomats, businessmen—and by extension, filmmakers—enjoyed the 20-day cruise to the Aswan Dam and the Old Cataract Hotel. There was a stark contrast between the grueling endurance desert crossings explored above and these more genteel excursions, where footage was often secured from riverboat decks, or among riverbank communities.

Thus, although Burton Holmes had secured footage of the Nile in 1906, and Alfred Machin, in the employ of Pathé, had traveled upriver for *Une Fête chez les Chillouks au Bahr al Ghazal* (*A Festival of the Chilluks, Bahr el Ghazal*, 1910), cinematic renderings became more commonplace in the 1920s. As a case in point, the Pathé Exchange produced *The Blue Nile* in 1925, offering glimpses of the waterway, ancient monuments near Wadi Halfa, and a camel caravan being unloaded. As we saw earlier, in 1927 on assignment for Harvard's Peabody Museum, anthropologist Frederick Wulsin found himself on the Nile, where he put together a few reels known as *Frederick Wulsin's Travel Footage of Africa*.[105] Funded by the Laura Spelman Rockefeller Fund, he took footage all the way to Rejaf, the terminus for boats on the White Nile, and continued into the Belgian Congo, filming zookeepers, an elephant training station, an officer mustering the Force Publique, and Mbuti locals. The film ends with Wulsin south of Lake Chad, in Fort Lamy, French West Africa, coincidentally where Amelia Earhart would later stop during her bid to fly solo around the world.

The next year the river again supplied the backdrop for a scientific excursion film, this time in the form of William O. Field's *Up the Nile to Central Africa* (1928). His primary goal was to secure museum-quality animal specimens for the Smithsonian's National Museum of Natural History, but Field used both still and motion picture cameras to document more generally what the Smithsonian archives describes as the many miles covered on his "expedition by steamboat up the Nile River into the Sudan," in addition to the Mosque of Muhammad Ali, ancient Egyptian ruins, and Dinka and Shilluk communities. Yet in a nod to the ubiquity of filmmaking artifice discussed below, Field later confessed that the film's sequencing was inaccurate, with scenes cleverly spliced together to conform to preconceived notions of where Nile River exploration "should" begin. In fact, rather than originating in Egypt, the crew traveled through the canal to Port Sudan on the Red Sea. There the crew boarded a train to Khartoum, and continued on a "chartered steamer up the White Nile to the head of navigation, then returned to Khartoum, and northward through Egypt to Cairo, and out."[106] Field was surprised by what he perceived as the indolence of locals along the way, a bias that continually pervades the film. According to one intertitle, "Here were the typical Sudanese people, strange mixtures of Semitic, Arabic, and Negro blood, well built and strong, yet lazy and childishly ignorant." Describing the Shilluk, Field hammered home widespread stereotypes of the lazy African, describing a village in

2. *The Scramble for Images: Strange Savages, Paid Primitives, Negotiating Natives* 69

which "the young men characteristically idled about leaving the women and children to do the work," and declaring later that "idleness" constituted the "main occupation" of male warriors.[107]

In 1926, Pathé News cinematographer Charles Charlton was on the ocean liner *Llanstephan*, accompanying the Smithsonian-Chrysler Expedition to East Africa. The Smithsonian had opened its National Zoological Park in 1889, but struggled to secure animals for its collection. Thus, with funding provided by Walter Chrysler, the goal of expedition leader and zoo director William Mann was to return home with a large selection of Tanganyikan fauna. His subsequent capture of an impressive 1,200 specimens, documented by Charlton's Pathé News cameras, served to enlarge the zoo's holdings by 50 percent.[108] Despite Charlton's experience in the business, he must have been thrilled to discover the identity of his fellow heavyweights heading to Africa on board the *Llanstephan*: the legendary George Eastman and Carl Akeley, who were traveling with somewhat different forms of specimen collection in mind. George Eastman had founded Eastman Kodak Company in 1892, marketing a flexible celluloid strip that revolutionized photography and the emerging motion picture industry. By 1921, with the meteoric growth of Kodak behind him and facing a government anti-trust suit, Eastman began extricating himself from daily management to pursue personal interests.[109] Increasingly absorbed by the great outdoors, Eastman asked Akeley to accompany him on an African hunting

Filming wildlife on the Akeley-Eastman-Pomeroy Expedition, 1926 (Image #412239, American Museum of Natural History Library).

trip. Akeley readily acceded, as he was eager to secure more diorama specimens for Akeley Hall in the American Museum of Natural History. When they set sail in 1926, banker and museum trustee Daniel Pomeroy had also joined what was officially named the Akeley-Eastman-Pomeroy African Hall Expedition. To add even more luster, Pomeroy also facilitated contact with Osa and Martin Johnson, who took part in the festivities once expedition members disembarked.

The expedition clearly blurred the lines between Eastman's desire for an old-school big-game hunt and Akeley's more targeted search for samples in the pursuit of science. In any event, an opportunity to secure riveting footage presented near the Gurumetti River in Tanganyika, where an enthusiastic Eastman hoped to secure trophies from "the centre of the greatest game country left in the world." The location, he mused, was simply "ideal as a place to hunt, kill or murder the wild animals which roam the plains and hills in countless thousands."[110] Eastman's primary goal was trophy hunting, yet he also hoped to replicate Alfred Klein's now-legendary lion-spearing sequence:

> I am sending this [letter] by a truck which is going back to Narok for forty natives who are coming down to execute a lion spearing stunt for us if possible. We hope we can get a very interesting affair out of it and some excitement. To show how little value these natives put on life, they only stipulated that any man who is disabled shall get the value of one cow.[111]

With an expedition now comprising Akeley, Eastman, and the Johnsons, there was no lack of cameras on August 2, 1926, as they followed the "forty spearmen" with great anticipation:

> They are of the Lumbwa tribe, and we had to bring them on trucks ... to a donga where we had seen lions.... They advanced slowly, making little noise ... because they did not want to have the lion get out too far in front of them. Besides the three trucks, we had the Buick,

Mrs. Akeley among the Lumbwa for a lion-spearing sequence, Akeley-Eastman-Pomeroy Expedition, 1926 (Image #412216 American Museum of Natural History Library).

2. The Scramble for Images: Strange Savages, Paid Primitives, Negotiating Natives

Osa's new Willys-Knight, Carl Akeley's two cars and Martin Johnson on his old Willys-Knight, Pat driving. I say "on" because he was perched on the back of the rear seat with his Akeley camera on a high tripod.... Akeley also had another of his cameras, and, of course, Audley and I had our Ciné-Kodaks and 1A's. The object was to drive the quarry out into the open so that the spearing could be photographed.[112]

These careful preparations yielded only a buffalo mistakenly speared in the bush. Although a lion did emerge when the Lumbwa beat some nearby grass, he quickly escaped. Two subsequent attempts were similarly disappointing, after which the expedition turned its sights on Simpson's Camp, 40 miles to the north. While the American explorers drove to Simpson's, it took the Lumbwa two days to trek to the site. Once everyone was assembled, expedition members cornered a lion through the aid of the vehicles, and with their high vantage point they signaled the Lumbwa, who quickly honed in on the hapless target:

It was a merciful death in that it was all over in a few seconds. As soon as he rose up out of the grass he was in full view of the camera, and Martin got a wonderful picture. Carl was a little further away as, with his wife driving, he was not justified in getting as close as Johnson, but he secured a good picture too. After half an hour of dancing, rejoicing and picture-taking the spearmen were keen for another lion.[113]

While Eastman and Akeley were filming their exploits in East Africa, world traveler and filmmaker Suydam Cutting and a team including Wilfred Osgood and Louis Fuertes, were busy exploring the Ethiopian hinterland to acquire "precise facts" and "specimens of animal life."[114] Cutting's expedition was sponsored by Chicago's Field Museum and the *Chicago Daily News*, but filming in Ethiopia still required diplomacy, for unlike the rest of Africa formally occupied by European powers (Liberia excluded), Ethiopia had actually crushed an earlier Italian invasion. We have noted that only the year before the Field Museum expedition, Regent Ras Tafari had welcomed Rosita Forbes and her cinematographer as part of his modernization campaign, and thus he similarly welcomed Cutting and crew to Addis Ababa, where they formally requested permission to film. "His manner was soft and quiet, but his personality projected force," noted Cutting. The conversation was perfunctory, conducted in Amharic through an interpreter. Exchanging a few pleasantries, the regent concluded with a cordial affirmation, "Yes, everything will be done to facilitate the expedition's progress."[115]

Cutting's team and a small corps of African porters traveled through the Arussi Plateau and "rolling, wooded country," where they came in contact with Galla (Oromo) villagers who "ran out to stare at us." Expedition members spent much of their time collecting animal specimens, including nyala, duiker, black bushbuck, and various bird species. But Cutting and Osgood managed to steal off to visit a Galla village, described by Cutting as a "primitive colony of thatched tuckels, surrounded by a sea of sodden mud and cattle dung. No men were visible and I feared our arrival might alarm the women and children." But in contrast to other explorers' reports that referenced the reticence of native women when confronted by expedition parties, here "the women calmly and boldly walked up and took stock of the first white men they had ever seen."[116] The composure of female villagers, though, failed to sway Cutting's preconceptions, for in his film *Abyssinia* he framed Ethiopians as irremediable Others, although the stereotypes affirmed by the intertitles are often belied by the images themselves. One scene in which villagers are casually walking to a marketplace is described as a "Market of wild Gallas—altitude 6,000 feet, just off the high tableland," attributing their perceived lack of civilization to an innate savagery compounded by geographical remoteness. The film also includes a retinue of servants and slaves catering to

Chief Ras Hailu of Gojjam Province, who offers hospitality to the crew.[117] Most viewers of *Abyssinia*, however, would have been unaware that this "primitive," if powerful, chieftain had, in fact, visited England just two years before to meet King George V. The two had traded insults for their mutual ignorance of the other's language, a minor dispute that was quickly laughed off.

In the summer of 1930, the Logan Museum at Wisconsin's Beloit College sponsored the Logan African Expedition to Algeria. Led by Alonzo Pond, the expedition was unique because Logan, a teaching museum, sponsored eight undergraduates to accompany Pond, along with Alonzo's wife, Dorothy, and photographer/filmmaker George Waite (*National Geographic* and *Milwaukee Journal* photographer).[118] The expedition's primary objective was to study 30,000-year-old shell heaps made by paleolithic peoples who survived on land snails. After months excavating south of Constantine, the party returned to Beloit with significant booty from the Saharan "land of the dead," as one newspaper phrased it. Approximately 36,000 flint fragments were carted out, along with 30 skeletons and other osteological remains deposited at Logan. Pond and Waite also took 700 photographs (47 comprising the lantern slide collection *Desert Sheiks*), and 6,000 feet of footage from which Pond pulled scenes for *Reliving the Past* (1930).[119] This film was wide-ranging in scope; on the one hand it served as a record of the expedition itself, with lighthearted scenes of Waite riding a camel and a crewmember celebrating a birthday at "Camp Logan." But Pond also wanted to convey the rigors of scientific inquiry, and thus Waite filmed excavation activities, including trench digging, screening of prehistoric ash, and so on. One drawback, according to Pond, was the conspicuous camera, resulting in Arab workers feeling overly self-conscious as they demonstrated work on a skeleton, and footage "so awkward and obviously posed that it is just funny."[120] Additionally, the film served as an ethnographic document of the culture in Biskra. Highlights included Berber caravans and the quotidian tasks of grain grinding, cous-cous production, pottery finishing and sheep shearing. Pond later tried to sell the footage to Eastman Teaching Films, but was rejected due to "edge fog," the shakiness of the hand-held camera, and simplistic shots that failed to "follow the conventional pattern of long shot, medium shot and close-up in order to register action."[121]

Despite the scientific nature of a portion of Pond's footage, the films that were the outgrowth of the majority of these expeditions were rarely fully integrated into scientific methodology or comprehensive data collection. Rather, they were designed to document and popularize the expeditions for museum trustees and the general public. Pond, for instance, toured Wisconsin exhibiting his film and lecturing on Algeria, with appearances in Beloit, Milwaukee and Rockford. We see the same goal to popularize scientific endeavors in the film *Harvard African Expedition of 1934*. Richard Pearson Strong, a tropical medicine specialist, had experimented with film on a previous African expedition. But now with sponsorship from the Belgians eager to test earlier findings of ophthalmologist Jean Hissette relating to African River Blindness, Pearson and crew traveled to the Belgian Congo's Sankuru River region. It seems that while Henry Mallinckrodt likely took the raw footage, Guido Kluxen edited the slick production. Although the film did document Africans being tested and treated, it primarily functioned as a chronicle of the laborious itinerary itself, with maps of the continent and the Congo, and shots of the various modes of transportation required to reach remote locations in Central Africa.[122] The overall impression one derives from the film is not how cinema might be integrated into cutting-edge scientific endeavors, but the distance from home traveled by the crew, and the primitive conditions under which they worked. Picturing difference, and not disease, was its primary *raison d'être*.

Paid Primitives: The Ethnographic and Ethnotacular Film

In many ways the impetus for ethnographic filmmaking emerged at the crossroads between two turn-of-the-century phenomena: the romanticization and commodification of exotic otherness, and the search for traditional cultures seemingly headed toward extinction. As I.C. Jarvie phrased it, "To the true romantic ... the only truly unspoiled and hence real people are those out of touch with civilization but in touch with nature: primitive people," a perspective which fueled cinematic salvage operations, albeit not without debate in the anthropological community.[123] There was a crucial third thread that provided impetus for the early visual recordings of non–Western peoples, and one which played a formative role in the development of cinema itself. Marta Braun has noted that French authorities struggled to reverse a perceived racial degeneracy following the country's 1871 defeat by Prussia, leading to government funding for Etienne-Jules Marey's studies in locomotion and physiology.[124] Marey's chronophotographic investigations into the morphological differences between African and European soldiers were conducted specifically with the aim of overhauling French military training.[125] These studies were followed up by what is generally credited as "the first ethnographic film." This was produced by French physician Felix Regnault, who made a female Wolof fashioning a clay pot the subject of a series of chronophotographs in the very year that saw the launch of commercial cinema.[126] Regnault, who claimed that the Wolof pot fabrication preserved on film represented the crucial stage between non-wheeled and wheeled pottery production, subsequently produced chronophotographic images of Wolof, Fulani and Diola (Jola) subjects squatting, walking and climbing trees.

These early motion experiments filmed in Europe were followed by Alfred Cort Haddon's 1898 filming of Mer cultural practices in the Torres Straits, an early experiment in location shooting for anthropological purposes. There were a number of subsequent landmarks in the evolution of ethnographic filmmaking, including Robert Flaherty's *Nanook of the North* (1922); the inauguration of 1920s anthropological teaching films; Marcel Mauss's Institut d'Ethnologie lectures promoting cinema's capacity to "record and preserve the facts"[127]; Jean Rouch's 1940s spirit possession films; the Musée de l'Homme's 1948 ethnographic film congress; and the 1952 founding of both the International Committee on Ethnographic Films and the Institut für den Wissenschaftlichen. Yet during this entire period, both before and after the institutionalization of the genre, ethnographic film expeditions were just as likely to be led by missionaries, adventurers, explorers and commercial concerns as they were ethnographers. Moreover, the release of what might be called commercial "ethnotaculars" guaranteed larger crowds and, ultimately, had a greater social impact outside the ivory tower.

By the early 20th century, salvage operations were underway to capture both the bizarre and the traditional on celluloid. Yet bulky equipment, climatic issues and other problems often stymied these pioneering efforts. We have already noted that footage taken by cinematographers Weber and Machin was rendered useless in 1897 and 1908, respectively. In a similar case, Adolf Friedrich, the Duke of Mecklenburg, discovered to his dismay in the Sudan during his German Central African Expedition (1910–11) that "a case containing almost all of my photographic films" had simply disappeared.[128] Around this time, Hans Schomburgk's first film experiments in West Africa also failed as "the negative stock he took out was not the right kind for the tropics," although by 1913 he was successfully producing the first ethnodramas in Togoland.[129] For his part, Karl Weule, professor of Ethnography and Prehistory at Leipzig University, was satisfied that at least a portion of his 1907 research footage of the Wakonda in German East Africa had survived:

As to the cinematograph, I must remember that I am a pioneer, and as such must not incur all the inconvenience involved in the imperfections of an industry as yet in its infancy.... I know, by those I have developed myself, that about two-thirds of my thirty-eight cinematograph records must be fairly good ... and that is a pretty fair proportion for a beginner.[130]

Other expeditions were more successful. In a famous example of early ethnographic filmmaking, the Berlin Anthropological Society sent Rudolph Pöch to the Kalahari to film "the oldest and most primitive surviving south African race," the Bushmen (San).[131] This would be neither the Western world's first visual encounter with the San, nor the last: by the 1860s Barnum's Museum was already displaying "Troglodyte Bushmen or Earthmen."[132] Pöch's footage, now collectively entitled *Bushmen of the Kalahari* (1908), was followed by other cinematic expeditions to capture the desert "Ur-race." In 1925, South African hunter and cameraman C. Ernest Cadle teamed up with cinematographer Paul Hoefler for the Denver African Expedition. Hoefler edited the resulting film, *The Bushman* (1926), but the overexposed production received tepid reviews. Cadle, though, returned to the Kalahari on the 1928 Cameron-Cadle Expedition, outfitted with two "Diamond T" trucks emblazoned with the expedition's name on the sides. Now teamed with Will J. Cameron, owner of a medical implements firm who apparently bankrolled the expedition, Cadle hired Fred Parrish as cinematographer and with five cameras they secured 30,000 feet of film of the Kalahari and the Belgian Congo.[133] In his later film lectures, Cameron highlighted what he described as the crude primitivity of the "Bushmen"—"a race so low in the human scale that they have a vocabulary of but 200 words." Indeed, to say that the San existed on a level equal to that of wild animals in terms of social organization would be, from Cameron's perspective, an insult to the latter: "It is certain they [Bushmen] are not so well organized, socially, as are the baboons, who always have their leader, and who keeps his outposts on constant watch."[134]

In general, "tribal" Africans were measured, prodded and poked during the colonial era to satisfy the ethnographic eye. Filmmakers in search of the exotic commonly used measuring tapes and other tools to note the contrasting stature of the San, Mbuti, Tutsi, and others. Aurélio Rossi capitalized on this leitmotif of extremes for his stencil-colored film *Au pays des colosses et des pygmées* (*In the Land of Giants and Pygmies*, 1925), with one intertitle comparing the oversized, primeval wilderness of Africa to the diminutive yet primitive Mbuti: "Deep in the equatorial forest, among giant plants and colossi of the animal kingdom, live the smallest representatives of the human race: the Mambutti."

An earlier instance of invasive objectivity harnessing both still and moving pictures to scientific research can be seen in anthropologist Frederic Starr's 1912 West African expedition, sponsored by Chicago's Field Museum. Starr had recently defended King Leopold II, earning him a dubious reputation for condoning atrocities during the Congo Free State Propaganda War. Nevertheless, in the autumn Starr and photographer/cameraman Campbell Marvin disembarked in Liberia, first trekking eastward to study the "native arts and industries, religions and folklore" of the Bassa people, and eventually working north to Sierra Leone and Morocco. Starr had been championing the use of cinema as an effective tool for scientific instruction for several years, although his experience on his 1906–7 Congo expedition resonated with that of others in equatorial zones—his footage was rendered useless due to humidity.[135] Despite this setback, Starr had begun incorporating motion pictures into his public lectures, and as he prepared to depart for Africa in 1912 he received encouragement from friend and filmmaker William Selig in Chicago. In fact, Starr's subsequent book *Liberia: Description, History, Problems* was dedicated to Selig, who had recently enjoyed success with his own Roosevelt safari film (discussed below), compelling

Selig's move west to continue producing jungle-themed features in Hollywood. If cinema was first introduced by Starr into many areas of the interior to document the cultural and physical characteristics of West African peoples, it was only one in an array of objectifying instruments. In addition to securing 14,000 feet of film, he used a variety of apparatuses to take measurements of 200 soldiers of the Liberian frontier force, and palmar and plantar impressions of 100 other native subjects.[136] This trove of data was complemented by the acquisition of 350 Bassa artifacts which were deposited in Cologne's Rauterstrauch-Joest Museum.

If measuring instruments were used to engrain cultural difference, ethnographic films also hawked other stark visual contrasts. "First contact" scenarios, despite their dubious ethnographic utility, became commonplace as filmmakers touted modern technological marvels and their supposed impact on primitive peoples. In 1908, for instance, Rudolf Pöch filmed a gesticulating "Bushman" speaking directly into the funnel of a gramophone, while Alfred Machin included a similar scene for *Une Fête chez les Chillouks au Bahr al Ghazal*. In Machin's film, the intertitle "The children are curious about a phonograph" is followed by a curious monkey who puts his head in the speaker and then lies down on the spinning turntable. This motif was exploited most famously by Flaherty in a very different setting for *Nanook of the North*, with an "uncomprehending" Nanook staring at a working gramophone and biting down on a vinyl record. Although not the first to peddle the theme, Flaherty's success no doubt prompted Paul Hoefler to incorporate the motif on his 1928–29 Colorado African Expedition:

> While the Masai have no music of their own ... like the people of all savage tribes, they go wild over American jazz. We had a great deal of fun with our phonograph. They could not understand where the sound was coming from and would gaze all about, looking for it. When we asked them what they thought made it talk, their reply was that we had cut off somebody's head and placed it in the box.[137]

Osa and Martin Johnson similarly put the phonograph front and center in *Congorilla*, with Osa playing a jazz record and dancing with "Pygmies" while Martin provides the voiceover: "About this time I said to Osa, let's give the boys and girls some modern jazz!" Because the theme became so entrenched it was inevitable that even a post–World War II explorer like John Brom would find it irresistible during his 1950s stopover in the Ituri Forest: "In the morning, Pygmies appeared around Brom's camp as he was preparing his cameras and recording equipment. They gathered around him and as they were talking to each other, Brom decided to record them and then replayed their voices. The older Pygmies were afraid but the younger ones were quite curious."[138]

The shift from late–19th-century time-motion studies to location shooting reflected the broader ethnographic impulse to document the folkways of African communities. Ethnographic films often featured de-contextualized group rituals and other cultural phenomena in their "native setting," which frequently involved filming communal dances. In the first few decades, these were generally the result of brief visits in the field. Melville Herskovits, for instance, conducted research in West Africa in 1931 and documented cinematically "some southern Nigeria types" including the Alake of Abeokuta, and a "Dahomean village [consisting] of groups of mud-walled, thatch-covered houses." But a primary focus of his Dahomean footage was the "'Nesuhwe,' or princely ancestral dance. This young man danced to illustrate this and other ceremonial dances, so that the motor behavior involved might be analyzed."[139] Colonial propaganda sometimes pushed in a similar direction, for very different aims. Working for the French Ministry of Colonies, for instance, R. Bugniet highlighted the gap between European civilization and "traditional" Africa in his 12-minute short *Cameroun* (1930s), featuring dances from the southern provinces of Akonolinga, Yaounde, Doume and Batouri, while obscuring the realities of French colonial occupation.

While many expeditions allowed limited time for fieldwork among African communities, in some instances research was conducted over several visits, as we see in the case of Marcel Griaule, who produced the shorts *Au pays du Dogon* (*In Dogon Country*) and *Sous les masques noirs* (*Under the Black Masks*) in 1938, as part of his now-controversial explication of Dogon mythology. In a few cases, decades of research led to a rich visual archive collected over the *long durée*. John Marshall, in the Kalahari intermittently throughout the second half of the 20th century (although sometimes banned for political reasons) amassed significant footage of the hunting expertise of the !Kung Bushmen for *The Hunters* (1957), *!Kung Bushmen Hunting Equipment* (1972), and other films.

A critical issue throughout the evolution of 20th century ethnographic filmmaking was the three-way relationship between cinematic eye, observer and observed. Jean Rouch proved to be a pivotal figure in the debate by re-conceptualizing the role of the filmmaker and the placement of the camera vis-à-vis the observed: now embedded within the social space under investigation—an approach termed *cinéma vérité* designed to provoke deeper truths from the subjects—the filmmaker now enters the frame and engages in open dialogue and discussion with his informants. Observation becomes interrogation. While the "Rouch-effect" proved revolutionary through his ground-breaking, collaborative style developed in *Moi, un noir* (*I, a Negro*, 1958), among other films, the observational paradigm proved surprisingly resilient. In 1972, Walter Goldschmidt was still repeating the familiar refrain: "Ethnographic film is film which endeavors to interpret the behavior of people of one culture to persons of another culture by using shots of people doing precisely what they would have been doing if the cameras were not present."[140] This ponderous (if pat) definition highlights the implied surveillance functions of the observational approach, subjecting Africans to the panoptic vision of imperial power even as it conflates Africans with surrounding wildlife. Filmmaker Donald Ker once spoke of the importance of a "blind" in his nature photography: "In order to secure the most interesting movies or stills of game, and at the same time study their ways, it is necessary to be entirely hidden, so that the animals are unaware of human presence."[141] Ker's position resonates revealingly with the subterfuge of Carl von Hoffman, who directed *Jungle Gods* and a commercially successful (if now forgotten) ethnographic study entitled, *Land of the Moors*. On one occasion, he attached a mirror to the camera lens to capture surreptitiously the action behind him,[142] while on another he tried to take advantage of a blind:

> I was only too keenly aware, however, that the Mahdies of Obdurman ... adhered more strictly to the ancient [Moslem prohibitions]. There, bakshish was of no avail, and I found it necessary to take motion pictures with the aid of a telephoto lens from a hidden retreat. When this concealment hindered me from securing satisfactory results, I was obliged to leave the blind and work in the open in closer proximity to my subject, with my back turned and my hand grinding the camera as I gazed in an opposite direction, the natives thus unwitting targets for my lens.[143]

Despite the examples above, and ethical considerations aside, the reality was that in the field expeditions were almost always high-profile events, with large motion picture cameras the focus of intense scrutiny by villagers. Indeed, to return to our previous example, Hoffman and team had to pre-schedule dozens of paid porters for each territory and secure film permits from colonial officials. And while Hoffman worked his way south from Cairo in 1925, Delia Akeley was traveling on her own Central African expedition, reporting in her diary that her arrival in the Ituri Forest to film the Mbuti caused quite a stir: "When we approach a village the tepoy men sing madly.... Everybody rushes out to see who is [being carried] and when they realize that I am a woman they yell and run after us."[144] To cite again Alonzo Pond and George Waite, there was little doubt about the visibility of their Algerian expedition as they filmed *Reliving the Past*, or that locals were honing their histrionic skills even as they conducted their normal, primitive tasks. Moreover, crewmembers themselves even felt the power of the return gaze: "We felt as though we were monkeys in a cage, for wherever we went in the cars we would be surrounded by several hundred Algerians, full of curiosity.... They play their flutes and sing their monotone songs. We paid them 32 cents a day."[145]

John Brom offered generous compensation to Mwana Katchunga of the Yambala to recreate a defunct social ritual for the benefit of the camera (courtesy Olga Brom Spencer).

Ironically, despite the veneer of gift-giving governing transactions between villagers and crew, many early ethnographic films designed to tease out the dynamics of pre-capitalist modes of production were, in fact, staged events enacted through an exchange economy. Of course, in the case of non-ethnographic films by commercial concerns, agreements were explicit and wages were higher (a phenomenon deplored by explorer-filmmakers who preferred "primitives" to "professionals"). After shooting *Rhodes of Africa* (1936), for instance, Gaumont set up a table and locals, "clad once more in rags and tatters," filed past to receive their wages. One crewmember managing the "moneybags" was accompanied by "two camp officials with pay sheets, a representative of the Department of Native Affairs and his clerk, a police officer, and a corporal. Some of the Matabele had earned as much as thirty shillings. Most of them departed with a pound or twenty-five shillings to their credit."[146] In contrast, those shooting ethnographic films generally deplored the "bribes" that had to be paid to Africans. In the case of Margaret Carson Hubbard filming *Leibalala (Sweetheart)* in 1925, a film that wove into the primary narrative of a Lozi wedding aspects of traditional culture, including fishing, mining and smelting, she soon realized she would be bank-rolling actual bride-prices.[147] With ad-hoc pay scales in place, there can be little doubt that in the multitude of reels displaying "primitive" Africans, villagers were often (over)performing for the camera, and indeed would have considered their white visitors little more than ethno-tourists. Of course, this allowed a small opening wedge for

Meru porters in the employ of Martin and Osa Johnson, expedition in Kenya, 1921 (Image #129101, American Museum of Natural History Library).

negotiation, a critical point often overlooked by film scholars. Olga Brom Spencer, who spent years in Africa with her husband, John Brom, in the 1950s, confirmed to this author that upon entering a village it was common practice to hold a palaver with a headman to negotiate fees (often goods) for services rendered. Yet whether the booty agreed upon ever filtered down to the rank and file is questionable.[148] Crewmembers could also work other angles to improve their lot, as Martin and Osa found out in Kenya:

> Our Meru porters arrived, and with their arrival our troubles began. They immediately struck for twelve shillings a month instead of the regulation price of ten. Much against his better judgment, Martin had to give in to them, because he was worried about the rains.[149]

In any event, transactions remained embedded within prevailing colonial power relations, generally involving low wages and frequently the protection of security forces. In the case of William Field, a native commissioner pre-arranged film shoots: "I think the [Dinka dance] cost the equivalent of one dollar and was equal to anything the Messrs. Carroll, White and Ziegfeld ever put on…. It should make an interesting companion picture to that of the war dance at Kodok." Traveling in the Sudan in 1910–11, Adolf Friedrich required the assistance of "fifty bearers and an escort of seven soldiers."[150] Thus, not surprisingly, when he was appointed governor of Togoland the following year, Friedrich guaranteed Hans Schomburgk's safety by requiring that all district commissioners help facilitate the movement of the huge expedition (including 120 paid porters), to "film scenes and plays of native life amongst absolutely virgin and unspoiled surroundings."[151]

Missionary Film: Christian Interventions in Africa

In many ways, missionaries were the advance guard for the European cultural engineering project in Africa. Often established before colonial occupation, Christian missions both Protestant and Catholic could boast of sustained involvement in the interior, and generally displayed a willingness to exploit cinema to achieve a range of objectives: while missionaries produced films to advertise their work in the field and expand their recruitment base, within Africa itself they often screened films for indigenous subjects to promote Christianity, bio-medical procedures, Western domesticity, mission education, and "healthful" recreation.

Within the Catholic world, both the White Fathers and Mill Hill Missionaries exploited the potential of the cinema before the independence era. Established in Algeria by Cardinal Charles Lavigerie in 1868, the Society of Missionaries for Africa (referred to as the White Fathers for their long white robes) spread its Order throughout much of North and Central Africa, establishing its presence through mission schools and hospitals in the Sudan, Uganda, Tanganyika, and Upper Congo. In turn, on the heels of the 1890s armed conflict between Protestants and Catholics in Uganda, St. Joseph's Missionary Society (Mill Hill) gained a foothold and expanded outwards from Kampala to the Nairobi escarpment, the Congo and Cameroon. In the multi-reel *Mill Hill Fathers Uganda Missionary Film* (1920), St. Joseph's touted its global outreach, with Bishop Biermans welcoming new missionaries from London who soon "depart for their destination in the Jungle." The film proceeds to highlight the perceived backwardness of Bugandan communities through its visualization of the cow bloodletting ritual and traditional judicial procedures.

Despite Mill Hill's early filmmaking experiments, cinema's standing within the religious community continued to be hotly debated. Indeed, by the 1930s, the Church was moving in two directions simultaneously. Many Catholics remained fearful of the medium—leading to the 1933 formation of the Catholic Legion of Decency (soon renamed the National Legion of Decency) to combat "immoral" tendencies—yet in 1936, Pope Pius issued the *Vigilanti Cura*, defining the official stance of the Church. While he warned "that the more wonderful the increase of the technique of the cinema, the more dangerous it has become to the hindrance of morals, to religion, and to the social itself," he also recognized its potential for good. Ideally, films must "conform to right standards, that they might incite the spectators to right living and education worthy of the name."[152]

Hence, by the late 1940s, the White Fathers were actively incorporating cinema in the missionary field through the driving force of Father Fournier. After spending much of the 1930s in Tunisia and Algeria, and traveling the length of Africa in 1946 on a Navy expedition, Fournier learned the art of filmmaking, touring the Belgian Congo, Rwanda, Kenya and Uganda with director Arch Oboler. Oboler was securing footage for *Bwana Devil* (1952), a jungle adventure film about the "man-eating lions of Tsavo" (the first feature shot in 3-D). In 1951, Fournier established the African Film Center in Washington, D.C., to facilitate distribution of Catholic films, and two years later crossed the Sahara from Algeria to Ghana on a 2,000-mile drive to film the work of the White Fathers, with later forays elsewhere.[153] These expeditions led to a set of films on various topics produced throughout the continent: *The Devil Fights Back* (shot in Rwanda) and *Candida* (Ghana) both highlighted the difference between polygamy and monogamy, with the implied destructive side-effects of the former; *La Touque* (Belgian Congo) showed creative African uses for oil drums; *The Catechist* highlighted the religious angle by detailing conversion experiences in Uganda, while *Seven Brothers of Thibar* continued the theme by focusing on a White Fathers' Tunisian mission station.

If Fournier's filmmaking projects were winding down by 1960, they were just beginning for others. The Maryknoll Society had arrived in Tanzania in 1946, building upon ground already broken by the White Fathers. Between the early 1960s and early 1980s, various "Maryknollers" produced films primarily in Tanzania, explaining the role of the church in a changing Africa. Given that many earlier missionary films commonly peddled stereotypical images of primitive Africans in traditional settings, the new orientation of the Maryknoll films produced at the dawn of the independence era is notable. Gone are loin-cloth savages—Africans now mill around wearing khakis and other casual wear; gone is the smug superiority of white Christians—one senses a creeping self-doubt in voice-over narrations; gone is the pressure to introduce European capitalism wholesale into Africa—Afro-Socialism is touted as a viable option for East African conditions; and gone is the omniscient white narrator—African Catholics now occasionally share the microphone. This interesting transition was in part facilitated by Maryknoll's close affiliation with Julius Nyerere, who was married in 1953 in Musoma Town in a ceremony overseen by Father William Collins.[154] One Maryknoll film, *Sons of Bwiregi*, is something of an open-ended reflection on the quotidian cultural tensions between polygamy vis-à-vis an expanding Christian sensibility. In *Ujamaa*, Father Art Wille discusses in his voice-over the debilitating drought and the impact it had on his thinking: "Living like this, so close to famine, is what made me try Ujamaa. Now in the years before Ujamaa, I had seen very little change. So when President Nyerere began to promote his idea of Ujamaa as a way for Tanzania to transform itself, socially and economically, well, I began to work for it." The struggle for survival is similarly the theme of *Kumekucha: From Sunup*, a film lauding the important role of women, including shots of water collection, native health care clinics and corn-shucking. A later film, *New Zimbabwe* (1982), departs dramatically from earlier films described in this chapter with its critique of

2. *The Scramble for Images: Strange Savages, Paid Primitives, Negotiating Natives* 81

White Fathers' film shoot in progress, Mali, date unknown (National Anthropological Archives, Smithsonian Institution, White Fathers Photographic Collection).

Cecil Rhodes and the 1923 disbursement of land to the minority white population. The film continues with ruminations on the racial and ethnic tensions palpable in newly independent Zimbabwe: "The challenge that faces the new government is not just its interrelationship with its white citizens; centuries of tribal rivalries also demand attention."[155]

In the Protestant world, images had long been incorporated in their African missions, through photographs, flannelgraphs and lantern slides. For late–19th-century missionary Mary Slessor, in fact, images served as a civilizing influence among the "tribe of headhunters," where she was stationed in Okoyong, Nigeria. Soon after her arrival, the eldest son of Chief Edem was tragically crushed by a log, leading the grieving chief to order the arbitrary arrest of a dozen men and women from a nearby village. Mary successfully pleaded for the release of one or two, and then threw her energy behind elaborate funeral preparations to pull attention away from those awaiting execution:

> She got Mr. Ovens to make a coffin for the dead boy, and two missionaries were hurried up from Creek Town with a magic lantern to honour the occasion still further. To uninstructed eyes it would all have seemed a bit of melodramatic farce, but in reality it was a grim struggle for human lives. And in the end she won. The last of the prisoners was released and only a cow was sacrificed at the grave.[156]

Missionaries by the interwar years were commonly incorporating cinema into their work in the field. The London Missionary Society (LMS), for instance, introduced cinema to its students at its South African school Tiger Kloof in the 1920s for educational purposes.¹⁵⁷ In the middle of the decade, some Tiger Kloof missionaries also provided assistance on *Livingstone* (1925), a commercial film written, directed and starring big-game hunter and filmmaker Marmaduke Wetherell, now known for setting up the faked Loch Ness photo. *Livingstone* (re-released as *Stanley* in 1933) re-enacted the explorer's famous meeting with Stanley and lauded Livingstone's efforts to abolish slavery and expand African education.

As village hospitals and schools were constructed in areas firmly under colonial control, some Protestants began to film the fruits of their labors—generally amateurish productions—to be brought back home for local church audiences. Coupled with lectures and slides, these films were greeted with great anticipation by congregations, and reinvigorated fundraising and recruitment. Yet their limitations led many missionaries in the interwar period to pool their resources to improve production values. In England, three societies experimented by collectively producing two films in West Africa and the Far East, followed up by *India To-day* in 1925. The positive response to *India To-day* led to the official launch of the Missionary Film Committee (MFC) on October 1, 1926, with T.H. Baxter as Secretary and support from five organizations: Church of England Zenana Missionary Society; Church Missionary Society (CMS); London Missionary Society; Society for the Propagation for the Gospel; and the Wesleyan Methodist Missionary Society. Baxter departed for Africa in 1927 with a cinematographer named Best to produce *Africa To-day*, that "had an extraordinarily successful four weeks' run at the Polytechnic Cinema. Since then it has been shown in about 100 towns meetings with warm appreciation and encouraging results."¹⁵⁸ Yet while the MFC enjoyed initial success, the global depression of the early 1930s soon eroded its efficacy. By June 1930, the CMS was exhibiting strains both financial and otherwise and rejected an MFC loan request of £310.¹⁵⁹ The crisis quickly deepened, leading to a July correspondence between the CMS and LMS commenting on the unfortunate "sparring" between societies and describing the MFC as a sinking ship.¹⁶⁰ Although the organization concluded that "propaganda through the co-operative showing of missionary films ... no longer justifies the time, energy and funds expended by the missionary Societies concerned," the MFC continued to limp along under "a considerably reduced scale" until 1932.¹⁶¹

As the Missionary Film Committee petered out in England in the early 1930s, there was increasing support for a similar organization to professionalize the genre among American denominations with a stake in Africa. The impetus came from different sources. The Missionary Education Movement supported the idea of ecumenical coordination to bolster film quality, and what was conceived as Catholic hostility in the Belgian Congo further prompted Protestant denominations to find common ground. The primary mover for what would become known as the Africa Motion Picture Project (AMPP) was Emory Ross of the Disciples of Christ.¹⁶² Ross was well acquainted with Ray Phillips and the Mines' Compound Cinema Circuit (see upcoming chapter) and the two had discussed the "civilizing role" film might play in Africa. Culling footage from 100 amateurish reels, Ross and the Africa Committee initially produced *Africa Joins the World* (1936), the success of which sparked the idea of sending a professional AMPP crew to the Belgian Congo and French Cameroons. Sponsorship came from the Harmon Foundation—a secular organization bank-rolling African American art exhibitions—and eight mission boards. With independent filmmaker Ray Garner hired as director/cinematographer (accompanied by his wife, Virginia), AMPP location shooting began after the couple arrived at the Baptist mission station in Mboko, Belgian Congo. Some AMPP films focused on medical missionary endeavors, with *Song After Sorrow* highlighting Eugene Kellersberger's work at the Bibanga leper colony, and the docu-drama *The Story of Bamba* touting Western medicine while exposing the effects of traditional "witchcraft" and superstition. *Children of Africa* and *A Day in an African Village*, in contrast, were framed ethnographically and provided more sympathetic portraits of traditional African life. In addition to detailing Protestant involvement in the Congo, the Garners also filmed the perceived benignity of colonial rule in *How an African Tribe Is Ruled Under Colonial Government*, showing "government methods in action, men and women as they fit into the colonial system; indistrial [*sic*] and raw material occupations; [and] the westernization of Africans as far as training goes."[163]

Missionaries, in fact, played pivotal roles in other cinema campaigns in Africa throughout the colonial era. In subsequent chapters we trace the Mines' Compound Cinema Circuit—which introduced cinema initially for healthful recreation among black miners on the Witwatersrand—and explore the joint role of Protestant missionaries and the Colonial Office in launching the Bantu Educational Kinema Experiment in British Africa.

The Reel: Artifice in Africa

The issue of cinematic artifice is one that has engaged filmmakers, audiences and scholars from the inception of the medium. As Africa increasingly became the site of location shooting, the question of "what was real and what was reel" played an important role in the marketing of films and in public debates over authenticity. Ironically, the more films were marketed as "real," the more they seemed to engage in subterfuge to reel in the audience. It was the wildlife film that largely opened the door to the widespread use of "fakery" when it came to producing both fictional and documentary films about Africa. In particular, the expense and risks of shooting on the continent led studios to take substantial liberties to pull a profit. While the above-mentioned *Roosevelt in Africa* was successful, for instance, it was not actually the first film released about the president's safari. In fact, as soon as Roosevelt embarked on his journey, Selig Polyscope quickly produced *Hunting Big Game in Africa* (1909), filmed entirely in Chicago with zoo animals and a Roosevelt imposter. In a case of life imitating art, the studio waited until receiving word that Roosevelt and company had indeed slaughtered their first lion, and the film was quickly released.[164] Although *Hunting Big Game in Africa* was initially popular, the release of the officially authorized *Roosevelt in Africa* the following year, filmed by Cherry Kearton in the real Africa with the real president, caused some embarrassment. Nevertheless, William Selig became the first major film mogul to move his studios to sunny Los Angeles, where he set up a menagerie to allow for the shooting of more "jungle adventures." The Africa theme, therefore, played a key, if underappreciated, role in the founding of Hollywood. If wildlife films were increasingly scrutinized by critics and audiences for possible fakery, films with a more ethnographic slant displayed their "constructedness" as well. We noted above that from the earliest years of cinema, ethnographic expeditions were highly visible affairs with native actors honing their histrionic skills. Yet the travel accounts of filmmakers often confessed to a certain amount of artifice. In his book *Africa Speaks*, for instance, Paul Hoefler openly spoke of the liberties he took editing the footage of his Colorado African Expedition of 1928–29: in his subsequent film *Africa Speaks* (1931) detailing "the first crossing of Central Equatorial Africa by motor truck from the Indian to the Atlantic Ocean," he re-routed the expedition west to east to generate excitement for the conclusion with lion hunts and the "exotic" Maasai.[165] Nevertheless, Hoefler omitted other forms of artifice used during production. Only with the publication of *Mr. Bernds Goes to Hollywood* decades later did we learn that after returning from Africa and contracting with Columbia, Hoefler painted a truck to match the original expedition vehicle, and with his crew took connecting shots of "lion country" and "gorilla country" in sunny California.[166]

There were other glaring examples of filmmakers trying to pawn off dubious stories about the "African jungle" to the American public. One prominent example was *Ingagi* (*Gorilla*, 1930) which led to greater scrutiny, public outrage and, predictably, huge profits. Produced by Congo Pictures, *Ingagi* was billed as the real-life exploits of Sir Hubert Winstead and Captain Daniel Swayne's 1926 humanitarian expedition into the Congo. Rumors of a gorilla-worshipping tribe had led the two men to Central Africa, where they witnessed the terrifying sacrifice of a virgin to a huge gorilla, who spirited away the struggling girl into the jungle. But during the premiere one of the female "Africans" was recognized as an actress from Central Casting, and soon the exotic "Pygmies" were exposed as Los Angeles schoolchildren. The hue and cry continued, and after the American Society of Mammalogists levied objections, the FTC opened an investigation which concluded that Winstead and Swayne "were both fictitious persons not existing in fact" and that scenes of Africa had been produced in the Los Angeles Zoo, using a man in a gorilla suit. But because the crowds kept coming due to a vicarious desire to see the farce, or perhaps the advertised "naked ape-women," the film eventually spawned the equally bizarre *Son of Ingagi* (1940).

Commercial films with faux–African backdrops were generally slower to appear than earlier actualities from the "real" Africa, but they satisfied the appeal of seeing savage Africans, wild witch doctors, and impenetrable jungles during the consolidation of colonial control. Yet the exposé of *Ingagi* shows that, in fact, critics by 1930 were becoming more circumspect, and even films which were undoubtedly filmed in Africa were scrutinized for their accuracy. As we saw with Hoefler, filmmakers sometimes confessed to a degree of artifice, but always played up the dangers of shooting in the "real jungle." Chaplin Court Treatt's *Stampede* (1930), produced with Stella and quickly re-released under the sensationalized title *Africa in Flames*, was another case in point. Four years earlier the couple had produced *Cape to Cairo*, detailing their motoring adventures, but their new release pushed against the boundaries of the travelogue in telling the story of a Sudanese tribe's struggle for survival. In the film, which was promptly sold to British Instructional and widely distributed, a young boy named Boru helps save a tribe from a debilitating famine. Billed as a documentary, Stella nevertheless spoke openly of the artifice of the filmmaking process and their effort to promote a bare-chested "Valentino-like" male African protagonist "to thrill the hearts of a good many female 'movie fans.'"[167] Nevertheless, a *New York Times* reviewer expressed doubts about the film: "Although Major Treatt strives to present his scenes in a forceful fashion, they are, more often than not, too theatric, lacking, as they do, spontaneity and truth. Granted that the participants are Arabs and that they are photographed in their native haunts, the different events strike one too forcibly as having been prearranged.[168]

Ironically, even travel lecturer and filmmaker Carveth Wells, who prided himself on his portrayals of the "real" Africa, found himself caught up in a reel scandal. Wells had worked as cinematographer on the 1928–29 Cudahy-Massee Expedition, with 1,976 artifacts carted out of East Africa to enlarge the Milwaukee Museum's holdings. Wells used his film of the expedition, *Hell Below Zero* (1931), in his travel lectures to correct a number of popular misconceptions about the continent, noting the existence of snow near the equator (on the Ruwenzori Range), and the fact that lions were prone to run away from visitors. Given his reputation, in 1932 he was hired by Century Productions to "synchronize, edit, and furnish the dialogue" for *Jungle Killer*, a film exposing the excessive cruelty visited upon African wildlife by big-game hunters. However, the film was itself exposed for being

2. The Scramble for Images: Strange Savages, Paid Primitives, Negotiating Natives

little more than a pirated copy of Frederick Patterson's *Shooting Big Game with a Camera* (1927), when a judge concluded that "the deliberate purloining of at least 1,000 feet of Patterson's film … was established beyond doubt."[169]

The first two chapters of this study have provided an overview of the introduction of cinema into Africa. While not exhaustive, they have described the role of circus performers, missionaries, explorers, colonial officials, anthropologists, private interests and others in exhibiting and shooting films for very different purposes. But how did Africans become full-fledged consumers of cinema in their own right? In the formative period before World War I, they were haphazardly introduced to the spectacle in bioscopes, mission stations and other venues. As ground-breaking as this was, it is important to note that while these sites were necessary for mass black spectatorship in Africa, they were not sufficient. This is because prior to the war, there appear to be no attempts to introduce cinema to Africans on a regional or colony-wide level. This situation was to change as social transformations wrought by the mining industry led to new opportunities for black spectators. Missionaries, as we shall see, played a crucial role in designing new cinema programs, censoring imported films, and negotiating with African spectators, mining officials and the British Colonial Office as the reels began to roll throughout southern Africa after 1920.

3

Silver Screens and Cities of Gold and Copper

The Mines' Compound Cinema Circuit

Prior to World War I, few whites perceived that within a decade the movie-going experience in South Africa would expand dramatically to include hundreds of thousands of black viewers. For the *South African Pictorial: Stage and Screen*, in which readers could peruse reviews of new Hollywood releases, the social life of black urbanites and miners seemed distant and unreal. In fact, into the mid–1920s this leading magazine covering Johannesburg's high society not only ignored the era's spectacular increase in black film spectatorship, but also virtually elided the existence of South Africa's blacks altogether, except when occasionally highlighting their perceived primitivity. Despite the popularity of the bioscope, the presence of Kodak which had opened in Johannesburg, and even an amateur cine-club formed by D.A. Macnair, most city dwellers perceived motion pictures as simply another popular recreation that would reverberate only within the white community.[1]

By the early 1920s, however, as a few local bioscopes led the way in welcoming African spectators (or surreptitiously admitting them), some missionaries, mining officials and white settlers expressed race-based concerns as they fretted over the possible impact of commercial cinema on the colonized. This chapter explores efforts to resolve these anxieties as missionaries Ray Phillips and Frederick Bridgman established first, in 1920, a limited bioscope program for African children in Johannesburg, followed by the Mines' Compound Cinema Circuit, one of the most extensive colonial-era film exhibition experiments implemented on the continent.

Transatlantic Progressivism and Idle Black Hands

In 1920 South African Prime Minister Jan Smuts declared that "one of the most tremendous social and political phenomena of our generation has been the migration of Natives into the large centres of South Africa. The future difficulties will not be with the raw Native in his village but in the great centres where are congregating hundreds of thousands of these people."[2] But for Frederick Bridgman of the American Board of Commissioners for Foreign Missions (ABCFM), industrial migration opened up new possibilities. While he agreed that the "evils" intrinsic to industrial compounds and townships could potentially contaminate village life, labor migration could, conversely, accelerate the Christianization of the countryside by piggy-backing the Gospel on the back of repatriated miners returning to the reserves.

Bridgman had moved to Johannesburg to revitalize Christianity and address the material and social needs of the city's black population. Two themes permeated his Social Gospel approach to urban missionary work: first, industrialization introduced new social problems—inner-city slums, wealth disparities and gender issues—requiring a pro-active, interventionist policy; second, "detribalization"—the perceived erosion of traditional tribal controls—compounded the problems of acculturation. As the influx of blacks into urban Johannesburg expanded, Bridgman sought Ray Phillips's assistance in constructing new social programs. A recent graduate of Yale Divinity anxious to pursue his calling, Phillips and his wife, Dora, departed for Durban in early 1918 and engaged in an intensive study of Zulu so that they might "soon pass for Zulus on a dark night."[3] Relocating to Johannesburg, Phillips galvanized Bridgman's plans to address the needs of the city's growing black population. As Clifford Scott has noted, ABCFM missionaries believed "Africans were facing a critical period of transition between agrarianism and industrialization, [and that] the form of industrial civilization which developed would be decided within the current generation." The new missionary focus on the "disorganizing effects of the urban-industrial complex,"[4] led to a flurry of programs on the part of Bridgman, Phillips, and James Dexter Taylor, an Auburn Theological Seminary graduate who had arrived in Natal in 1899 to bolster the Zulu mission.[5]

One of Phillips's targets was the black male *petit-bourgeoisie* increasingly disillusioned by the political climate of the late 1910s, which he hoped to capture by way of the Joint Councils of Europeans and Natives, formed in 1921 as a clearing house for interracial discussion.[6] European members, in addition to Phillips, included Frederick Bridgman, Jan Hofmeyr, Howard Pim, Walter Webber and Henry Taberer, the latter two representing the liberal arm of the Chamber of Mines. Representatives of the educated African middle class included newspaper editor Richard V. Selope Thema and union activist Allison W.G. Champion.

As early as 1915, Bridgman had formulated plans for an institution servicing Johannesburg's fledgling black *petit-bourgeoisie* to be built along the lines of the YMCA. With Phillips's assistance, the Bantu Men's Social Centre (BMSC) opened on Eloff Street Extension in 1924, and became the hub for white philanthropy on the Rand.[7] Phillips believed the BMSC supplied a crucial bulwark against the looming possibility of a race war, claiming to have heard members of the African intelligentsia in "calm, dispassionate" tones that "made the blood run cold," discussing the "desirability" of opening the compound gates to let mine workers "wipe the white man off the map."[8] The BMSC included black members on a sub-committee, but was chartered to ensure that whites retained control of policy.[9] Philips openly admitted that his role of reformer constituted a modern form of social engineering:

> So instead of preaching merely to men to help them to become changed spiritual creatures—instead of washing the inside of the cup only and putting it down—we today have a vital concern about the outside of the cup, the physical man and his surroundings. The whole man, spiritually, mentally, and physically, his surroundings, his work, his play, must be made clean and wholesome and conducive to the greatest possible development.[10]

It was the class and gender makeup of the BMSC's membership that has led most historians to focus on Phillips's interaction with the black male *petit-bourgeoisie*. Understanding pre-apartheid liberal reforms, however, requires a more in-depth look at Phillips's attempt to address slumyard conditions and leisure activities. For Phillips and Bridgman alike, images would come to play an important role in their program for African betterment. Bridgman emulated the social exposés of Jacob Riis in New York by displaying a set of his own photographs depicting the squalor of Johannesburg slumyards to City Hall. Although this indictment of substandard housing led to a slight improvement, the end result of such telling exposures was massive municipal slum clearance and the forced relocation of thousands of Africans to peri-urban locations.

One of the keys to reforming the outside of the African "cup," argued Bridgman and Phillips, was to meet the recreational needs of urban Africans of all backgrounds. The lack of "constructive and wholesome" leisure time, they believed, was shared by the juvenile underclass, gold miners and the African *petit-bourgeoisie*. All three, according to Phillips, suffered "detribalization" as they struggled to make sense of a region in transition: "Like the 'fade-out' on the moving picture screen, the old days are going, giving place to a new order. The rapid change is responsible for severe strains in every department of native life."[11] Responding to these strains required not just Sunday morning sermons, but ongoing activities to address constructively the recreational needs of African children, "semi-detribalized" industrial laborers and town "sophisticates." Phillips retooled Puritan theology for South African conditions in a 1920 lecture, "Native Leisure Hours," declaring that in a congested labor center like Johannesburg, "The devil was finding altogether too many things for idle black hands to do."[12] Yet Phillips tempered this conclusion by arguing that Africans should be given more access to the fruits of civilization, including viable recreational and leisure activities. Thus, Phillips and Bridgman would focus not on the labor time of African workers, but the time spent away from work, those spaces in one's waking life normally reserved for play, passion, and personal pursuits.

For missionaries, moralizing leisure time meant moralizing "idle" time, but for black intellectuals like Selope Thema, increasingly pushed to the margins in the heyday of 1920s liberal reform, one senses the deep feeling of loss as the influence of the West impacted with traditional African forms of leisure:

> Africans, like Europeans, are very fond of recreation. In the days of our ancestors recreation was a part of our national life. Dancing, hunting and cattle racing were games in which grown up men indulged. The little boys, besides herding the livestock, passed their leisure time in wrestling, sham fighting, swimming and bathing, racing and dancing. But with the coming of Western civilization these things have been forgotten, and as the result many men, women and children spend their leisure hours in things which do not matter in life. In the urban areas where there are no recreation grounds of any kind for the Africans the situation is tragic. Here one finds men and women, boys and girls, indulging in all manner of evils.[13]

Cinema as Antidote and Uplift

Prior to the BMSC, Phillips targeted poor children in townships and slumyards engaged in juvenile delinquency or experiencing significant hardship. As I note in the next chapter, 1920s street gangs in Johannesburg and elsewhere evolved skills for independent living through watching silent Westerns at bioscopes despite little discretionary income. In a white-dominated society, American commercial cinema had an impact on South Africa that, to date, has been little studied. Yet visitors noted signs of America's potent cultural influence: one American advertising agent in Port Elizabeth, for instance, was shocked by seeing "broad-brimmed hats," and hearing "American slang, American talkies, [and] American songs,"[14] while anthropologists pointed to the expanding recreations open to town Xhosa, including "tennis [and the] bioscope."[15]

Phillips was appalled at the lack of attention paid to children's recreation. He first attempted to rectify the situation by organizing the Wayfarers and Pathfinders (equivalent to the Girl and Boy Scouts) and building playgrounds as healthful alternatives to the dusty streets. In addition, with assistance from City and Suburban mine that offered use of vacant land near the slumyards, soccer, hockey and volleyball were introduced to instill in children the value of working as a team. Phillips's next experiment, beginning in either late 1919 or early 1920, was an "uplift" cinema for African children. Obtaining permission from municipal officials, Phillips blocked off two streets in the New Doornfontein ghetto district for weekly recreational events where slumyard children, dismissed by one citizen as the "dregs of the Johannesburg melting pot," were now treated to free bioscope shows.[16] His reasoning resonates with that of American social worker Jane Addams, who had initiated a similar "nickel theater" in Chicago: Johannesburg juveniles, like their European immigrant counterparts in American municipalities, lacked basic recreational amenities and were thus corrupted by urban vices in their spare time. What little recreation there was came in the form of the cheap thrills of local bioscopes, exhibiting what Phillips decried as "low shows," including Hollywood melodramas and cowboy thrillers.

As we have seen, commercial cinema had come early to South Africa, with approximately 150 bioscopes operating by 1913, including Johannesburg's Orpheum, Empire Theatre and Carleton Theatre. William Schlesinger consolidated the bioscope business under the banner of African Theatres Trust and his film importing/distribution company, African Films Trust. Because of his monopoly, by 1918 British films were virtually non-existent in South Africa, and most films in distribution were actually of American origin. For missionaries like Phillips it was the new African exposure, children especially, to what he considered Hollywood's degrading images of the white world that most worried him.

The archives are silent as to precisely what films Phillips screened in New Doornfontein, but years later the BMSC began hosting Friday evening shows exclusively for children, with *Tarzan the Mighty* (1928) proving popular among township youth. Yet according to Modikwe Dikobe, who as an adolescent enjoyed these events, the films may not only have failed to stem the tide of delinquency, they might even have fueled it: "It was at these shows that boys in particular learned gangsterism," he claims. "They prized Tarzan as a daring man and emulated Our Gang to prove that they were town boys." Moreover, as children departed the BMSC to return to Vrededorp, Doornfontein, Prospect Township, City Suburbs, and Sophiatown, they "left a sparkling trail of urine along Eloff Street, making the street their own, until group by group they dwindled from Eloff Street and drifted to the suburbs where they lived."[17]

Class Formation on the Rand

Phillips struggled to address child welfare and later to co-opt the black *petit-bourgeoisie* through the BMSC, but membership was unfeasible for the Witwatersrand's hundreds of thousands of miners.[18] During the planning stages for the Centre, Phillips spoke in cinematic metaphors of the desperate need for targeting the swelling industrial workforce:

Our black friends here were still wearing the fig-leaf when the first missionaries arrived. Like the flower on the moving picture screen which grows from seed to flower in a brief five minutes, so these black people are now springing into man's estate. The influence of industrial centres, chief of which is Johannesburg, is largely responsible for this super-hot-house growth.[19]

Phillips pondered the "seething resentment" building up in the mining community. Deploring the lack of suitable compound recreations and looking for alternatives to gambling, whoring and drinking, Phillips recognized that deeper causes of discontent stemmed from the subordinate position of black miners who suffered differential treatment. Indeed, in 1920, 40,000 disaffected miners took to the streets protesting poor wages, a strike broken when cordons were thrown up around compounds and workers (mis)informed that other mines had resumed operations. The industrial action failed due to the lack of an effective central command, but what was more ominous to Phillips was that the suspension of the strike failed to dispel its underlying causes. The problem, he thought, was that the only white "friends of the native" were radicals like Edward Roux who fomented racial/class hatred by raising the banner of communism. Moreover, "Communists," he declared, "are quite openly directing propaganda from Moscow, employing Native agents [who spread] seeds of revolt among the black proletariat."[20]

Conversely, Phillips perceived little in the actions of South African authorities to ease his mind. The state, whose "policy it is to 'keep the damned nigger in his place' ... has done little for the native except to give way grudgingly, here and there a little when compelled to by native agitation."[21] Thus, in mid–1920, flush with the success of his New Doornfontein bioscopes, Phillips moved to experiment in dozens of compounds scattered along the Reef.[22] Although he first introduced soccer, workers were generally too tired for strenuous activity after stints underground. Thus, given the increasing radicalism of black miners, coupled with the recalcitrance of industry officials, the success of his next experiment—film exhibitions for miners—was anything but assured. Phillips was more than gratified then, when "whirlwinds and hurricanes of joyous enthusiasm greeted this new venture."[23]

Bhayisikop

Western metaphysics is predicated on the notion that light and sight offer privileged glimpses into the universe by illuminating its secrets. Religious metaphors similarly highlight halos and burning bushes—contributing to discursive formulations of a Dark Continent in need of Christian *enlightenment*. In an early account of Phillips's bioscopes for miners, the headlamps of his motorcycle and projector as he arrives at a compound invoke the light of the Gospel lifting the *benighted* from their savage state:

> The night is dark as I approach a Mine Compound with motorcycle and side-car outfit. I need all the light given by the two lights of the machine as I leave the main roads and approach the gate of the compound. The twisting, bumpy road would be hard to follow had I not been over the ground often before. The low walls of the compound are seen and I pause while the gate is being opened. Within are from four to seven thousand young black men from all over South Africa—from the Cape Province, from Basuto Land and Swaziland, from Portuguese East Africa and from far-away Northern Rhodesia.... The white man provides the work, and the Devil provides the recreation for these fellows. Well the Devil takes a back seat to-night. I chug through the gate with my motor and the fun begins. No sooner is the sound of the motor heard than the magic word is shouted out by a hundred joyful throats, "Bhayisikop" (bioscope). Other hundreds take up the shout and add cheers.... Black rushing forms

shoot by me all running for the same spot before a white painted space on the compound wall. Before I stop a thousand men have already seated themselves on the ground and are waiting for the performance to begin. I quickly arrange my projector while the thousands gather around. "Tulani" I shout (meaning that I wish the babbling in a dozen different languages to cease). Silence reigns supreme. I explain what the first picture is going to be.

The cathartic release following this passage, with its aura of an evangelical tent meeting, is the projector piercing, literally and metaphorically, the African gloom: "Then the whole happy crowd goes off on a trip around the world, viewing images of "the crowded folk of China or India,… the surf-riders of Honolulu … the reindeer drivers of Lapland,… [and] the immortal Charlie [Chaplin]."[24] During the last half of 1920, Phillips independently funded and operated his informal film circuit *gratis* at several compounds. But as one newspaper reported, these popular screenings, although "consistently advocated, caused much anxiety for authorities."[25] In late November the finance company Rand Mines Limited distributed a questionnaire to mine managers inquiring about the desirability/feasibility of institutionalizing films for compound entertainment.[26] Reaction was mixed. Officials who had yet to host Phillips's showings, such as those at Robinson Gold and New Modderfontein, were generally opposed, as well as those with objections to the "meddling" of proselytizing missionaries.[27] In one account, Phillips described his encounter with a mine manager ("Mr. X"), who "never had time for missionaries":

I went to see him; introduced myself; gave him my card.
"So you are another of these … missionaries!" he fired at me.
I said I was a missionary.
"Well, what do you want? Be brief!"
I told him I wanted his permission to come to his compound and give his native workers a programme of moving pictures. I explained what I was doing for other compounds.
"Nothing doing!" he snapped.
I remonstrated, courteously, said I knew he was interested in the welfare of his men, and surely wouldn't object to allowing them to have a good time. He looked up again from his desk.
"How do you propose to sell tickets?" he asked.
"I'm not going to sell tickets," I answered.
"How're you going to take up your collection?"
I explained we were not going to take up a collection.
"Well, what're you going to get out of it?"
I told him we were going to get nothing out of it except the satisfaction of giving his workers a wholesome good time and of discovering whether the films had the same appeal for his natives as for the others.
"Do you know what happened to the last fellow who tried to put on a stunt for my natives?"
I didn't know.
"Well, we had him taken off to the lockup." And he glared my way.
I stuck, and finally he gave in, with various threats as to what would happen if he caught me trying any monkey-business among his natives.

Phillips, though, reported a remarkable change in Mr. X following the show after the manager witnessed the miners' gratitude and excitement. "When are you coming up again?" he asked. "Say, but those fellows enjoyed that!"[28] Nevertheless, another official doubted that "natives in general understand them [bioscopes], or are much interested in them at present." This is an early articulation of what would become a popular colonial myth—namely, that the cognitive tools necessary to grasp the meaning of moving images are racially coded—a myth repeated by colonial officials *ad nauseam* throughout much of Africa.[29]

The negative responses submitted by officials at some mines, though, contrasted with those by managers at Modderfontein B. Gold, Nourse Mines, Knight Central and Crown Mines. One applauded the "great success" of Phillips's shows, an opinion seconded by another who reported that films were received with "great satisfaction and pleasure [by] the natives, who have asked for more frequent visits."[30] Phillips, it seemed, had a way of winning over those in the industry. After a meeting at New Modderfontein in January 1921 to promote the circuit, for instance, managers there did a *volta face* and lined up fully "in accord with his ideas."[31]

Phillips was not actually the first to offer cinema to South African miners. In fact, his crusade to "pre-occupy the field" of film exhibition on the Rand was, in part, a reaction to fly-by-night commercial venues, camped outside compound gates, targeting industrial workers.[32] Despite anxiety over the provisions for, and popularity of, these "unwholesome" images for blacks, industry memos reveal these business concerns suffered from the lack of discretionary income available to potential viewers. As early as 1919, a Mr. Dunbar charged modest admission fees for Hollywood shorts in a tent pitched outside Knight Central's compound walls, an event which was apparently well patronized. But other itinerant showmen fared less well. Mr. Patz, for instance, who charged only nominal fees outside Crown Mines, closed down after a few showings. The manager of Ferreira Deep similarly reported that a man named Daniels held two shows outside his compound, but failed to make the venture remunerative, bringing in a total of only £11 for both evenings.[33] While no records have surfaced listing what films were shown in these venues, Phillips, sounding a general warning about the seductions of commercial films, complained of the "low-grade, suggestive stuff that seemed to be gleaned from the gutters of the world; the worst products of English, American and continental studios."[34]

At East Rand Proprietary Mines, for years the world's largest gold mine,[35] manager Edward Grant was surprisingly receptive to motion pictures and purchased a DeVry Portable Projector. On Phillips's advice, he put together programs including "pictures of Native Life, Educational films, Nature Studies, humorous pictures, etc." The mine also pioneered Safety First films detailing how tragedies could be avoided in the shafts.[36] Safety was indeed a crucial issue: one American observer in the 1930s noted that the industry averaged eight fatalities a week, with scores more injured.[37]

In early 1921, the Native Recruiting Corporation (NRC), which had been launched in 1912 to supply the mining industry's labor needs, agreed to fund free weekly bioscopes with an initial outlay of £1,500 for projectors and supplies. While Phillips supervised the undertaking, the NRC retained ownership of all materials and charged mining houses £2 per showing to offset operating expenses and rental fees for films secured from African Films Trust.[38] The NRC's participation was critical for two reasons: first, it reflected the success of Phillips's shows; second, film exhibitions could be expanded dramatically to reach all the Witwatersrand mines, something that Phillips working alone could not hope to accomplish.

To reduce costs, mines were organized in groups of five, based on proximity, with each group serviced by a single projector. On the whole, mining officials were amenable, provided the films would not be solely of a religious nature and that Phillips would oversee censorship of scenes "unsuitable" for black audiences. By mid–March, Phillips, who had now been given a Chevrolet by the American Board to manage film distribution, reported regular showings at 32 mines, with more to follow.[39] Beginning at dusk, films were shown under the night skies in a central area of the compounds, using either whitewashed walls, painted sheet iron, or white bed sheets strung up between two poles for screens.[40] Sheets, while suffering from wind undulations and billowing, had the benefit of being viewed from both back and front. Projectionists, who often doubled as mining officials, were charged with more than just changing the reels. In addition to enforcing a "remain seated" policy during performances, they began each showing with an introduction, with further commentary during the screenings. Projectionists unfamiliar with African vernaculars enlisted *mabalans* (native clerks) to interpret the action, and silence was enforced with a threat to postpone or suspend the shows if audiences were noncompliant. Reports indicate that attendance was excellent, often numbering in the thousands, and sometimes included mine managers and their families, who "appear regularly to see the fun." Even cooler temperatures failed to deter audiences, and despite complaints on the part of officials about a rise in chest colds in inclement weather, every "native who can possibly get there sees the pictures." In fact, if one is to believe Phillips's hyperbole, temperatures actually rose as "natives crowd[ed] together," reaching the "boiling point when an exciting film is being shown."[41]

The programs, running approximately 90 minutes, were diverse and, at least initially, downplayed religious themes. For Phillips, uplift through moving images required didactic films as well as imagery culled from around the globe. A variety of material, he believed, would facilitate African acculturation to the bewildering complexities of modern life. But acculturation was to be tempered by a dose of local interest films. *African Mirror*, South Africa's first newsreel series, which premiered May 5, 1913, presented images familiar to many miners, such as first-aid instruction, traditional dancing, and commercial agriculture.[42] A sampling of early programs offered in May 1921 reflects Phillips's determination to intersperse entertainment with didactic material:

Program #7
(1) Interesting Incidents Here and There
(2) Art of Alpine Mountain Climbing
(3) African Mirror (#350 and #382)
(4) Prize Performing Ponies
(5) Uncle Sam at Work
(6) Mountains of St. Gothards
(7) Northern Sports Under Southern Skies

Program #10
(1) Jungle Joy Ride
(2) The Dionnes (Acrobats)
(3) Lt. Rose and the Royal Visit
(4) The Only Way (Safety First)
(5) African Mirror (#338)
(6) Graphic (#957 and #958)[43]

An expressed aim of what was now officially termed the Mines' Compound Cinema Circuit (MCCC) was to promote "wholesome" alternatives to the cowboy films increasingly available for urban cinemagoers. Images of the Wild West, though, were not excluded entirely, but often worked the documentary angle as attested to by films such as *Cowboy Sports, New Cowpuncher*, and *Cattle Breeding in Brazil*. Although Phillips would soon include Hollywood films in the MCCC, he believed that commercial cinema, because of the profit motive, tended to cater to base instincts and exhibit the "least ennobling" characteristics of the West. Yet if the programs were put together sensibly, this hurdle could be overcome to benefit the thousands of spectators on the Rand:

> We have often thought that one of the main things which the natives get from our bioscope shows on the Reef is a sense of discrimination. Occasionally the films are stories in which a villain and a hero contend for honours. White men are shown as heroes, also as villains. We have both in the white race, unfortunately, and it is just as well for the native people to know it, and early.[44]

It was Phillips's opinion, of course, that Africans lacked any real sense of American history, but some Africans may have been more knowledgeable about the history of race relations in the American West than white observers supposed. On a visit to South Africa, Eslanda Robeson (spouse of Paul Robeson) was intrigued when several chiefs "asked pointed questions about the Indians in America (that surprised and impressed me), are they still on reservations, do they have the vote, has their property ever been returned to them by the government?"[45]

By October 1921, Phillips noted that with the exception of Roodeport, the Witwatersrand, Wit. Deep, Knights Central and Luipardsvlei, all mining houses were now included in the circuit, with a total of 177 shows for that month. In November, despite several rainouts, the number increased to 198.[46] Although the chamber charged the mining companies only a nominal operating fee, Luipardsvlei still remained hesitant. A November 1921 Rand Mines memo, though, shows that Phillips had not only overcome the last vestiges of resistance within the Chamber of Mines, but had won its open endorsement. Addressed to Luipardsvlei manager Andrew Cohen, the mining house was encouraged to reconsider: "I shall be glad if you will take into consideration the advisability of falling into line on your Mine with what is being done on other mines of the Reef in regard to giving the natives Cinema shows at regular intervals." By doing so, officials there could "reduce ... native labour wastage and, in consequence, the costs of recruiting."[47]

If 1921 was a watershed year for black spectatorship in South Africa, Phillips was not willing to rest on his laurels, for he now began sending films to industrializing areas north of the Limpopo. Films followed the path blazed by Cecil Rhodes's 1890 Pioneer Column making its way into Mashonaland to secure the mineral rights claimed by the British South African Company. Although Southern Rhodesia's limited deposits never promised huge returns, this foray resulted in a burgeoning mining sector tapping gold, chrome, lead, copper, and asbestos. And like South Africa, where there were mines, there were men, and where there were men, there would soon be movies.

The larger mining interests invested in square compounds built of wood and iron for black workers. Soon, though, due to African discontent over living conditions (compounds lacked privacy, suffered temperature shifts, and were built to guarantee worker "control and discipline"), officials ordered the construction of *chitando* huts as more permanent abodes, partially as a recruiting enticement. Unfortunately, the rapid expansion of the mining sector and improved housing in the early 1900s was offset by fluctuating yields, leading to declining real wages for African workers.[48]

Given Southern Rhodesia's often disappointing profits, coupled with industry's cost-cutting strategies in the late 1910s, it is all the more remarkable that in 1921 Que Que's Globe and Phoenix gold mine signed on to the MCCC, offering film showings on Wednesday and Saturday evenings. These programs were foundational for mass black spectatorship in Southern Rhodesia, for prior to 1920 the few existing bioscopes (often multi-purpose theaters) such as Bulawayo's Empire and Salisbury's Drill Hall, Posada

Rink Bioscope, and Grand Theatre, either restricted African patrons to balconies or excluded them altogether.[49] But after the Globe and Phoenix contracted with the MCCC, Arcturus gold mine followed, and by the end of the decade films were a staple of black recreation at mines throughout Southern Rhodesia, including base mineral mines such as Shabani.[50]

The MCCC continued to push against Rhodes's northern frontier of railroad construction. The Wankie Colliery, first connected by rail to Bulawayo in 1903, shipped films north to Northern Rhodesia's Broken Hill lead and zinc mine around 1923. By this time European-only theaters had opened in Broken Hill, Lusaka, Livingstone, and Bwana Mkubwa, exhibiting the same African Films Trust commercial films distributed to bioscopes in South Africa and Southern Rhodesia. The pattern set in those areas was replicated here: while whites watched films indoors, black employees at Broken Hill enjoyed the MCCC celluloid spectacles under a night sky. But these outdoor shows, originally for miners only, were soon opened to Railway and Town employees, with audiences numbering between 600 and 1,000 per show, often dwarfing the number of whites watching films in commercial theaters.[51] Although these venues provided entertainment for black miners and towndwellers in 1920s Northern Rhodesia, the 1930s depression temporarily stalled opportunities for black spectatorship due to predictable cutbacks. But by 1936, colonial officials there once again gave consideration to the recreational value of the cinematograph. In April the manager at Broken Hill offered an old silent projector, which had seen service years before, for "Native Welfare" work. Yet due to difficulties finding proper accommodations, machine operators, and adequate electricity, it took 18 months for the district officer to put together two experimental exhibitions. Although he confessed that the "films were rather dull, and the projection hardly perfect," the indoor show at the railway compound and the outside show at the fenced-off enclosure near the town's water tanks "were literally a 'roaring' success." Ticket fees were modest, and despite the fact that the shows were not advertised for fear of huge crowds, both quickly sold out. The railway compound hosted 249 viewers, with hundreds more camped outside, while at the town performance there were 272 ticket buyers, with others peering over the fence.[52]

Northern Rhodesia's copper industry to the north of Broken Hill offered another fertile field for moving images. In the strip of land just south of the Belgian Congo, early 20th century "discoveries" of reddish-orange ore by European prospectors were made easier because Africans had long been working surface deposits there. In 1923 Northern Rhodesia's copper industry shifted into high gear as prospectors realized that yields might rival those of the Belgian Congo's nearby Katanga region. Although one missionary emphasized the differences between the Transvaal's sprawling compounds and the Copperbelt's modest structures—"still small settlements which have just emerged from the primeval bush"—Copperbelt officials nevertheless hired welfare officers to organize leisure activities. In 1928, Roan Antelope, in conjunction with the Mine Welfare Department, introduced bi-weekly MCCC showings for approximately 1,000 miners. Given the strenuous nature of underground work, the Copperbelt's director of recreation had found it "difficult to interest the native in recreation. The latter will attend a moving picture exhibit and is measurably enthusiastic about football, but otherwise indoor and outdoor sports and games have no continuous attraction for him."[53] The increasing importance accorded to film is reflected in the fact that, in 1933, even with the economic downturn that left Northern Rhodesia's mining industry in dire straits, the Nkana mine acquired a projector and signed on to the MCCC.[54]

This era was characterized by one industry newsletter on the Copperbelt as the "rip-roaring thirties." Whites enjoyed Greta Garbo and other stars in the comfort of new venues like the Nkana Cinema (renamed Rhokana Cinema) and Roan Antelope Hall in Luanshya.[55] The latter had a seating capacity of 540, with upholstered tip seats and individual copper ashtrays. Floors and walls were constructed with selected Rhodesian teak, and windows glazed in amber cathedral glass.[56] In contrast, black miners and townspeople thrilled to the exploits of Hollywood heroes by the hundreds under the stars, consistently braving the streets and poor weather to get a glimpse of the latest bioscope attraction. Despite this radical asymmetry, by this time mining officials and government representatives were coming to a consensus that cinema fulfilled vital functions both on the mines and in newly urbanizing areas throughout southern Africa.

The Social Control Thesis: Industrial Efficiency, Uplift and Cultural Broker

Historical literature in Africa has generally ignored the dramatic rise of mass black film spectatorship, or has sometimes dealt with the phenomenon in a reductionist way. A number of scholars have made passing references to the MCCC, emphasizing the symbiotic relationship between the mining industry, with its perceived need for the social control of miners, and Phillips's desire to provide cinematic uplift in the compounds. While social control certainly was an explicit goal of both Phillips and Chamber officials, the foregoing discussion has exposed early reluctance within the industry itself during the fitful period of its implementation. Moreover, while a social control analysis properly demands that we question the deeper roots of Phillips's outward humanitarianism, it fails to account fully for the complex motives behind his cinema program, resulting in an under-theorized (if suspiciously convenient) appraisal of the MCCC.

In Phillips's line of thinking, social control was a necessary complement to social welfare work in all urban environments, informed as much by the city/country dialectic during rapid urbanization as it was by explicitly racial concerns. His conception of social control resonated with theoretical formulations of the Chicago School of Sociology: "There is always a breakdown of community standards of behaviour and conduct developed under rural conditions which made possible adequate social control. A major problem of city life concerns the creation of an urban counterpart of the rural social standard; an urban pattern of acceptable behaviour, socially motivated."[57] By the end of 1921, once the MCCC was institutionalized with most Rand mines brought into the fold, film showings clearly inculcated a degree of industrial discipline and were tailored in part to satisfy the need for a compliant workforce. Indeed, this phenomenon explains its rapid extension into the Rhodesias in the early 1920s as the industry introduced, as van Onselen has noted, a "form of cheap mass entertainment" for black workers.[58] On the Witwatersrand, the MCCC came to play an even more dramatic role during the 1922 White Miners' Rand Revolt. On January 2, a work stoppage by white workers protesting the possible elimination of the Colour Bar quickly engulfed nearby gold mines, threatening national stability. During the strike, approximately 25,000 strikers virtually paralyzed the Rand before Smuts concluded the dispute through the military option. Yet from the strike's inception, deeper fears had plagued mining officials, white settlers and missionaries, with the *Rand Daily Mail* on January 7 foreseeing a recipe for disaster:

> Assuming that the mine stoppage has become general—whereby the vast majority of the whites on these fields would be thrown out of work—the repatriation of the natives would, it

is said, have to begin almost at once. To keep so vast a number of Kaffirs idle would not only increase the standing charges on the industry ... but would increase the threat to public order.[59]

Thus, while black workers were soon repatriated to the reserves in part as a cost-cutting strategy, primarily it was due to the potential demonstration effect of the general strike. A corollary to this was Phillips's perspective: "It was the hope of the extreme element among the [white] strikers that the natives would become so restive that they would break out and destroy property and wreck the mines."[60] Idleness, many whites believed, had been the devil's workshop for the 200,000 black miners during normal leisure hours, and Phillips and officials alike feared more aggressive anti-social behavior as operations were temporarily suspended. But while most black workers were thrown out of work, it was not true that all were idle for the duration. *South African Pictorial: Stage and Screen* reported that at Robinson Deep, "Mine boys, relishing the change from underground to surface work, sing and dance as they work."[61]

Moreover, there is little evidence to suggest that black miners were fomenting unrest, for, as the *Rand Daily Mail* grudgingly admitted in the article "Natives Quietly Happy," there had been no documented cases of violence by blacks following the stoppage,[62] an assertion reiterated by the director of Native Labour, who remarked that "the Natives are remarkably law-abiding."[63] Nevertheless, a pro-active chamber implemented massive repatriation, so that by January 25, 27,702 workers had been sent home, with many more languishing in the compounds as peripheral observers to the white-on-white class struggle. But mining officials were determined to curtail black restlessness among those remaining behind or awaiting repatriation, and Phillips readily complied with their requests that he "speed up" film showings at the mines.[64]

This opium-for-the-masses strategy, however, ran into complications when white workers, on March 7, assaulted black miners at New Primrose Mine expressly to instigate discord. In fact, smaller interracial clashes had been reported earlier; but the escalation of attacks caused more alarm and led to denunciations of the white-on-black violence by government and mining officials. After rifle-bearing whites attacked New Primrose, resulting in several black fatalities and injuries, rumors of possible nighttime reprisals circulated the area.[65] White homeowners on mine property quickly abandoned their abodes, fleeing to the tops of nearby mining dumps. Meanwhile, Phillips moved rapidly into the fray, contacting projectionist V. Futcher, who serviced New Primrose, Geldenhuis, Simmer & Jack, and Rose Deep, requesting he work an emergency shift. Phillips and Futcher compiled a two-hour program primarily of Charlie Chaplin, Buster Keaton and Larry Semon comedies and rushed to New Primrose. The miners were clearly in a state of high dudgeon, and sounds of the "war dance" and the "clanging of new weapons" could be heard some distance from the compound gates as they neared. But gaining access to the compound proved difficult given the army cordon thrown up around the perimeter. Thus, Phillips required special entrance authorization from government forces to enable the movies to work, as he phrased it, in "the direction of peace."[66] Although the nervous compound manager greeting them at the gate claimed "the natives didn't want pictures; they wanted blood," Phillips suggested his specially tailored program was sure to turn their minds from thoughts of revenge. At the same time, a heated debate was under way in the compound between black miners over whether or not to allow the missionary and projectionist inside. Eventually, however, the gates opened, exposing a veritable "munitions plant," and the two proceeded to load the reels as sullen miners looked on:

> For a moment only the silence continued, then uproar! Listeners far outside the compound trembled. Were the natives coming out? It was an attack, an attack by the film comedian on

the outraged feelings of the New Primrose workers. Soon all the 4,000 were shouting themselves sick with laughter as they watched Charlie ... and others do their funny stuff. Never was there such a treat; so many laughs. At the end of two hours the compound was limp and weak from shouting, the vengeful spirit had long since vanished, and the great crowd bade us good night in the usual joyous way—many still laughing. There was no murder that night at the New Primrose.[67]

Three days later, on March 10, special night passes were issued to leading Chamber officials such as Charlers Villiers and Henry Taberer, allowing them to be out at night during the military curfew. It was a testament to Phillips's strategy of pacification through film that he was included in this select group.[68] Furthermore, a Chamber memo the same day reaffirmed that "it is of the highest importance at this time that native mine labourers should be encouraged to remain in their compounds and that their leisure should be pleasantly occupied," and requested that all 14 circuit projectionists be extended permits to expedite the film showings.[69]

Ironically, Phillips's actions during the Rand Revolt earned him the standing distrust of radical opinion on both sides of the color line throughout the 1920–30s. For white miners, Phillips was already under suspicion for the MCCC catering exclusively to blacks. Furthermore, his New Primrose intervention had foiled the strategy of extremists to goad African miners into causing chaos across the Rand. But scattered attacks on his paternalistic liberalism also later appeared in *Umsebenzi*, organ of the increasingly black-dominated South African Communist Party.[70] And others in the working class movement could be heard disparaging Phillips as the "minion of the mines"; even William Ballinger, who had struggled to organize black workers along British trade union lines, asserted that Phillips was responsible for "getting him kept out of the compounds for five years."[71] Nevertheless, some black *petit-bourgeois* members of the BMSC rushed to defend Phillips, arguing that "it has been proven time and time again that there are Europeans who are really 'white' in their hearts."[72]

The industry credited the MCCC for improving workplace efficiency as well as defusing the rising tide of discontent. High on administrators' grievance lists from the earliest days was poor job performance due to the debilitating effects of chronic dissipation. Before the Boer War, miners had few leisure activities other than consuming homebrews concocted illegally in the compounds, or wandering off in search of women. One missionary complained that workers were "rapidly acquiring the vices of the white man, and the love of strong drink is getting such a hold on them that it is perfectly appalling."[73] The popularity of these activities, according to one historian, led to "a large percentage of the workforce ... incapacitated when work resumed on Monday morning."[74] One early remedy, recognizing the futility of blanket prohibitions, was to monopolize the field. According to Alfred Xuma, "The Mines introduced kaffir beer into their compounds partly to provide them with certain vitamins,... and partly to prevent their natives from going outside and getting drunk. They have reduced the absences through Monday mornings by the introduction of kaffir beer by something like 80 percent."[75] This figure is questionable, for the Liquor Act which prohibited non–Europeans from drinking without permits may have actually led to an expansion of shebeens. In any event, mines to the north suffered similar problems: officials noted that weekend binging in Southern Rhodesia's compounds led to fights and Monday absenteeism. Black elites also complained about drinking and inter-ethnic mixing, which they believed weakened traditional tribal controls. In Bulawayo, G.G. Ndzotyana complained, "The influx of boys and girls into town is a serious menace, especially boys who have returned from the mines. Those youths far from parental restraint find it easy to indulge in immoral diversions and in beer drinks. It is evident they have learnt new customs from alien tribes."[76]

After launching the circuit, Phillips declared that films boosted industrial efficiency and worker morale in the mines. Although some historians have stressed the complicity of Phillips and the industry in this regard, it should be noted that some officials actually questioned the efficacy of movies in achieving Phillips's goals. In December 1921, for example, the manager of New Goch mine, refused to "pay for the pictures in his compound unless it can be proved to him that they are going to 'increase the working efficiency of his boys.'" Phillips, who had just convinced Luipaardsvlei to join the circuit and was working hard to bring remaining holdouts like New Goch in line, responded, "We believe that anything of this kind which tends to keep the natives from drink and gives them a healthy outlook on life—something wholesome to think about and talk about—is bound to increase their working efficiency"; nevertheless, he confessed, "It is a hard thing to prove by figures."[77] Most officials, though, assumed that film showings reduced the tendency to drink in off-hours. Managers at the Globe and Phoenix added another variable into their cost/benefit analysis. Investing moderately in the film circuit, they reasoned, not only made "inroads into the total number of cases of Monday morning hangover," but also reduced the fracases in the compounds that had been an by-product of weekend binging.[78]

These two issues—defusing discontent and increasing industrial efficiency—have provided easy pickings for social-control interpretations of the MCCC. Phillips advocated the latter to mining management while bragging about the former in his treatise *The Bantu Are Coming*. But unlike officials who supported the circuit merely to ensure a dependable workforce, Phillips conceived of cinema showings as a larger Progressive program of social and moral uplift by redistributing leisure to the working class. "It is not enough to teach the Natives to work effectively," he declared. "They must be taught to play healthfully."[79] And while officials fought inebriation in the compounds to combat inefficiency, Phillips opposed it for reasons of physical and moral hygiene:

> A person's conscience is easily lulled to sleep. What one knows to be wrong before a drink of alcoholic beverage of one sort or another is quite a different thing after one has taken the drink. Alcohol puts the conscience completely out of order, lulls to sleep one's capacity to make clear-cut judgements; and the animal in man is therefore released to do as he wills.[80]

Other components of Phillips's perspective need mentioning. First, as circuit supervisor he advocated a variety of films to familiarize Africans with Western culture and values. Carefully selected imagery would, he believed, help industrial workers recently torn from "traditional" surroundings acclimate to the modern world. Second, films were potential transmitters of a Christian ethos. While early on religious themes were largely absent to allay suspicions of mining managers, Phillips increasingly incorporated them throughout the 1920–30s. But mining houses remained suspicious of evangelization. Some years after Phillips handed over his duties to his successor, the industry co-opted the circuit to suit more narrow aims: "The only avowed aim is to entertain," stated a 1953 Chamber memo. "In fact, no 'propaganda' films are allowed and no religious films are used. As a result, the chief type of film used is the Hollywood 'Western.'"[81] The MCCC, then, had come full circle: through a curious cinematic dialectic, the circuit designed in large part to wean the African from the Western, was now showing primarily Westerns.

Phillips also perceived bioscopes as a cultural/racial mediator, as was the case in 1928 when he hosted an event for secondary- and college-level Afrikaners, featuring a (black) Glee Club and *The Changing African*, a four-reel missionary film tracking African recruits from "Native Kraals" to urban-industrial centers. Although Phillips claimed that "the Dutch have a reputation in this country of being anti–Native," and believe in "keep[ing] the Nigger in his place," the hall was full. *The Changing African*, often shown on the MCCC, departed from common ethnographic constructions of primitive blacks by illustrating vividly "the black man's work in the white man's mines and factories;... the disreputable slums where a large part of the black population is sinking to a state far below the old heathen level; the low wage and consequent impossible economic position; then what religious and social agencies and labour organizations are attempting for the welfare of the blacks."[82] As Phillips and other missionaries showed the film to young Afrikaners they provided running commentary on black life in villages and mines.

Hoping to convince whites of the "need for Christian service among the native hordes in Johannesburg," Phillips introduced a "pure South African Native" to say a few words following the screening. Richard Selope Thema addressed the color line directly, recalling a trip to England where he met a little girl who had "never seen an African like myself. She looked me over, disapprovingly, then went to her father and said, 'Daddy, this man hasn't washed his face!—glancing down—'nor his hands!'" Eliciting only a "suppressed laugh," Selope Thema then recounted his response: "I explained to the little girl just how it was; how the African sun had burned us people pretty badly. Then I went on to tell her my impression of the first white man I ever saw. It was in the Northern Transvaal. An English gentleman visited our tribe. I was a badly excited boy when I saw him. 'Why!' I told my little brothers. 'Here's a man who has been skinned—alive!'" Phillips noted that following this story "a real laugh came from the white listeners. The contact had been made. From this time on every word the speaker said was listened to with keen attention," as Selope Thema described Africans struggling to adapt in a new environment.[83] In a "few well-chosen sentences," Phillips declared, the African guest speaker "created just the right impression." A member of the audience then spoke up: "Our opposition to the kind of thing your film deals with is due to pure ignorance. We simply have not known of the things you have been telling us tonight. You will find that we are as keen as anyone else when we are shown what the need is and how we can help."[84] Social control theorists critique the many strategies of elites to maintain power. But one limitation is the assumption that the aims of those at the top of the hierarchy have been realized. Furthermore, even in the compelling case of New Primrose—which certainly qualifies as social control—no critic has bothered to suggest a more favorable outcome. Had Phillips not deployed his cinematic arsenal, black miners might have responded to the provocation by pouring out of the compounds and initiating a race war, resulting certainly in body bags, mass arrests, and tightened controls on black labor. Had there not been social control, white extremists would have succeeded.

Thus, the social control model, like the social order it critiques, suffers from a "top down" approach that presumes a sweeping domination of the colonized, without analyzing how meaning is constructed or contested at points of culture contact. African viewers were often able to confront images on their own terms, negotiate between different possible readings, and, in rare instances, to "speak to power" not only about their film-watching experience, but of the broader racial dynamic in which black spectatorship was framed. In short, much of African reception theory has unwittingly replicated the tendency of colonial officials who denied the ability of African audiences to engage critically the cultural messages encoded within Western cinema. Simplistic social control interpretations of Phillips's vision for film, then, while properly questioning missionary claims of selfless altruism, ultimately serve as reductionist critiques of the MCCC, and foreclose avenues for further investigation.[85]

Race, Representation and Restriction

The same era that saw the rapid proliferation of cinema for black viewers also saw the implementation of film censorship to restrict the free flow of film to these new consumers. European cries for censorship were often imbued with the paternalist discourse of trusteeship because of Africans' putative susceptibility to the seductions of the image—an issue explored in more detail later—thus requiring "friends of the native" to filter out the unwanted detritus of Western culture. In 1931, *South African Outlook* opined that commercial films displaying images "far from the average life of the European community" should be a cause for concern for those entrusted with "backward" peoples' moral development:

> The shameless exploitation of what Hollywood calls "sex appeal" has been too much for India, China and Japan, which have protested effectually and with State aid have established their own film-making concerns. If Bantu Africa were articulate, it would follow suit. It is not, and the decent-minded European population must speak for the Native people.[86]

Given these pressures, a cumbersome three-tiered censorship system evolved fitfully in South Africa following World War I and was seemingly honed to perfection in the next two decades. By the mid–1920s, imported films for *all* audiences were screened for possible excision by a local Cape Town Censorship Board. Yet the board, which took over the duties of the Bioscope Advisory Committee following passage of the 1917 Cinematograph Film Act, was nothing more than a Provincial body whose limited mandate only highlighted what concerned citizens perceived as the deplorable lack of a national censorship policy. Thelma Gutsche, for example, argued that, ironically, the banning of films in the Cape often served as an added inducement for spectators in other provinces to see "forbidden fruit."[87]

It was in the second stage of review that the nexus between race and representation appeared: a Transvaal Board of Censors evaluated films destined for general black audiences (miners/townsmen), to be passed or banned by Inspector Brown of the Johannesburg police. Finally, for those films making their way specifically to the MCCC, representatives from the American Board could make yet further cuts and, if desired, replace offending scenes with alternative ones shot by the missionary board itself![88] Whether or not missionaries actually inserted their own footage into pre-existing films is not known, but clearly this level of redundancy in censorship procedures was designed to guarantee that only those images deemed appropriate by the white community would be seen by African eyes. Yet while this three-tiered system initially suggests excessive control, it probably reflects more the decentralized, *ad hoc* nature of the whole enterprise, and certainly reflects that not all white observers could agree on what constituted "undesirable" images.

For this reason, the 1931 Entertainments (Censorship) Act No. 29 offered reform by replacing the local Cape Town Board with an official Board of Censors for the Union appointed by the Minister of the Interior, which would also be located in Cape Town. The decisions of this central organization were intended to cover the Rhodesias as well, although, as detailed below, officials there complained that censorship in South Africa was dangerously lax. Generally composed of seven members, the new board also reflected a shift in official thinking from an emphasis on censorship to film classification, and explicitly distinguished between "different classes of individuals":

> Certificate A: Approved for general exhibition to anyone, without age or colour restrictions.

Certificate B: Approved for European audiences only.
Certificate C: Approved for Europeans and Non-Europeans, but excludes Natives.
Certificate D: Approved subject to any condition or restriction as to age or sex of person before whom such film may be exhibited.[89]

Within a few years, though, a loophole led minister Jan Hofmeyr to amend the act. In February 1934, he advocated more stringent requirements given that the current law allowed private societies to show "censorable" films, and failed to "prevent natives forming themselves into such a society and ... becoming susceptible to subversive propaganda."[90] This fear of destabilization, in fact, was already present in the wording of the original act, which had empowered the board to reject any film that "in its opinion, depicts any matter that prejudicially affects the safety of the State."[91] Hofmeyr's campaign led to the 1934 "Entertainments Censorship Amendment Bill," which prohibited the showing of films *anywhere* in South Africa without explicit authorization of the Board of Censors.[92]

Officials in the Rhodesias following World War I were likewise scrutinizing what they considered to be unsatisfactory policies in South Africa covering cinema exhibitions for black audiences. A more rigorous system of differential censorship, they hoped, over and above that of the South African Board of Censors, was needed to stave off suggestive images. In his study of colonial cinema, James Burns highlights an evolution regarding those images perceived as most problematic by colonial officials. While screen violence topped the list during the war, there was a newfound obsession with representations of white women by the late 1920s.[93] Because black subjects were perceived as requiring special consideration, white fraternal organizations and women's groups spearheaded a thorough censorship code that distinguished between races. The 1932 Entertainments Control and Censorship Bill, deemed "overdue" by the Colonial Secretary, superseded antiquated 1912 legislation that had only authorized the police to intervene following negative reactions to a premiere, rather than requiring producers to submit films for review.[94]

Officials in the Southern and Northern Rhodesian Criminal Investigations Departments (CID) also investigated images on local marquees as well as citizen complaints about "offensive" scenes approved by South Africa. In 1927, the Northern Rhodesian CID fretted that the 1912 Cinematograph Proclamation failed to cover the circulation of cinema posters. The problem was not indecent images that could be "the subject of [regular] criminal proceedings, but rather of such posters as might be fairly innocuous if seen only by Europeans but would be distinctly undesirable for display in places ... accessible to natives."[95] Similarly, the head of the Northern Rhodesian Censorship Board worried, "The type of picture that might be passed as suitable for exhibition to natives [in South Africa] might not always be desirable for exhibition to native audiences in this territory."[96] Broken Hill mine manager A.P. Marriot agreed. A pioneer in Northern Rhodesian bioscopes, he nevertheless imposed further censorship on all African Films, Ltd. movies imported for his black employees. Presumably this system was still in place a year later when he began sending the films north to the Copperbelt. Northern Rhodesia's director of native education, Geoffrey Latham, joined the fray by demanding segregated exhibitions throughout the colony, urging officials in Lusaka, Broken Hill and Bwana Mkubwa to "satisfy themselves that any chances of natives seeing films intended for exhibition to Euros only should be reduced to a minimum." Latham later began working full-time on an alternative to commercial cinema as educational director for the Bantu Educational Kinema Experiment, and in so doing secured a prominent role in the history of colonial cinema.[97]

It should be noted that interwar racial anxiety over images in southern Africa paralleled movements for differential censorship in tropical Africa and throughout the broader colonial world. In the Gold Coast, prior to 1927, censorship powers were vested solely in the police under the Cinematograph Exhibitions Ordinance.[98] In October of that year, administrators formed a Board of Control, comprising prison and customs officials, as well as staff from local schools and missionary societies. The board, headed by the secretary for native affairs and the inspector general of police, emphasized that films passed by the British Board of Film Censors in England needed still further review, and might be entirely unsuitable for British Africa.[99] The British Board was an NGO formed by the industry for self-regulation, but censorship decisions were based on the assumption that audiences were English. In contrast, the Gold Coast's Board of Control was largely an outgrowth of the 1927 recommendations of a Colonial Office Conference on "Cinematograph Films." At this meeting, Kenya officials explained that under the Stage Plays and Cinematograph Exhibition Ordinance of 1912, all films there were censored by a Nairobi board consisting of two members of the East Africa's Women's League and a policeman. "Nothing touching on the colour question or anything detrimental to the native race is allowed to be shown," they assured the delegates, and the "censoring of films generally is given the most careful scrutiny."[100] Films were either designated for "non-natives" only, banned completely, or given viewing certificates for all audiences. In the event that a consensus was impossible, the film in question was submitted to the superintendent of police, whose decision was final.

The apparent stringency of African film censorship reflects the struggle to establish hegemony over the flow of visual media to the colonized. As Poonam Arora demonstrates, race-based censorship was also a common feature in British India as colonial officials either excised images inciting violence and disrespect for whites, or prohibited the colonized from seeing films altogether.[101] Indeed, in 1929, the British secretary of state for the colonies appointed a Colonial Films Committee to consider a more uniform system of censorship in the colonies and dominions, which recommended that "a single censorship board should be established in each territory, consisting of one or two members, one of whom should be a member of the Education Department of Native Affairs. In Tropical African Colonies an African should, where possible, be a member of the censorship board."[102] Such measures reflect colonial administrators' efforts to restrict the proliferation of images which might foment unrest.

A closer look, though, reveals vulnerabilities in the system. Africans often took advantage of the predictable leakages and enjoyed films "banned to natives." What seemed to be an ever-tightening noose of interwar censorship, then, begins to look more like a failed attempt to put a brake on the inevitable, as profitability for private enterprise ran up against broader concerns for political control. Phillips himself discovered in the mid–1930s that South Africa's bioscopes often ignored Censor Board requirements. Visiting venues exhibiting films banned for Africans, he discovered many failed to post the compulsory notice "Natives are Not Admitted to the Performance," and that Africans frequented the establishments. A proprietor confirmed Phillips's findings: "This censorship is a farce. We don't exclude anybody. The educated Native is a better patron than many Coloured or Poor Whites." Nor was the lack of posted signs an oversight; printed programs for upcoming showings at four non–European bioscopes similarly failed to distinguish between those films passed and those banned for Africans.[103]

A few years later, at a Native Juvenile Delinquency conference, Phillips spoke on the failures of censorship enforcement. Exhibitors, he complained, failed to bar Africans from seeing banned films like *The Sin Ship* (1931), *Why Change Your Husband* (a.k.a. *Red Hot Sinners*, 1931), *Gay Divorcee* (1934) and *Bad Girl* (1931). Phillips also decried inconsistent criteria for making censorship decisions: "Not infrequently, films are shown which anyone even remotely acquainted with current productions will recognize as hardly suitable for exhibition to Native youth." Particularly rankling were *Blonde Venus* (1932), with the byline "What could she do? She loved two men at once!," which included a striptease out of a gorilla suit; and *What Price Hollywood?* (1932) in which Mary, a young down-and-out waitress/actress, is willing to do about anything for her big break.[104]

Fears of inadequate censorship plagued British territories north of the Limpopo. In Southern Rhodesia, CID Superintendent Brundell aired his dissatisfaction in 1927 not just with the Union Censor Board in Cape Town, but also censorship procedures further down the chain. He was furious that young American Board missionary Arthur Adams was wielding the knife, unofficially, for the third tier of review, despite an earlier promise by African Films, Ltd., that films for blacks would not be shown without explicit approval by the South African Native Affairs Department (NAD). Apparently NAD had quietly entrusted the tedious work of image excision to missionary expertise, a decision Brundell denounced as "unsatisfactory and illegal."[105] Although American Board representatives were generally diligent, Brundell feared that giving missionaries control over censorship gave them too much decision-making power without oversight. Ironically, while administrators in British territories expressed dissatisfaction with South African censorship, the Colonial Office doubted the ability of colonial CID's to quarantine unwanted images. Due to the lack of consistent licensing distinctions between white and black viewers in the British Empire, the Colonial Films Committee in London argued that pressures for profits, coupled with appeasement of white settler demands for new movies, potentially allowed blacks to see almost any film:

> In the smaller areas [colonies] it is not easy to find responsible officers with time to view films, and the task has sometimes been left to less responsible subordinates. Again, a conscientious officer may have felt bound to pass a film of which he disapproved, because if you banned it the cinema would have to close, as there was nothing else to show. A film suitable for Europeans may be unsuitable for natives, and the demands of the former may be insistent.[106]

In other instances, simple programming mistakes led to films being exhibited to Africans that were meant for European consumption only. On the Copperbelt, one such lapse caused an "uproar" when black spectators were shown a complete 35mm program designed for whites, rather than the heavily censored 16mm version. Most alarming was that horror films were accidentally shown in their entirety.[107]

Perhaps one black contributor in a letter to the editor of the *Rand Daily Mail* summed up best the inevitable seepage of images through the regulatory net. Taunting South Africa's Censor Board, which banned *From Here to Eternity* (1953) and *Pinky* (1949) for Africans, this "Cinema-Fan" asked, "Why don't the censors realize that by hook or by crook we still manage to see these pictures? Remember, some of us can 'play white.' Others have European friends with 16mm films at which [sic] we are invited. So Censors, please make up your minds and give us a break."[108]

The Expansion of Black Spectatorship

Despite censorship and film classification, the mid–1920s saw a corresponding increase in viewing opportunities for blacks throughout South Africa. Even Phillips's 1926 furlough failed to slow the exponential rise in black spectatorship at commercial bioscopes, on the MCCC, and elsewhere. One observer described Phillips's temporary replacement, American Board recruit Arthur Adams (nicknamed "Bioscope Man" by black miners), so "ultra-American in temperament and speed that he found even Johannesburg slow." As we have seen, despite being a newcomer Adams wielded the censor's blade, yet he was equally adept at restocking the MCCC with new films and distributing them along the Reef. Mabel Carney, head of the Department of Rural Education at Columbia University's Teachers' College, once reported that she had accompanied Adams on a "tearing drive of 70 miles up and down the Rand delivering motion pictures to the various mines."[109]

This flurry of activity on the Rand paralleled developments elsewhere. In addition to films pushing their way into the Rhodesias, by early 1929 no fewer than 40 other locations were hosting showings, including South African Railway compounds, leper institutions in Pretoria and Emjanyana, the women's wing of the Johannesburg jail, Diepkloof Reformatory for juveniles, the Pass office for Native Police, and the Johannesburg Native Hospital.[110] Seven years later this number had expanded to an astonishing 83 exhibition centers outside the mining sector.[111] In all locations, excepting the railway compounds where a collection was taken, screenings were free; funding was secured jointly through Chamber of Mines' contributions ($30,000 per annum) and the American Board's Social Service Department.[112] Lovedale Missionary Institute also began showing films, both to its students and to neighborhood children, with Phillips helping to locate suitable silent pictures.[113] It would be impossible to tabulate the number of spectators at all these locations, but if one considers collectively the Rhodesian mining centers, the Witwatersrand compounds, and almost 100 other locations, we can assume that the MCCC alone was now providing millions of Africans with their first look at the magic of motion pictures.

Phillips, though, was still not done. In the early 1920s, he identified yet another untapped audience in the peri-urban Native Locations, and stressed the need in these crowded areas to do for African residents what municipalities in the U.S. and Canada were doing for their local populations:

> The leaders arrange Community nights for the whole community, getting the whole town to sing together or enjoy a social evening. They [organize] special Festivals and Pageants, and Dramatic plays [and] they censor and direct the showing of special programs of bioscope shows.[114]

"Every [South African] municipality," Phillips argued, "should provide its native people with the pleasure and educational advantages of well-chosen bioscope films."[115] As a result, several cities signed on to the circuit for Location showings, including Durban, Benoni, Randfontein, and Krugersdorp.[116] The rationale for extending the MCCC to municipalities with Chamber funding was based on two premises. First, the latter three Locations contained quarters for married miners; second, the "annoying" presence of children and women at compound shows, Phillips argued, created a disorderly atmosphere; Location showings were thus implemented to deter these non-miner populations from frequenting compound showings. Many city officials, it seems, echoed these sentiments.[117]

In some cases, however, officials objected to free showings in the Locations. In 1936, the Pretoria City Council and the Public Health, Native and Asiatic Affairs Committee, which were considering showings for local townships were taken aback by a Native Recruiting Corporation letter: "The films we have found to be most popular with the natives are cowboy pictures, straightforward comedies without any love sentiment, or any other picture with a lot of action in it." The superintendent of Locations, fearful of rising juvenile delinquency, responded firmly: "I am opposed to films with plenty of action. Wild gangster pictures and cowboy pictures do not tend to improve the native mind."[118] The Pretoria Joint Councils similarly suggested that the possible "undesirable effect[s] on Native children of cinematograph films" was a "national and not a local matter," and suggested the issue be bounced back to the SAIRR for consideration.[119]

It is unclear how the issue was resolved in Pretoria, but in Johannesburg the Chamber handed over responsibilities for free bioscopes in hostels and Locations to the NAD, just as talkies were being introduced.[120] The arrival of talking pictures caused a ripple in the MCCC. As early as 1933, Phillips could hear the death knell for silent movies, with worrying implications: "When we are forced finally to supply 'talkie' films to the mine compounds, it is going to be even more difficult than it is today to find sufficient suitable films for presentation to the Natives."[121] Despite this assessment, talkies were introduced almost simultaneously on the compounds and surrounding Locations. On May 25, 1936, the Sub-Nigel screened the first talkie for miners,[122] and a week later, Marabastad opened the first Location talkie with an introductory speech by the deputy mayor, chairman of the Native Committee of the Kroonstad Town Council.[123] Ironically, some African elites expressed dissatisfaction. The *Bantu World*, for instance, railed against what it considered offensive programs:

> Most of the films shown in our locations are undesirable ... and undesirable characteristically. Westerners, highway robbery, thefts and flirtatious love are predominant. These pictures have done more harm than good. The free bioscope in our "Zoos" is a monotonous menace to social advance. The cinema to many people is no longer for occasional entertainment, it is rather daily bread.[124]

Fortunately for Phillips, grievances concerning compound and Location showings became someone else's problem. In February 1935, he hand-picked his successor, J.E. Hallendorff, and departed to finish his Yale dissertation (although he returned to South Africa for a time upon completion). Hallendorff, the son of Swedish missionaries, spoke Zulu fluently and was, Phillips said approvingly, "mechanically minded."[125] Hallendorff would play a key role in the MCCC throughout the 1940s and into the apartheid era. A report for the third quarter of 1942 shows the circuit survived surprisingly well during the war. Hallendorff recorded an impressive 1,149 showings, with most mines on a weekly schedule and approximately 1,500 spectators in attendance per show. At Government Areas South Compound, however, audiences were much larger, with 6,000–8,000 spectators on average. Hallendorff bragged about the 1,723,500 film-goers from July through September, but admitted that these figures failed to count for redundancy: "Like Europeans, some natives are regular cinema 'fans,' and they attend the shows week after week." Hallendorff, like Phillips before him, continued to expand the scope of the MCCC, as venues like hospitals, the Modderfontein Dynamite Factory, Largo Collieries, Witbank Collieries, and Native Military Camps at Spaarkwater, West Vlakfontain and Reitfontein were added.[126] Cinema, it seems, had come to Black Africa.

From the Manger to the Cross: Bringing Religion to the Mines

Compound managers were generally suspicious of missionaries and were concerned that Phillips would introduce religion into the mines. As a result, American Board representatives were careful to include several genres in each program. In the mid–1930s education and travel films (*India Today, Canada's Evergreen Playground*) were interspersed with serials (*New Adventures of Tarzan*), comedies (Larry Semon, Charlie Chaplin, Harold Lloyd, Buster Keaton, and Our Gang shorts), Safety First films, dramas (*Peter Pan*, *Robin Hood*, *The Thief of Bagdad*), "native African life" sketches produced by missionaries or mining officials (*Industrialization of the African*, *Pickaninny's Christmas*, *The Gorilla Hunt*, *The African Witch-Doctor and the Way Out*, *From Red Blanket to Civilization*), and Westerns (*The Golden Stallion*, *Cactus Trails*, *Ambushed*).[127]

Despite the reticence of managers, Phillips also included religious and morality films, including *The Ten Commandments*, *Les Miserables*, *Pilgrim's Progress*, *Passing of the Third Floor Back*, and the controversial *From the Manger to the Cross* which, in spite of an ambivalent reception in the white world, was destined to have one of the MCCC's longest shelf lives. The film appeared at a turning point in early film history. Premiering in America in 1912, it was an expensive four-reel production riding the wave of new feature length, historico-religious dramas like *Pilgrim's Progress* and *Damon and Pythias*. Remarkably, the Kalem Company sent 42 crewmen and actors with director Sidney Olcott to film on location in Palestine for a dose of realism.

It was precisely what one writer described as the very "tangible solidity" of the scenery and Biblical characters that elicited criticism from clergymen, who argued that direct Biblical interpretations profaned the Scriptures. The film's commercial release also caused condemnation among those who questioned charging admission for religious films, with a London newspaper inviting religious opinion on the suitability of religious themes for commercial uses.[128] Most respondents who had seen the film approved, claiming "it was no more irreverent than the use of sacred subjects in art and was likely to bring home to people the beauty of the Bible's teachings," while those who had not passed an adverse judgment. To appease critics, Kalem announced showings would be limited to town halls, churches, and institutes.[129]

Although the Pope banned the viewing of religious films prior to its European release, in January 1913 the Johannesburg newspaper *The Star* announced a preview for religious leaders and the media. After receiving considerable praise, Johannesburg's Empire scheduled a public premiere on Sunday, February 9. Mixed reactions followed, for while many seats were filled, some complained that Sabbath showings constituted sacrilege. When the theater moved opening night up to Saturday, a few town council members tried again to force a cancellation, although without success, and the film was screened to favorable reviews.

Prior to its Cape Town release, however, clergy and the press condemned its "very grave and indeed fatal blemishes.... In the latter part, we see Judas hanging from the bough of a tree, Christ being scourged, black weals being indistinguishable on His body and limbs and Herod with his men at war for setting Him at naught and mocking Him. Even to one who has witnessed much of the brutal realism of life," the writer complained, "these scenes are revolting."[130] Indeed, the very corporeality of the backdrops and the film's characterizations were crudely contrasted to the sacred Biblical intertitles. Using a heavy-handed dichotomy between good and evil, for instance, Judas is dressed in black as he betrays Jesus to Herod.[131]

Mixed reviews failed to stop Phillips from incorporating the film in 1920, which had "a profound effect on the Natives, and so impressed have the Europeans been that requests have been made for the film to be shown to European employes [sic]."[132] Thelma Gutsche has argued that despite its ambivalent early reception, the film "eventually attained a popular success which has never been surpassed."[133] Curiously, though, she reported in 1938 that the film had disappeared for a decade and had only recently resurfaced to be modified into a talkie. Three years before, though, it was still in rotation on the MCCC, and 1938 BMSC Monthly Reports list a showing for Good Friday, asserting the "picture has attracted huge crowds and is worth seeing."[134] This disparity suggests that Gutsche, despite her encyclopedic knowledge of South African commercial cinema, failed to stay abreast of the ever-expanding MCCC. *From the Manger to the Cross*, then, appealed to towndwellers and miners for 20 years or more. This conclusion leads to tantalizing questions: what films proved most popular with migrant workers and townsmen? Did gender, class, or ethnic affiliation play a part in determining what films would have staying power in municipal and mining compounds? Were there identifiable genres that viewers consistently found particularly offensive or confusing? In fact, these questions vexed white contemporaries like Phillips, Taberer, and Hallendorff, as much as they interest the modern historian, for ultimately, as James Burns suggests, officials and missionaries were "committed to transforming African societies, and though their agendas ranged from selling soap to saving souls, they shared the common hope that motion pictures might prove an efficient and potent tool for influencing African audiences."[135]

Satisfying the Discriminating Palate

In 1924, Phillips affirmed that a "larger proportion" of miners attended shows than ever before, with spectators registering "distinct disappointment" when bad weather forced cancellations.[136] And when MCCC projectionists showed films that proved confusing, miners "walk[ed] miles the next night to the compound where the picture is to be shown, in order to put their minds straight."[137] If this is true, it suggests that even those films that viewers had trouble understanding failed to stem the tide of expanding black audiences.

Reports of the incredible popularity of the bioscope were not restricted to the Rand, but merely underscore a similar refrain heard throughout southern Africa. But we also see the frustration of film supervisors and distributors trying to satisfy viewers' increasing cinematic sophistication once the initial novelty had worn thin. By the mid–1920s, Phillips was already warning the NRC that new initiates were quickly becoming devoted habitués of the bioscope:

> We are finding it increasingly difficult to keep pace with the improvement in taste of the compound audience. When we first began, any picture which showed motion of any sort was satisfactory. To-day, however, there is a critical taste which will not tolerate a program unless it is really good. To obtain these really good films, and in sufficient numbers to satisfy the discriminating palate of these compound groups, means much search among the films stocked by the local African Films, Ltd., at Killarney.[138]

Not surprisingly, though, spectators and supervisors held different views on what genres should be made accessible to blacks. The Western led all genres in the interwar period despite strong competition from comedies and the emerging gangster genre. While many whites expressed concern over the violence, Phillips and MCCC supervisors recognized that the Western's popularity among miners made their inclusion virtually *de rigueur* for any program to attract large crowds.

The appeal of the Western, though, was often equaled by the appeal of Charlie Chaplin. Indeed, following the 1914 split-reeler *Kid Auto Races at Venice, Ca.*, in which he introduced his iconic "Tramp" persona, Chaplin dominated the field of comedy around much of the globe and in colonial Africa. Phillips showed Chaplin films on the compounds prior to his celebrated deployment of them during the Rand Revolt, and they remained a cornerstone of the MCCC for years. Even in Southern Rhodesia, where mining officials often complained about lax censorship in South Africa, Chaplin comedies were "generally favoured as most suitable for showing to native audiences."[139] And when the Tanganyika Director of Education pondered opening a "native-only" theater in Dar es Salaam, he emphasized that "experience so far tends to show that the African enjoys a Charlie Chaplin picture and is completely bored by one specifically produced with the intention of edifying him."[140] Moreover, we have seen that in West Africa Chaplin was already an iconic figure by the mid–1920s due to the distribution of his films in the Gold Coast and beyond. As a result, by the early 1930s popular "concert party" performer Ishmael "Bob" Johnson, who was touring the Gold Coast with his vaudeville act, was incorporating the Chaplin "shuffle" and other components of his slapstick comedy into his own routine.[141]

Chaplin's ubiquity in Anglophone Africa seems to have been tempered somewhat during World War II when Britain's Ministry of Information organized the Colonial Film Unit (CFU), which rarely showed Chaplin films in their entirety; rather, ignoring plot development, random scenes were spliced together for "harmless" entertainment. At issue was imagery deemed morally undesirable or incomprehensible when seen by African eyes, a concern that ruled out the following:

> Chaplin or some other character dressing himself up as a woman; scenes which showed the police in a bad light; scenes in which a priest or clergyman was a figure of fun. Also, it was useless to send out films dealing with matters of which the audience would have no knowledge. Fun and games in the snow do not look so funny to an audience which thinks the snow is sand wonders how it sticks together. Similarly, the elaborately fitted dentist's chair is a perfect centre-piece around which to build a humorous film, but only for people who recognize the setting.[142]

But the CFU edits failed to stop the Chaplin phenomenon. In 1947, a journalist in Lusaka noted, "At present, Charlie Chaplin and pantomime artists are easily the favorites of audiences who squat under the stars to see the films," and by the mid–1950s, they were being shown again in their entirety.[143] Anthropologist Hortense Powdermaker reported that Copperbelt residents responded "most enthusiastically when Chaplin glided into a graceful rhythm" in *The Rink* (1916), exhibited by a mobile cinema truck making the rounds of Northern Rhodesian villages.[144] Hence, Koyinde Vaughan's assertion in 1960 that in villages and towns such as "Accra, Freetown, Kumasi, Lagos or Nairobi, Charles Chaplin and many popular stars are household names," is correct.[145]

Chaplin's reception among Africa's colonized underscores the fluid interpretations to which Hollywood films were subjected. For white liberals like Rheinallt-Jones, interracial understanding required recognizing how images reflected the underlying assumptions of those who produced them: "African humour is not the same as European and their morality and beliefs are distinctive."[146] Thus, it should not surprise us, any more than it surprised white supervisors that Chaplin films were "read" in light of local experiences. Rand miners nicknamed Chaplin "SiDakwa," or "Little Drunken Man," a designation Phillips joked was chosen "untruthfully and we fear libelously."[147] Similarly, Powdermaker found Copperbelt residents referring to Chaplin as "Kaumuntu," a Bemba expression for a diminutive, sexless man, and not quite "normal." Held up as a foolish and good-natured clown, elders considered Kaumuntu mere children's entertainment, and criticized Chaplin for saving himself from difficult situations not through his wit, like the African "trickster," but rather through childlike naïveté.[148] Interestingly, images of Chaplin were even formative in the evolution of African customs: in Northern Rhodesia, one mask in the Gule wa Mkulu dance of the

Nyau secret society apparently evolved from Chaplin's onscreen personas.[149] Clearly Manthia Diawara's claim that European officials believed "distributing commercial films, such as those of Charlie Chaplin, would harmfully introduce Africans to film's powerful means of persuasion," is broad and unsubstantiated.[150] Chaplin, in fact, proved popular among a wide range of African audiences, and with the exception of the limitations imposed by the CFU in the 1940s, his films enjoyed wide distribution throughout the colonial world. Indeed, as early as 1925, for instance, Africans in the Gold Coast were flocking to see Charlie at the Accra Picture Palace, where this iconic figure was greeted with shouts of "Charlee! Charlee!" as he ambled onto the screen.[151]

Phillips and mining officials exploited another genre that evoked excitement among African viewers. "No comedies or cowboy films obtainable anywhere," Phillips informed the Chamber of Mines, "are so universally enjoyed as films showing simple black folk with black skins, in their homes, about their daily tasks, at their dancing, hunting, etc. Compound managers have repeatedly asked for more and more films of Native life."[152] Phillips combed the inventory of South African distributors, picking shorts like *Zulu's Pomp*, *A Zulu's Devotion*, *Events in the Life of a Zulu Chief*, and *Piccaninny's Christmas* for the MCCC. He also imported the Johnsons' *Simba: The King of the Beasts* from Kenya, and "native life" footage from Madagascar. But as with European films, Phillips found that increasing sophistication led to a demand for "new stuff, which we would have to make ourselves." The Chamber thus authorized Phillips's purchase of a cumbersome French camera, and later a more portable DeVry unit. Traveling through the northern Transvaal, Portuguese East Africa and elsewhere, Phillips captured tribal life in African reserves, and by 1932 had compiled 30,000 feet of footage which could be spliced together for MCCC films. Unfortunately, these rare images seem to have disappeared, but records indicate that before the war they enjoyed heavy rotation. Projecting the cultural expressions of indigenous peoples on the screen, Phillips discovered, often served as comic relief for migrant workers and provided a curious juxtaposition of the strange and familiar:

> The Natives in the Congo, Northern and Southern Rhodesia, are of course not, at present, engaged in large numbers on the Witwatersrand Gold Mines. They are, however, Bantu folk; some, as the Fingoes and Matabele, being close relatives of our South African Natives. And the fact that the customs, dances, and habits of the photographed folk are somewhat different from those in South Africa makes the film much more interesting and amusing than otherwise.[153]

Just as "white" images might be greeted with disdain or confusion, "native sketches" of rural Africa were also subject to a range of reactions. It is difficult to reconstruct fully the nuances of African reception to seeing scenes of village life on the screen, but what is clear is that the humorous sense of both distance and proximity made possible by a newly mediated reality was not shared equally. In 1924, mining official William Gemmill asked Phillips whether specific films were more popular in certain compounds than others. In those films "where the percentage of Portuguese Natives is high," Phillips responded, "the percentage of Natives attending the shows is higher." And he found a less-than-enthusiastic response from many Xhosa and Sotho, who were under-represented in many films: "You are showing us pictures all the while of the Zulus, the Swazis, and the Shangaans," they complained, "why don't you show us pictures of our homes and our wives and children?" Thus, while some Xhosa and Sotho frequented the compound shows, Phillips found many "sleeping in their room, [or] roasting meat."[154]

For the Sotho, this omission was rectified somewhat in 1929 when recreational assistant

P.C. Van Haght brought his own amateurish films into Crown Deep to gain the confidence of miners: "He is becoming keenly sensible of the opportunity presented there for getting into touch with Natives from every corner of the subcontinent. A small Cine moving-picture apparatus, the property of Mr. Van Haght, with pictures taken by him in Basutoland and elsewhere, has been the means of making him immediately the centre of interested groups."[155]

Ambivalence among the Xhosa, however, played out in various ways in succeeding years. In an urban anthropological study of the Xhosa in East London, two anthropologists found that while industrialization fostered new interpersonal relationships, the politics of leisure reflected entrenched intra-ethnic divisions based on "Red," "School," or "Townsman" patterns of preference.[156] In fact, the bioscope was at the center of a passionate controversy, pitting more traditionally minded Xhosa against those who gravitated to the West:

> [The Reds] said that reading a book or a paper was learning lies, and learning the knowledge of how to oppress them and rob them of their money. Mention of attending a bioscope was hated so much that if one did so they would never trust one again. They said the bioscope was the main reason for the theft among School people.[157]

Clearly, neither white supervisors nor black spectators constituted a monolithic bloc during this period of expanding black spectatorship. In addition to whites' subtly contrasting ideologies of uplift versus efficiency, Africans were divided along gender, class, and both inter-ethnic and intra-ethnic lines, distinctions which did not diminish when images were culled from African settings.

Witchdoctors and Other Impurities of the Spectacle

By the post–World War I era the European civilizing mission was in retreat, and evangelical exhortation was increasingly becoming obsolete. The ensuing fear of detribalization, espoused by missionaries and others suggested now that perhaps the African needed *less* Europeanization. Hence, C.T. Loram warned that "in the past, western civilization has been imposed upon non-western peoples without much forethought and with an almost complete disregard for consequences."[158] While a degree of African acculturation was still perceived as desirable, there was a newfound desire to preserve rather than destroy tribal culture. Cultural fossilization had its limits, however. In particular, polygamy and witchcraft were deemed odious, for, as one missionary declared, "No one in Africa has more power over the natives and their lives than has a witchdoctor."[159]

Traditional religious beliefs emphasized ancestral spirits that effected change in the material realm. Personal afflictions and social calamities were often blamed on the spirit world and witches; conversely, spirits could be invoked by dingaka calling for animal sacrifices to help recover from loss. Whites like Rheinallt-Jones despaired at the influence wielded by these practitioners, and levied blame on the African belief in witchcraft, in conjunction with variables like "wars, destruction of wild animals, and the slave trade," for the depopulation of the sub-continent.[160]

For Phillips, what remained of value in the civilizing mission could be found in health, hygiene and medicine. *The African Witchdoctor and the Way Out*, a film he produced in the early 1920s targeting both African audiences and American church groups, critiqued Zulu medicinal practices and, by extension, promoted Western medicine. With American Board backing, Phillips began shooting near Durban for the film which opens with the documentary realism favored by the ethnographic gaze, but concludes by confirming the superiority of Western medicine. Hoping to film Hlambisinye Shangase (a Zulu diviner/herbalist) for the "native medicine" segment, Phillips, James Dexter Taylor, and Dr. McCord struggled to convey bulky film equipment to Shangase's kraal deep in the bush. Some 40 miles outside Durban, rutted roads forced them to abandon their automobile and rely on local Zulus as porters and guides as they trod mile after mile under a baking sun.[161]

Nestled in a hillside, Shangase's kraal boasted 25 grass huts, nine wives, and numerous children. Expecting an exotic headman dressed in full regalia, Phillips registered visible disappointment when the "witchdoctor" emerged from his domicile where he had been receiving patients dressed in "a dirty white shirt and [an] ill-fitting pair of white man's trousers." According to Phillips, "He look[ed] very common and ordinary." Just as the ethnographic gaze relied on visual markers of racial/cultural difference for its *raison d'etre*, Phillips's film needed to emphasize distinctions beyond mere differences in medical techniques, and it thus became necessary to reconstruct the past in order to condemn it. The crew convinced the reluctant diviner to allow himself to be filmed in his "regulation witchdoctor's outfit" to add a dash of realism. Shangase changed in his hut and delighted his visitors by re-emerging adorned in fabulous skins, hair festooned with igwalawala feathers, and "hands full of potent charms and medicines."[162]

This poignant scene recalls similar cultural border crossings and other contaminations abounding in European exploration literature. While most first-contact reports exploited the "shock of the new" as Westerners opened new markets and saved souls, in other instances the expected contact with exotic Otherness gave way to a dull recognition of the Same. David Livingstone, for instance, was flabbergasted by the Kololo during his 1851 Central Africa expedition: "Many of the people were clothed in European manufactures, one had a dressing-gown on, and a red worsted nightcap." In this case trade had clearly preceded the flag, for long before the Scramble, Mambari slave-traders in the Zambezi Valley hawked Western clothing imported on Angolan slave routes.[163]

Phillips's film, a reconstitution of an imagined African past, resonates with Walter Benjamin, who spoke of the dialectical tension between film's ability to "shatter" tradition on the one hand, and its unique capacity to recall and resurrect the myths of the past, on the other. For Benjamin, who highlighted the critical function of mechanical reproduction, perception functions by "get[ting] hold of an object at very close range by way of its likeness" rather than through the use of empirical or first-hand observation. Foreshadowing McCluhan and Baudrillard, Benjamin emphasized the viewer's new relationship with reality. Just as "an ancient statue of Venus ... stood in a different traditional context with the Greeks, who made it an object of veneration, than with the clerics of the Middle Ages, who viewed it as an ominous idol," we can imagine that Phillips's intended audience viewing the practices of the witchdoctor would receive such images in a radically different context than that in which they originally evolved.[164] This context in Phillips's case—also supporting a claim of Benjamin—is politically charged. In fact, reconstructing the primitive connoted much more than an innocent resurrection of tradition; it banished the activities of the diviner from their original social context and embedded them within the broader field of colonial power relations. With the image, denigration replaced veneration.

It is here that the question of authenticity is raised. Clearly Phillips was not simply documenting the activities of the witchdoctor in the sense of portraying the Real as given, but rather was engaging in what pioneer documentary filmmaker John Grierson described in a famous phrase as the "creative interpretation of actuality." But while postcolonial critics concerned with authenticity might dismiss the careful staging of the divination sequence, it is important to note that Phillips himself was equally concerned with verisimilitude, but verisimilitude grounded not in the existence of an enduring referent (the diviner normally eschewed his traditional garments), but rather in white colonialist fantasies of what a proper witchdoctor *should* look like. Thus, it was Shangase's own cultural border crossing—his sporting of casual western attire—that seemed to Phillips to emit an aura of in-authenticity that had to be countered through the reconstruction of now-defunct social forms. From his perspective, in order to tell the truth about the world, the Real had to be repackaged before it could be projected.

Phillips reconstructed the perceived primitivity of his subjects in an effort to preserve for posterity those traditions and customs seemingly headed for extinction. In a similar example of the obstacles ethnographic cinema had to overcome from its very inception, British anthropologist A.C. Haddon made the first ethnological film in 1898 of an initiation ritual dance of the Torres Strait Islanders. Using a Newman and Guardia camera and wax cylinder phonographs to capture his subjects' speech and songs, Haddon was forced to come to terms with the paradox of pre-existing stereotypes versus rapidly changing late–19th century realities. Apparently the dance had already died out following missionary intervention, and Haddon resorted to begging the islanders to recreate the ritual using cardboard replicas of ceremonial masks.[165] Similarly, Martine Loutfi relates a story that resonates with this vexing issue of authenticity:

> The practice of using local people as actors in supposedly authentic events seems to have been widespread in the early years of the cinema. Raoul Grimoin-Sanson, a pioneer of North Atlantic filming, recalls how he arranged with a French general to film a fake battle involving some two thousand men on horseback. Obviously, the reality of the world that was supposed to be communicated through films was manipulated and what the audience saw was a spectacle in which document and performance were inextricably intertwined.[166]

So it was with Phillips, who recast Shangase as timeless primitive while the diviner ministered to his patients in full regalia. "This is what we wanted!" chortled Phillips with camera rolling. Yet the corrosive influence of the West was not entirely eviscerated with the shedding of the witchdoctor's casual wear, for the crew soon noticed that the traditional medical procedures themselves were also compromised by cultural impurities. Shangase, demonstrating his medical technique on a tubercular knee of a patient, pulled a small, sharp object from his bag and cut the knee with a series of small jabs and rubbed one of his "bitter concoctions" into the wounds. Phillips remarked on the patient's stoicism, who suffered the tribulation in a pained silence. But for Phillips—not to mention Dr. McCord—the horror of the treatment was compounded when a member of the crew picked up the tiny blade and discovered it was the "rusty stay from a woman's corset!"[167]

In another instance, Shangase announced that he would be interested in seeing McCord's method for treating patients whom he could not heal, including one child with a club foot and another with paralyzed legs. McCord was surprised to find Shangase "gravely using a stethoscope" in these cases. As McCord's own stethoscope had been left in the car, he borrowed the instrument and put it to a patient's chest, to no avail. Unscrewing the receiver, he was shocked when a "nest of small spiders" and dirt spilled out. Phillips' colorful descriptions of these episodes suggest that his anxiety over these illicit cultural borrowings rivaled his concern with the procedures themselves. As David Slavin has argued, "Fears of pollution and corrosion displaced fascination with exotic Others."[168]

In the same way that white masters long enjoyed secret dalliances with their black slaves, the transgression of the racial/cultural divide in Phillips's case had another component that suggests that his concern about Shangase's use of Western medical instruments was dictated not so much by the *act of transgression* itself, but rather by who retained the power to cross the border. Hoping to secure more footage for *The African Witchdoctor*, the filmmakers asked Shangase how he would treat the headache of another patient. With the young woman kneeling before him, Shangase parted her hair, selected a knife (not the corset stay), and cut a three-inch gash on her scalp, with the blade scraping the exposed skull as blood poured down her face. It was, Phillips said, simply the African method of "letting out the pain!" But this time the African's sorcery was countered by McCord's own act of transgression—"white magic." Having limited medicines at his disposal, McCord quickly dispensed "an immediate and powerful antidote," which "reliev[ed] the pain like magic, for her smile on her face last[ed] until we [left]." His instant remedy, it turned out, was 10 shillings in silver. One can only imagine the effect this bizarre scene would have had on African spectators had McCord's medico-magical intervention made it into the final cut.[169] In any case, the fact that it was the white filmmakers who initiated the border crossing explains Phillips's approval of this pecuniary prescription.[170]

Although *The African Witchdoctor and the Way Out* enjoyed distribution on the MCCC, it is unclear whether the American Board released it for distribution in America to bolster missionary recruitment. Quite possibly, the members were less than impressed. In 1924, Phillips wrote to the board that he was finishing another film, *The African in Transition*: "It is a great improvement on the 'Witchdoctor' film which we sent you a year or so ago and the fate of which is unknown to us. What happened to that film? Did you have a private funeral for it and bury it one dark night in the basement of the Congregational House? Dr. McCord had no reply to his proposition that he send another copy or two or three more if necessary."[171]

In colonial systems structured around notions of purity and exclusion, change and mutation required careful management. In Phillips's case, the embalming of African life proceeded on two registers. The first was the temporary reconstruction of African traditions which fulfilled the narrative requirements of *The African Witchdoctor*. The second was the cinematic representations of these reconstructions, etched indelibly in celluloid. The irony, of course, is that Phillips, perhaps more than any of his white contemporaries, was acutely aware of the enormous changes in Africa's social fabric inaugurated by the large-scale migrant labor system. While many officials and industrialists both expected and welcomed change as a necessary component of the civilizing mission, the profound disruptions wrought in the cultural sphere as black recruits moved to industrial centers was cause for alarm. Unexpectedly, though, it was not images of the "modern" that seemed to capture most miners' attention, but rather images of America's heroic and mythic frontier past.

4

You Don't Know Jack

Hollywood, Hybridity and the African Cowboy

In *Africans on African-Americans*, Yekutiel Gershoni relates a discussion he once had with historian L.H. Gann. The most popular films among African miners in Northern Rhodesia's Copperbelt, Gann informed him, were Wild West films, and their "favorite recreation" was simulating American cowboys.[1] While many African film scholars marginalize these experiences, cowboy films were adaptational tools by which migrant laborers and newly urbanized blacks distanced themselves from African rural life, subsumed ethnic differences, resisted time-work discipline, and constructed the very type of "dialogized, fragmented, and multiple consciousness that goes with urban life."[2] Moreover, just as Hollywood demarcated the frontier as a male preserve, industrial zones in southern Africa where films were shown during the interwar years were noteworthy for their male-only work compounds.[3] Westerns, in fact, offered a visual template for the construction of new male identities in imperialist milieus in which power was forcibly divested from traditionally patriarchal communities.

Locating African agency in the cultural practice of film-going requires looking at two related themes that have dominated interpretations of black spectatorship. The first reduces audiences to passive victims of cinema's overriding powers of ideological persuasion, while the second constitutes a crude inversion of this logic by resurrecting hidden forms of subaltern resistance.[4] Both typologies often fail to account for the nuances of actual viewing practices, especially as black spectators enthusiastically yoked the hagiographical dimensions of the American cowboy to emerging African forms of urban sociability by dressing up as cowboys, co-opting Country and Western musical idioms, and incorporating the Wild West into evolving dance styles.

White response to the African cowboy phenomenon was mixed. Many industry officials and colonial bureaucrats considered the genre a harmless diversion, but others feared its potential to challenge colonial authority if black spectators chose to identify with Indians or outlaws. Following Homi Bhabha, this chapter suggests that it was the very production of hybrid identities, as dynamic engines of disruption, change, and reconstitution that exposed the inherent instability of the colonial project as much as overtly resistant readings of the Hollywood code. As Bhabha puts it, "Mimicry is at once resemblance and menace."[5]

America's Wild West and Africa's "Cultural Driftwood"

In one of Africa's very first film reviews, the *Standard and Diggers' News* of April 6, 1895, reported that Johannesburg was stunned by Edison's Kinetoscope showing Buffalo Bill "in one of his quick-firing expeditions."[6] Distributors in southern Africa were soon importing celluloid cowboys and "horse operas" initially for the ocular pleasure of white settlers and the colonial elite, a pattern modified in the 1910–20s when some bioscopes began catering to black miners and township residents.[7] These urban bioscopes often attracted young street toughs, with Pretoria as a case in point where gangs like Frisco Ranch, Texas Ranch and the Upper-Cut Ranch ruled the streets.[8] And in Durban, the *abaquafi*, described by Absalom Vilakazi as "cultural driftwood" who often labored in the mines on weekdays, were notorious for their "absolute lack of respect for old traditions."[9] More than any other genre, cowboy films induced powerful behavioral affectations on miners and adolescents who began sporting Western fashion: a colorful handkerchief around the neck, cowboy hat perched on the head, and pants tied below the knee to imitate breeches. Often an acoustic guitar or harmonica completed the image. This style, adopted initially for urban African settings, was soon conveyed to outlying villages by those who had completed contractual obligations on the mines and were repatriated home to African reserves, where the cowboy theme was quickly imitated, with some variation.

This was no regional fad. Even in Monrovia, where a missionary reported in 1935 that "practically no one … has seen a moving picture," there was a rickety projector African spectators lovingly christened "The Wild West."[10] And in Leopoldville on the eve of independence, segregated theaters served as headquarters for the "Bills," a gang heavily influenced by Buffalo Bill films and Gene Autry's fashion sense.[11]

The presence of Africans in bioscopes featuring films that glorified gunslingers and horse thieves led to significant missionary concern. Frederick Bridgman and Ray Phillips feared that African townships and Locations constituted breeding grounds for vice and iniquity, replicating the social dislocations that plagued industrial/urban centers back home.[12] While missionaries oversaw censorship of excessive gunplay or Indian attacks on whites during the third tier of review, Wild West films were nevertheless included on the MCCC and remained a staple for years. In fact, by 1935, when Phillips and the Chamber handed over responsibilities to the Johannesburg City Council,[13] there were over 50 Westerns on the circuit, including *Cactus Trails* (1927), *The Golden Stallion* (1927) and *Ambushed* (1925). The weekly outdoor showings elicited an effusive response among the African working class as the sun went down and projectors turned on. The heroic arrival of the Western star, identifiable by his pearl-handled guns and white horse, was greeted with thunderous appreciation, an appeal heightened by the arrival of talkies in the 1930s.[14] Sound bolstered the excitement of the visuals, according to one cinema supervisor, for "the action is followed by the sound of galloping horses, bellowing of cattle, roaring of guns, and the peculiar cowboy songs and calls."[15] By World War II, the genre had spread beyond the Anglophone world and was fully entrenched in urban African social life. In Angola, officials concerned about the politics of social intermingling consistently enforced segregation. Restoration Cinema and National Cinema in downtown Luanda may have catered primarily to white settlers and the *assimilado* colonial elite, but at the latter African patrons were admitted if they remained behind the screen and watched films from the rear. But with the construction of the Colonial and Ngola cinemas, designed for the indigenous population, Africans were no longer allowed into theaters outside of African districts. These racial differences paralleled programming disparities: while dramas commonly screened at white theaters, cowboy films were standard fare in black neighborhoods, leading one African resident years later to recall "the most dreadful westerns," noting too that many Africans emulated the American frontier style.[16]

African audiences paid close attention to the action and shouted warnings to the hero as the enemy approached. In Luanda, viewers yelled, "Olha p'ra 'tras! Olha p'ra 'tras!" ("Look behind you! Look behind you!"),[17] and in South Africa, MCCC projectionist Archie Crawford noted that Africans universally hailed the screen protagonist as "Jack," or "Lo-Jack," and cheered their celluloid hero as he "galloped into town, shouldered his way through the bat-wing doors and bellied up to the bar." But this constituted mere foreplay for the more central action of "a barroom brawl with Jack either beating up or shooting down every badman in sight."[18] Jack also set his sights on other frontiers to the north. Phillips exported censored MCCC Wild West films (often Western documentaries) to the Rhodesias in part to counter the appearance of objectionable films there, as well as to provide new forms of recreation for Africa's black proletariat. Yet even these films could elicit consternation among white observers; cowboy images included in weekly programs in the mining areas of Que Que, Shamva and Wankie prompted some officials to complain about "gambling, abduction of females, and gun play."[19] Nevertheless, following exhibition at the Wankie Colliery, the films were shipped to Northern Rhodesia's Broken Hill mine, where open-air showings were implemented in 1923.[20] Notably, it was the oldest mines in operation in the Rhodesias, employing the highest percentage of "detribalized natives," which were among the first to invest in film showings. Wankie dated from 1904, and Broken Hill began active operations in 1906, soon emerging as Northern Rhodesia's first profitable venture in the extractive industries.[21] For many industry officials in the 1920s, films were a potential antidote to the disruptive side-effects of detribalization and proletarianization as Africans filled the ranks of the industrial workforce, but fears remained over the advisability of offering Westerns to miners.

The MCCC programs, with Wild West films included, continued their march northward and by 1928 had been introduced into copper-yielding areas skirting Northern Rhodesia's border with the Belgian Congo. The director of recreation for mining interests on the Copperbelt despaired that other than the cinema, only soccer held any attraction for most workers.[22] Thus, the Luanshya and Nchanga mines initiated bioscope shows for their workforce, constructing crude outdoor theaters in the compound recreation blocks to accommodate large crowds.[23] Shown weekly, these programs were highly anticipated events eliciting a voluble interaction between copper miners and screen heroes. The turnout was impressive: in 1931, an average of 1,200 spectators attended each showing in Nchanga, while roughly 2,000 attended in Luanshya.[24]

White observers of outdoor bioscope shows throughout southern Africa were often startled by thousands of black spectators screaming their approval for the hero as the violence unfolded: "A curious feature of all the African exhibitions," one mused, "is that no matter who the cowboy star is, he is universally hailed as 'Jack.' Whole audiences roar the word 'Jack' as each daring exploit wins him a laurel, or each fist lands on the villainous chin of the bad man."[25] Concurring with the Copperbelt's director of recreation, Roan Antelope Copper Mine manager Cecil F. Spearpoint reported that many recreational experiments met with little success due to the "apathy of the natives." But the bioscope was different; he noted that in the mid–1930s audiences frequently numbered 2,000 and generally gave "the most applause" to fight sequences. Even worse, according to Spearpoint, "Whenever there occurs a fight between two natives, the crowd which quickly assembles shouts, 'Jack—Jack—Jack.'" This phenomenon seemed proof that cowboy films "are entirely unsuited to a native audience, they do not understand them, cannot follow the plot or theme, and undoubtedly invariably get the wrong impression."[26] This negative assessment of African film literacy, though, seems rather ungracious considering problems of cultural translation and the previous censorship imposed on the films, often rendering narratives unintelligible. Nevertheless, Spearpoint's complaint about African comprehension would be echoed throughout southern Africa, with one Southern Rhodesian official offering this perspective in 1950:

> The operator of the mobile cinema told me that people like cowboy films best.... The cowboy films certainly cause uproarious amusement at times and the reason is easy to find. For long periods the audience sits completely bemused by pictures without action but with continuous meaningless (to it) dialogue: then violent action occurs, and the audience is released from its embarrassment and its bemusement and reacts almost hysterically. The fact is that the people are so glad to have something they can understand that they make a lot of noise when it happens.[27]

While many missionaries and officials railed against the pernicious effects of the Western, others believed they provided a harmless release from the tensions of townships and mines. Even Phillips, in selecting MCCC films, was soon suggesting that "Cow Boy films and adventure stories are shown with effects which are probably not very detrimental."[28] In September 1935, when he returned to the United States, he even mailed three Westerns to South Africa to be added to the MCCC.[29] Following World War II, when officials began scrutinizing the popularity of the gangster genre among the African underclass, a panelist at the Film in Colonial Development conference largely concurred with Phillips, declaring that in British Africa the "Western provides plenty of good wild fun with little danger and is generally popular."[30] More common, however, was the mixed opinion expressed by the likes of Rheinallt-Jones, who appreciated the short-term gains of a contented workforce, but fretted about a possible hidden down-side to exposing workers to a barrage of violent imagery:

> We have no evidence on the effects of films upon the native mine workers. My own impression is that they invariably side with the hero and the forces of law and order in Wild West films: this is confirmed by Dr. Ray Phillips and Mr. E. Hallendorff, but there is no information as to the ultimate effect. The sharp increase in the use of firearms and knives in criminal assaults on the Reef suggests the possibility of the influence of the cinema. It would be valuable to have research among mine natives on this subject.[31]

For some critics, fears of screen violence fueling detribalization through Africans mimicking the least savory ways of the white man were misplaced. From their perspective, cowboy violence actually paralleled the "primitive passions" of traditional Africa. For the South African Director of the National Bureau of Educational and Social Research, the "Jack" trend had ominous undertones:

> I notice that preference is given to "Wild West" pictures which are regarded as innocent amusement for natives as well as for European children. I have a feeling, however, that many of these pictures showing violent action, come so near the natives' way of primitive reaction, that these pictures might much more readily incite natives to acts of violence than they would in the case of European boys and girls who have grown up in the atmosphere of a civilized home.[32]

As in South Africa, the African enthusiasm for the Western on the Copperbelt often extended beyond mere adulation to emulation. Colin Beale of the Edinburgh House Bureau for Visual Aids was either unaware of the phenomenon or simply underestimated the creativity of African spectators when he stated, "The Western films in which there may be a lot of revolver shooting are much less harmful—there are no revolvers here and so no temptation to imitate."[33] In fact, those closer to events on the ground were often frightened by the capacity of the African to emulate the action. A contributor to the British Ministry of Information journal *Colonial Cinema* reported on "groups of African boys, dressed in home-made paper 'chaps' and cowboy hats, carrying crudely carved wooden pistols,… running around the native quarters of any industrial town in Northern Rhodesia shouting 'Jeke, Jeke, come on Jeke.' … Sometimes the boys affect a more sinister appearance, with a black mask over the eyes and a wooden dagger in the belt."[34] Louis Nell, who decades later served as director and cameraman for the Central African Film Unit, recalled a similar phenomenon while growing up as the child of a mining developer at Roan Antelope. Film heroes, he said, were called "Jackie" and found "many mimics" in the compounds: "Owners of [bi]cycles would play at 'cowboys' and emulate their hero by wearing some sort of home-made cowboy garb and charging round the compound using their cycles as steeds."[35]

The etymology of the name Jack is one of the more intriguing mysteries of colonial cinema in Africa. Two theories can be gleaned from the historical record. According to Cecil Spearpoint, an early Western entitled *Jack* had left an indelible impression on Roan Antelope's miners, leading to the indiscriminate naming of every Wild West hero on the silver screen. But Northern Rhodesian District Officer Harry Franklin later asserted that Western star Jack Holt was the inspiration for what he called the "Copper Belt Cowboy" phenomenon.[36] Of the two claims, the latter seems more likely, as I have failed to locate a pre–World War II Western entitled *Jack*.

Another theory that might be advanced is that Jack Hoxie, rather than Jack Holt, was the archetype for the term. While Holt certainly starred in Westerns during the interwar years, including *The Mysterious Rider* (1927) and *Sunset Pass* (1929), Hoxie's output was more extensive, and he starred exclusively as a cowboy during this period. By the early 1920s, he had become one of Universal's most prolific and popular Western stars. It may also be that it was simply the name of a protagonist on the screen, rather than an actor's name, which gave rise to Jack. Hoxie fits the bill here as well. An informal survey of Hoxie films produced between 1921 and 1933 reveals that in no fewer than 22 (out of 56) he plays a justice-seeking protagonist named Jack.[37] The fact is, Jack was an exceedingly popular pseudonym for Hollywood actors as well as for screen heroes. Just as African spectators indiscriminately cheered "Jack," many Western stars themselves adopted the moniker: Charles John Holt ("Jack Holt"); John Hartford Hoxie ("Jack Hoxie"); Addison Owen Randall ("Jack Randall"); and Jacob Benson Luden ("Jack Luden"). Clearly then, a similar process of stereotyped identity construction lies at the very core of both the celluloid frontier and the "real" frontier, for in America's Wild West old identities could be remolded beyond the confining institutions of Europe's highly stratified society. From early dime novels to "Buffalo Bill's Wild West" and beyond, the reproduced frontier delighted American readers and audiences, especially in the East, as cathartic forms of mass media and performative ritual during the industrialization of the continent.[38] Perhaps, after all, the "Jack" phenomenon in Africa was simply a reflection of a larger process of cowboy self-fashioning already set in motion in the studios of Hollywood.

White Power and the Invasion of the Body Snatchers

How are we to apprehend this mimetic impulse of colonial Others, this African appropriation and manipulation of America's postbellum myth of origins? Michael Taussig, Paul

Stoller, Graham Huggan, and Fritz Kramer have initiated a lively debate over similar African examples of identity metamorphosis.[39] Taussig, for example, notes the satirization of European culture in the Ivory Coast's *statues colons*—wooden figurative sculptures mysteriously sporting European garb—and even Nigeria's *mbari* huts housing mud statues of white people wearing eyeglasses and speaking into microphones, and mud sculptures caricaturing western consumer products such as bicycles and sewing machines.[40] Even more germane to the *faux* cowboy phenomenon, however, are the more embodied forms of European simulacra found among West African Yoruba dancers engaged in an ostensibly ironic performative mimicry, dancing frenetically in "ersatz tuxedos and evening gowns,"[41] or Hauka spirit-possession in Niger in which entranced mediums sacrifice dogs and eat poisonous plants while adopting the stiff mannerisms of French colonial officers: erect postures, salutes, about-faces, and the mechanized movements of military drill formations.[42]

What, then, are we to make of these oddly displaced (re)presentations of white identity in African settings? Taussig takes his cue from Walter Benjamin and places these cultural transactions in the context of what he calls the "magical power" of replication: "I want to dwell," he says, "on this notion of the copy, in magical practice, affecting the original to such a degree that the representation shares in or acquires the properties of the represented."[43] Drawing upon the long tradition of sympathetic magic in both Western and non–Western cultures, he elaborates on his conception of mimesis by postulating that a copy has the power to usurp or adversely influence the original from which it is forged. This immediately brings to mind two related questions: Is power truly a zero sum game, as this sense of mimesis seems to imply, wherein the efficacy of the copy and that which it represents are locked in a perennial struggle? And if so, are there precedents for such? One paradigm that comes to mind is the cruel effectiveness of a voodoo doll, whose power is in inverse proportion to the ebbing fortitude of the intended target. Or to borrow a film analogy, one recognizes in Taussig's formulation a rough colonial equivalent of the *Invasion of the Body Snatchers* (1956), in which alien forces engage in bodily possession in order to destroy the very hosts they emulate. His point, in short, is that the mimetic behavior of the Other directly targets the repressive structures of colonial authority.[44]

In the African construction of Jack, one can indeed detect a degree of anti-colonial or proletarian resistance channeled through African film-going practices. Just as 19th-century English workers developed quotidian forms of refusal when faced with the cold imposition of industrial time-work discipline, the subtle resistance of African males migrating to town and mine was not lost on industry officials and colonial bureaucrats. Listen to one official in Northern Rhodesia's capital of Lusaka, for example, complaining that

> the local effect of showing these "cowboy" films to native audiences is plain to see on every street. The popularity of cowboy shirts, 10 gallon hats and the rest of it. Harmless? Of course. But what possible grounds exist for persuading anyone that it is only the harmless side that makes a mental impression. The idea that to stand and speak to anyone with hands in pockets, lounging, and possibly giving the hat … an insolent backward tilt is to show a high degree of sophistication, is hardly a desirable trait to encourage in our local natives.[45]

While not as spectacular as the radical endgame solutions implemented by the Luddites or even the Mau Mau, such "insolent" behavior does suggest at least a hint of embryonic African resistance to foreign rule. White elites, of course, frequently noted the "pernicious" effects of cinema, but the concern expressed above over bodily adornment and "bad attitude" shows that just as fundamental was the struggle over who would retain jurisdiction over the signifying practices of the body. Ironically, Western fashion as early as the 1920s served as a testimony to an urban African sophistication, a self-constructed sign of status and manhood; it offered common ground for those of different ethnicities on the street who, invoking the negative assessment of Vilakazi, had "no address, culturally speaking."[46] Status, it must be stressed, has always been inscribed upon the body, whether by cicatrization, tattoos, makeup, or outer integuments. But it is precisely when the forms of Western fashion breach the specific social context in which they "should" be embedded—in this case the American frontier—that they are potentially transformed from relatively innocent duplication of social custom to more purposive acts of defiance.[47] As we have seen earlier with the encounter between Phillips and Zulu healer Shangase, the replication of visual cues in very different circumstances imbues otherwise mundane objects and forms with new political overtones. Context is everything.

But this interpretation of cowboy mimesis as an exclusively parodic or counter-hegemonic act, is in the end of limited efficacy for our purposes. Taussig's celebratory postulation of mimesis as a symbolic gesture directed by the colonized exclusively at the colonizer is based on an implicit ethnocentric bias; as Eric Gable and Graham Huggan warn us, "We tend to ventriloquize our own desire for subversion."[48] In our almost compulsive search to recover traces of colonial contestation, we must be wary of theoretical models that fail to engage the nuances of the everyday identity politics of the colonized.

Following this line of thinking, Huggan has criticized Taussig for conflating the consequential, if subtle, distinctions between mimicry and mimesis. Mimicry, Huggan contends, is first and foremost a disruptive or parodic imitation directed by the copy toward its originary form, while mimesis is best conceived as a form of symbolic representation existing within a broader field of cultural mediation between "different worlds and people."[49] Huggan's argument parallels Stoller's interpretation of the Hauka's appropriation and ritualistic redeployment of French mannerisms in Niger, who argues these mimetic acts must be theorized not as a strategy to destabilize or destroy the "original," but on the contrary, as a means of "tap[ping] into the extraordinary power [of ruling whites to] be recircuited for local uses."[50] Power is reconceptualized here as a generative force rather than a zero sum game, and capable of being redeployed effectively by the underclass for purposes other than direct resistance to colonial rule.

It is this conception of power and identity as a manipulation of signs that clarifies the various levels of meaning embedded within Africa's cowboy semiotics. Drawing upon the cinematic imagery of America's postbellum frontier, Africans appropriated the paraphernalia and panache of Wild West heroes to construct new urban identities to distance themselves from those left behind in local villages. This rural/urban tension can be heard in the response given to an anthropologist who queried one resident of East London, South Africa, about the desirability of town versus country life: "It is too dull in the country. It would be better if the Government established some bioscopes and made it attractive."[51] Ultimately, though, it was workers' new-found involvement in the cash nexus that led to significant intra-racial tensions between working-class migrants and indigenous elites in the reserves and urban Welfare Societies. For Americans, the frontier myth looked backward; for Africans, the theme was forward-looking, helping to construct new cosmopolitan identities that reflected the growing divide between old ethnic bonds that historically ruled the countryside, and new forms of social affiliation in the streets of the urban-industrial metropolis.

Of Class and Cowboys

While for white Americans the Western functioned as a nostalgic trope justifying nation-building through westward expansion, for Africans it provided a ready cache of images for negotiating the demands of modern life in imperialist milieus, as well as a release from the drudgery of life on the lower rungs of the industrial ladder. Crucial to the experiences of Copperbelt cowboys in towns and industrial frontiers was a changing sense of identity as ethnic differences were, to some extent at least, relegated to the background. Fueling this new form of subjectification was southern Africa's industrial revolution lorded over by European powers that implicated the nascent African proletariat, and even the urban underclass, in a cash economy. The link between the novelty of Western vogue and Africa's changing socio-economic order must be emphasized, for, as Jean Baudrillard argues, fashion is linked to the spectacle and is integral to societies structured around a money economy and stratified by class:

> In effect, fashion does not reflect a natural need of change: the pleasure of changing clothes, objects, cars comes to sanction the constraints of another order psychologically, constraints of social differentiation and prestige. The effects of fashion only appear in socially mobile societies (and beyond a certain threshold of money). Ascending or descending social status must be registered in the continual flux and reflux of distinctive signs.[52]

It is worth noting that Frederick Jackson Turner also believed that while the frontier was the determining factor in American development, it functioned in part through a process of self-fashioning. Western settlers, he argued, were faced with negotiating the strange new environment of the frontier, wherein Europeans were both metaphorically and literally stripped of their raiments and reduced to a basic struggle for survival. Fired by an intensely individualist ethos, these trailblazers overcame both natural impedimenta and nearby savages as they created a new world in the West.

In contrast, African spectators, while perhaps exhibiting similar instincts for survival, collectively corralled Western fashion as part of a larger group ritual. Films were watched *en masse* with audiences numbering in the thousands, and spectators formed cowboy-inspired gangs that patrolled streets and townships, correlating the putative freedom of the American frontier with their own newfound sense of social (and geographic) mobility in the urban milieu. For many whites in Africa, of course, such freedoms, especially during the period of swelling urban populations, promised little more than higher rates of delinquency and a potential threat to white rule. In 1947, one concerned citizen writing to *The Natal Mercury* complained bitterly about the dangers of showing Africans "fantastic exhibitions of gun law ... love scenes and scantily-clad women." Pulling no punches, this author who signed his editorial "Stop the Rot," suggested that the "qualification most needed to make the Native into a good citizen is discipline."[53]

Equally important, though, as James Burns has pointed out, is that even urban African elites, no doubt dismayed at their loss of traditional controls over young town-dwellers and migrant workers, often joined the rising chorus in arguing for stricter race-based censorship.[54] Thus, the corrupting influence of the Western became a leading topic at a 1947 African Provincial Council meeting in Luanshya, where councilman Harrison Chungu despaired that "these films are leaving a very bad impression on the children and it is easy for them to imitate." Chungu concluded that "the showing of 'Jacks' and people fighting should entirely go off because even for the adults they are infectious; they affect their minds."[55]

Circumstantial evidence for the inherent dangers of imitative behavior among the lower orders was, in fact, not difficult to find. In Mufulira, six African adolescents arrested for robbery and assault claimed that they were merely acting out violent scenes from American films.[56] Similarly, a 1949 South Africa commission studying growing township unrest reported that "responsible native leaders had complained to them that films shown to Africans portrayed 'cowboys, crooks and pickpockets,'" and that the "scholars and young children attending these film[s] try and imitate what they see, with the result that they are initiated in crime at an early age."[57]

Nor was film-fueled criminality restricted to southern Africa. In Sapele, Nigeria, residents were terrified when an avid cinema fan going by the long-winded moniker "Lucky, the new Sheriff in Town" threatened patrons with a sawed-off shotgun at the Olympia, the town's only cinema. Predictably, Lucky's good fortune quickly ran out when he was fatally shot by unimpressed police right outside the foyer.[58] Moreover, tensions between African elites and young spectators failed to diminish following decolonization, as we see in the case of Nigerian social outcasts called "toughians" who wore Western attire, terrorized townspeople and called out to each other using nicknames like "John Wayne," "Texas," "Django," and "Nevajojo."[59] Elites in Burkina Faso (formerly Upper Volta) complained of similar problems in coping with the country's boisterous underclass. Following independence in 1960, both outdoor cinemas in Ouagadougou retained their architectural layout in which less expensive seats (concrete benches) for the urban poor were situated in the uncovered pit located directly in front of a whitewashed concrete wall serving as film screen. Despite the name "la place des indiennes" given to these third-class seats filled with gang members and street hustlers, the whooping and hollering invariably was in support of popular Western icons pacifying the frontier. Pointedly, what African elders in higher-priced first- and second-class seats found particularly objectionable was the proclivity of these "indiennes" to try to "relive the films."[60]

Tall Tales of Passive Reception and Triumphant Resistance

African leaders, historians and postcolonial filmmakers, pushing for cultural independence and frustrated with American control of the continental film market, have long condemned Hollywood's hegemony over African viewers. Kwame Nkrumah, channeling Clausewitz perhaps, once declared that the culture of the colonizer is simply war pursued by other means to pacify Africa: "Even the cinema stories of Hollywood are loaded. One has only to listen to the cheers of an African audience as Hollywood's heroes slaughter the red Indians ... to understand the effectiveness of this weapon. For, in the developing continents, where the colonialist heritage has left a majority of illiterates, even the smallest child gets the message contained in the blood and thunder stories emanating from California."[61] Nkrumah's decision, then, to nationalize Ghana's film industry after leading the country to independence in 1957 should come as no surprise.

Onookome Okome, himself a spectator of colonial cinema in Nigeria, underscored Nkrumah's claim. Growing up, he witnessed the ideological transition from the mobile cinema shows organized by the British colonial government to those later organized by transnational corporations. While the Colonial Office after World War II exhibited propaganda and instructional films to bolster colonial development schemes, privately funded cinemas of the post-independence period were designed to ensure the largest possible audience with the goal of flooding African markets with British consumer goods.[62] It was through the latter phenomenon, Okome asserts, that the Western infiltrated rural areas and destroyed the integrity of traditional life.[63] Cowboy films glorifying the whitening of the American frontier, he suggests, led inexorably to forms of self-loathing for people of color, a sentiment seconded by Nwachukwu Ukadike who argues that films were a "powerful tool for indoctrinating Africans into foreign cultures, including their ideals and aesthetics."[64] The basis for these strident attacks is not difficult to locate. Indeed, the fundamental aesthetic guiding the cowboy genre can be construed as encapsulating, in compressed form, the general parameters of late–19th-century European expansion, which had dire consequences for Africa following the 1884–85 Berlin Conference. As Tom Englehardt brusquely describes it, "The viewer is forced behind the barrel of a repeating rifle and it is from that position, through its gun sights, that he receives a picture history of western colonialism and imperialism."[65]

Not all theorists, however, share this belief in the inability of black audiences to engage critically Hollywood's Wild West machine. Manthia Diawara has called for black spectators to deconstruct the cultural identities imposed upon them, while bell hooks has echoed this call for resistance by invoking the putative power of the gaze to counteract strategies of domination.[66] The film-going experience, she argues, opens a unique space for spectators—in her case those doubly stigmatized for being born both black and female—to engage in a liberatory counter-gaze.[67] A resistant reading of a film allocates new powers to the cinema consumers, offering them alternatives to a demeaning identification with the tools of their own domination. Reflecting a shift in film studies from structure to agency, this increased attention to audience reception broadens our understanding of the cultural interface between product and consumer, between text and interpreter.

Proponents of spectatorial resistance, attempting to reveal what one might call ocular examples of James Scott's "weapons of the weak," have left no stone unturned in recovering traces of subaltern agency expressed through film reception. Rob Nixon has explored post–World War II patterns of film-going in popular township cinemas such as Odin and Balansky's. In urban ghettos suffering from the strictures of apartheid, many youths were making an identity transition from a subculture of masculinity informed by American cowboy-worship, now considered by some to be an outdated fad, to gangster-worship. Tsotsi gang members flocked to the new releases, identifying with Hollywood screen toughs such as Humphrey Bogart and Richard Widmark. This phenomenon, Nixon argues, implies "young male Sophiatowners ... energetically resisted the moral resolution of Hollywood gangster movies."[68] But were these viewers truly abandoning the moral drive of these films by engaging in acts of resistant identification? Members of the "Americans," one of Sophiatown's toughest gangs, did indeed sport "straw hats, elegant cardigans, brown and white shoes and narrow black trousers called 'Bogarts.'"[69] And following the release of Richard Widmark's *The Street with No Name* (1948) in non–European bioscopes, *Drum* editor Anthony Sampson noted spectators' admiration for Widmark's "bad guy" character:

> The cinema was packed with tsotsi's, shouting and cat-calling. I was the only white man. As I sat down, between Bill and Can, I heard a murmur behind me of "Laanis," the tsotsi word for white men. Everyone was talking Afrikaans, tsotsi slang or Chicago-ese. A man in a straw boater and a green and yellow shirt turned around to us from the next row, snarling as he chewed gum. "Say, ain't youse the Drum guys, brother?"[70]

Mac Fenwick has applauded Nixon's analysis of South African urban blacks' appropriation and "plundering" of the Hollywood gangster figure.[71] This claim of triumphant resistance through oppositional readings, though, may be called into question. While representatives of law and order generally triumphed over the criminal element, it was evident in most gangster films that audiences were expected to identify with the outlaws. In fact, it was the overwhelming popularity of the Prohibition-era underworld that was partially responsible for the 1934 Hays Code restricting depictions of graphic violence and, tellingly, "imitable" crimes. For this reason Bogart's roles shifted from villain to hero, with his characters retaining many of the shady but romantic qualities of the gangster. Furthermore, in the case of Widmark (and James Cagney and Edward G. Robinson), the genre's *noir* underpinnings ensured that regardless of the outward resolution of the films where moral retribution is visited upon the bad guys due to industry pressure, the urban underworld was surreptitiously glorified. Township gang members, then, read these texts in roughly the way in which they were intended: criminal endeavors, the films insinuate, offer to marginalized populations a means to move up the social ladder when socially acceptable avenues have been foreclosed.

If the aforementioned examples of resistant readings to Hollywood should be viewed with caution, unearthing concrete examples of resistance to the Western has proved even more daunting. The specter of anti-colonial struggles fueled by cinematic renderings of bank holdups or stagecoach raids may have raised concern in colonial settings—indeed, one projectionist wondered if "black mineworkers identify the Red Indians as black people"[72]—but many agreed with Rheinallt-Jones that "the Wild West film best suits their [mineworkers'] needs."[73] The colonized more commonly critiqued propaganda-instructional films, despite *Drum* magazine contributor Lewis Nkosi's later claim that his adolescent years were spent deconstructing the Western:

> I definitely identified with the weak ... people who were unarmed. Not because they were particularly black, or because I knew anything about Indian culture versus white culture, but simply because they were unarmed and I saw the same forces ranged against them, the same technologies ranged against them, that seemed to be in play in my own particular situation.... It is possible that the color element also came into it.[74]

We shall revisit the counter-gaze in the context of labor recruiting and propaganda films, but here we must recognize that theorizing "resistant readings" as the dominant mode of cross-cultural reception often fails to account for the full range of micro-politics involved as African audiences put cowboy flair to work in local settings. Whether stereotyping African film-goers as helpless victims of Hollywood's ideological warfare, or, conversely, as triumphant insurgents deconstructing cinematic narrative to break the bonds of colonial oppression, these two positions are ultimately reductionist and occlude the intra-racial tensions of a world undergoing rapid industrialization and urbanization. Moreover, both positions posit an overdetermined white/black dichotomy: the cultural imperialist school denounces Hollywood's hegemony and the irrepressible power of a united "white" world using images as a form of warfare, while the spectatorial resistance school champions the ability of all "blacks" to challenge that very power through a visual praxis.[75] Yet Africans prior to the independence era rarely perceived the colonial project within such binary terms. In South Africa, for instance, black ethnics readily distinguished between three "white" populations: Afrikaner, British, and American. Hortense Powdermaker perceived a similar distinction in Northern Rhodesia in ascertaining the popularity of the genre: "The cowboy," she maintained, "is white, but not European."[76] Where cases of resistant viewing did occur, white populations were generally played off against one another: the African underclasses gleefully co-opted and emulated American cowboy machismo to subvert the authority of Afrikaner settlers and British officials.

Rather than positing uniform, unchanging and ahistorical African cultures countering, through deconstructive readings, the cultural invasions of the white world, we must be sensitive to what Stuart Hall describes as the continuous production of identity that occurs within, rather than outside, representation itself.[77] Identities, Hall argues, are never stable entities but are constructed through the very forms of media commonly believed to "reflect" them. But how is such a thing possible? Below we look at how the attributes of the American cowboy were appropriated selectively as ready tools by the African underclasses in constructing new hybrid identities.

The Africanization of America's Frontier Myth

It is precisely the inherent instability of regimes of representation that allows us to reconstruct vestiges of African agency despite the overwhelming affective power of the cowboy genre. The scant traces available suggest that, in fact, it was the image of the West itself, as much as the subjectivity of the African underclass, which underwent modification even as Africans flocked to see the latest blood-and-thunder thrillers.

In a study of cross-cultural comprehension by Elihu Katz and Tamar Liebes, 50 small groups in Israel viewed the 1980s television drama *Dallas*—an urban, 20th-century Western with corporate overtones. The focus groups were composed of Russian and Moroccan immigrants in Israel, kibbutz residents, and Israeli Arabs. Their responses were then compared with those from target groups in Los Angeles to discover the "critical apparatus marshaled by lower middle-class groups of varying ethnicity" as they decoded the values and meanings embedded within the episode.[78] Viewers, they found, do not passively absorb the meanings and messages of foreign media, but rather bring their own social experiences to bear in the process of cultural translation. Moreover, this process of incorporation "is filtered by group dynamics—in conversation with significant others—and can be done in a variety of ways: by affirmation or negation of the moral of a story, for example, through identification with a character, or by some more critical judgment."[79]

This interpretation bears remarkable affinity to bioscope showings of Westerns throughout southern Africa. Shows were interactive and voluble events, with spectators loudly contributing their own piece of the puzzle as their hero Jack resolved conflicts with Indians and outlaws on the American frontier:

> "I know this cowboy. He does not play with anyone except his brother."
> "They all fear him because they cannot fight him."
> "Oh, that man will soon receive a blow."
> "He has let that man go because the man is a weakling."
> "Ahass! One! One! Waan!"
> "Look at that other man!"
> "Oh yes, that is the only man who can fight Jack!"
> "Look at his ears, they indicate that is a furious man!"
> "That man in feathers is a Negro!"
> "No. You do not know Negroes! He is a red Indian."
> "Look at that man! He is smoking opium."
> "What is it for?"
> "Oh, so you do not know that it removes the sense of fear."
> "Hmm, Jack is very clever, he can fight them all."[80]

Inexorably, African audience interaction led to the "Africanization" of America's frontier myth, a phenomenon recognized by Powdermaker studying socio-cultural adjustment on the Copperbelt. "The cowboy," she said, "has become part of the African world and has even taken on African characteristics. He is supposed to have witchcraft, to be the son of a "big" man, and to show traditional respect toward his elders."[81] Others were less sanguine that respect for traditional authority was upheld during this transformation of Hollywood's Wild West genre. In Tanganyika, for instance, one investigator of African town life complained, "The cult of the cowboy clothes is the safety-valve of the dangerous mob element which is always likely to be part of Dar es Salaam. They are unformed Hitlerjugend, as yet, their uniform jeans and wide hat, their march the gun-on-the-hip cowboy slouch, waiting for a Feuhrer to give respectability to their longing to be admired, to be feared, to have a place in the sun." Yet even this believer in the relative malleability of African audiences confessed that, after a few years of "direct imitation," the Jack trend was modulated by "[local] peculiarities, such as the uchingo jeans drawn down tight to well above the ankle, like shrimping pants, and drain-pipe thin."[82]

These inter-cultural transactions extended beyond mere fashion to other idioms. In South Africa, Bhaca and Zulu dancers in Durban and Johannesburg incorporated cowboy fashion in the Isicathulo dance choreography. This Gumboot dance, involving synchronized foot stamping and hand clapping, evolved as a leisure pursuit on the mines and spread throughout southern Africa as workers were repatriated. Dressed in broad-brimmed cowboy hats, bright red shirts with tassels, black trousers and boots, these hybrid cowboy-dancers could be found as late as 1970 performing to the sound of acoustic guitars in Johannesburg's gold mining compounds.[83] Similarly, in British territories, distinctly new hybrid forms began to emerge by the 1950s. A.L. Epstein discovered that workers relaxing around industry-funded Beer Halls devised a new musical style derived from the American singing cowboy: "Young men," he said, "dressed in gaily-coloured open-necked shirts, and wearing cowboy hats, squat on the ground or move around strumming a guitar and singing the latest Copperbelt 'hit-numbers' or otherwise seek to gain the attention of the bakapenta, the 'young ladies of the town.'" These popular numbers that were sometimes made into gramaphone records, Epstein noted, exhibited heavy influence from the "'hill-billy' type of cowboy song, but are clearly reinterpreted in terms of African musical idiom."[84]

Of course, some whites attributed new hybrid cowboy identities to African ignorance of "real life" in 20th-century America. At a Central Province Teachers' Refresher course in Lusaka, the colony's chief information officer stated,

> apparently large numbers of Africans still believe that Cowboy films portray the present American way of life. Several teachers said that if it was widely publicized that "cowboy" life in the form shown in the films ceased as long as forty years ago in America and that it is merely "playacting" ... then Africans would appreciate that they were not observing present day habits and activities of "European" Americans.[85]

Others contradicted this, arguing that cowboy films were popular because they were virtually the only pictures available, and the only ones comprehensible by a population with only rudimentary English skills. "The African [male] in the towns," claimed one official "has come to expect the cowboy picture and he does not, we believe, relate it to any particular form of real life."[86] African elites, though, emphasized class differences between themselves and the masses: "We ourselves understand that these films are only plays and that Europeans do not really behave in the way the pictures show. Some of us like them, others do not bother to attend because they get no benefit from them and their desire is to be educated by films."[87] In any event, the cowboy genre still resonates in 21st-century Africa in interesting ways. In 2005, an American art collector scouring Ghanaian villages for traditional artifacts was surprised by the following question from a local resident: "Do you own any horses?"[88]

This debate calls for broader consideration of the cultural distinctions negotiated by African spectators: To what extent were images of the American frontier alien impositions? For Okome, foreign films undermined local Nigerian institutions because they depicted a strange white world completely outside the African purview:

> The first set of images that local populations saw was of white faces, doing outlandish things in their environment. These film images were far removed from the social reality of the indigenous people. As an art form the film medium was not native to these people and since it was brought to them by the same people who colonized them, this form of art was seen as something outside of their social life.[89]

From this perspective, an overwhelming cultural chasm divided cowboys and American consumers of Wild West images from African audiences. In fact, though, it is not apparent how even the average American read the Western, for the mythic construction of the frontier has two discernible strains pushing in opposing directions, suggesting that, for American audiences, cowboy films provided different forms of belonging and identity. Virginia Wexman describes the genre as "steeped in … American patriotism" and an idealized construction of national origins based on the Jeffersonian "sanctity of the family farm."[90] Yet as Eric Hobsbawm emphasizes, the Wild West "only lasted a short time, its heyday falling between the Civil War and the collapse of mining and cattle booms of the 1880s," and cannot be understood outside its individualist and male-dominated ethos where "beyond the frontier of farm-settlement and city there were no families."[91] It was precisely the cinematic renderings of the lone male maverick pacifying the cactus-filled landscape, of course, which dominated most films of the genre. Thus, for many Americans, the Western hearkened back to a seminal moment in postbellum national development—when the pressures for (white) political reunification and territorial expansion were at a premium due to the bitterly divisive legacy of the Civil War.

This account of the film-going experience among American viewers indicates that a somewhat different process of self-fashioning was at work for Africans who knew little, if anything, of the historical evolution of the United States. Workers in Johannesburg and other mining centers were certainly not relocating families to areas of frontier settlement nor riding on lone horseback through canyons and prairies. Nor, as we have seen, were these filmic representations of the open frontier viewed quietly in isolation. Rather, compound and Location bioscopes were intensely social gatherings bringing together thousands of spectators of varying ethnicities, reinterpreting the American frontier through the prism of local cultural peculiarities.

Despite this cultural divide separating the mythical American frontier from the life experiences of the African colonized, several features of commonality can indeed be gleaned that provided a means by which the African rank and file were able to identify with the screen images. Powdermaker offers two such points of convergence. First, the repetitive and stereotypical quality of the cowboy drama parallels the oral tradition of African storytelling in which "the brave hero, always on the side of the good people, fights hard, sometimes infatuates a girl, and always triumphs through his manly strength." Walter Ong sees this polarity as endemic to the structure of orality in non-literate cultures. Just as villains require constant vilification, heroes require veneration reinforced throughout the narrative.[92] The second point of convergence is, in fact, situated within the first. According to Powdermaker the strong identification with "Jack" was due not only to the ritualistic nature of African folk tales, but because "intertribal wars were part of African life, and success in fighting was one way of gaining prestige."[93]

A very different line of convergence might also be suggested here. In addition to the robberies and shootouts that provided much of the action, one of the hallmarks of the Western, especially with the inauguration of location shooting, was the physical landscape of the Plains and prairie. Films played up the dramatic and arid topography of the West with its rolling hills, scrub grass and winding rivers. Comparing the contours of the American West to rural areas in southern Africa, one cannot help but notice a similarity. From the Ciskei up through the rural landscapes of Zimbabwe and Zambia, one hardly needs to stretch the imagination to understand how Africans would associate the frontier with their own environment, an association which may well have been lost on more cynical observers.

While these arguments are suggestive, they still fail to explain fully the pervasive popularity of the genre in industrial areas where workers and townsmen constituted a detribalized population removed, to some extent, from the steadying influence of traditional folkways. There were, in fact, other themes in Western narratives that spoke more immediately to miners and urbanites. The railroad, for instance, so prominent in Wild West films, no doubt held a fascination for those recruits in southern Africa's industrial centers whose transition from peasant to proletariat was generally facilitated by railroads chartered to transport new recruits to the mines. Similarly, Western storylines featuring mining camps, gold strikes and boomtowns surely resonated with miners in Johannesburg and elsewhere. In particular, *The Gold Stallion* (1927), on the MCCC rotation as late as 1935, must have elicited amusement as the plot revolves around a search for a lost gold mine.[94]

Another interpretation might be forwarded for the seemingly anomalous attraction of the American frontier for those living in urban ghettos and industrial compounds. In *Violent Land: Single Men and Social Disorder from the Frontier to the Inner City*, David Courtwright argues that the migration of young males in search of opportunity in the American West led to violence in the frontier beyond the reach of familial or legal restraints. Ironically, this violence has been replicated somewhat, Courtwright avers, in the modern inner city where those same restraints are often deplorably absent.[95] A similar manifestation can be discerned in southern Africa where industrial centers like the Witwatersrand and the Copperbelt, with their expanding populations of migrant workers and townsmen, doubled as both frontier boomtowns and modern municipalities. Will Wright's contention then, that "the cowboy became more popular as America became industrial," holds for southern Africa as well. Young males migrating from rural kraals embraced the freedom from social controls promised by the Wild West films and appropriated characteristics of the frontier as they engaged in the process of cowboy self-fashioning.

This chapter has recast those spectators embedded within the process of southern Africa's nascent industrialization and urbanization as active agents in constructing new forms of subjectivity. Although hybridity has gained currency in post-colonial studies for theorizing identity formation in the peripheries, we must heed the warnings of Brah and Coombes, who remind us that the expression has often "resulted in an uncritical celebration of the traces of cultural syncretism ... without paying adequate attention to economic, political and social inequalities."[96] Similarly, Rod Edmond has characterized Bhabha's championing of hybridity and cultural indeterminacy as a "disturbing political blindness," thus failing to appreciate the destructive side effects of unequal power relations,[97] while Aletta Norval notes that the difficulties of living a life of indeterminacy was nowhere more evident than in apartheid South Africa, where the Coloured community faced ostracism from both sides of the color line. Author and ex-gang member Don Mattera, for instance, was doubly stigmatized, initially by the "reclassification trauma" in apartheid's early years. Due to his mixed heritage (a Griqua grandmother and Italian grandfather), he was categorized as "Mixed" or "Coloured." That this racial classification placed him above his black brethren was of little consolation; rather, racial coding simply drove a wedge between himself and his "true African heritage." Accepting the dubious privileges of being Coloured would have been tantamount to accepting the entire edifice of white supremacy, and for this reason he rejected the label in favor of "black South African."[98] His second stigma was imposed not by the state, but through an insult unwisely, if casually, hurled at the adolescent gang leader by another township youth. Tellingly, this affront also alluded to the "impurity" of Mattera's identity, but in a context that resonates with the theme of this chapter: "I mused as I passed Mukkadam's butchery. His son Ghalab, had tasted the wrath of my fists inside the classroom after he had called me Hopalong Kaffir—instead of Cassidy because of the way I used to walk."[99] Mattera's obvious displeasure in suffering derogatory accusations of impurity, either as a Coloured or black cowboy, suggests that we celebrate his hybridization with peril if we fail to investigate the broader workings of colonial power that often dictated terms of identity through forced displacements and racial classifications. Despite these warnings, however, there are reasons to disassociate the African cowboy from the more problematic forms of hybridity most commonly discussed in the postcolonial canon. First, the mimesis of the African cowboy functions on the level of sign manipulation, rather than being the product of miscegenation. As such, it is both mutable and reversible. Second, the spectator-cum-cowboy remained in control of the resulting hybrid form, even reinterpreting the Wild West to suit his needs. Finally, while Bhabha has been taken to task for not paying due attention to the political realities of asymmetrical power arrangements, it is worth noting that the Wild West itself was never truly the sanctuary for a white American masculinity that it claimed for itself, and one expressed through early Western films.

Not surprisingly, Bhabha himself has spoken of the American frontier as the very site where the common stereotype is shown, in his words, to be "as anxious as it is assertive."[100] For it is precisely in those frontier areas where illicit mixings and insecure cultural borders were so prevalent that one finds the need to assert, and to reassert *ad infinitum*, the myriad justifications for white domination in the face of the savage Other: "The American border," Bhabha tells us, is the "cultural signifier of a pioneering, male 'American' spirit always under the threat from races and cultures beyond the border or frontier."[101] The secret of the Wild West, and one that runs counter to the narrative thrust we see depicted in countless films, is that it was always an arena of indeterminacy and self-fashioning.[102] Richard Hofstadter, then, ruminating on Frederick Jackson Turner's famous frontier thesis, was perhaps more correct than he knew when he declared that its emotive appeal was its very "property of plasticity" that allowed it to be put to a variety of purposes in diverse contexts.[103] Throughout much of Africa, images of the American frontier served as adaptational tools for townsmen, miners and street youths forging new bonds of community and affiliation.

5

From Red Blanket to Civilization

Movies and Migration in South Africa

In 1925 Henry Melville Taberer, native labor advisor for the Native Recruiting Corporation (NRC), prepared a screenplay on the Transkei that would become a staple for black spectators in South Africa. Initially entitled *Native Life in the Cape Province*, Taberer's labor recruiting film would be produced along the same lines as one already in rotation in Mozambican recruiting zones, and provide "a representation of the development of the South African Native—one of the greatest factors in the industrial progress of South Africa." During production, Taberer re-titled the film *From Red Blanket to Civilization* to reflect more accurately the projected "development" of the African. There appear to be no extant copies of the film, but Chamber of Mines' memoranda as well as a surviving storyboard open an aperture on the link between labor recruiting, African migrancy and the introduction of cinema into outlying areas of the Union.

While the historiography on South African labor migration is voluminous, many scholars assume a seamless transition to an effective, if super-exploitative, system of labor recruitment following the creation of the NRC under Chamber of Mines' auspices in 1912.[1] Saddled with discriminatory legislation and huddled into overcrowded reserves, we are told, Africans were powerless to resist the chamber's hegemonic sway in its relentless search for black labor to service the Witwatersrand. This narrative has much to tell us. Yet the fact that the chamber's extensive film propaganda campaign targeted the very areas where rural impoverishment should have allowed for little resistance, suggests a more nuanced story. In part a case study of African response to the propaganda program in the Eastern Cape, this chapter complicates the picture of migration and recruitment, for it was against the backdrop of a perpetual labor shortage that chamber officials resorted to producing and showing films as a recruiting device. Designed to coax rather than coerce, this strategy to sell South Africa's industrial revolution in the bush had the important secondary function of introducing hundreds of thousands—perhaps millions—of Africans to motion pictures for the first time. This chapter has four objectives. First, it contributes to our investigation of early African film spectatorship, exploring the conditions under which the colonized in reserves became consumers of the bioscope, rather than mere "hewers of wood and drawers of water." While miners and township sophisticates enjoyed Chaplin and cowboys thrillers as early as World War I, in villages it was mining recruiting films in the 1920s that provided many Africans with their first exposure to the cinema. Second, the chapter examines how the chamber produced films to enhance efficiency and workers' health for those already toiling in the shafts. Despite their obscurity today, South Africa's propaganda films shown in mining compounds were, in fact, a pioneering example of colonial cinema in Africa. Third, this chapter reveals that to retain audiences, mobile film units relied on the contribution of indigenous interpreters and headmen who had their own stake in perpetuating the migrant labor system. But while newspaper accounts of black spectatorship smugly recounted the spectacle of Africans running in terror from moving pictures projected on outdoor screens, NRC memoranda provide a revealing counter-narrative, showing that viewers critically engaged the films, and that officials took these responses seriously in calculating production/exhibition decisions. Finally, evidence presented here may also assist future research on African perceptions toward wage labor, a field requiring more attention to the micro-negotiations found in a variety of occupations. As Birkenbach and van der Merwe note, "It is generally accepted by psychologists that an organization's reward structure and pay practices will have important implications for employees." However, they add, "It is not surprising to find little or no research on perceptions of pay practices in the South African context.... There are few guidelines as to how the Black worker may perceive reward assumptions and pay administrative practices."[2]

Migration and the Witwatersrand Labor Supply

Historians differ on whether the dominant pressures for labor mobilization in South Africa were located within the political or economic realms. But in most cases, they both highlight "push" factors and other forms of forced extrusion from the reserves, generally only footnoting strategies of recruitment developed by the mining industry. Admittedly, "push" catalysts leading to the exodus of workers bound for diamond and gold mines, white farms and railroad construction sites were numerous. Foremost among them was the crippling overpopulation suffered by the Tsonga, Tswana, Zulu, Xhosa and others squeezed into the reserves. With the erosion of political autonomy due to annexation or conquest, African peoples succumbed to pressures to become integrated into the (inter)national economy. Maputoland, for instance, offered a ready reservoir of Tsonga laborers as up to half of its able-bodied males at any one time were away in the Orange Free State, Natal, or the Transvaal.[3] Africa's rinderpest scourge of the mid–1890s forced many Africans off the land, although many Transkei residents traveled to the mines with "extreme reluctance" due to harsh conditions in late–19th-century compounds.[4] Cecil Rhodes's 1894 Glen Grey Act imposed taxes as yet another incentive to bring Africans into the cash nexus: "You will remove [Africans] from that life of sloth and laziness: you will teach them the dignity of labour and make them contribute to the prosperity of the State: and make them give some return for our wise and good government."[5] We will return to these compulsions below to highlight the difficulties Africans in the Transkei and Ciskei faced as they attempted to retain a sense of community and autonomy.

As Alan Jeeves notes in reference to more mundane strategies for labor procurement, though, many studies have remained silent.[6] Recruitment, in fact, played a significant part in industrial development since the discovery of diamonds in Kimberley, when Africans were barred from holding digging licenses and the Griqualand West Administration sent labor agents to secure unskilled recruits throughout Bechuanaland. The corruption that developed as labor touts worked to gain the support of local chiefs was replicated in the anarchical first years of recruiting for the Witwatersand mining houses. In 1899, A.S. Poultney secured 1,000 Tswana laborers from Ngamiland, and his methods are instructive for the way stratified monetary rewards informed evolving class relations in rural districts:

Poultney found difficulty at Segomi's Stad in recruiting for his Association.
The working classes ... were not unwilling to visit the mines. He explained to them the advantages of a year's work at fifty shillings monthly and free rations.
Many were curious to see the white man's big city. But ... their owners refused to let them go without heavy payment. The only way out of this difficulty was through bribery and corruption, and Poultney took it.[7]

Miners who were "sold" to recruiters often made poor employees—demanding higher wages, refusing underground work, or simply deserting upon arrival. This propensity for disaffected workers to break contract led the Volksraad, in 1895, to enact a Pass Law to "have a hold on the native whom we have brought down, be it from the East Coast, South, or from the North, at considerable outlay to ourselves."[8]

Other forms of recruitment, however, offered more tangible rewards for individual recruits, their families, and their communities. The industry extended cash and cattle advances, leading villages in the Cape to become increasingly dependent on the "cash injection which the black miners provided."[9] William Beinart argues that Pondoland chiefs used cattle advances for recruits' families not only to profit from industrial development while lessening its impact on villages, but also to ensure that migrants would return home.[10] Another strategy to prevent desertion and encourage cyclical migration was deferred wages to be paid upon completion of contract, a scheme with the added bonus of helping workers resist temptations that depleted their wages.

The importance of all this, however, is that the loose infrastructure put in place for labor recruitment failed to stimulate the flow of labor to the mines in sufficient numbers to satisfy ever-increasing demand. In fact, the lack of an effective central recruiting organization left mines and touts competing, and the advertised benefits of mine work failed to overcome the resistance of Africans who wished to be at home for the harvest and retain a stake in the rural homestead. Consequently, several recruiting organizations emerged to rectify what the Joint Councils decried as the "unsatisfactory results [of unregulated recruitment] both to the mines and the native labourers."[11] The failure of the Rand Native Labour Association (RNLA) to eliminate individual recruiters led to the Witwatersrand Native Labour Association (WNLA), formed during the Boer War to monopsonize African recruitment. While WNLA officially opposed the practice of bribing headmen to supply cheap black labor for the mines, corruption continued in a lesser capacity.[12] Furthermore, target areas for the WNLA were predominately northern regions such as Mozambique, the Rhodesias, Nyasaland, and even equatorial regions, until President Botha banned tropical recruiting in 1913 due to excessive mortality rates. It was the formation of the NRC in 1912 that proved instrumental for industrial recruitment and found favor among most mining houses. But the ever-increasing manpower needs in the gold mining industry, despite the influx of hundreds of thousands of workers onto the Rand in the 1910s–20s, served as incentive to conjure up yet new enticements for potential recruits. We have seen that Ray Phillips first introduced films in the company compounds, but by the late 1920s, many fresh recruits, in fact, already had some experience with the cinema, for the success of the MCCC led to a spate of recruiting films produced by the NRC to expand the industrial workforce.

Kwateba: Race, Recruitment and Migrancy

South Africa was not the only fertile recruiting zone for the Witwatersand gold mines. In 1899, in fact, Mozambique alone accounted for approximately 60 percent of its unskilled mining labor. Early on, there were strong incentives for these north-of-the-border recruits. A primary attraction for Thongo men migrating from Mozambique was that work on the mines would enable them to secure money for a bride-price.[13] By 1904, the fact that two-thirds of the labor supply still derived from Mozambique led the chamber to introduce Chinese laborers to offset domestic shortages, a policy eliminated within a few years due to the hostility of both Botha and British liberals.[14]

By 1912, following the formation of the Union, the system of African recruitment was anything but stable. WNLA had come under attack even by its own member companies, driven "out of almost all of its recruiting centers except Mozambique."[15] Newly appointed to lead the Transvaal Native Labour Bureau and stimulate domestic recruiting within South Africa, Henry Taberer met with Edward Dower, secretary of native affairs for the Cape Province, to devise a program whereby "voluntaries" (unrecruited Africans) headed for the mines would be transported and fed *en route* free of charge through government loans.[16] Taberer assisted in the founding of the NRC once most Transvaal's mining houses agreed to eliminate independent recruiting. With Charles Villiers as chairman and Taberer as general superintendent, the NRC was to reduce recruiting costs and competition by bringing within its fold all the Rand's mines, and extend its reach throughout the Cape Province, Basutoland, Swaziland and Bechuanaland.[17]

During the ensuing period of tightening labor controls, reduction of wages, and the expansion of South African recruiting, migrancy became more firmly entrenched within the reserve economies. From its Johannesburg offices, the NRC oversaw the processing of recruits in district branches and local sub-offices. Although the number of voluntaries increased, the NRC opened up a significant catchment zone in the Eastern Cape for new recruits, areas that a few years later would be specifically targeted by recruitment films. By 1922, for instance, while Basutoland, Swaziland, and Bechuanaland had one branch each in Maseru, Piet Rietief, and Pietersburg, the Cape Province (including Pondoland) had 14 offices, including branches in Kingwilliamstown, Queenstown, and Umtata, each with several sub-offices. The table below showing the number of recruiters working in each district gives an indication of the increasing importance of the Cape in the industrial migration system following the formation of the NRC:

Cape Province:	321
Transvaal:	24
Basutoland:	14
Natal & Zululand:	13
Swaziland:	12
Bechuanaland[18]:	7

Taberer served as mediator between the chamber and those Africans doubling as peasants and proletarians within dual economies. Born in the Eastern Cape and fluent in Xhosa, he gained a remarkable degree of trust among African workers undergoing partial proletarianization. In 1913, he played a key role in calming angry black miners during a general strike initiated by white workers, and his popularity extended into the countryside due to his constant travels in the reserves.[19] Locals who found his surname difficult to pronounce referred to him as "Teba" and the local NRC branch offices as KwaTeba (Teba's Place). Years later, in homage to Taberer, the entity created by the merger between the WNLA and the NRC became known as TEBA (which doubled as an acronym for The Employment Bureau of Africa).[20] Taberer's prominence among Africans during his lifetime is remarkable considering his position as the NRC's general superintendent during the years the chamber reconstructed the cheap black labor system in the mines through the increasing rigidity of the Colour Bar. His approval rating in part reflected his role as advocate for those who wished to bring their families with them to the mines, although industry for the most part resisted this plea.[21]

In 1922, Taberer commented on the difficult task of recruiting. "It has taken many years of hard work," he said, "to educate the native of British South Africa to come and work on the Witwatersrand."[22] But, in fact, it was becoming clear that yet more needed to be done to satisfy the manpower needs of the mining houses. In 1924 the Chamber of Mines appointed William Gemmill as general manager of the chamber, the WNLA and the NRC, while Taberer, with his skills as mediator and recruiter, became the NRC's native labor advisor. This administrative reshuffling within the NRC set the stage for introducing images as part of the industry's recruiting arsenal.

From Red Blanket to Civilization

By the time the NRC built upon the MCCC's success to produce its own recruitment films, South Africa's film industry had evolved significantly. In 1909, bioscopes began to proliferate in major cities, and soon Johannesburg had cinema fever and enjoyed no fewer than 20 full-time picture palaces in addition to the opening of "bio-cafes" and even "Jollyrinkoscopes."[23] Rufe Naylor, riding success with his Tivoli Picture Palace and Pavilion Picture Palace, launched Africa's Amalgamated Theaters in 1911. Not to be outdone, Edgar Hyman's Empire Theatres Company established a chain of theaters, and his African Film Syndicate facilitated distribution. The result was what Thelma Gutsche has called "suicidal competition" that was only concluded by the entrance of insurance magnate Isidore Schlesinger. Arriving in Cape Town in 1894, Schlesinger had made a fortune in insurance, and moved to dominate the entire South African film industry in April 1913 through African Theatres Trust which purchased or otherwise absorbed the Union's leading cinema companies. He then moved into the world of film production to jumpstart the making of "South African films for South African audiences."[24] As a case in point, Schlesinger's African Film Productions (AFP) produced *African Mirror*, South Africa's first series of topical newsreels that ran until 1984, and which were often included in the MCCC in its formative years. In March 1925, following the success of earlier WNLA films for Mozambican recruitment, Gemmill contracted AFP to produce *From Red Blanket to Civilization*.[25] Propaganda films such as these were believed to best meet their desired goals through brevity, and were to be included only as a segment of longer programs of primarily entertainment shorts and cartoons. Nevertheless, *Red Blanket* was an important example of what Gregory and Piche refer to as industrial paternalism—in this case a strategy designed to bind the interests of the migrant workforce to those of the gold mining industry.[26] Nor was the film designed to denigrate tribal life. Rather, *Red Blanket* required a delicate balancing act to promote circular migration by advertising the benefits of the mines while providing a positive portrayal of idyllic tribal life in the reserves. This dualism was crucial, for a film that critiqued customary obligations and peasant economies ran two risks: first, spectators imbibing the message might precipitate rapid westernization and the "drift into town"; second, it might conversely foster a counter-reaction and spark wholesale resistance to the entire system of labor migration.

Red Blanket is divided into roughly three sequences constructed through a decidedly teleological and Eurocentric perspective. The first sequence—what I refer to as the "primitive" phase—portrays an array of traditional African activities. The second sequence—the "transition" phase—presents African social progress in the context of two forms of education, followed by a third—"modern" phase—featuring African migrant workers against the backdrop of an industrializing Witwatersrand.[27] The film was remarkable for its time because cameraman Carrick, no doubt due to Taberer's standing within the African community, was allowed to film some of "the most closely guarded ceremonials of the Transkeien natives."[28]

The film opens with establishing shots of the Transkei and "a large native kraal," followed by scenes of "Native National Ceremonies" practiced by "uncivilized natives." The first is the Ntonjane dance, which young women complete before being considered eligible for marriage. This rite of passage requires that pubescent girls be sequestered in the house of a female relative, while outside the "jaka" (young girls) congregate for a dance lasting, intermittently, several days. The primitive sequence continues with a "marriage ceremony as performed amongst the Amaxosa and which differs slightly from that obtaining amongst the Fingoes," followed by other traditional customs such as a "Kaffir Beer Drink," a deer hunt, and circumcision dances. Next, a group of boys perform a Kwedini dance, and women perform the Umdudo marriage dance in which rows of men and women move in place, jumping vertically and vigorously shaking their bodies. While the men are almost naked and shorn of war paraphernalia, women remain in full dress throughout. As these lively scenes conclude, viewers see traditional "women's activities such as carrying wood and water in the village and weaving intricate baskets." The final two shots of the primitive sequence show, first, a native stick fight between two boys, followed by an African court scene at the kraal of Victor Poto, paramount chief of Western Pondoland.

The narrative construction of the primitive sequence embodies interwar concerns with disappearing cultures shared by missionaries, anthropologists and many Africans themselves. Noticeably absent are demeaning depictions of traditional life—Rhodes's "life of sloth and laziness"—so familiar to scholars of European imperialism. Instead, *Red Blanket*'s carefully constructed ideological edifice shows traditional communities living in peace and harmony: the tribe is primal; it is the realm of the pure and authentic and its social spaces are uncorrupted by the rush and tumble of the modern. Basic needs are taken care of in the village: rites of passage are celebrated by the community; males play-fight as youngsters in preparation for future roles as buck hunters; women excel in the domestic arts; and a native judicial court at the end of the sequence emphasizes traditional social controls necessary for tribal unity. But if the tribe is artificially elevated as a land of bliss, it also suffers from an inability to progress unassisted beyond the static realm of the simple and the primitive. Outside of time and history alike, the tribe can only experience lasting social transformation through European intervention.

Taberer describes how the film feeds into the transition phase: "Hereafter the picture shows that while ancient native customs are rigidly adhered to in parts of South Africa, the march of civilization is reflected in the education and industrial development of the natives." We now see the "younger generation of natives" training in mission schools, such as St. Matthews Mission, located near Keiskammahoek (Taberer's birthplace), as well as St. Cuthbert's Mission in Tsolo, which became widely known in the 20th century for its Weaving School for women. It is notable that *Red Blanket*'s transition phase opens with mission schools, as they constituted the first sustained arenas of contact many rural Africans had with Western culture. Only following this contact with whites, the film implies, can Africans continue other forms of education required to join world civilization. Poignantly, the second section of the transition phase includes a native agricultural college, and scenes of "the advancement of the native at his own home" at Umtata's Native Agricultural School. "The [agricultural] show," Taberer is careful to note, is "entirely organized and controlled by the natives themselves."

The modern sequence incorporates two new elements into the narrative. First, Africans are introduced into areas well beyond their traditional habitat; second, their contact with the modern is framed within a topos of well-defined socio-economic hierarchies. The sequence opens with "natives working at the wharf at East London," followed by, at long last, the "recruitment for and control of native labourers on the gold mines." Highlighted are the NRC's Johannesburg headquarters, a "typical Mine Compound," and the BMSC where "the more progressive natives on the mines are enabled to enjoy some social life." The BMSC of course, while influential within the black community, never had more than a few hundred full-time members, although certainly more enjoyed its amenities. Nevertheless, this site for social gatherings and recreation comprises an important narrative device in the film, for it constituted one of the few acceptable arenas wherein (male) members of the African *petit-bourgeoisie* could air grievances and engage white philanthropists.

Ultimately, then, the message conveyed is that while the quaint pastoralism of traditional African communities offers a critical space for nurture, it fails to provide a roadmap for meaningful social progress. For the civilizing process to flourish, Europeans must be introduced into the narrative, and even then the civilizing mission transpires within a predominately male African setting. Women remain in the reserves, serving as willing marriage partners managing food production, while men leave home and join the unskilled industrial army. Those few literate blacks who attain a higher level of learning or standing in the community, usually through the beneficence of missionary education, are welcomed into organizations like the BMSC to assist in racial uplift. While chiefs preside over tribal communities, young males are given opportunities for limited personal development in the mining sector. The social effect of this bias toward young males, leaving women to cope with the quotidian affairs of tribal life, can be seen in the report of one NRC agent who, arriving in Tongaland, was struck by the "advanced" state of the male population, while "strangely enough ... the women are most backward, probably the most backward in South Africa."[29]

The revealing title change—from *Native Life in the Cape Province* to *From Red Blanket to Civilization*—introduces to some extent the dynamism of social advancement, but there are nevertheless important lacunae in the narrative. Missing are scenes of repatriation at the termination of labor obligations, wherein the worker is expected to discard his provisional identity as industrial worker and to don the red blanket once again to be reincorporated into the day-to-day subsistence economy of the reserves. Images of repatriation, so important to a migrant system tailored to retard the drift into town while yet securing its labor needs for industrial interests, would have to wait until the next spate of propaganda films in the 1930s.

Red Blanket's discursive strategy of inscribing the tribe as a primordial feature of African life also distracts the spectator from the often harsh socio-political realities undergirding South Africa's system of oscillating migrant labor. Pointedly missing from the film was any reference to the 1911 Colour Bar that institutionalized the industry's racial divide, or that migrancy actually led to massive disruption in the countryside. Areas in southern Africa affected by migration often experienced a disproportionate decrease in production because of households suffering from the absence of breadwinners.[30] As men left villages for the mines, women and children were left to restructure the division of labor, or women themselves migrated to cities in search of husbands or jobs.[31]

The degradation of the Transkei and Ciskei reflected the role played by discriminatory legislation and other pressures in the conversion of pre-capitalist economies into vast reservoirs of cheap industrial labor. This ecological decay is worth exploring briefly, as reserves were used both as subjects for recruiting films, as well as target areas for exhibition. Direct colonial rule in the Transkei was achieved in the late–19th century. The subsequent erosion of peasant self-sufficiency was accelerated by devastating droughts, cattle losses, rising food prices, taxes, and the 1913 Land Act. Population growth and declining resources further burdened the region,[32] leading the 1915 Beaumont Commission to conclude that existing land set aside for Africans could at best support one half of the Union's black population.[33] But this was stating the obvious: an official in the Transkei had already despaired years earlier that "Natives in this and other districts are virtually insolvent."[34]

The gap in *Red Blanket* between life on the reels and life on the reserves is even more pronounced when one looks at the Transkei in relation to the 1894 Glen Grey Act, which introduced individual land tenure as a civilizing agent. Although a small stratum of peasants benefited, the plan largely failed due to land scarcity. What *Red Blanket* fails to mention is that in 1929, when the film was enjoying wide distribution, there were 11,000 Transkei families with no land of their own for agricultural pursuits, which "hinder[ed] the more enterprising Natives."[35] Sensing the rural decline, the chamber conducted an agricultural/nutritional survey in the Ciskei and Transkei, which ironically determined Africans would fare better if they stayed on the land rather than migrate to the mines. Yet industry officials consistently ignored the increasing impoverishment despite new exposures by Margaret Ballinger and the 1943 Witwatersrand Mine Natives Wages' Commission.[36] Tellingly, the latter found a positive correlation between areas with egregiously low agricultural production and high mining recruitment figures, showing that underdevelopment led to competition for mining jobs, thus keeping wages artificially low. Moreover, lower industrial wages led to shorter intervals spent in tribal lands for males who tried desperately to earn needed cash.

The effects of restrictive legislation and migration later also had a dire impact on one of the very institutions depicted in the transition phase of *Red Blanket*. During the apartheid years, when government officials required that all mission schools teach Bantu Education or lose funding, St. Matthews Mission tried with little success to maintain its independence and be self-sufficient. As a result, young men in the region flocked to the mines, leaving behind crumbling structures that continue to erode with the march of time.

The industry, nevertheless, complained incessantly of a labor shortage. And for this reason *Red Blanket* went into wide distribution throughout the Eastern Cape upon release in 1925. In addition to being shown at various recruiting stations throughout the Transkei and Ciskei, it premiered for white audiences at London's Wembley exhibition. A print was soon provided to the Society for the Propagation of the Gospel in Foreign Parts, and the International Labour Office in Geneva even hosted a showing in December 1928. Ray Phillips began showing *Red Blanket* on the MCCC along with similar AFP films such as *Industrialization of the African* and *From Kraal to Mine* that rehashed the positive spin on industrial migration. The latter consisted of short "native sketches" of KwaZulu-Natal, the Ciskei, Basutoland, Pondoland, and the Northern Transvaal.[37] Presumably many of these films began to fall out of favor among MCCC audiences by 1937 as talkies had long been the norm.

AFP and the Kernel

From Red Blanket to Civilization, as we have noted, was not the first recruitment film for the South African mines. In 1920, as Phillips was beginning to experiment with cinema in the compounds, AFP produced *The W.N.L.A. in Portuguese East Africa*, with Portuguese subtitles. As late as 1936, African labor from all Portuguese-held territories still constituted roughly 20 percent of South Africa's entire black workforce on the mines. The attraction of touring cinema shows beginning in 1920 may have contributed to a steady traffic of Mozambican labor, although it is difficult to assess the relative weight of the "carrot" in the form of visual propaganda, vis-à-vis the "stick" of economic desperation and political pressure.

During this period, AFP began producing other documentary/propaganda films. Between 1916 and 1922, due to the wartime slowdown of imports, the studio pumped out 43 films targeting primarily white audiences, although there was apparently some cross-racial seepage. *Peeps into Basutoland* was an early example, during the shooting of which a cameraman who raised the ire of local villagers was virtually expelled, for reasons that are unclear.[38] It is also unclear whether this film is identical to *Glimpses of Native Life in Basutoland*, which was still on MCCC rotation in 1936.[39] In any event, by 1924, AFP had produced topicals, publicity films, and a Safety First film for the MCCC, but the following year the company expanded its activities with the production of *Red Blanket*, which helped to forge a symbiotic relationship between the production company and the NRC.[40]

Although NRC general manager William Gemmill applauded existing recruiting films as "having great value," several years after *Red Blanket*'s release he contemplated producing new, refined propaganda films for the touring circuit, for two reasons.[41] First, in the words of the Chamber of Mines' president, "Our requirements in the way of native labour are constantly increasing. A year ago my predecessor told you that 195,000 natives were needed to work the mines at maximum economy. To-day, we have 200,000 at work, yet need more."[42] But propaganda would have to be delicately handled, for Margaret Ballinger touring the degradation of the Ciskei noted that in many cases, "All prefer to starve together" rather than migrate for work.[43] In addition, audience reaction needed to be taken into account. NRC field reports suggested that, due to ethnic animosities, not all images of Africa's tribal life were suitable for all audiences. For instance, one recruiter warned Gemmill that audiences in the Cape Province, while generally displaying "extraordinary enthusiasm" for *Red Blanket*, would nonetheless "resent any reference to East Coast natives,"[44] while a superintendent suggested "it would appeal more to the Bechuanaland natives if their own people appeared on the picture; if possible no Portuguese, Shangaans, Xosas or other tribes should be included in the film, as the Bechuana is prejudiced against these tribes."[45]

To increase recruiting, Gemmill now recognized that mining propaganda needed to take into account cultural peculiarities, a conclusion which, unfortunately, implied significantly greater expenditures and more sensitivity to disparate tribal customs. In effect, films would have to be produced in different locales in order to capture the distinctive cultural practices of each area. And there were additional problems of fidelity that arose when Europeans depicted African societies, an issue that consistently plagued colonial filmmaking. William Sellers, for instance, while producing health films in Nigeria to fight hookworm and tropical diseases, warned that filmmakers featuring local customs required a deep understanding of tribal nuances: "Strict accuracy is vital in all scenes and particularly so in the production of local films, where thorough knowledge of local habits and customs is essential. Mistakes in this direction, however slight, may turn the most serious film into a roaring comedy."[46]

NRC superintendents similarly noticed the tendency for "local color" scenes to elicit derision and laughter among African audiences. Whether even strict accuracy would be sufficient in meeting recruitment quotas was still unknown, though. One Northern Transvaal recruiter denied that showing "local dancing [or] tribe ceremonials" would have any positive effect on recruitment at all: "Briefly our purpose should be instructive and not to amuse," he said. "If we must amuse our audiences we can secure some of the Comics from the African Theatres Trust." In what would prove to be a rather perceptive assessment of the primary concerns of potential recruits, this recruiter maintained that "dances and ceremonies among the Transkei natives created widespread interest and merriment; but did not in any way suggest to the natives that the Gold Mines provided pleasant and lucrative work."[47]

In September 1930, Gemmill elicited reports from district superintendents concerning what scenarios would be most likely to strike a responsive chord in their local populations. These memos provide the historian with a rare glimpse of some of the concerns voiced by potential African recruits and their families when considering work in the mines. Superintendents, as we shall see, were clearly acting on the assumption that even African neophytes to film technology were capable of fairly sophisticated visual cognition when it came to reading filmic images, an issue over which colonial filmmakers would argue for decades.[48] Based on first-hand recruiting experience in their respective districts, the memos display a remarkable degree of unanimity, suggesting that Africans were more likely to respond favorably to scenarios providing more than the vague "civilizing" promises proffered in *Red Blanket*.

Before exploring these field reports in more detail, however, it will prove instructive to look at a similar film proposal written not by a NRC field recruiter, but by an administrator at the Chamber of Mines. Owen Letcher, former editor of the *South African Mining and Engineering Journal*, had previous film experience working with AFP on the comedy *A Madcap of the Veldt*. Although he would later assist in producing the mining portions of Gemmill's slated film, Letcher's own proposed storyboard, which was ultimately rejected, hearkened back to earlier colonial stereotypes. It begins with an "Introductory Caption": "In the old days before the establishment of law and order in South Africa under the whiteman's rule, the country was periodically ravaged by despots like Tchaka [Zulu]. Intertribal wars were of frequent occurrence and no man's life or property was secure." The film was to open with an epic tableau "similar to that which appeared in the well-known South African film the *De Voortrekkers* [1916], showing hordes of savages in war dress."[49] The next caption, accompanying "scenes of carnage," continues Letcher's myopic denigration of tribal life:

> In those days possession of cattle and kraals, etc., was only secured by fighting and there were of course many thousands of people killed in tribal raids. To-day the native is able to obtain money by peaceful work, and his kraal and women folk, cattle, etc., are secured and protected by forces of law and order created by the whiteman.

Subsequent scenes showed African miners drawing their pay and remitting these hard-earned wages to families back home. These earnings would serve as a civilizing agent and bring tranquility to village life, in contrast to what Letcher referred to as the "bad old days."[50] It is unclear whether he was aware that his depiction of tribal society was at odds with the romanticization of African life in *Red Blanket*, but the NRC passed on his proposal.

In contrast to Letcher, superintendents in the field pressed for a more pragmatic approach to propaganda and recruiting, with more attention paid to working conditions in the mines. While many expressed an appreciation for earlier recruiting films like *Red Blanket*, based in part on the excitement generated in villages by the cinema tours, they argued that Gemmill's project should detail industry arrangements for pay, provisions, accommodation, and recreation. Moreover, superintendents concerned about the general antipathy and distrust many Africans felt toward Western bio-medical techniques argued for the necessity of health care scenarios. One memo went further, stating that to counter prejudice, any "hospital scene should show the native nurses in attendance."[51] This belief that Africans responded more favorably to seeing Africans rather than Europeans on the screen (in addition to Africans ministering to their own kind) would soon become a critical axiom of colonial filmmaking with the Bantu Educational Kinema Experiment.

In accordance with the mining portion of Letcher's storyboard, the profit motive was what superintendents felt Africans would respond to most readily. Recruiters advised Gemmill that attention should be paid to the minutia of payday, deferred pay, and "native remittance" arrangements being honored in workers' home districts. Two storylines sent in by superintendents also enumerated the putative benefits of cash wages for recruiting purposes. The first, from the superintendent of Kokstad, suggested that the most effective imagery for his district would include

> a very poorly clad Bechuanaland native arriving at the Mine; at work in the Mine; meal time; at play (such as football, "Safety First" ambulance work, Gymnastics, swings, etc., as at present at Robinson Deep, Ltd.), and lastly well dressed with a roll of rugs and suit case for returning home, well pleased with himself.[52]

The second storyline, from an Umtata recruiter, agreed that the principle urge for Africans to migrate was their wish to earn money. However, he included other benefits accruing to miners in a cash economy. Because money was needed for the purchase of dowry cattle to secure a wife back home, he suggested a "humorous courtship scene" near the beginning of the film. Later, after mining sequences highlighting pay arrangements, the "well-dressed young recruit returns to his village to purchase cattle and presents for his family." This recruiter seems to have noted that for many African communities, a spell on the mines for young men had become a virtual rite of passage before marriage. Thus, his final scene suggests that in addition to creating desirable class disparities, a money economy might even enhance a miner's sexual attractiveness to village women:

> A number of well-dressed returned recruits approaching a group of native girls being courted by native youths in ragged clothing whose advances are being accepted by the girls until the latter notice the approach of the group of recruits. The girls then leave their erstwhile swains and accept the blandishments of the new arrivals who present the girls with presents of dooks and sweets.[53]

The importance of providing Africans with images of material advancement was thus central to the thinking of those recruiting for the Rand mines. Although there is a dearth of material relating the actual conversations between potential recruits, their families and NRC representatives, the responses from superintendents indicate that terms of favorable remuneration, rather than an abundance of tribal imagery, would more readily entice recruits to sign six-to-nine month contracts as industrial wage workers.

Referring to his slated project as "the most important form of native propaganda yet undertaken by this country," Gemmill devised an expensive yet clever way to incorporate mining arrangements in the film while acknowledging crucial African cultural distinctions to boost recruitment. By February 1931, he had ironed out the final details with AFP. Given the number of scenes to be shot and the immense geography to be covered by the mobile film unit, the chamber clearly had faith that a flood of willing recruits would offset high production costs. Under the supervision of Letcher and Taberer, AFP was to begin shooting the film's key mining segments, nicknamed *The Kernel*, which would include mining accommodations, feeding, safety standards and pay arrangements. This section, filmed on the Rand, could be shown to all audiences, regardless of ethnic affiliation. Next, seven different tribal sequences would be culled from the following areas:

1. Basutoland
2. Bechuanaland
3. Swaziland and Northern Zululand
4. Natal and Zululand
5. Transkei and Pondoland
6. Portuguese East Africa
7. Pafuri and Northern Transvaal.[54]

These local flavor segments would then be spliced onto different copies of *The Kernel*, making for seven distinct propaganda films tailored specifically for each region. Gemmill expected the project to take 11 months to complete, a prediction that turned out to be hopelessly optimistic.

By June 1931, the mining segments had been completed and Gemmill's team set off to shoot in the seven designated zones. A June monthly report from Pietermaritzburg noted the film crew hard at work. As was the case elsewhere in Africa, the arrival of the cinema truck reportedly "created great enthusiasm" in local communities, for the crew also offered bioscope shows for village entertainment while they took footage of "real native life." Unfortunately, NRC reports fail to list exactly what titles were exhibited, but in a revealing case of colonial infantilization, Felix the Cat cartoons seem to have been regular fare. Indeed, the use of cartoons for adult African spectators was not uncommon during the colonial period. Phillips regularly included them on the MCCC, and in the Belgian Congo Catholic missionaries produced the animated cartoon series *Les Palabres de Mboloko* because they equated adult African mental acuity with European children.[55] But cartoons also risked the potential for blowback. Congolese soldiers watching Donald Duck cartoons during the Second World War, for instance, threw stones at the screen, claiming they were being ridiculed: "Animals don't talk," they shouted; "whoever saw a duck in uniform?"[56] The discourse of the "African as child" also fueled accounts in white newspapers of indigenes acting in "irrational" ways to seeing moving images for the first time.

By July, the Northern Transvaal, Natal, and Zululand sequences were complete, and Taberer reported that "the native chiefs and their people responded very readily to our calls upon them for their assistance."[57] But if film crews were generally welcomed, it was not always the case. In the High Commission Territories, things proceeded less smoothly for Taberer's crew. In Basutoland in particular, they experienced difficulty procuring the blessings of Paramount Chief Nathaniel Lerotholi. After some deft negotiations, the filmmakers finally secured the needed footage and headed out to shoot in Northern Zululand, Tongaland and Swaziland. However, Swaziland presented Taberer with a rather different set of challenges even before shooting began.

Selling South Africa's Industrial Revolution in the Bush

Taberer's concerns about Swaziland were linked to the economic reverberations caused by the Wall Street Crash. One of the ironies of Gemmill's grand project was that during the early stages of shooting the South African economy was reeling from macro-economic shockwaves. Kimberley first felt the effects of the contraction when the diamond trade virtually collapsed, followed by slumping agricultural prices that devastated Afrikaners and Africans alike on the veldt. The gold mining sector soon found itself with a rare glut of workers, unable to place the many willing (and sometimes desperate) "voluntaries" hoping to sign on. Taberer visited Swaziland during the depression's early days and reported that residents were "not understanding [and were] unable to appreciate why the Industry could not accept them for work when they were anxious to come forward on account of bad economic conditions." Thus, Taberer waited until he arrived in Stegi in eastern Swaziland before taking footage for the new film. Indeed, it must have been rather embarrassing to admit that he was making a recruitment film for an organization that was currently turning away applicants!

These odd circumstances were only temporary, however. While Gemmill's project bogged down somewhat during the bleak months of late 1931 and early 1932, the mining industry enjoyed something of a recovery after the government abandoned the gold standard. In fact, by June AFP had completed the Northern Transvaal portion, spliced it onto a copy of *The Kernel*, and started touring in that territory. Tragically, on June 5, Henry Melville Taberer passed away from pneumonia, a serious blow felt not only in the NRC offices and mining compounds, but throughout the reserves as well. Presumably the NRC was soon signing up new recruits in the Transvaal where the film was being screened, yet a March 1933 report from Umtata by new native labor advisor Henry Wellbeloved shows that the seeds of recovery, which had begun to take root that year, were uneven and slow to yield significant gains for many Africans:

> The natives right throughout are appealing for work and hundreds are turned away from our offices every week.... Mr. Moore had orders for fifteen natives only, the rest were being turned adrift. This state of affairs prevails right throughout the Territories, and I have no hesitation in saying that all our requirements for the Winter will be easily met.[58]

Economic hardship also led to delays in filming and post-production on other versions of the film. Despite some delays, though, Gemmill received word in March 1935 that five had been completed—*Natal, Ciskei, Basutoland, Pondoland,* and *Zululand*—almost five years after first conceiving the project.[59] As recruitment needs finally leveled up to pre-depression levels, these films went into distribution in their target areas.

Select Europeans were also provided special showings. At *Basutoland*'s screening in 1933 in Umtata (Transkei's administrative center), Matatiele, Kokstad, and Flagstaff, whites praised the "care and attention given to the mine natives," and urged that a copy be sent to South Africa's parliament, or perhaps even London to advertise the country's mining sector.[60] Although it is unclear whether the NRC followed up on these suggestions, two years later Wellbeloved did in fact screen *Basutoland* before a 500-strong audience in Geneva. Promoting the beneficence bestowed by the industry on Africa's laboring masses, Wellbeloved reported an upbeat response, hearing it "frequently remarked that more had been learned from the film than from all the speeches made in the conference and in committee."[61]

By 1937 recruitment tours were underway in full force as cinema lorries snaked their way through the South African interior, exhibiting the expanded *Kernels* to tens of thousands of Africans in the reserves. One journalist lauded the NRC's efforts to advertise "to Natives the advantages of working on the Witwatersrand gold mines," and declared the project a success in the Butterworth District: "Great interest is being taken in the show by

Natives of all walks of life and in spite of some very cold evenings there have been excellent attendances." This assessment seems accurate, for even in the winter weeks between June 27 and August 14, 1937, each show averaged 809 spectators.[62] A Queenstown paper reported that for the film showing in that municipality, "There was a great crowd present, and the picture was thoroughly enjoyed by everybody. The picture showed the thoughtfulness of the treatment meted out to them throughout the great venture. There were many "Quoiks!" as the train steamed away with its load of adventurers."[63] One Cunning Moor student even composed a letter to recruiters, thanking them for the "beautiful things on the Bioscope":

> Well! These Europeans shewed us marvellous things about the Mines, the towns, the Chiefs of Northern Transvaal of various tribes.... They pleased the 1. Men 2. And young men that had never seen the Mines 3. And old women 4. And women 5. And boys 6. And girls 7. And children.[64]

At these shows in outlying villages, where recruiting films were interspersed with comedies and cartoons to attract locals, many neophytes reportedly reacted in ways predictable to those unfamiliar with the medium. One writer claimed that in some districts where film was entirely unknown, the "assembled audiences rose as a body and inspected the back of the screen to discover what had happened to the people they had just seen."[65] Others apparently ran in fright from Felix the Cat, believing that the animated feline was a ghost. The use of cartoons, as well as the newspaper accounts highlighting what seemed to be a childlike response to seeing moving images for the first time, situates the film showings within the broader ideology of paternalism permeating the thinking of white elites in the interwar period. An equally dramatic incident of first-contact folklore was later recounted by NRC projectionist Bill Larkan. He was stationed at the top of the Drakensberg Ridge, in Mokhotlong, Basutoland—the "loneliest place in the British Empire." The first to bring cinema to the area, Larkan had to use pack mules to carry his Homelite engine, poles, screens, projectors and reels:

> One show on the border with Leribe gave us one of our most amusing incidents. I was showing an old film *Fight between a Lion and a Tiger*: the last scene shows the lion kill the tiger then, seemingly, walk towards one on the screen, place his front paw on the body of the dead tiger, then give a mighty roar. As this happened the screen and poles came tumbling down towards us, as the people in their terror leapt up and scattered. It took about an hour of gentle talking and persuasion over the mike to convince the people that this was only a film and no wild animals were present, and that they should return to view the rest of the show. Next day, when we gaily rode off to hold our show at the next village ... we were met by a delegation comprising the village headmen and some elders. They addressed my propagandist (the late Ezakiah Mpe) thus: "Listen, man, tell this white man of yours to take your bioscope and all the wild animals he has with him, and leave our area. We do not want people being eaten by lions here." After almost falling off our horses in mirth we took the better part of two hours of talking to convince the committee that we did not have any wild animals, only pictures.[66]

This tale resonates with one told by Ray Phillips about the MCCC's experimental stage. During a "snake film" in the compounds, spectators watched a puff adder and boa constrictor with "bated breath." When suddenly the film cut to a shot of a large, black snake moving rapidly toward the camera, the "natives jumped to their feet and rushed backwards, treading on their friends and bowling the row of European guests over on their back."[67] All these anecdotes of the Africans' frightened reactions made good press for the white public. Yet it might be noted that the jumpiness of those Africans attending nighttime outdoor showings was not entirely unwarranted. In 1951, a recruitment film in Mahalapye Stad, Bechuanaland, was interrupted by a (real) night adder slithering between the viewers' feet. According to reports, though, the crowd simply dispatched of the snake rather quickly and the show continued.[68] No doubt events like this were a frequent occurrence as reels rolled under darkened skies.

While evidence from the reserves indicates that there was usually significant African enthusiasm for the cinema, one district superintendent admitted that exuberance for *The Kernel* was often tempered by a degree of distrust of the touring crew's motivations by the more traditionally minded:

> The average "red" Native is skeptical about the machinations of the European in matters of this kind, and it took considerable explanation to convince them that they were being given a free show in which they would be interested; but, once persuaded to attend, they became the most interested spectators, who will assist us immensely in any future propaganda work of this kind.[69]

Thus, although Africans did indeed become "the most interested spectators," they did not do so without reservation. In fact, as white audiences eulogized the treatment of new recruits depicted in the films, concerns voiced by black audiences in Natal reveal that many articulated very specific concerns about working conditions on the Rand. Indeed, it is likely that a number of these viewers had already worked a stint on the mines, and their shared experiences served as insightful counterpoints to the propagandistic thrust of the films. Several viewers lodged complaints about the pay scale for shoveling, for instance, a job known to require a great expenditure of energy. While the film tried to soft-pedal the grueling nature of the task for obvious reasons, spectators commented that due its strenuous nature the rate of remuneration should be increased. The topic of work-site injuries led to similar complaints that the proposed disability compensation package was inadequate. Some members of the audience also declared that the practice of debarring older men from going to the mines amounted to age discrimination, while still others expressed trepidation as to how the politics of ethnicity would be played out on jobsites and in the compounds. Specifically, they stated that the chamber should be vigilant in assuring that "boss boys" and "indunas" (low-level foremen) not be of a different ethnic group from those over whom they wielded authority.[70]

There is also reason to believe that despite glowing reports on the popularity of the shows, the films did not always succeed in selling themselves, much less the benefits of mine work, without extra inducement. Superintendents believed that just as the films were designed to attract men to the mines, part of the touring operator's job should be to attract villagers to the exhibitions. Several means were devised to accomplish this. Loudspeakers, generally attached to the cinema lorry roof, announced upcoming shows in the afternoon. Loud music was also played to build suspense and interest, with one superintendent working to increase the audio to a radius of three miles to "call up the audience."[71] It was "not 'advertisement' but 'attraction,'" he argued, "which draws an audience." The NRC also had sweets printed with the words "KwaTeba," which officials nicknamed Kaffir Mottoes, distributed to women and children.[72] These strategies were often used in tandem: sweets were promised to children in advance, music and announcements played over loudspeakers, and even searchlights attached to tall flagpoles pierced the gloaming to generate excitement before the show. In another case, a recruiter reported that in Swaziland and Northern Zululand, competition with asbestos and coal recruiters, in conjunction with the long distances spectators had to walk to get to the shows, required even more substantial incentives: free meat and beer for the audience.[73] One cinema operator summed it up best: "Out in the country much depends on the forcefulness of the advertising."[74]

The NRC, it should be noted, was not alone in using some of these techniques. Similar strategies became common throughout the colonial world in Africa and beyond as officials and missionaries introduced a new visual culture of consumption to sell commodities, encourage Western hygiene, and promote rural development. William Sellers of the Colonial Film Unit, which had been formed originally to promote Allied war aims in World War II, similarly argued that loudspeakers were necessary to attract large crowds. But some methods led to frustration among colonial officials who felt that subject peoples were too uncharitable, a refrain we have encountered before. In a similar context elsewhere, Europeans showing off cinematic technology around 1920 were frustrated at the tepid response: "It does not pay to advertise in the New Hebrides," one official grumbled, "we had to bribe the Cannibals with tobacco to come to our show."[75]

Notwithstanding all these enticements to secure large audiences and more workers, NRC recruiters would have been incapable of fulfilling desired quotas without the active support of local headmen and indigenous assistants, hired as translators and commentators, who traveled with the crews. Although headmen were prohibited from recruiting, the practice was ongoing and "clearly an essential part of the chain connecting mining companies to the potential mineworker in the countryside."[76] The schedules of the mobile units, in fact, were designed to capitalize on the influence of local elites. Arriving in a village around midday, recruiters scheduled afternoon meetings for approximately four o'clock with the headman and his people, during which they spoke glowingly to potential recruits and families about the benefits of mining for young men, and explained contractual expectations. And one recruiter reported that his "exhaustive propaganda address" in Natal was reinforced with a speech made by his African representative, Prince Matholegwaqa Peter Zulu. Zulu's services had been offered the NRC by his brother, the acting Zulu paramount chief. At an earlier recruiting meeting the chief himself had addressed those attending, criticizing the Zulu's lack of support for the gold mines, and urging them to "change their minds." Upon his offer to be of more assistance, superintendents requested that he speak to leaders of all the nearby "closed areas," and encourage them to request that new NRC branches be opened.

Following afternoon recruiting meetings, dinner commenced around 5:30 while music played over the van's loudspeakers. As twilight fell projectors rolled. Similar to many MCCC showings, a white sheet, suspended between two tall poles, served as a screen. With audiences often numbering 3,000, spectators sat or stood on both sides of the sheet, while recruiters kept up a running commentary. C.H. Cooper, a European official who traveled through Zululand with the Natal crew, was known for his forceful comments in the vernacular, described by his superintendent as "pungent propaganda."[77] Frequently, however, indigenous assistants like Peter Zulu took to the loudspeakers to broadcast commentary in the villages. In the Cape Province, a head clerk by the name of Stone Matanga gained quite a reputation on the circuit and was lauded by his superior as "a most capable propagandist who not only explained the picture but took full advantage of the occasion to advertise the advantages of working on the Mines."[78] Indeed, NRC officials consistently credited charismatic African commentators with boosting recruiting in each district. The shows created quite a stir in the countryside as crowds responded to the loud music and thronged to the strange moving picture attractions. Regardless of their interest in industrial work, hundreds of people, young and old, walked miles in anticipation of the big event. At one showing in Natal, 40 or 50 Zulu elites from the district were present, accompanied by mounted and foot regiments. And occasionally, enthusiastic spectators even traveled to nearby venues on subsequent nights to see the films again. Thus, while critiques were often forthcoming over the minutia of pay arrangements, safety conditions, and the like, recruiting bioscopes (with cartoons) clearly evolved as a popular pastime and leisure pursuit in local villages. In 1940, a Graskop monthly report estimated an impressive 20,000 spectators, the "bulk of whom were admittedly women and children" because so many men were already working in the mines. But even so, the shows were considered useful as "women can and do exert their influence upon the [remaining] menfolk, urging them to go out and work."

These accounts show that white perceptions of African spectatorship operated on two registers simultaneously during the colonial period. The first included print media's familiar cinematic sensationalism—accounts of primitive Africans reacting in humorous ways to motion pictures, and/or depicting Africans as incapable of understanding what was screened before them. It is this phenomenon that almost all historians and film scholars continue to critique today. But the second, more subterranean, register is that industry officials soon realized, due to audience response, that black spectators often made for keen observers who articulated perceptive comments about working conditions and pay scales, or critiqued films depicting ethnic groups other than their own. In sum, had Africans displayed no capacity to read motion pictures, there would have been no reason to produce propaganda films in the first place, and certainly no need to revamp the programs at great expense after reports filtered in from the *Red Blanket* touring circuits.

The Dust That Kills: Film Propaganda on the Rand

Recruits who signed up with the NRC following the conclusion of the film showings usually traveled to Johannesburg by rail. These trains—often converted cattle cars—made round trips from the countryside to the Rand where fresh recruits were dropped off, and those finishing contracts entrained for departure. On a visit to South Africa, Eslanda Robeson spoke of the return trip in graphic terms: "We saw a mine train ... from Joburg with its tragic burden of Africans who have served their term in the mines. Some broken in health, some coughing, some with the beginning of the dreaded phthisis. All exhausted, "worked out".... All with the pathetic little cash which will be eaten up by taxes and fees."[79] While historians have tended to focus on precisely these issues of taxes and fees and other forms of racial discrimination, a few have highlighted worker health and job site safety, issues of particular concern to those working on the mines.[80]

Tourists were not alone in recognizing the telltale signs of silicosis afflicting many miners. Industry officials initially argued, though, despite noticing the coughing and shortness of breath, that the steady repatriation of workers to the countryside provided a natural bulwark against long-term risks. Yet there were good reasons for addressing the problem through the implementation of safety procedures: first, for recruiting to pay dividends, or to entice those who had completed contractual obligations to return, workers had to be convinced that their health concerns were receiving attention; second, worker reproduction required maintaining a base level of health among the workforce; and third, insurance companies for mining houses had their own interests, especially following the 1911 Miners' Phthisis Act, which guaranteed some compensation for suffering workers.

Ironically, it was Louis Botha who first prodded the industry to establish more effective health services. Impelled by the state and also faced with the potential cut-off of tropical labor recruits due to high mortality, Crown Mines' chairman Samuel Evans traveled to the

Panama Canal on a fact-finding mission. The canal zone had been a death trap for West Indians,[81] but pneumonia and yellow fever had been spectacularly combated through the medico-interventions of health supervisor William Gorgas. Evans convinced Gorgas to come to Johannesburg in 1913 to investigate conditions on the Rand, an assignment that resulted in a "scathing" report.[82] Gorgas's recommendations included building more spacious compounds, providing healthier provisions, and hiring a competent medical officer to oversee health services.[83] Although these were not immediately implemented industry-wide due to predictable employer resistance, Rand Mines/Central Mining asked Gorgas to recommend someone to run their medical staff, leading to the hiring of Alexander Orenstein, Gorgas's former Panama assistant, as sanitary superintendent. Orenstein initiated an array of reforms, emulated by other mining houses, including waterborne sewage in the compounds, appointment of full-time medical officers, and new medical facilities.

Orenstein and Phillips believed the MCCC could reinforce new health programs with a dose of prevention. By December 1921, AFP had produced three films under the aegis of the Prevention of Accidents Committee of the Rand Mutual Assurance Company. The most successful of these, *The Dust that Kills*, was directed by Orenstein himself, who took footage at Ferreira Deep with the support of manager Paul Selby. The film, describing how protective gear and other safety procedures could prevent silicosis, premiered at Johannesburg's New Bijou Theatre on February 10, 1921,[84] followed by a showing for the Scientific and Technical Societies.[85]

Fire was also a leading cause for concern, and led to attempts to address the issue through the use of cinema. Initially, short films made by the Prevention of Accidents Committee dealt specifically with the threat in the compounds and the dangers of throwing lighted Cheesa sticks into shafts. Soon Phillips submitted a longer film promoting fire safety to Orenstein and the Rand Mutual Safety First Committee; simultaneously, the Compound Managers' Association was coming to a consensus that a robust set of films "would serve a good purpose in impressing upon natives the necessity for care underground in connection with the prevention of fires."[86] Rand Mutual and AFP thus continued to produce Safety First films for the MCCC so that, by the mid-1930s, quite a number were on rotation, including *What to Do in Case of Fire*, *How Accidents Happen*, *First-Aid—It's Easy to Learn*, and *Safety-First on the Mines*. The latter stressed the importance of wearing hard hats and good shoes in the shafts, the dangers of mishandling hot wires, detonators and fuses, how to avoid train and tramway accidents, and the hazards of inebriation. Until the mid-1930s, these films were silent and narrated by a compound manager or African commentator. In 1940 the Safety First Committee responded to the popularity of talkies on the compounds with *Pas Op Wena!* (*Look Out, You!*), sounded in *fanakolo* (or "Mine Kaffir").

Imaging the Wise and Foolish African

AFP frequently constructed storylines that were among the earliest examples of the "Mr. Wise and Mr. Foolish" or "Two Brothers" genre. In these simple formulaic plots, the "silly native" is injured or contracts an illness due to negligence or moral failing, while the "wise native" serves as role model and comes to his rescue. As James Burns has noted, this theme "offered a simple, stark contrast between the hero, who is rewarded for embracing the modernizing project of colonialism, and the villain, whose intransigent traditionalism inevitably brings suffering and hardship to himself and his family."[87] By the 1940s it had

5. From Red Blanket to Civilization: Movies and Migration in South Africa 149

become a template for colonial filmmakers. *First Aid—It's Easy to Learn*, for instance, relied on precisely this emplotment to engage its audiences.[88] Tea Market Expansion Boards also exploited the theme: AFP's *Mr. Tea and Mr. Skokiaan* (1939) juxtaposed the tea-drinking "sober native" with his corrupted counterpart who imbibed stronger spirits. Purportedly, after each show, audiences chanted, "Tea is GOOOOOOOOOOD for you!" In Nyasaland, too, where the hoods of Tea Market vans were adorned with the words "Drink Tea," this type of advertising reportedly met with success. When the vehicles stopped in a village, European operators gave a speech over the loudspeaker, lauding the benefits of drinking tea rather than beer. According to one African educator:

> Europeans showed the people how to make tea, and he allowed schoolboys only to drink free of charge. We enjoyed hearing the story of the brave Ramosa, the tea drinker, and Nzima, the beer drinker. In the evening everyone came to see the cinema.... I am very grateful for this Tea Board, because we Nyasalanders are understanding about tea.[89]

The crude characterization of wise and foolish Africans was easily appropriated for a joint anti-syphilis program undertaken by the Red Cross and South Africa's Department of Public Health. In September 1938, a Red Cross committee had reviewed and rejected a number of foreign films on the topic as unsuitable for Africans.[90] By September 1939, Joseph Albrecht, recruited by AFP's Isidore Schlesinger, had finished his screenplay and was busy filming *The Two Brothers*, with African talent. It premiered at Johannesburg's Empire Theatre in February 1940 with the launching of a Red Cross health drive, and was subsequently shown on mining compounds and other venues for black audiences.[91] Alan Jeeves argues that this campaign, initiated to assuage white fears in South Africa as well as to educate blacks about VD, was part of a broader campaign waged on both sides of the Atlantic to publicize previously taboo topics relating to sex and public health.[92] The film's perceived success led the British Ministry's Colonial Film Unit to re-edit *The Two Brothers*, titling the "shorter, simpler version" *Mr. Wise and Mr. Foolish Go To Town*, for exhibition in Nyasaland and Northern Rhodesia.[93]

The film opens with two brothers from Zululand, Enoch and Charlie (re-assigned traditional African names in the edited version) in courtship scenes. Enoch (Mr. Wise) engages a woman in "proper" conversation, while Charlie (Mr. Foolish) wakes up late, emerges from his hut, and approaches a different woman in an overly seductive manner. The men, hoping to marry their new sweethearts, are instructed by their headman that a bride price must first be secured by earning cash wages in Johannesburg. Both Enoch and Charlie subsequently find employment in town, but both, in fact, fall prey to the pleasures of the flesh. Enoch is seduced by a woman in a white uniform, while an inebriated Charlie hands money to a woman and disappears with her off camera. Unfortunately, Mr. Wise and Mr. Foolish both contract syphilis, a plight about which they commiserate when they meet up again weeks later. A mutual friend castigates them for their indiscretions, and pulls a leaflet from his pocket entitled *Syphilis*, containing information on European methods of combating the disease. Enoch thanks his friend, but Charlie spurns the sage advice and storms out of the room.[94]

Mr. Wise and Mr. Foolish are then rendered seeking treatment in predictable ways. Charlie visits a traditional Inyanga (Zulu herbalist), who accepts money in exchange for a suspicious bottle of liquid. Enoch instead wisely visits a local hospital, a sequence that poignantly begins with several disturbing close-ups of patients suffering from hereditary syphilis. In a nod to the new imperative of colonial filmmaking, Albrecht included among the European staff an immaculately dressed black male nurse. Enoch receives his injection and makes a full recovery, but Charlie, who has temporarily gone into remission, returns home only to suffer a horrible relapse.

The final segment, subtitled "TEN YEARS LATER," shows a prosperous Enoch, who despite his accommodation to Western bio-medicine, has re-integrated into his community and is shown standing next to his family, a field of maize, and his cattle. In contrast, Charlie is sick and has several wives who shout at him to "shut up" as he begins to cough uncontrollably in a hut. When Enoch and family visit Charlie, one of Charlie's wives displays lesions on her face while standing next to their son, who is apparently sick and blind.

A number of moral admonitions are present in the triumph and tragedy of *The Two Brothers*. But as Alan Jeeves and Megan Vaughan have noted, male sexual propriety was not among them, for both brothers were guilty of promiscuity while in Johannesburg. Nevertheless, viewers were expected to interpret the film's message that Africans should abandon indigenous treatments and embrace Western medicine in order to be cured and prosper. Moreover, the storyline has the added burden, reminiscent of *Red Blanket*, of encouraging modernization while idealizing tribal life. In this film, though, while mining is encouraged, the city is properly a white enclave whose complexity tends to debase rural Africans. Phillips, back in Africa and reporting on MCCC showings of *The Two Brothers* in 1940, dwelled on this dual concern with cities and sickness: "You will note that we have made much use of the film *The Two Brothers*. This is a very impressive film showing the dangers of town life and the rapid and easy spread of syphilis; the waste of money through the patronage of the inyanga for medicines for the treatment of this disease, and the manner in which, over a long period of time, the disease can be cured."[95] Viewers were thus expected to understand that indigenous treatments were insufficient, while simultaneously submitting to rural social controls. This, surely, was a delicate ideological balancing act. In the end, *The Two Brothers* reflected the deep ambivalence about Africans in the city for various reasons, including Europeans' own perceived vulnerability to contagion from syphilis and other diseases in urban areas. Yet the irony of this fear among both state and industry officials is that the "color" of the disease was, in fact, "white," as syphilis was a product of urban-industrial centers inhabited overwhelmingly by Europeans.[96]

White proponents of the segregationist Stallard doctrine, though, were not the only ones concerned about unfettered urbanization. In fact many African males, distressed about the erosion of indigenous communities, were themselves increasingly equating European culture, urbanization and industrialization with disease and corruption. This notion was popularized by Sesotho authors K.E. Ntsane, S.S. Matlosa and A. Nqheku through the "makgoweng" ("Land of the Whites") motif, a migration theme explored in such film classics as *African Jim* (a.k.a. *Jim Comes to Joburg*, 1949) and *Come Back Africa* (1959).[97] Thus, *The Two Brothers*' narrative device of the black seductress was not simply a fantasy of white propagandists; rather, the film borrowed cleverly from a theme pregnant with meaning in both European and African communities.

If the city was an arena of corruption for males, the film partly levies blame on black women for being the agents of the brothers' destruction. African males were expected to have some presence in industrial zones and city centers, in marked contrast to African women who could hold fewer claims to such freedoms. Minding the rural kraal, not the urban sprawl, should be primary among tribal women's concerns. Therefore, as Jeeves notes, *The Two Brothers* betrays a "deep hostility to women."[98] The film's representational strategy, then, with its caricature of dangerous urban women and wise and foolish men, supports to some extent Vaughan's contention that *The Two Brothers* exemplifies the tendency of colonial filmmaking to retain the "Africans are different" theme by regurgitating colonial stereotypes. But the wide distribution of both versions of The Two Brothers leads inevitably to a host of questions: Were the films effective in attaining their goal? How did viewers respond to the storylines? Did viewers identify strongly with Enoch, the wise African?

Such questions are difficult to answer, but provisional conclusions may be gleaned from the sparse evidence available. According to one early researcher, the *Mr. Wise and Mr. Foolish* formula succeeded in portraying the latter as a buffoon. The "silly native," claimed Gutsche, was always the subject of "much mirth on the part of audiences."[99] Phillips, moreover, presents further evidence for the film's effectiveness in actually modifying behavior, rather than simply tailoring a "subject-position" for impressionable viewers. Not only was the film "greatly appreciated [with] requests ... that the film be shown again," but "reports come from hospitals and clinics on the Reef that, after the showing of the film, there is a rapid and gratifying increase of patients coming for examination and treatment."[100]

A more varied reaction was discernable, however, in Northern Rhodesia following a showing of *Mr. Wise and Mr. Foolish* to a literate crowd (not the target audience) in Lusaka's Welfare Hall. At the request of the Rhoasa Sub-Area Anti-Venereal Disease Committee in 1945, information and public relations officer William Vernon Brelsford tried to gauge African comprehension of visual propaganda. Brelsford elicited reaction by awarding prizes to the best essay on the film's theme. Some respondents underscored the misogynist thrust of the narrative by suggesting methods for tighter controls on the movement of women in town, akin to the Belgian Congo's system of requiring that all women carry passes to enter municipal areas.

Reception also took less predictable forms, however. In the previous chapter I suggested that, contrary to the claims of Diawara, commercial cinema was less conducive to resistant readings than propaganda films. As a case in point, examples of discernible spectator resistance surfaced in the essay-writing contest in Lusaka. One participant in Brelsford's experiment brilliantly turned the tables on the morality tale of the two brothers contracting syphilis after traveling to town. To prevent such an occurrence, he suggested, the government should "improve conditions in the villages so that men would not be forced to expose themselves to the diseases of the towns." Another essayist asked wryly whether only Africans suffered from the disease, as they were the only group depicted in the film, while another expressed verbally his surprise that Mr. Wise should catch VD from a "hospital nurse."[101] In fact, the "nurse" was most likely intended to be a maid, but this anomaly reflected the persistent problem of visual literacy and translation in colonial cinema campaigns.

Questions about inter- and intra-racial cultural transmission were crucial in the colonial world, and it is notable that while propaganda films like *The Two Brothers* may have succeeded somewhat in expanding awareness of communicable diseases throughout parts of southern Africa, still unforeseen controversies erupted, exposing the limits of documentary filmmaking and the tension between European and African conceptions of fiction and non-fiction:

> The screening of a hygiene film, lent by the Durban City Health Department, at a convention of native chiefs ended in an uproar when one of the characters acting the part of a man suffering from venereal disease was recognised by the chairman. "That is my nephew," he cried in astonishment. "What is he doing in a film like this? I never knew he had been sick."
> "Mmm.... He's related to me too," called out the general secretary. "It's a disgrace to our family." The uproar continued until at the order of the president of the Native Congress the film was stopped.The lights then went up, and there sitting on the platform was the offending

member of the family, who is secretary of the Bantu Sports Club in Johannesburg. He explained that the film was purely health propaganda and that he had never had a day's sickness in his life. Nor had his brother who took part in the film. But many of the simpler native chiefs would not believe him. We've just seen the history of your sickness with our own eyes," they protested. "How can you tell such lies?" If, as he said, the "film was purely a fairy tale, what was the use of showing it as though it were true?" they demanded. The Durban Medical Officer of Health has now been asked to suppress the film.[102]

If it was true that familiarity could breed contempt when audiences recognized actors on the screen, it was, as we have seen with *Red Blanket*, equally true that cultural idiosyncrasies could as well. In fact, Brelsford concluded from his experiment in Lusaka that *Mr. Wise and Mr. Foolish* "was not an outstanding success with African audiences [in Northern Rhodesia] on several technical grounds, mainly that of being made in a strange terrain and with actors of distant tribes." The "unRhodesian street scenes of Johannesburg with tramcars and skyscrapers," Brelsford discovered, "only caused sniggers in the audience rather than exclamations of wonder."[103] Brelsford is telling us what we already know: that the explosive issue of cultural peculiarities, in fact, consistently plagued colonial filmmaking and exhibition, resulting in conflicts in the MCCC and leading the mining industry to retool recruitment films at significant expense.

Predictably, the issue of medical treatment for VD also arose, as Brelsford noticed many Africans incorrectly expecting a single injection to cure the scourge. "The African," he warned, "has a sometimes surprisingly different approach to Venereal Disease from that of the European."[104] These thorny problems of cultural translation in Brelsford's deliberations in 1947 would rear their head again the following year when the BFI hosted the Film in Colonial Development conference in London, with an opening address by Arthur Creech Jones, secretary of state for the colonies, and talks by notables such as documentary filmmaker John Grierson and the Colonial Film Unit's George Pearson.[105] As the next chapter demonstrates, though, the very questions posed for conference panelists and participants—how best to utilize and tailor cinema for illiterate colonial subjects—basically rehashed those that framed the search for a responsible British film policy years earlier.

Britain expended considerable energy to establish an official, consistent policy toward colonial filmmaking and film exhibition. But despite the conferences, the critiques and all the false starts, evidence suggests that officials in both the private and public sectors continued to believe that motion pictures offered an effective tool for mobilizing and educating Africans like those laboring in the South African gold mines. In fact, films remained an important part of the labor recruitment arsenal well after the introduction of apartheid in 1948. In 1974, for instance, in response to Malawi pulling out 100,000 migrant laborers from the Rand, the Chamber of Mines set up a new Public Relations Media Division to complement the existing TEBA Film and TV Unit. In a revealing description of the chamber's recruiting strategy during this period that shows remarkable continuity with *Red Blanket*'s earlier narrative strategy of romanticizing tribal life while advertising the putative benefits of mine labor, TEBA produced newsreels shown throughout the Union by "field representatives [to] familiarize families at home with the mining environment as well as keeping workers in touch with happenings at home."[106]

6

Image Imperium

The Origins of British Film Policy in Africa

The crisis of the Great War led to new experiments in filmmaking on several fronts. A notable example was the USSR, where film was pressed into service to improve production and transform citizens into willing participants in the world's first modern socialist experiment. In 1918, the Soviets established the Division of Photography and Cinema, and in 1919 promptly nationalized the film industry. Within two years they could boast of dozens of "agitka" (agitational) shorts and propaganda features, including *For the Red Flag* (1920). With over 100 languages to contend with in their vast territory, the Bolsheviks hoped to achieve instantaneous ideological conversion through motion pictures.[1]

Before the rise of the motion picture industry, images of various sorts were already playing a role in tying Britain's colonial possessions to the metropole. As early as 1887 Britain's Imperial Institute opened galleries "to illustrate ... progress in our Empire" through film-strips and slides, as well as providing a center to study the resources of the peripheries.[2] By World War I, though, moving pictures in Britain had not only gained on these forms of visual edification, but had clearly surpassed them. During the conflict, Britain yoked the cinematograph to the needs of the state, although with less resolve than the Soviets.[3] To stimulate production domestically, for instance, the Ministry of Agriculture sought to reach English farmers more quickly and effectively by producing and exhibiting agricultural films.[4]

With the 1920s cultural solidification of the medium, efforts were made to broaden its pedagogical possibilities, especially with the 1925 Cinema Commission of Enquiry,[5] which led to the rapid proliferation of projectors in English schools.[6] Cinema advocates also began looking beyond England's borders to extend the reach of the film industry, stimulate colonial economic development, and most importantly, build ideological consensus for empire.[7] As early as 1913, officials were pondering a grand exhibition site to highlight the country's overseas holdings, an idea brought to fruition with the construction of Wembley Park in northwest London to host the colonial exhibitions of 1924–25. Cameramen for British Instructional Films combed Africa (the Gold Coast and Nigeria in particular) before and after the Wembley exhibitions with the aim of promoting Britain's colonial holdings. *Zanzibar and the Clove Industry* (1925), *Black Cotton* (1927), and *Oil Palm of Nigeria* (1928) were prominent examples of Empire Series films promoting agricultural successes, while *Blazing the Trail* (1929) focused on the construction of the Gold Coast's new harbor facilities at Takoradi.

By 1935 a number of colonial officials and missionaries were expanding the reach of cinema yet again with the idea of making films in the colonies for colonial spectators in Southern and Central Africa. This project aimed to satisfy the somewhat paradoxical directive to aid "tribal society in the two-fold struggle it is making to preserve the old traditions and adapt itself to the modern world."[8] But before turning to the Bantu Educational Kinema Experiment (the subject of the next chapter) it is necessary to explore the tangled roots of the project dating back a decade, to the search for a comprehensive and constructive film policy for the British Empire. Examining these debates on the "films question" which engaged the upper echelon of the Colonial Office and British missionary circles, requires looking first at three pervasive themes of interwar discourse: economic protectionism and development, the impact of cinema in India on the broader colonial world, and African education.

Protection and Development

In March 1927, president of the Board of Trade, Sir Cunliffe-Lister, took to the Parliament floor to read the proposed Cinematograph Films Bill to restructure the British film industry. "To-day," he thundered, "films are shown to millions of people throughout the Empire and must unconsciously influence the ideas and outlook of British people of all races." Unfortunately, he noted, due to wartime retrenchment "only a fraction, something like 5 percent, of the films which are at present shown in the British Empire are of British origin."[9] Cunliffe-Lister was not the only one fretting about America's stranglehold on worldwide distribution. Film producers and others were rethinking domestic cinema policy, arguing for abolishing blind and block booking, and imposing quotas for British films to bolster the domestic industry and enhance political/economic colonial stability.[10] By the time the act was passed, however, the quota only applied to domestic exhibition, for African dependencies were already locked into long-term contracts with distributors like AFP, which supplied primarily American films.[11] Cunliffe-Lister subsequently encouraged colonial governments to "follow the lead given by the Home Government in this matter, if not by adopting the quota method, then by some other effective means such as a preferential scheme of duties."[12]

Protectionism, in fact, had been deemed crucial enough to be explored by the Imperial Conference in October 1926 (which was itself the subject of a Pathé Gazette film showing statesmen emerging from 10 Downing Street and posing for a group shot), and by Sir Robert Donald in particular who was also investigating America's hegemony. Areas under British rule, he despaired, had become targets for Hollywood's detritus, for "the pictures which are not fit for exhibition in America are dumped in the overseas markets." To make matters worse, this "stupendous world industry, of mushroom growth, has been built up, or is controlled to a large extent, by men who are either of foreign birth or are hyphenated Americans." Donald warned his readers that "Americanization" could lead to destabilization, especially because "the propaganda is all the more telling because it is unconscious."[13] Protectionist support for the domestic film industry by conservatives like Donald and Cunliffe-Lister was only part of a larger imperialist strategy by Colonial Secretary Amery and Prime Minister Baldwin to fight chronic unemployment and realize economic windfalls from the empire. In fact, it was out of an unsuccessful bid to impose tariffs that motion pictures were conceived as a way of stimulating domestic consumption of Empire goods in England. For this reason, by the mid–1920s elites were hoping for an expanded role for British cinema both in England and abroad. Conservatives hoped the Cinematograph Bill would strengthen the domestic film industry, lead to a greater awareness overseas of all things British, and advertise at home through a "National Movement," the benefits of consuming British Empire foodstuffs.[14] In 1926, the newly formed Empire Marketing Board (EMB) was working to "bring the Empire alive" in England through an extensive propaganda campaign: "Buy British" included building awareness of Empire goods through sales drives and Empire Shopping Weeks, banner-heading EMB on newspaper advertisements, posters, and leaflets,[15] and providing English schoolchildren with "pleasing pictures of workers picking cotton, cutting copra and harvesting tea."[16]

Stephen Tallents, who authored *The Projection of England* and was appointed to oversee the EMB, hired John Grierson—the "father of documentary film"—to head the bureau's Film Unit. Ironically, given the EMB's conservative origins, the department, in Grierson's words, was "left-wing to a man. Not many of us were Communists, but we were all socialists."[17] Grierson, in fact, looked approvingly upon the USSR for recognizing early the propagandistic possibilities of moving pictures, and bragged that the EMB was "the only organisation outside Russia that understands and has imagination enough to practice the principles of long-range propaganda."[18] Despite his political leanings, Grierson exhibited little opposition to British imperialism and, instead, ruminated on the putative dividends of a kinder, gentler empire whose fruits would be harvested equally by colonizer and colonized. "The principle effect [of the EMB] in six years," he declared, "has been to change the connotations of the word 'Empire'":

> Our command of peoples becomes slowly a cooperative effort in the tilling of the soil, the reaping of harvests and the organisation of a world economy. For the old flags of exploitation it substitutes new flags of common labour; for the old frontiers of conquest it substitutes the new frontiers of research and world-wide organisation.[19]

Leopold Amery hoped the EMB could educate a British public untrained in the nuances of international trade and colonial geography, for many consumers apparently believed that California tinned fruit was an Empire product.[20] He therefore put "Cinematograph Films" on the Colonial Office Conference agenda for May 1927. At this gathering, which included Under-Secretary of State for the Colonies Ormsby-Gore and colonial secretaries from the dependencies, a prominent topic was censorship, which has been treated earlier in this study. But members also resolved that a more constructive role for cinema should be sought, for films are "the best way of describing one part of the Empire to another."[21] Subsequently, in 1929 Amery appointed a Colonial Films Committee, which reported in 1930 to the Colonial Office on three points of reference: (1) the use of the cinematograph as an instrument of education; (2) the supply and exhibition of British films; and (3) censorship in the colonies.[22]

What the report omitted was precisely what was meant by "educating" the colonized. The committee did suggest that "to the millions of unsophisticated people of Africa who are unable to read and write, moving pictures must be a most impressive vehicle of instruction. By no other means could greater progress be made in giving them the foundation of general knowledge of the outer world, upon which a more elaborate form of education may, later on, be built up."[23] But this still left open the precise purpose of this education. What was clear, though, was that cinema, for Amery, could educate the African in two types of consumption. First, imported British films could be marketed and thereby expand film-going as a regular leisure activity; second, non-commercial films could help stimulate the African purchase of British manufactured goods.

Amery's interest in films for the colonies was consistent with his overall approach towards development. The same year that he formed the Colonial Films Committee, he pushed through the 1929 Colonial Development Act to "aid and develop agriculture and industry in the Colonies, Protectorates and Mandated Territories."[24] Through the use of cinema, then, new modes of production could potentially be coupled with new forms of consumption. For this reason, while much of the 1927 Colonial Office report emphasized censorship and control, the 1930 majority opinion of the Colonial Films Committee pushed in a new direction, that of redirecting the purchasing habits of British subjects. But another reason for this change in emphasis was the liberal influence of the new secretary of state for the colonies, Lord Passfield (Sidney Webb), on the Colonial Office.[25] A majority of the Committee of Colonial Governors who considered the report also threw their support behind a more constructive role for the medium: "The Conference is convinced that the cinematograph has very great possibilities for educational purposes in the widest sense, not only for children, but also for adults, especially with illiterate peoples."[26] Not all committee members, though, supported the proliferation of film, especially in areas of Africa where motion pictures were just arriving. In the dissenting opinion of Hesketh Bell, former governor of Uganda and Northern Nigeria, the lack of an effective censorship apparatus had already weakened British colonial rule in India and threatened to do the same for Africa.

From Jewel to Thorn: Lessons from India

In the same year as Amery's Colonial Films Committee report, India's colonial regime was delivered a shock by the 1930 declaration of independence and Gandhi's Salt March. For most officials, these disruptions pointed to the tragic breakdown of respect in the jewel of the Crown for British authority. For Bell, they added fuel to his withering opinion of the 1930 Colonial Films Committee report:

> Although we know that a vast deal of harm can be done even to civilized persons by the display of bad pictures, the injury which can be done to primitive people by the exhibition of demoralizing films, representing criminal and immodest actions by white men and women, can hardly be exaggerated. The success of our government of subject races depends almost entirely on the degree of respect which we can inspire. Incalculable is the damage that has already been done to the prestige of Europeans in India and the Far East through the widespread exhibition of ultra-sensationalistic and disreputable pictures, and it behooves us, therefore, while there is yet time, to see that the same harm shall not be repeated in our Tropical Empire.[27]

Whether cinema had already ruined the East by 1930 is debatable, but it had indeed made an early arrival. The first recorded performance dates to Bombay's "cinematographe" in July 1896, followed the next year by screenings in Madras.[28] The contours of the earliest exhibitions mirrored those of the Cape Colony, the Transvaal and elsewhere, initially catering to elites through touring circuses, music halls, and vaudeville. In addition, itinerant exhibitors offered programs with themes highlighting Christianity, European exploration, and the coronations of British kings. Soon, however, Indian and African paths diverged, for purveyors of European films increasingly included enterprising Indians themselves.[29] Indians also made inroads into production, with Dadasaheb Phalke's feature film *Raja Harischandra* (1913), launching Bollywood and blazing a trail for a burgeoning national cinema, as a 1929 trade bulletin made clear:

The production of feature films in India exceeds in number and footage, that of the United Kingdom, a fact which is not generally recognized. In 1925 the production of feature films in the United Kingdom was 34; in 1926, 26; and in 1927, 48. The approximate number of feature films produced by Indian concerns (excluding Burma) in 1924–5 was 60; in 1925–6, 111; and in 1926–7, 108.[30]

This upper-class entertainment soon spread to all social classes as cinema was injected into Indian cultural life.[31] But film-going remained a primarily urban diversion for several years. In the 1920s, the Indian Cinematograph Committee reported that "the cinema has as yet scarcely touched the fringe of the vast rural population," a pattern that began to change in the half decade before the talkies.[32] The government sponsored railroad cars to be used for a traveling cinema circuit, bringing American, Indian and British commercial films to rural areas. Shows were offered in the evening air to villages situated near train tracks. According to estimates, during this period an astonishing six million spectators watched the films, which sparked a new approach toward film.[33] State intervention had been broached as far back as 1918, when Sir Stanley Reed, vice-president of the Indian government's Publicity Board, estimated that "the cinema could reach ten times the number of people than the traditional magic lantern show could," but his proposal was postponed temporarily due to the colonial government's *laissez-faire* orientation.[34] Yet by 1937, there were no fewer than 1,236 government-funded traveling cinemas in India, showing films that, according to one critic, were "defective in every respect ... produced and exhibited to the semi-educated."[35]

In the late 1920s, Bollywood productions ranked the most popular among Indians, although the Cinematograph Committee claims it was especially favored by the "less cultured classes." *The Birth of Krishna*, representative of the mythological genre, proved to have universal appeal among Hindus, while Muslim themes were rarely treated given sectarian differences and prohibitions concerning religious imagery. But American films also brought in large crowds. By 1930, reportedly the most popular film ever shown in India was Douglas Fairbanks's *The Thief of Bagdad* (1924), with Chaplin films right behind.

The expansion of Indian spectatorship led inexorably to the issue of image control. In 1918 the government passed the Cinematograph Act, establishing censor boards in Madras, Bombay, Calcutta, and Rangoon. But officials in Britain and India often accused the boards of being "weak and inexperienced,"[36] and were frustrated by the lack of centralized control, with one complaining that "in India the commission of many dacoities and other crimes of violence can be traced to the influence exerted upon the impressionable and imitative minds of Indian youth by the exploits of a film villain or even hero."[37] *The Guardian* in Madras also denounced "the evil influences of unwholesome sex films [on] the public mind,"[38] a complaint echoed by other papers and the National Council of Women.[39] The British Social Hygiene Council (later represented in the Bantu Educational Kinema Experiment) also blamed cinema specifically for "lowering [India's] standard of sex conduct, and thereby tending to increase the dissemination of disease."[40]

The hysteria in India over the effects of commercial films on the East soon spread throughout England. In August 1926, the *Leeds Mercury* published a scathing article by Constance Bromley of the Calcutta Opera House, describing how white women especially were imperiled by the eroding respect for British authority:

> It is the presentation on the film of white women in objectionable poses that gives rise to an attitude of increasing disrespect on the part of the native.... It is not the films only which require a more careful censorship, but the posters which ... show a dark-skinned Mexican

abducting a lovely white girl.... There can be no doubt that the exhibition of such posters and films is bad for the prestige of the European in India.[41]

Only a few weeks later, Hesketh Bell reiterated Bromley's fears about the "deplorable effects of the 'pictures' in the Far East," an editorial read by government officials such as Leopold Amery. "Until the cinemas laid bare the worst sides of the life of the white man most of the natives were ignorant of the depths of vice which afflict certain sections of white society." But Bell's harangue went further, expressing anxiety about the potential for political agitation resulting from cinema's subversive tendencies: "Whatever may be the effect of Communist agents in the Far East there can be no doubt that the relations between Europeans and natives, especially in the large towns, are very different from what they used to be.... There can be no doubt that the way for Communistic influence has been facilitated by a powerful and novel element: cinema."[42]

One possible solution, of course, was to centralize and tighten the censorship apparatus. But some colonial officials argued that exploiting the educational possibilities of the medium would be more desirable, and more effective, than simply implementing racially coded restrictions. Although many whites believed India was already too saturated with commercial cinema to make such a plan feasible, one writer applauded an instructional film, *A Tale of Gurgaon*, for its "uplift" work in "raising the standard of living and increasing the produce of the soil in India," specifically because the "people who appear in the film are actual villagers, just living their ordinary life before the camera."[43]

By the mid-to-late 1930s colonial officialdom in India was finally moving toward addressing the recommendations made by the Cinematograph Committee a full decade earlier, arguing that "production should be promoted of films in India subjects." But according to C.W. Jardine of the Indian Board of Trade, by necessity the government itself would have to subsidize the production of films. He warned, though, of the potential for blowback, as it might produce strong opposition within India itself. Nor could India's indigenous film industry be trusted to produce films lauding British rule; on the contrary, by the 1930s Bollywood was inserting subtle nationalist propaganda, which often escaped the scrutiny of colonial officials, into otherwise banal melodramas and mythological epics.

Thus, those interested in advancing the cause of British colonialism in India through cinema had their backs to the wall for several reasons. The relatively early introduction of commercial films from America endangered the authority of whites by depicting demeaning imagery from the West. But instructional/propaganda films sponsored by the British government risked being accused of bias against Indian nationalist aspirations. To make matters worse, Indian commercial films were often imbued with, however subtly, the gathering tides of revolutionary discontent.

Nor did the British "Empire" genre of the 1930s succeed in doing for the colonies what it was apparently doing for the metropole. Spectators in England admired these productions which dovetailed nicely with other visual propaganda of the day, emphasizing British benevolence for dark-skinned subalterns. But reception in the peripheries to these ideological constructions proved troubling. R.T. Peel, for instance, secretary of the Public and Judicial Department in London's India Office, received a warning of possible "misreadings" of *The Charge of the Light Brigade* (1936), which takes place in a fictitious northern Indian province called Suristan. "It has occurred to us," officials noted, "that the name 'Suristan' can only be interpreted to mean 'The Country of the Swine' and, since everything points to its identity with Afghanistan, this point will be noticed and give great offense to Muslim sentiment."[44] This may have been an unintended affront on the part of the scriptwriter, but

Prem Chowdhry details how films like *The Drum* (1938) were explicitly designed to support Britain's divide-and-rule strategy. This film, which portrays Muslims as "fundamentalist, backward, and anti-national," succeeded in raising agitation in Bombay among what the police derided as "mostly young Mussalmans of no importance."[45]

Those concerned about the tensile strength of empire in India proved prescient, as the British colonial project there disintegrated in the early post–World War II years. But two decades earlier, Hesketh Bell was arguing that, while India might be lost, perhaps there was still time to learn from British mistakes in the East and salvage Britain's standing in Africa: "Much harm has already been done, but, owing to the complete authority possessed by colonial administrations in such matters, it is still within our power to prevent the spread of this dangerous influence and especially stop the introduction of demoralising pictures into those great African territories which are still unaffected." Despite his tone, which sent shockwaves through Colonial Office circles, no one seems to have followed up on his suggestion that in order to "avoid the risk of the Colonial Censor's veto, … film producers might … prepare concurrently two versions of the same film story—one for general exhibition and the other for display in countries where restrictions are advisable."[46] Rather, those who produced films for Africans would soon create films uniquely designed for the "primitive" mind, an experiment requiring not only an intimate knowledge of the Other, but a theory of social development and differential education in which colonial cinema could be grounded.

African Education at the Crossroads

Broadly sketched, virtually all schools for the colonized in the subcontinent had, for decades, been under the controlling influence of missionaries of various stripes. Although one missionary claimed, "Bible teaching was the backbone of all our school efforts," the three R's were also emphasized in most curricula.[47] Prior to World War I Britain's Colonial Office generally preferred a hands-off approach to educating the African, mostly providing financial incentives to mission schools through the grants-in-aid system. Theoretically, this should have provided some sway over educational policy, yet most schools remained outside the jurisdiction of colonial officialdom.[48] Mabel Carney, whom we encountered earlier on the Witwatersrand traveling with the "Bioscope Man," suggested that "governments … entrust nearly 90 percent of all educational activity in the continent to missionary direction."[49] But by the 1910s, three changes were underway that would prove foundational for colonial cinema. First, colonial governments were becoming more involved in educating their African charges; second, local vernaculars often replaced English as a means of instruction[50]; and third, the Bookerite model of industrial education was increasingly touted as "the solution to Africa's problems."[51] Indeed, it is telling that at the Edinburgh World Missionary Conference of 1910, missionaries were encouraged to study closely Tuskegee's and Hampton's pedagogy to explore its applicability to Africa.[52] This new orientation was reflected in Booker T. Washington's own stark judgment on haphazardly transplanting "European" education to Africa:

> A friend of mine who went to Liberia to study conditions once came upon a negro shut up within a hovel reading Cicero's orations. That was all right. The negro has as much right to read Cicero's orations in Africa as a white man does in America. But the trouble with the coloured man was that he had on no pants. I want a tailor shop first so the negro can sit down and read Cicero's orations like a gentleman with his pants on.[53]

The proliferation of vocational curricula south of the Sahara in the interwar years owed its success to the attractiveness of the doctrine across the white political spectrum. Missionaries were concluding that as an added component to indirect rule, the manual arts could resolve the dilemmas of detribalization, while white settlers believed the Bookerite model promised a more compliant black population.[54] For those in government, though, efficiency and cash-crop production were crucial. In cotton-producing Uganda, for instance, a commission appointed by the secretary of state for the colonies emphasized, "Farming is not merely the most important aspect of African life. It is the foundation on which African culture and education must be built.... School books need to be 'rural' in outlook, containing stories about plants, animals, farmers and markets."[55]

At the core of these educational reappraisals was the conviction that societies must move through discrete stages of social development—modernized agriculture the necessary precursor to industry—a perspective championed by two books on opposite sides of the Atlantic. In 1917, as Charles T. Loram published *Education of the South African Native*, Thomas Jesse Jones released his study on *Negro Education* in America.[56] Both were destined to wield tremendous influence over African education following World War I.[57] In particular, Joseph Oldham, who had risen to prominence in 1910 as secretary for the Edinburgh Missionary Conference, and as editor of the *International Review of Missions*, inaugurated a "formidable era of educational cooperation" with a review of Loram's and Jones's treatises on industrial education.[58] In 1919, in conjunction with the Conference of British Missionary Societies and missionary bodies in America, Oldham encouraged Jones to head a commission to study education in West and South Africa. Oldham himself subsequently toured America to get a first-hand look at black institutions, and met with Jones and the Gold Coast's James Emman Kwegyir Aggrey, who was currently teaching at Livingstone College in North Carolina.[59]

In a sweeping 1920–21 West African tour, Jones promoted his industrial agenda by critiquing the earlier missionary bias toward literary training. Spending more time advertising the putative benefits of the manual arts for blacks than studying existing colonial educational policy, the commission traveled to South Africa where Jones teamed up with Loram, who was serving on the Native Affairs Commission. Jones proceeded to meet with John David Rheinallt-Jones (himself the son of a minister) who applauded his "remarkable work in the creation of a better spirit amongst the 'radical' Native."[60] Jones, in turn, went on to applaud Ray Phillips's focus on urban leisure and the MCCC, which was still in its early stages but already showing signs of success:

> It is evident that the value of these shows is not only in diverting the minds of thousands of Natives from less helpful subjects, but also in giving to them pictures of activities and life that will influence their own actions and, through them, the actions of hundreds of villages scattered far and wide.[61]

Jones led another African tour in 1924, but by this time his impact on policy could already be seen in the Advisory Committee of Native Education in Tropical Africa organized by the secretary of state for the colonies in 1923. In fact, the two were connected through the labors of Major Hanns Vischer. After retiring as Nigeria's director of native education, Vischer traveled with Jones on the second tour, while simultaneously serving as secretary of the Advisory Committee on Native Education, which included the likes of Oldham and Frederick Lugard.[62] Due to the desire of both missionaries and the Colonial Office to better understand Bookerite philosophy, Vischer also followed in Oldham's footsteps on a short tour of American institutions, including Tuskegee, Hampton, Penn, and rural Alabama schools.⁶³ The Colonial Office soon offered Jones the post of director of education for the colonies. He refused, but Vischer took the position.⁶⁴ And it was Vischer who would be among the first in colonial circles to propose the use of the cinematograph in the peripheries not only as an educational aid for schools, but more generally as a tool for colonial development.⁶⁵

Oldham, who penned the findings of the Advisory Committee on Native Education, stressed the need for "co-operation between Government and other educational agencies." But just as importantly, the committee defined its pedagogical theory of "adaptation" which proved enormously influential, with colonial education departments subsequently struggling to put into practice its recommendations of "Africanizing" rather than "Europeanizing" their indigenous students. "Education," declared Oldham, "should be adapted to the mentality, aptitudes, occupations and traditions of the various peoples, conserving so far as possible all sound and healthy elements in the fabric of their social life, adapting them where necessary to changed circumstance and progressive ideas, as an agent of natural growth and evolution."⁶⁶ As one of the primary architects of trusteeship in the 1920s and as chief ideologue of the Bantu Educational Kinema Experiment in the 1930s, it is helpful to dwell on Oldham's understanding of the need for interracial cooperation, social progress and colonial education in the empire. Education for Oldham was not a mere adjunct of imperial control, but rather lay at its very core. "The term education," he stressed, "is used in a wider sense than the activities of the school."⁶⁷ In 1923 he had served on the Royal Hilton Young Commission studying Kenya. The result was not the rubber-stamping of Amery's conservative leanings favoring white settlers, but rather, as William Roger Louis coined it, a "rogue commission" that refused "Amery's lead on economic problems … [and] reopened the political question."⁶⁸

At the core of the White Paper drafted by Oldham was the declaration of "native paramountcy" and "trusteeship," two concepts that dominated interwar discourse on the "native problem": "In the administration of Kenya His Majesty's Government regard themselves as exercising a trust on behalf of the African population, and they are unable to delegate or share this trust, the object of which may be defined as the protection and advancement of the native races."⁶⁹ Oldham's vision for African development was education and controlled modernization under the tutelage of missionaries and colonial educators, and thus it was no coincidence that his treatise *The Remaking of Man in Africa* focused heavily on education. But when it came to subject peoples, he emphasized that instruction should not lead to a class of "over-educated" graduates. Indeed, it was precisely this tendency in an earlier era, Oldham argued, that resulted in the bitter recriminations of "trousered" Africans breeding discontent among the young. Rather, the school must serve to reintegrate students into the broader indigenous community for the betterment of the whole:

> Experience of work among rural communities in many parts of the world has shown the importance of educating the community as a whole…. Where the school touches only the children, it takes them further and further away from their parents and their homes and brings suffering and mental unrest to old and young…. Education must include parents as well as children and relate its message to every side of the village life.⁷⁰

When the cinema lorries started rolling for the Bantu Educational Kinema Experiment (BEKE) in the mid–1930s, the new paradigm for African education had been crafted: under the rubric of trusteeship, Africans would, however paradoxically, be both "remade" and "Africanized" through the manual arts, with communities rather than individuals serving as the prime focus. But in the decade between the 1925 Memorandum of the Advisory

Committee on Native Education and the commencement of the BEKE, the path was littered with several stillborn film proposals and two localized experiments in utilizing cinema to facilitate colonial consolidation.

Colonial Cinema, the British Empire and Intruding Chickens

In 1926, an enterprising Nigerian put on a number of cinematograph shows, projecting old films from an enclosure onto the whitewashed gable of a house. These events would undoubtedly have been lost to historical memory but for the presence of William Sellers, propaganda officer for the Nigerian Colonial Services. Sellers had already been experimenting with ways to impart instructional material to locals, but his attempts to incorporate lantern slides, he confessed, were "very disappointing indeed except with comparatively highly educated Africans." Dubious about Africans' ability to make sense out of still pictures which were usually turned "the wrong way up in an effort to focus ... on the picture," Sellers believed that films might prove useful providing there were allowances made for African cinematic illiteracy, and if they were locally made.[71] Pressing events in Lagos soon led him to put theory into practice when a plague called for broad co-operation in reducing the rat population. *Anti-Plague Operations in Lagos* (1929?), Sellers's health film illustrating the way in which rats spread disease, was one of Britain's first films produced in the colonies for educational purposes.[72]

The effectiveness of the narrative, Sellers himself later stated, suffered somewhat from broken continuity as a result of Africans' lack of exposure to the medium. He became intrigued by the fact that at several showings "illiterate members of the audience" made reference to a chicken pecking in the dirt. There were, thought Sellers, no fowl featured, and he suspected that "Africans must have mistaken the chicken for something else in the film." Upon closer inspection, though, he discovered that indeed an "intruding chicken" had appeared in one corner of the screen and then moved off.[73] And thus was born one of the most enduring tales of African reception to colonial films: Africans, he argued, were virtually incapable of correctly decoding the broader intended message or theme of a film, instead focusing on the immediacy of inconsequential fleeting images. Decades later, for instance, one of the primary recollections of a Central African Film Unit (CAFU) cameraman who had worked in Zimbabwe was that "Africans would laugh at anything, like a monkey running across the set."[74] Similar stories abounded throughout the continent and served as smug justification for the cinematic paternalism of the colonial era.

Sellers concluded from the reaction not that Africans had a keen sense of observation—picking up what he, in fact, had missed—but rather that "illiterate people have their own way of looking at a picture":

> Educated people normally focus their eyes on a point a foot or two in front of the screen, and by more or less glancing at the picture we are able to appreciate the entire scene as a whole. The same thing happens when we use our eyes for reading. We see a word, a group of words, or even a whole line, and are not conscious of the individual letters. This is only possible because we focus our eyes a little distance in front of the page. The eyes of illiterate people are not trained to see non-stereoscopic things in this way. They focus their eyes flat on to the screen and they can scan the picture and analyse it in detail. They fasten their gaze on to any movement in the scene to the exclusion of everything else in the picture.[75]

What was needed, argued Sellers, was a "special and restricted technique" of filmmaking for colonial subjects, a perspective that guided him when he launched an experimental health and welfare campaign using his own motion pictures with the aid of the Colonial Development Fund. Sellers initially retro-fitted two vehicles in Nigeria with generators and projectors, but in 1931 a mobile van was built to specification in England and imported to the colony.[76] The Nigerian Health Services Department, hoping to reap benefits from the cinema, soon sponsored its own propaganda unit with Sellers at the helm, allowing for mobile film tours throughout the colony.[77]

It was in Nigeria, then, that the ruling paradigm of colonial cinema for African spectators was established: for films to be effective, they must have slow tempos and simple, smooth narratives. Reverse shots, cross-cuts or other radical changes in perspective were to be eschewed, such as the opening establishing shot of Sellers's own anti-plague film which began with an "aerial view of a Lagos slum, before 'zooming in' on a rat scurrying among the rubbish."[78] Close-ups, while sometimes necessary for making the obscure appear larger on the screen, should not be casually "pitchforked into a film every few seconds as is normally done for the purpose of avoiding monotony in shots of fair length."[79] Indeed, Sellers's later experiments in showing Africans huge close-ups of mosquitoes sucking blood had supposedly backfired, as "people became alarmed and enquired about the country where the people had to contend with such wicked looking monsters."[80]

The mosquito was another variant of the familiar topos of primitive African film reception during the colonial period. Timothy Burke relates a story told to him by an aging Zimbabwean advertiser who had witnessed a program for educating villagers about malaria in the Zambezi Valley. A Rhodesian health officer had constructed a two-foot *papier-mâché* mosquito for the presentation, but villagers informed him that his good-intentioned concerns were irrelevant given that their own mosquitoes were so much smaller.[81] Opposing interpretations of these responses immediately suggest themselves. On the one hand, colonial officials may have been correct in their estimation that Africans simply misunderstood the intended message in the film or demonstration. Or perhaps, to cite a famous controversy which cuts to the core of problems inherent in participant/observer ethnographic fieldwork, Africans may have simply been playing a hoax on their interrogators in the same way that Derek Freeman has claimed that indigenes intentionally led Margaret Mead astray in *Coming of Age in Samoa*.[82]

Further experiments in instructional films for Africans were set in motion by Oldham and the Native Education Advisory Committee when they invited biologist Julian Huxley to East Africa to "advise upon certain aspects of native education." In 1929, Huxley hosted two showings for black audiences (as well as one for whites at Nairobi's Government House). Each included three films provided by the EMB corresponding to different levels of comprehension, to gauge the value of visual propaganda and educational films among adolescents. *Cotton-Growing in Nigeria* (originally titled *Black Cotton*) was considered the most accessible for African schoolchildren because, as Huxley affirmed, it starred "people like themselves, engaged in familiar occupations." *Fathoms of the Deep* was considered to be more difficult as it introduced many children to animal life under the sea. *The Life of a Plant* introduced several novel elements: the entire lifecycle of a nasturtium was illustrated through time-lapse photography, microscopic images showed structures invisible to the naked eye, and botanical processes such as pollination were carefully explained.[83]

The morning of the first exhibition, in Moshi, Tanganyika, Huxley explained what the boys of the Government School could expect. Following his introductory talk, they walked with the school's marching band five miles from the school in Old Moshi to New Moshi where the only cinema in town was located. Although most students had taken only one year of English, essays written after the screening reflected their ability to digest the material:

> M. JUMA: The first cinema which was shown to us was the cotton which is obtained in the part of Africa which is called Nigeria, and how the people of Nigeria pick up the cotton. And how they separate the cotton seeds from the cotton by the way of ginning machines. And how they weave clothes.
> STANISLAUS: And then how flowers can bear. First of all the bee take a little medicine in a masculine flower on his feet and put in a woman flower and it can bear the seeds.[84]

According to Huxley, only one "attempted to <u>explain</u> the speeding-up of the plant film[,] though I understand from Mr. Chandor that most of the older boys seemed definitely to have grasped the principle."[85] Chandor, no less than the famed biologist, determined that "cinema could be a most important instrument for awaking the young African mind." It should be noted that one student aligned himself explicitly with the deeper ideological implications of Huxley's experiment: "We found that the people of Nigeria are now civilized as I saw the women picking the cotton from the pods and put in the sacks, and how they gin it by machines called gins."[86]

Kampala was next on the itinerary for Huxley's EMB experiment. Director of Education E.G. Morris reserved the primary cinema hall in town, and invitations went out to different groups. Turnout was greater than anticipated, and spectators "filled the body of the Hall, and many had to be accommodated in the gallery, which it had been intended to reserve for Europeans; and even some [Africans] had to be turned away." The large crowd was more diverse than the Tanganyika showing. Present were boys from Makerere College, Kisube and Budo Intermediate School, and the Government Normal School and Industrial Training Department. Also girls from Gayaza and Cook's Maternity Training Centre at Namirembe were on hand, and even younger schoolchildren. Estimates were that 75–80 percent of those present had never before witnessed motion pictures. "The reaction of the audience were [sic] extremely interesting," Huxley wrote. "During the first minute or so of the cotton film they were very quiet. Partly, I think, the whole thing was new and for the moment incomprehensible[;] partly, the opening of the film is rather dull":

> When, however, a number of natives began to appear on the screen to pick, carry, and load the cotton, the audience began to get wildly excited. They applauded, stamped with their feet, laughed, shouted, explained to each other; the noise was particularly deafening when anyone was seen on the film doing a hard job of work. It was completely impossible to make myself heard, and in any case I was so overcome by laughter that I should have found it difficult to carry on with my explanations.[87]

Many of the Baganda's essays, according to Huxley, displayed higher writing and comprehension skills due to the presence of Makerere College students. Overall, he concluded, "There is great scope for the use of educational films in Africa. The African enjoys the film with an almost childlike delight; he will come to see a film where he would not attend a lecture." But the value of motion pictures, he believed, went far beyond mere classroom instruction for children: "Films can be profitably used both as an adjunct to school education, and for adult education and propaganda. For the latter purpose they will in the present state of tropical Africa be much the most powerful weapon of propaganda which we have at our command."[88]

In October 1929, Huxley met Dr. Arthur Rutherford Paterson, deputy director of medical and sanitary services in Kenya, who had already begun his own filmmaking experiments. A few years before, Paterson had been called in to conduct an anti-hookworm health campaign among the coastal Digo people. According to Huxley, the campaign, which included digging nine thousand latrines, had almost eliminated the scourge and led to "an increase in the efficiency of Digo labourers, and in the amount of land under cultivation in the reserves."[89] Paterson's own film of the project, *Hookworm Campaign on the Kenya Coast* (referred to hereafter by its popular name, *Harley Street in the Bush*) produced in 1926, showed the building of the pits, with white doctors and black assistants moving from village to village examining residents. The film also contrasted sanitary and unsanitary huts, and showed health lectures to Africans. Interestingly, during the later stages of the campaign, cinema itself was used to secure the desired buy-in from local villagers:

> Proceedings in a new village were opened by a showing of the film, with running commentary; and this broke the ice, so that the doctors could get on twice as fast with their real work. With a little training beforehand in the photography, and a good deal of skilled assistance in the cutting and titling, such films could be of enormous assistance in all those numerous cases where the understanding and feelings of the general population need to be enlisted before a reform, be it medical, agricultural or social, can be properly carried out.[90]

For his film, Paterson probably used as a template *Unhooking the Hookworm* (1920) by the International Health Division of the Rockefeller Institute. This film was not only displayed in the American South, but also enjoyed distribution in several African colonies.[91] In the BEKE of the 1930s, the topic would be revisited yet again during its second stage of production in the form of *Tropical Hookworm* (1936). Paterson's film, though, may be the first produced by the British in Africa for Africans, for educational purposes. Its apparent success in local villages, evidenced in the fact that "the natives were delighted to see themselves on the screen, and were impressed by familiar examples," led the Medical Department to follow *Harley Street* with another on the causes and dangers of malaria. In fact, James Russell Orr, who a few years later would hatch his own colonial cinema scheme, told Roland Venables Vernon at the Colonial Office that Paterson credited *Harley Street*'s success to the fact that Africans saw themselves represented, a determination that would weigh heavily on future colonial cinema campaigns: "Dr. Paterson ... told me that he had exhibited his films among the Masai, who are, of course, the most backward of our tribes. He tells me that they found difficulty in understanding the film until they saw themselves or their cattle in the picture[,] when the whole subject became quite clear to them."[92] Soon Kenya's agriculture and veterinary departments followed suit with films on crop-growing instruction and Western methods of animal husbandry, also using local Africans as talent.[93]

The pioneering filmmaking experiments of Sellers and Paterson in West and East Africa, respectively, while important for cinema's dissemination, were both limited in scope, addressed primarily local needs, and thus lacked a coordinating body to oversee production of films deemed suitable for broader colonial audiences. But by 1930 there was a discernible escalation of interest within the Colonial Office, educational circles, missionary bodies, and, of course, the film industry to harness motion pictures to imperial pursuits—not simply to open new markets, but additionally to reap social and cultural benefits from the new medium.[94] Two commissions worked to bring film onto the national agenda in England. The first, as we have seen, was the 1929 Colonial Office Films Committee, which had pushed for race-based censorship within the colonies but expanded its recommendations to include using cinema as an educational tool. The change in emphasis reflected Britain's shifting political landscape when, in June 1929, Lord Passfield preserved the basic structure of the EMB, but "gave the terms of reference [for colonial cinema] more of a bias in the direction of the cultural and educational possibilities of the film."[95] The second, the 1929 Commission on Educational and Cultural Films, concluded that cinema "for good or evil" had become "a powerful force in national life, which should be used constructively in the interests of education in its widest sense."[96] The result of its investigation was the commission's 1932 report, *The Film in National Life*, leading to the formation of the British Film Institute (BFI) the following year to increase the quality and scope of films both domestically and within the empire.

"Making Native Peoples Happier, Healthier and More Useful"

Between 1930 and 1934 no fewer than five proposals for cinema programs targeting colonial audiences circulated the Colonial Office, none of which came to fruition. In 1930 Geoffrey Barkas, who had co-directed the wartime documentary *Q Ships*, recommended the creation of a small government cinema bureau to produce a "constant supply" of films for overseas dependencies, a plan which fell on deaf ears.[97] The next year James Russell Orr outlined his more ambitious vision of a chain of movie houses in East Africa, premiering health propaganda, British newsreels and agricultural instruction based on the Bookerite model. As director of education in Kenya, he had explicitly modeled education in the colony along Tuskegee lines.[98] In 1930 he was appointed assistant secretary for the commission on educational and cultural films. Consequently, the Africa Society invited Orr to speak at the Royal Society of Arts in April 1931, and it was in his speech on "The Use of the Kinema in the Guidance of Backward Races" that he first laid out his vision for a colonial cinema to rival the dangers of existing films. The need for intervention sooner than later was due primarily to "the evil influence of the public kinema house, which to the backward races is something novel and attractive." And in one of the more startlingly candid statements linking cinema with colonial hegemony, he lectured on the "major principles" that could be inculcated in African populations through film: "1) Loyalty; (2) Discipline and obedience to authority; (3) Courage; [and] (4) Self-Sacrifice."[99] This plan would have required that colonial governments provide 120-foot × 200-foot sites for cinema houses to be constructed by the Colonial Office in black townships.

While Orr pushed for realization of his scheme, competition was already emerging from within official circles. Roland Vernon served as assistant secretary of the Colonial Office and represented that body on Amery's Colonial Office Films Committee. Vernon had actually attended Orr's lecture before the Africa Society, and, in fact, was busy drafting his own proposal for an experiment "with regard to the potentialities and risks of the cinema as an instrument either of education or of recreation among more primitive races, or under cultural conditions widely different from those of Europe or America."[100] His plan, conceived at the end of 1930 and submitted to the Rockefeller Foundation the following July, envisioned obtaining expert assistance from education specialists like Hanns Vischer and ethnographers such as J.L. Myers of the Royal Anthropological Institute. Vernon contemplated films on the following subjects for exhibition to mixed audiences in Malaysia, his target area:

General Education and Geography:
  a. Daily Life; scenes, arts and crafts.
  b. Homes and Houses, arts and crafts of other races at similar stages of development.

Nature Study and Its Application:
  c. Nature study of the territory selected for the experiment, showing its plants and animals, together with comparative scenes from other regions.

Economic and Cultural:

d. Higher Culture. From the Near East to Europe—development of arts and crafts, industries and commerce on other lands.

Agriculture:

e. Illustration of methods in general use related to botany and biology as well as to comparison with other civilizations.

Hygiene:

f. Health—Origins, transmission and avoidance of disease (certain films of this kind are known to be available with valuable results to native races at various stages of development).[101]

While Orr and Vernon hoped to begin work in their respective territories, both plans foundered primarily due to lack of funding. Another intriguing proposal for cinematic uplift originated from outside the Colonial Office. In 1932, Beresford Gale, a British-born black filled with what one official in Africa described as a "burning desire to help his coloured brethren," contacted Vischer with a plan to outfit a lorry in England with films, projectors, and a "dynamo" capable of bringing moving pictures to local villages in West Africa. Gale was also a naturalized American citizen and member of the Improved, Benevolent and Protective Order of the Elks, and hoped to establish local chapters along the African coast for "mutual Friendly aid and social uplift," and to "couple with this idea that of industrial, social, and hygienic education through Motion Picture[s]." One official approvingly declared that no indigenous resistance would result, and that, indeed, the "people of the Coast welcome all such overtures which could be made for their social betterment." He informed Vischer that Gale's program could replicate film experiments tried elsewhere with success:

> The idea of the Moving Picture lorry is nothing new or experimental, and its advantages and blessings away from first-class towns have been mamifold [sic] even here in England, and it is hoped that in helping to widen the scope of education and enlightenment in Africa a great step forward might be made in assisting Government in the herculean task which lies before it of doing for Africa what has been done so well for Canada, Australia and many of the other possessions for it has been conclusively demonstrated, time without number that governing an intelligent class of people, wherever situated, is far easier than governing the benighted and ignorant.[102]

Gale's plans, though, were never implemented. Vischer suggested that he consult further with the educational directors of the African possessions in question, but warned him that, while he was given the green light to proceed by the Colonial Office, no financial assistance could be expected from London.

The BFI soon entered the crowded field when it formed the Dominions, India and Colonies Panel in 1934, with Thomas Drummond Shiels as chairman. Arthur Paterson, who had already pioneered *Harley Street in the Bush* and replaced John L. Gilks as Kenya's director of medical services in 1932, was invited to submit his own proposal to the panel.[103] Paterson, in fact, was already working on other modes of visual propaganda by authoring illustrated books for African audiences, emphasizing the benefits of a "more prosperous peasant" in the emerging global economy (a perspective paralleling that of Joseph Oldham). In *The Book of Civilization: Part I*, he articulated from a colonialist perspective how an emerging Africa could best meet its own needs by meeting those of Britain.[104] For Paterson,

Western standards of cleanliness could be obtained through increased education and consumerism, which would boost African living standards: "Well, what is necessary? Two things are necessary: good education and enough money. But how much money? Certainly more than the average African possesses at present; because soap, clothes, furniture, pots which can be cleaned, houses which can be kept clean, and the water supplies which are necessary if we are to clean them cost money; and education costs money." *The Book of Civilization: Part II* clarified how meeting the needs of one society could resolve the problems of another. Illustrations show white British laborers at work in factories and loading ocean containers with manufactured goods, with the caption, "The men who make the cotton cloth, and the ploughs, and the bicycles ... need potatoes, and maize, and hides." Other illustrations show Africans loading raw materials onto the ocean containers for the return trip to England. The proper education for the African, then, was manual training to increase their "usefulness" and boost the empire's productivity. For Paterson, relations between colonizer and colonized in the world economic order entailed not structural domination, but rather symbiosis, and this was nowhere more evident than in a drawing of "The African Countryside as it Might Be," a serene, rolling landscape complete with farm houses, carefully tilled fields, and a few cattle. The image, one recognizes immediately, is indistinguishable from an idealized English panorama, or perhaps even Kenya's White Highlands, but bears little resemblance to the bitter realities of landless Kikuyu.[105]

Paterson took up the panel's offer and submitted "Suggestions with Regard to the Production of Educational Films for East African Natives," that largely reiterated the ideological thrust of his *Book of Civilization*. The primary purpose of colonial cinema, Paterson stressed, should be to "make the native peoples happier, healthier, and more useful." Of the three, usefulness was deemed paramount "based on the assumption that the African can never be as happy or as healthy as he might otherwise be unless he is in a position to take advantage of what European, American, and Eastern manufacturers can do for him by supplying him with those products of heavy industry and with such hardware and textiles as he cannot produce for himself." But appropriate education for Africans, Paterson mused, could also foster, or awaken, new needs and desires that could be satisfied through consumption: "An immediate object of propaganda, therefore, must be to demonstrate what we mean by a fair standard of living in such a fashion that it may appear desirable, and a second object must be to demonstrate how it can be achieved." Specifically, Paterson targeted what he perceived to be three perennial deficiencies in traditional East African culture: (1) general outlook; (2) agriculture, animal husbandry and trading; and (3) management of the home and care of the children. His list of proposed film themes reflected these priorities:

1. Work at the Veterinary Training Depot
2. Work at the Demonstration Small Holdings (homestead, ploughing, manure, cultivating, etc.)
3. Preparation and Marketing of Hides and Skins
4. Preparation and marketing of glue
5. Preparation and marketing of wattle bark
6. Cotton
7. Coconuts
8. Homebuilding
9. The Out Houses
10. Food
11. Children (Feeding, Clothing, Washing, General Care)

12. The Bush School
13. Small domestic Water supplies[106]

Included in Paterson's proposal were rough storyboards for three films—*About Cattle*, *About Crops*, and *About Water*. The storylines are similar in that each exposes the perceived ignorance, poverty, and wastefulness of African life, juxtaposing scenes of decayed villages with scenes of improved lifestyles resulting from the introduction of Western techniques of husbandry, cultivation and domesticity:

About Cattle

Any poor African village, early morning. The village awakes, the cattle are driven out to graze, pictures of exceedingly poor cattle and exceedingly poor clothed people and children. Closeups of poor cattle and poor children.

Pictures of poor grazing, the cattle wander about.

Milking, exceedingly poor results. Marketing, few are sold and the hides fetch no price. The unsold cattle return to the village to die. Poor cattle refused as a "bride price."

Pictures of a fine herd of native cattle at the Ugong Veterinary Depot. Bulls, close ups of the best native cattle[,] good bulls and poor bulls side by side. African veterinary instructor arrives in village home from leave and tells the story of the veterinary centre. He is next seen at the veterinary centre with his old parents and all the family with him, then pictures of work at the veterinary centre always with the old people being shown round. The film ends with a poor bull and a good bull side by side.

The next film scenario, *About Crops*, opens with Paterson's characteristically bleak perspective on "native life," complete with "a poor village, poor people, dirt and squalor, poor cattle in the usual enclosure in the centre of the village, dung all over the place." But as with *Harley Street*, his emplotment of primitivity versus modernity is given something of a self-referential, postmodern twist when form becomes content and the film itself demonstrates the benefits of visual propaganda:

The native agricultural demonstrator arrives and after talking and showing some good produce he has with him, arranges for a cinema show that night. Night falls with familiar scenes and the show begins. It uses scenes from the demonstration small holding at Kalete. The show over, the people ask for demonstrators who arrive.[107]

Paterson's proposal found favor within the Dominions, India and Colonies Panel, as well as the Colonial Office, which hoped to secure Colonial Development Fund backing. The failure of the plan to materialize, however, was attributable to the economic squeeze of the depression and the appearance of yet another rival proposal known as the Bantu Educational Kinema Experiment, which could boast American involvement as well as crucial missionary support from both sides of the Atlantic. Moreover, Oldham's theory of adaptation provided the ideological thrust that yoked the pedagogical potential of the cinema to the new orientation of African education that departed from mission-led Bible teachings or the three R's of the past. The belief that missionaries were uniquely attuned to the nuances of primitive cultures due to sustained culture contact was commonplace during this period, and surely strengthened the bargaining power of the founders of the BEKE. In fact, at the International Institute of Educational Cinematography, a League of Nations body formed in 1928, the question of how missionaries might prove helpful in designing a cinema for the Other had been explicitly addressed:

After having studied the problems that arise from the use of the cinema among peoples of a like mentality and civilization, we now desire to study the problems of the use of the cinema among peoples of a different culture and mentality, i.e.[,] among the backward races and those of a different civilization to that of the Occidents. Missionaries are in a position to furnish us with very valuable data on the use of cinematography among the backward races, either because they themselves use the cinema as a means to further their task of civilizing and assisting ... because they are constantly in touch with the natives—especially the young—and are thus qualified to say what influence, good or bad, the cinema has on the natives, or because in carrying out their duties as priest, teacher, doctor, propagandist, etc., the missionaries can indicate the ... kind of films ... that would be the most useful for the intellectual and spiritual elevation of the natives, especially the young.[108]

Missionaries concerned about colonial educational policy and the disturbing social effects of industrial migration in Southern and Central Africa, were thus destined to play a critical role in pioneering the first broad-based experiment in colonial cinema for African audiences, with the assistance of the British Colonial Office and a myriad of others interested in the use of cinema among "backward races." And it was precisely due to what the League of Nations envisioned—experience in the field fired with the necessary missionary zeal—that would propel their vision forward as the Bantu Educational Kinema Experiment.

7

Films of Africans, Made in Africa, for Africans, Under Effective Control

The Bantu Educational Kinema Experiment

Scholars studying interwar propaganda have rightly highlighted motion pictures for refining the tools of the trade, often illustrating how the spectacle was exploited by the Soviets and Nazis, or examining how the West achieved global cultural hegemony through block-booking and control of international markets.[1] Another fertile field explores colonial cinema—especially the making of films in the colonies for the colonies—in framing the European engagement with overseas possessions. Britain, while lagging behind authoritarian regimes in exploiting state-produced propaganda domestically, produced movies for the colonized to bind its subjects to the metropole. By the conclusion of World War II, the British Ministry of Information (MOI) had commissioned the Colonial Film Unit (CFU) and the Mobile Propaganda Unit to sell the European conflict to its African Allies.[2]

The forerunner of these projects was the Bantu Educational Kinema Experiment (BEKE), the first large-scale effort at producing films in the colonies for indigenous spectators, initiated by missionaries and officials to combat a crisis brewing in Northern Rhodesia's Copperbelt.[3] Several features of the project should be noted: (1) it was largely a product not of the Colonial Office, but of missionary concern about the rural side effects of Copperbelt labor migration; (2) Soviet film propaganda provided early inspiration; (3) indigenous spectators readily imbibed propaganda on a range of issues, but critiqued the films when they ran counter to individual expectations or community mores; and (4) the BEKE reflects hitherto unappreciated government involvement in African education.

Assessing the BEKE in building consent and imposing Western development initiatives requires understanding that the project was less a realization of a finely tuned strategy for British hegemony than it was an *ad hoc* response to conditions on the Copperbelt and labor reservoirs that serviced it. Indeed, whether instructional/propaganda films actually succeeded in discernibly improving African village life is highly debatable, but they did, however unintentionally, act in concert with commercial bioscopes and mining compound programs in creating new patterns of African leisure and consumption in the interwar years.

The Copperbelt Crisis

The Colonial Office worked haltingly to construct a "responsible" film policy for British Africa between 1926 and 1935. But the realization of the BEKE in the mid–1930s ultimately required the broader contribution of missionaries who had concerns about the mining sector's "disorganizing" impact on Central Africa. The industrial presence there can be traced to the Scramble for Africa, when the British South Africa Company (BSAC) descended upon the kingdoms of Lobengula and Lewanika to secure concessions for the right to exploit minerals in their respective kingdoms. Initially the region's mineral wealth was believed to lie in Mashonaland. As the BSAC extended its control, land north of the Zambezi was expected to serve as a native labor reservoir and buffer zone for competing Europeans, but the discovery of copper just south of the Congo led to "freebooting explorations" by feverish prospectors.[4] The Kansanshi Mine, already worked by the Kaonde, offered yields through 1910 but other areas also showed promise for future excavation. Discovering surface deposits near where he had shot a buck, William Collier laid claim in 1902 to what would eventually become the Roan Antelope Mine.[5] Weeks later, Collier was led by a local to an African digging site near Ndola, which Collier subsequently named Bwana Mkubwa,[6] and by 1905 the region was being referred to as the Copperbelt.[7] The Copperbelt suffered stiff competition from Katanga's Union Minière, and Anaconda, in Montana.[8] Moreover, because the extent of Copperbelt deposits was unknown the 1910s saw a decline in the mining industry, although in 1920 Selection Trust and Copper Venture re-evaluated dormant concessions. Revitalization was assured by engineer Raymond Brooks who began exploiting ore at Nchanga (soon the world's second-richest copper mine), and by prospector James Moir who discovered deposits in Mufulira in 1922. Moir would later be honored in a compelling 16-minute film tribute in 1961, as described in this synopsis:

> A monument to Moir had already been erected at the mine when in 1960 word came that the man long thought dead was still alive. Moir never saw the modern Mufulira; he steadfastly refused to leave his home deep in the Rhodesian bush where, though nearly 80, he was still prospecting. It is the happy story of a man who said six months before his death: "I've led a full life in the bush and if I had to live it over again I wouldn't change it—not a minute of it. I've no regrets."[9]

By the 1930s, the Anglo-American Corporation and Rhodesian Selection Trust dominated the region, accompanied by familiar refrains for cheap African labor. These developments paralleled the 1924 transfer of authority from the BSAC to the Crown, and the implementation of indirect rule. Re-establishing "Native Authority" was accorded greater urgency with the depression, as tribal institutions undergoing erosion were incapable of coping with large numbers of wandering and discontented individuals filling urban-industrial zones. White observers had difficulty deciding which was worse—the Copperbelt's migrant labor system with its attendant detribalized population, or the temporary breakdown of that system in the early 1930s. Either way, these dual concerns prompted missionaries to publicize the downside of Northern Rhodesia's industrialization.

This crisis precipitated the 1932 Copperbelt Commission under American missionary John Merle Davis to study the rapidly changing social order and craft a missionary response. One of the outgrowths of the commission was the proposal for the BEKE which proved timely given the dialogue within the Colonial Office on the feasibility of harnessing the powers of the cinema for development. As the first large-scale experiment in colonial cinema in the subcontinent, the BEKE targeted primarily adult illiterates in Copperbelt recruiting zones. In addition to ascertaining the African's ability to imbibe information through moving images, the project sought to rebuild tribal structures through colonial development initiatives.

The earlier 1928 World Missionary Council in Jerusalem had highlighted similar issues faced by the missionary community. One conference panel was devoted to "Christianity and the Growth of Industrialism in Asia, Africa and South America," with an address by R.H. Tawney who argued that the West's industrial problems received inordinate attention, and called for greater missionary awareness of socio-economic stresses in developing areas: "[As] profoundly as the setting of history, race, religion and economic environment differ in East and West, the social and ethical issues raised by industrial civilization are increasingly common to both."[10] H.A. Grimshaw, in "Industrial Revolution and Primitive Peoples," agreed and encouraged the International Missionary Council (IMC) to form a "Department of Economic and Social Research and Counsel" in Geneva, linking missionary societies together. With a Social Gospel orientation, John Merle Davis was appointed director of the bureau when it opened in 1930.

In September of that year, Effie Jamieson of the Woman's Missionary Society of the United Church of Canada related to Joseph Oldham the vast changes she saw in Northern Rhodesia, specifically in the villages that serviced the Copperbelt:

> Even a traveller could not escape the endless talk of this new mining area, in personal conversations, as well as from business and mining interests, one heard of it but I will quote only a few incidents. The Rev. Ray Phillips, whose work in the Johannesburg mining area is so well known to you, said that the mining men whom he knows well because of his associations, speak of this area with great enthusiasm as the "New Witwatersrand" of Africa, only that it will be on a much vaster scale. In the press, on the trains, in the hotels, everywhere the subject was on everyone's tongue.[11]

Jamieson proposed a united front of missionary boards to avoid "the scandal presented where 200 struggling churches vie with each other, thus weakening the whole cause of presenting a vital Christianity."[12] Oldham then spoke to the federation of British missionary boards working in sub-tropical Africa to urge cooperation for a broad-based study of African acculturation, and an investigation into the effects of the mining industry on "native life" in the region, which, in turn, prompted John Merle Davis's Department of Social and Industrial Research to conduct an investigation.[13] Davis was an ideal candidate for the job. He had studied the American acculturation of Japanese immigrants, and his Social Gospel roots ran deep: his mother was Sophia Strong, cousin of Josiah Strong,[14] and his sister Clara had married Frederick Bridgman and worked with her husband in South Africa.[15]

In October Oldham contacted Rheinallt-Jones to discuss with the secretary of the SAIRR what was now becoming a continent-wide concern among missionaries and colonial officials.[16] There is a "pressing need," Oldham asserted, for "meeting the spiritual and social needs of the masses of natives congregated in mining centres":

> No attempt has been made to consider this in any large way. Apart from the Bantu [Mens'] Social Centre at Johannesburg begun by Dr. Bridgeman [sic] and carried on by Ray Phillips, most of the efforts by the missions are isolated, small and far from adequate to the need. Large new problems will arise as a result of the big mining developments in Northern Rhodesia.[17]

Oldham, explicitly crediting Jamieson for raising "the whole question of the importance of the problems arising from mining development," suggested there were "two aspects of the problem: (1) the labourer himself and the conditions under which he works and (2) the effect upon the villages all over Central Africa from which the labourers come."[18] Impressed by the scope of the IMC research project, Rheinallt-Jones recommended Phillips as an advisor.

Phillips, of course, was already acquainted with the Copperbelt and had been sending films to the Rhodesias for years. He informed Oldham that duties in Johannesburg precluded him from leaving for longer than a month, yet the possibility of "getting in on the ground floor" and extending the reach of social welfare programs proved irresistible: "I should like, if it were deemed wise, to visit the new mining fields to the North, for it may be possible that some scheme of cooperation on a social work basis might be worked out in which we could have a share from here." Coincidently, only a week before Phillips had entertained the manager of Ndola's Roan Antelope Mine, and had agreed to train the firm's welfare worker to help "capture the leisure-time interests of the Native people" on the Copperbelt.[19]

In January 1931, Davis completed a tour of southern Africa and began seeking funding for the study. Writing to Thomas Jesse Jones, he emphasized his commission's focus on the effects of industrialization on Northern Rhodesia's nascent working class, but stressed it was of the "highest importance" to explore conditions in Katanga where the Union Minière and other mines had established a stabilization policy to ensure labor reproduction, and in the Transvaal where Phillips had convinced mine owners to invest in the MCCC. Davis admitted that the "three estates" at work—"Government, Industry, and Missions"—had a "disintegrating influence upon native life," but suggested that "integration" could follow if the three worked cooperatively, and if Protestants paid more attention to urban-industrial centers.[20]

The Copperbelt Commission reflected something of a paradigm shift in colonial thinking. Oldham in part blamed "detribalization" on earlier "missionary assumptions ... that the African cultural concepts, systems of values and tribal controls were all parts of a heathen way of life which must be completely superseded by Christian ways of life imported from Europe and America." It was the "modern science" of anthropology, he asserted, which had exposed the weakness of this position, leading to a re-evaluation of missionary focus.[21]

In addition to Phillips, Davis recruited Leo Marquard, and Mabel Shaw, principal of the Livingstone Memorial Girls' Boarding School. Carnegie Corporation provided primary backing, with Phelps-Stokes Fund support. In 1932, the team toured South Africa, the Rhodesias, and Katanga, investigating industrial areas, speaking to mining officials, and visiting recruitment zones like Basutoland, the Ciskei, and the Transkei. The result was *Modern Industry and the African*, credited by Frederick Cooper with "pushing beyond the usual" in its call for improving rural areas ravaged by migration, and recognizing urbanized and proletarianized Africans not as temporary sojourners in towns, but rather as permanent fixtures deserving of social institutions to help them acclimate.[22] The commission called attention to the disintegration of traditional folkways among those cut off from rural communities, and challenged missions to rebuild social life in urban settings along more "wholesome channels." Additionally, missionaries were asked to "exert their influence in and shape their activities toward rural stabilization and the strengthening of the economic foundations of Native society" by "control[ing] the direction and speed of these changes" and improving the efficiency of African agriculture.[23] This required more attention be paid to the whole community and not just an educated mission elite, a feat to be accomplished through adult education, even "if it means slowing down temporarily on elementary education."[24] It was this prescription that led the missionary community to join hands with the Colonial Office in launching the first broad-based study of African reaction to moving pictures.

Copper, Kinema and Carnegie

Ray Phillips, as we have seen, not only initiated one of the continent's largest cinema programs, but was an avid filmmaker himself. As he explained in a memo to the Chamber of Mines, a primary consideration in accepting Davis's invitation to serve on the Copperbelt Commission was the "golden opportunity I would have of obtaining some more good stuff for the [Mines' Compound] Cinema Circuit." Phillips shot ample footage of villages and towns throughout Northern Rhodesia, and by the time the commission reached the Copperbelt's eastern fringe, he had taken 3000 feet of negative and wired Johannesburg for more. Procuring another 2,400 feet, he succeeded in getting more "good stuff" in both Rhodesias, especially points of interest such as Morgenster, Hope Fountain, and Dambushawa.[25]

In "Education and the Copper Belt," the section of the Copperbelt report penned by Davis, Phillips's cinematic social welfare was affirmed to be "deserving of careful study":

> For a number of years, under the direction of Rev. Ray E. Phillips, and with the generous support of the Transvaal Chamber of Mines, a semi-weekly film service has been provided for the workers of more than fifty of the mines. More recently this service has been very widely extended to include many industries, schools, societies and missions in various parts of the Union of South Africa, and even reaching points in Southern and Northern Rhodesia.... The possibilities of the constructive use of the cinema are being studied by the Colonial Office. This is obviously a field in which extensive experiment and testing must be carried out under expert leadership.[26]

Davis wanted to build upon Phillips's success yet push cinema in a new direction—focusing on didactic topics rather than general uplift and recreation. Among adult, unschooled Africans especially, he argued, cinema could impart information more quickly and effectively than the written word, and the limitations of classrooms could be overcome because "through a large part of the tropical year the cinema can be used in the open air without the need of a special hall." Cinema was thus introduced in Central Africa at a time when African education was accorded greater interest by colonial officials. Describing colonial cinema in rather stark terms as using "the flank rather than the frontal attack," Davis suggested a range of topics that might be addressed, including "hygiene, sanitation, Government Administration, religious and moral instruction, economics, agriculture, art, child nurture, land utilisation, trade and commerce, geography, travel, natural science, physics, biology, physiology, [and] astronomy."[27]

By January 1934, Davis had submitted to the Carnegie Corporation a grant proposal on behalf of the IMC for an "International Study of the Cinema." Divided into three sections, Davis envisioned, first, an investigation of censorship in different countries, along with a study of educational cinema. Second, three countries "at different cultural levels" would be studied "intensively" to determine the social impact of the medium. Third, experimental films would be produced/exhibited among the colonized to determine effective strategies to impart visual information. For the study, Davis suggested, (1) the USSR, due to its "marked success" in exposing "illiterate and primitive groups to the cinema"; (2) Egypt, a homogenous society with some experience in cinema health campaigns; and (3) Northern Rhodesia, a colony undergoing "disintegration" due to European contact, but still redeemable if wide-reaching adult education campaigns could be implemented quickly.[28]

Through Hanns Vischer, Davis met Major Leslie Alan Notcutt who had already developed his own amateur colonial cinema as early as 1926 to maintain a contented, migrant labor force on his sisal plantations. An effective estate manager, Notcutt believed, needed less an intricate knowledge of the crop than a willingness to "obtain, and maintain, native efficiency," a stance that explains using film to boost morale.[29] Notcutt soon produced amateurish films himself, and was "astonished to find how remarkably attractive these proved to the natives, so much so that the idea entered my head that there might be commercial possibilities in the establishment of native cinemas with films of their own."[30]

In England to study film production and the feasibility of generating inexpensive films, Notcutt read about Julian Huxley's experimental film showings. His decision to move in this direction was "clinched" by Frank Melland, an ex-magistrate in Northern Rhodesia, who argued that cinema could foster inter-racial cooperation, and who "advocate[d] projecting England by means of carefully taken films before the Bantu races." In Melland's view, Africans would attain a deeper understanding of modernity by seeing images of Europe; and conversely, "Good films of Africa would help England to understand the races she is governing."[31]

Notcutt, although inspired my Melland, believed that "natives are very much more interested in films of themselves or of other natives than in films about Europeans," a belief that would emerge as a key ideological underpinning of the BEKE. The Colonial Office confirmed that "[Notcutt's] object was not primarily anthropological in taking films of natives, though no doubt what he did would have some such interest. He was simply concerned to produce suitable films which he was sure the native would be ready to look at."[32]

Davis was excited about Notcutt's ambitions and prior experience, and asked him to draw up a plan for the Rhodesian segment. Davis's Carnegie proposal envisioned a three-year study with a $128,000 budget, and Notcutt acting as Northern Rhodesia field director. An acquaintance of Notcutt's declared the experiment "colossally important," touting him as a "composite genius in native psychology, cinema, education, organization and applied science."[33] Notcutt put these skills to work for Exhibit A: "to produce film in the vernacular in Africa, using African actors and African stories. These films would be for entertainment, but they would carry educational lessons—on sanitation, proper methods of cultivation, the dangers of superstition, etc." Davis and Notcutt's "flank attack" would cloak the heavy hand of colonial development in African allegories, using indigenous actors to lessen resistance:

> Since the actors would be native, the speech native, the setting and motifs native, the lessons they are to derive from the films would come naturally and not from without as something imposed by the foreigner. The original obstacle all foreign education presents would be avoided. Even the methods of presentation would be kept in the native tradition as much as possible.[34]

Davis soon secured BFI and Colonial Office support and formed a sub-committee including Roland Vernon, and T.H. Baxter of the Cinema Christian Council. Vernon had earlier submitted his Malaysian proposal to the Rockefeller Foundation, from which he received no satisfaction. Baxter, though, as we saw in Chapter 2, had previous experience filming in Africa, and had concerns that resonated with Davis and the Copperbelt Commission. In 1927, the London Missionary Committee had sponsored his Cape Town to Nairobi tour, resulting in *Africa To-day*, a film targeting missionary audiences "to bring home the result of the impact of European civilization on the primitive African, and to indicate what is to be the general result of this impact in the course of another generation or so."[35] The cause of this disintegration was explored in a segment entitled "The Call of the White Man's Kraal," warning of the social effects of labor migration. Baxter compared the phenomenon to England's early industrial age, but argued that "in Africa the consequences are deeper for it is chiefly the men who leave, often for years, sometimes never to return."[36]

It is unknown what Baxter thought of the Davis/Notcutt proposal, but Vernon as committee chairman "damned it." He declared, "It appeared to me to involve the setting up of a kind of Hollywood in Northern Rhodesia with all kinds of attendant perils. African natives were to be encouraged to come and show their capacities as 'film stars'; the film was to be used as a means of teaching Africans the folly of their superstitions [and] belief in witchcraft."[37] Davis, though, had already submitted his proposal, although Vernon expected the Carnegie trustees to give it the *coup de grâce*.[38] What he failed to realize was that Carnegie had previously supported the Copperbelt study, and had an interest in black education, adult education, and the use of cinema for illiterates. Andrew Carnegie himself, in fact, had donated generously to Tuskegee[39] and British colonial educational institutions.[40] Furthermore, in the mid–1920s, Carnegie director Frederick Keppel had corresponded with James Dexter Taylor, who had touted Ray Phillips's MCCC and Durban's municipal compound showings.[41]

Keppel had also broadened the foundation's focus by hiring Nathanial Peffer, author of *New Schools for Older Students*.[42] When Davis submitted his proposal for his international, comparative study of the cinema, it was Peffer who perused it and suggested limiting its scope to Africa:

> I wonder whether the project might be halved. The experiment in Rhodesia has much to be said for it, but is it dependent on the larger, general studies? I doubt whether within the time limits set much could be learned from a world study in regulation, etc., even from the Russian methods.

Peffer adjudged that the Rhodesian segment of the experiment was capable of "standing on its own," and estimated the cost for the scaled-back version at $55,000.[43] By the time Davis resubmitted the proposal in November 1934, Vernon and others in the Colonial Office were beginning to rethink their objections. Indeed, those who had earlier preferred Paterson's proposal believed that while "the objects of the two schemes were identical," the "comprehensiveness" of the Davis plan was laudable, as it recognized the need for cultural themes and saw cinema as a leisure activity. In reality, though, the proposals had subtle differences that escaped the attention of the Colonial Office.

Paterson couched the African malaise in terms of an unchanging primitivity which required modification from without for the civilizing process to flourish. Notcutt, as we will see, may actually have agreed with Paterson, but Davis was moving toward a more nuanced perspective that viewed African stresses as stemming primarily *from* culture contact with the West without effective colonial institutions to direct social change. The logical extension of this position was that, while Paterson virtually rejected African traditions *in toto*, Davis extolled many of the virtues of a pre-industrial African past (excepting polygamy and witchcraft), and hoped to re-establish rural social cohesion by promoting agricultural efficiency in the countryside. Moreover, Davis's belief that mining was altering irrevocably Africa's social fabric led him to extend the plan to include areas beyond Northern Rhodesia that served as labor reservoirs for the copper mines, as well as colonies like Kenya where eroding race relations were demanding a rethinking of colonial policy. Thus, while his revised proposal omitted Egypt and the USSR, the Africa portion expanded to include Northern Rhodesia, Nyasaland, Tanganyika, Uganda, and Kenya.

As the proposal was being revised, Davis searched for an educational director to run the mobile units and gauge African response to the films. His first choice was the Reverend Neville-Jones, principal of London Missionary Society's Hope Mountain Mission and School in Southern Rhodesia. When Neville-Jones declined, Davis suggested Geoffrey Chitty Latham, former lieutenant, native commissioner, and first director of native education in Northern Rhodesia.[44] In the mid–1920s Latham had seemed intent on keeping Africans away from moving images, but by the early 1930s his interest in expanding African education led to his re-appraisal of the medium, and he accepted the position. Moreover, Davis now found a more favorable response when he resubmitted his proposal to Vernon and the Colonial Office, and in December Carnegie approved $55,000 for the project.[45] Additional modest grants were forthcoming from Roan Antelope Copper Mines, Rhokana Corporation, and Mufulira Copper Mines, and on March 1, 1935, the BEKE was officially born.

At the Seventh Imperial Social Hygiene Conference, Davis declared the experiment "essentially a missionary undertaking,"[46] but, in fact, an array of institutions were brought into play, including the BFI, the British Social Hygiene Council, the British Board of Education, and Gaumont-British Instructional Films. The Advisory Council was chaired and vice-chaired by Lord Lugard and Thomas Drummond Shiels, respectively, and members included Joseph Oldham, Hanns Vischer, T.H. Baxter, Roland Venables Vernon, Major Granville St. John Orde-Browne, and anthropologist Audrey Richards.[47] Davis also elicited advice from others. Alfred Hoernle, who was advocating increased segregation in South Africa to stop the labor drain from the reserves, suggested to Davis that the scheme, with "suitable adaptation," might be applicable to the Union. Ray Phillips and Davis also continued to correspond on the MCCC and the BEKE, and scholar Isaac Schapera, considered a leading expert on the "native mind," was invited to submit film proposals. More surprisingly, given the monochromatic racial makeup of the BEKE, Paul Robeson was invited to sit on the Advisory Council, but he refused.[48] In short, when the BEKE launched it was a veritable "who's who" of colonial administrators, missionaries, amateur filmmakers and anthropologists hoping to (re)direct the social transformation of 20th-century Africa.

Davis, Notcutt and Latham were also acutely aware that cinema in India had become politicized, and wanted to "occupy the field" of African film production/exhibition to ward off the "pernicious" effects of commercial cinema—to fight film with film. Edward Thompson's musings about cinema's impact in India were scrutinized, and Davis contacted the Madras Film Appraisal Committee, which sent its report on developing "public taste" among Indians as a censorship alternative.[49] The African territories in question, of course, were contacted to elicit their support for the "scientific study of the effects of various types of film upon the native races in [each] area."[50] The experiment, in fact, had been broached at a Nairobi Conference of East African Directors of Education, where representatives concluded that the experiment could make a "useful contribution."

Competition arose over where the BEKE should locate its production facility. James W.C. Dougall, Kenya's liaison between missions and government,[51] agreed with the chief native commissioner and Arthur Paterson that the experiment should be headquartered in Kiambu, Kenya, to provide access to "backward reserve conditions and the de-tribalized life of the reserve locations in Nairobi." But Tanganyika's deputy director of education, Albert A.M. Isherwood, offered a hotel in Old Moshi or an abandoned German sanitarium in Vugiri to base its operations. The latter location was more centrally located, and soon Notcutt, Latham and a small field staff sailed for Tanganyika.

BEKE: First Phase

Embarking on the project's first phase, the BEKE issued a report detailing its new pedagogical strategy. Modernity, it argued, was descending too abruptly upon a people incapable of being acclimated to the West through traditional strategies: "The stream of African life was running too swiftly, the demands put upon the native for cultural readjustment were too heavy to be met by the old methods alone." Cinema offered a new approach toward several overlapping strands of education: (1) Phelps-Stokes's differential education, wherein Africans would be trained to fill the lower ranks of society requiring less literacy; (2) Oldham's theory of adaptation, targeting the specific needs of non–Western students; and (3) Carnegie's emphasis on adult education, with particular relevance to Africa where the new missionary approach sought explicitly to bridge the gap between elders and the mission-educated.

The BEKE was implemented at the beginning of the talkie revolution. Accommodating this technological shift required taking into account the numerous languages spoken in the five target areas, and thus the BEKE made use of the economical "sound-on-disc" method, first pioneered by Emile Berliner and Léon Gaumont years before. This allowed for narration of the storylines on phonograph discs produced in English, Swahili, Sukuma, Kikuyu, Luo, Ganda, Nyanja, Bemba, and Tumbuka, for screening in different locales.

A variety of films would be produced specifically to gauge reaction to different genres: educational films would be sub-classified as instructional, story-instructional, and cultural, while entertainment films would include comedies and farce.[52] Notcutt and Latham hoped to discover which types of films appealed to the "mentality of different types of African— the educated, the partially detribalized native, and the primitive villager,"[53] and consequently, how cinema could meet Britain's development needs without fostering resistance. Questions absorbing the Advisory Council included the efficacy of sandwiching educational/instructional films between entertainment films, and whether Africans had the attention span to imbibe lessons from the films. The Reverend Spanton argued that the African's memory is "vastly keener than the white man's, especially in regard to the things he sees." But this disparagement of European mental acuity was actually rooted in a perceived disparity between the civilized European, whose head is full of complex ideas, and the *tabula rasa* of the primitive native: "His mind," said Spanton, "is more or less virgin soil and unusual ideas take root in it."[54] Ultimately, Davis, Latham and Notcutt envisioned laying the groundwork for a chain of Bantu Cinema Houses in East Africa and Northern Rhodesia, to exhibit films produced under "adequate control." The goal was not simply to construct storylines to pass censor boards, but to produce those "of a type possessing real cultural and educational value, or healthy entertainment of a kind suited to Bantu audiences."[55] Education directors in the African territories offered support, yet remained dubious about its feasibility, arguing that the films would have "little or no commercial significance, at any rate for a very considerable time."[56]

The project was given coverage in the British media. BFI's *Sight and Sound* noted that corporations sensing the commercial possibilities plied the council with requests to show industry films free of charge. Lever Brothers, Austin Motors, and Cadbury Brothers, for instance, shipped *Port Sunlight*, *This Progress*, and *The Night Watchman's Story* to East Africa in August 1935. It is unclear, though, whether these films were ever included in the traveling BEKE exhibitions. The *International Review of Missions* also published periodic updates on the experiment's progress.[57]

In Africa, too, the press noted the upcoming experiment. In "Harnessing the Cinema as an Ally in Native Development," *East Africa* explained that the BEKE had "no intention of making the programmes purely educational. They are, first, to be attractive. Native comedy and tragedy will be shown, also Native occupations and interests, but it is expected to weave in something that has definite educative value." *Crown Colonist* described this as "helping the African to adapt himself to the new ideas, morals, customs, and laws which Western Civilization is introducing," while *Congo Mission News* applauded efforts to discover "what the primitive African, still uncorrupted by films not intended for him, can most enjoy, and what benefit him best."[58] South Africa's *Cape Argus* and the *Rand Daily Mail* also reported sporadically on the BEKE cinema tours throughout British Africa.[59]

Notcutt initially suggested a series of interrelated films, collectively entitled "Health, Prosperity, and Happiness," offering a "two-fold advantage: (a) it enables each film to be more specialized as we can refer to subsidiary matters in films that have gone before or are to follow..., and (b) we attract the same audience to come again to the next performance." The series would open with an introductory film affirming that only through the white man could African prosperity be secured, and only through Christianity could happiness be attained:

<u>Synopsis for Introductory Film</u>

1. Darkness[.] "In the beginning God created heavens and the earth, but it was dark."
2. Dawn at Sea. "And God said let there be light."
3. Seascape and Beach, dissolving to bare hills. "God said let there be sea and land."
4. Tree ferns, braken, then forest, then fruit trees and then maize and Mtama. "Then God covered the land with trees, and gave fruit and grain. Then God said there shall be life."
5. Fishes "—and he made the fishes in the sea and lakes and rivers."
6. Crab, lizard, bird, hen, duck, goat, cow, dog, cat, monkey. "God took some fishes and made them into animals to live on the land."
7. Elephant grass, a negro appears in a skin, comes out and stands with back to camera. "Then at last God made man."
8. Dissolve in a white man alongside the negro. White man in identical skin to negro. "God made the black man and the white man." Black out.
9. Fade in five gourds in a row. "Five gifts were offered these men for them to choose one. The gifts were HEALTH, PROSPERITY, HAPPINESS, STENGTH, and WISDOM."
10. Black hand reaches out and takes fourth gourd. "The black man chose STRENGTH. He said that with strength he could have all he wished for."
11. White hand reaches out and takes the fifth gourd, and as he takes it the other three gourds vanish. "The white man chose WISDOM for with wisdom he also had HEALTH, PROSPERITY and HAPPINESS. Black out.
12. Scene of fighting: "The Black men had no prosperity because they were always fighting."
13. Scenes of sickness. "They had no health for all their strength."
14. Scenes of witchcraft. "They had no happiness because lacking wisdom they became prey to evil spirits."
15. Fade to blackout. "But the white men, who had chosen wisdom, had all these things. Friends—"

16. Natives in a group go forward to a white man. "—These white men will give us of their wisdom. Let us goo [sic] gain wisdom, thereby gaining Health, Prosperity and Happiness."
17. Native seated round white man[.] "White man, give us wisdom, we seek Health, Prosperity and Happiness."
18. White man. "To gain prosperity you must change your ways, you must learn from us better agriculture and animal husbandry; we will gladly teach you. To gain health, you must first be prosperous; then you must have better houses, live more cleanly, and eat better food. To gain happiness you must escape the evil spirits and in our churches learn the word of God. Follow me those who seek wisdom."
19. Some natives follow. Some stay behind. "And some followed and learnt wisdom. Others stayed behind like silly children."
20. Black out. "WHICH WILL YOU DO?"[60]

Notcutt's sententious allegory was never made into a film. The archives are silent in respect to what Latham and Davis thought of the script, but presumably they concurred with a British official in Zanzibar, who was ruminating on BEKE's suitability for the island: "I would ... express the opinion that the popularity of the films among native audiences in this Protectorate will depend almost entirely upon the extent to which the Mission bias predominates. If there is too obvious an intrusion of a Christian proselytizing element it is probable that the films will arouse little interest."[61] In fact, in a letter to Ruth Rouse of the World's Student Christian Federation, Davis himself addressed this issue, but argued that positive reception among Africans hinged more on the politics of race than religion:

One basic difficulty in the whole problem is that practically all films carrying a religious message depict white people or Europeans in the Western social and economic setting. This, of course, greatly detracts from the pictures. What is needed for use among the non–Christian peoples of the world is an interpretation of Christian principles and life in the medium of their surroundings and using their own nationals as actors.[62]

The efficacy of uplift through motion pictures also became a topic of discussion as the BEKE solicited opinion from colonial officials, missionaries, and anthropologists. In Kenya, James Dougall warned that for the Kikuyu and Maasai, there "must not be too much 'uplift.' Entertainment is the most important side of the Experiment."[63] Notcutt and Latham, of course, hoped this issue would be resolved by balancing out instructional/propaganda lessons with cultural films and comedies.

Notcutt and crew produced 13 films during the first phase, although they rushed production on the initial seven to enable Latham's exhibition team to begin its tour. The first film, *Post Office Savings Bank*, was a story-instructional propaganda film touting small-scale savings institutions introduced by British colonials. Latham and Notcutt chose the screenplay that fit best with the BEKE's ideological underpinnings—effective films must convey their message through a visual story, using African actors, and avoid tribal peculiarities that might alienate neighboring tribes. The screenplay also included a favorite device of American action films—a chase scene—to test African response and to whet the appetite of cinema sophisticates in the towns.

Framed in the familiar Mr. Wise and Mr. Foolish format, the film depicts two plantation workers returning home after receiving their wages. While the wise African deposits his money into a post office savings bank, the film focuses primarily on the foolish African who buries his money under his hut floor. Unfortunately, a thief views this ill-advised hoarding and later purloins the wages while the worker is away at a dance. Discovering his loss the next morning, the foolish African speaks to his neighbors, who report having seen a stranger in town. On his way into the village accompanied by a neighbor who claims he can identify the thief, the foolish African meets his wise counterpart, who shows him how he manages his own money. This sequence includes a brief description of the workings of the bank for the benefit of the audience. The thief is then spotted and a chase ensues. The crook is finally cornered and eludes his pursuers by climbing a tree, a strategy that fails when a branch breaks, sending him crashing to the ground in a fatal fall. We will explore below the way Africans read this particular morality tale and forced a revision to the film.

Latham wanted a variety of topics to gauge reaction on the tour. *Tax* explained the colonial administration taxation system, while *Tanga Travel* showed Tanganyikan scenes of a harbor, mission center, ceremonial dance, shipwreck, Arab dhow, beer shops, tea houses, churches, prisons and railways. *Hides*, produced in Korogwe, lauded the advantages of drying hides in the shade over traditional sun-drying. *Tea,* an increasingly popular beverage, showed women working on plantations picking leaves, weighing baskets, and tasting and packing the final product.

Another film addressed the widening generational/cultural gap, cast in the fictional tale of a chief who, visiting a relative, recognizes the value of mission education and returns home to propose to elders that a similar school be built in their village. *The Chief* has a poignant scene of elders consulting with the local witchdoctor, who rightly understands that the proposed mission would constitute a challenge to his authority. Despite his opposition, the school is built, but the chief soon falls ill and is taken to a hospital to receive an injection. As Notcutt and Latham describe it, "The elder who accompanies him thinks he is dead" when the chief faints from the injection:

> The witch-doctor thereupon calls a meeting, and induces the people to believe that the chief died because the school teacher had bewitched him in order to secure power for himself. The school teacher is compelled to submit to ordeal by poison. Just as he is about to drink the poison the chief arrives, cured. He asks for an explanation, and then enquires if the witch-doctor is sure that, since he was innocent, the school teacher would not have died if he had drunk the poison.

The witch-doctor replies that the teacher would not have died. The chief thereupon hands him the pot and says, "Well, drink it yourself!" The witch-doctor hesitates a moment and then, throwing the pot down, runs away.[64]

The final film, produced before the first displaying unit left in September, was designed to test Western techniques of screen humor for indigenous audiences and to provide comic relief: *First Farce* follows the pranks of a "naughty" African boy. Notcutt and Latham noted that the intent was primarily to entertain and to test the slapstick genre, with the scenario including mostly "standard film jokes" strung around a loose story. They hoped the film would serve to attract new villagers to the shows and break the monotony of the instructional films.[65]

Davis was elated that, just prior to Latham's first cinema tour, the Missionary Conference in Central Africa recognized the need for a new approach for engaging Africans, urging "all Rhodesian missions to co-operate in our cinematograph experiment."[66] This was no casual endorsement, for when Latham first sailed for Africa, he had been handed a letter critical of the whole affair. The missionaries penning the critique were "imbued with the idea that everything connected with films is undesirable," and that "night entertainments encourage immorality."[67] Latham heard similar concerns when arriving in the Copperbelt, but by the time the BEKE brought its exhibition lorries to the area the issue seems to have faded in favor of a willingness to exploit the "educative" possibilities of the medium.

Latham's first tour began on September 4, 1935, and ended on February 13, 1936, after covering 9,000 miles. Initially the crew traveled through Tanganyika, Northern Rhodesia and Nyasaland, and in December Kenya and Uganda were added to the itinerary. The team gave 95 performances before a total of approximately 80,000 Africans, 1,300 Europeans, and an unspecified number of Indians. According to estimates, 90–95 percent of the spectators were neophytes to film, although in coastal regions and industrialized areas like the Copperbelt, many more had familiarity with the medium. The projector was packed into a trailer, pulled by a Ford, which bounced around considerably as it was hauled along rutted or washed-out roads that proved nearly impassable. The crew consisted of two Europeans— Latham and projectionist Peter Woodall, and four Africans—Jackson the driver, Alphonse, Mulishu, and Hamedi, who often used a loudspeaker to supply additional commentary when the sound-on-disc system failed, or when supplementary explanation was deemed necessary. Latham and Notcutt often arranged to have European observers on hand to record the reactions of locals to the films. Unfortunately, much of this valuable material was apparently misplaced when the BFI library in London later relocated from Dean Street to Charing Cross Road.[68]

Latham and crew exhibited films almost exclusively in large clearings or other outdoor venues, with white sheets strung up between bamboo or metal poles. Although the intent of the BEKE was to obscure somewhat the ubiquity of colonial power through the use of African actors, the programs generally ended with an "interest" film shot by BEKE cameraman Captain Coley in England entitled *White People, Part One* (later films included *White People, Part Two* and *White People, Part Three*), including scenes of London, "white activities" such as the Trooping of the Colour military march, polar bear hunting, and acrobatics. In May 1935, Notcutt also decided that the BEKE, touring exclusively in British colonies, should "follow the custom of showing a picture of the King at the end of [each] performance." Latham subsequently ordered four leaders with scenes of royalty, and African spectators were expected to sing the national anthem. This finale, following instructional/ propaganda films such as *Tea* and *Tanga Travel*, showing Africans going about their daily tasks and improving their lot, served the multiple functions of giving credibility to development schemes, acquainting African spectators with the customs and activities of Europeans, and ultimately reconciling viewers with the long reach of colonial power.[69]

Other films produced during the first phase included *Soil Erosion*, under the guidance of Moshi Agricultural and Forest Officers, showing the dangers and causes of soil erosion, and how to combat it. *Gumu* was the one attempt to make a feature film (seven reels) with cultural and humorous elements that expanded on the lessons of the soil erosion film, and condemned the "drift into town." As it was precisely this migration pattern, with Africans making their way to burgeoning urban-industrial areas, which had supplied the stimulus for the 1932 Copperbelt study and the BEKE itself, the film is worthy of closer scrutiny.

Gumu tells the story of an African "garden boy," recently widowed, who turns into a hero when plantation wages are stolen from a crude safe on the estate. As a way to satisfy (or co-opt) the newfound African desire for Hollywood conventions, the hero discovers the culprit and a thrilling chase scene ensues. Because Latham and Notcutt were afraid of wounding African sensibilities by making the thief suffer undue punishment, he miraculously survives a fall from a hundred-foot cliff. In general, Notcutt and Latham had touted cinema's ability to "tell the truth" about the world in their desire to correct damaging images of the white world presented by Hollywood. The improbable survival of the culprit in *Gumu*, however, shows the degree to which the BEKE was forced to sacrifice verisimilitude to appease African sentiment.

Gumu's hero collects his reward and heads for the "bright lights of the city." Unfortunately, the attractions of town life consume his resources, and the bride price of his second marriage (to a Muslim town girl) pushes him back into poverty. When he decides to depart the city, his wife, whom he apparently divorces unintentionally due to his ignorance of Islamic custom, stays behind. However, upon returning to his village, the hero implements an effective program of planting, composting, and anti-erosion measures, enabling him to prosper once again. As a colonial morality tale, the film warned of the dangers of town life, and advised Africans to better their lot not by leaving the village, but by grafting modern agricultural methods to existing peasant farming practices.[70]

BEKE: Second Phase

Despite the adversities Latham and crew suffered on the tours—the first expedition, for instance, they "encountered and overcame formidable obstacles in the shape of unprecedently [sic] prolonged rains, washed-out mountain roads, cloud bursts, broken lines of communication and mechanical difficulties"—Davis reported to the Colonial Office that schedules had been met, and that Africans of "widely differing types" responded to the films with enthusiasm.[71] Yet the project found itself perpetually short of funds, and by the time the BEKE's 3rd Advisory Council met on July 30, 1936, Lugard announced that the experiment had reached a "serious crisis." Major Orde-Browne of the Royal African Society, however, justified the expenditures to date, stressing that the "propaganda work that had been undertaken by the displaying unit had been vital, though non-remunerative." Latham, in fact, had already applied for £3,000 from the Colonial Development Fund (CDF), which was subsequently granted, but the endowment contained a stipulation that Kenya, Uganda, and Tanganyika contribute £250 each. As hosts of the project, Tanganyika officials readily agreed, but Kenya and Uganda released the funds with reluctance.[72] From across the Atlantic, the Carnegie Corporation extended an additional $5,500.

A portion of the Interim Report evaluated African audience reaction, as interpreted by European spectators including missionaries, district officers, settlers, and anthropologists like Godfrey Wilson. While many applauded the films' educational potential, some complained that Africans were incapable of deriving anything useful from the images. Many condemned the pace, one arguing that both "action and speech were too quick." In one interpretation, an official claimed that women "are the people who can be swayed by cinemas rather than by any other form of entertainment." The problem was, of course, that in some areas in Central Africa women attended the shows in smaller numbers. Thus, as a district commissioner put it, "I consider that if women could be persuaded to attend the shows it would materially help adult education." Finally, a few Europeans objected to the use of cheap Hollywood devices: "Films shown smacked too much of the cheap American film type," one opined. "The thefts, fights, etc., were unnecessary thrillers."[73]

Topics considered for the BEKE's second phase, however, were altered as much by the terms of the CDF's grant as they were by the criticisms above. Because the fund was not authorized to finance projects of a purely educational nature, the BEKE requested that its application be considered on the grounds that native production in the colonies could be stimulated through motion pictures. As a result, with a few exceptions, the subsequent themes were agrarian-related as reflected in the titles *High Yields from Selected Plants, Coffee Marketing, Preserving Eggs, Coffee Under Banana Shade, Farm Implements, Cattle and Disease*, and *Msukumu Farmer*.

The push to increase agricultural efficiency was designed to resolve two plaguing problems. First, white officials and missionaries had concluded that mining migration led to rural degradation; second, slash-and-burn cultivation currently in use in Northern Rhodesia and elsewhere created a traditional migrant pattern of its own. Families in sparsely populated areas stayed on the move, making state-building more problematic for colonial administrators.[74] It was not until the 1950s that many authorities began to acknowledge that, in fact, shifting agriculture often produced greater long-term benefits than the settled plow agriculture introduced by colonial governments.

The narrow range of films produced during the experiment's second stage constricted somewhat its original mandate, which was precisely to provide a variety of genres to test African reaction to motion pictures. In fact, in a March 1936 missive to Notcutt prior to CDF involvement, Davis mentioned he was "feeling for some time the importance of our developing a few films that are distinctly related to our missionary programme as such." He worried that failure to produce such films would lead to a declining interest in the project by the missionary bodies involved.[75] Davis even pondered a remake of *Pilgrim's Progress* in an African setting, although his desire to promote missionary investment in Africa through motion pictures failed to materialize.[76] Given the suspicion with which many Africans regarded Christianity, Davis's failure to move *Pilgrim's Progress* beyond the planning stage may have been fortuitous: two decades later another generation of missionaries and colonial officials on the Copperbelt and in the Congo were confronted with a paradox over a different version of *Pilgrim's Progress* as they were forced to negotiate the delicate politics of cinema, race and religion in a colonial setting:

> After a film of the Pilgrim's Progress had been shown in a school at Nchanga during 1958, children asked their teachers: "Why are there no black people in Heaven? All the angels were white." One child wrote in his essay: "I have never seen a picture of Christ helping a black man." But another had been deeply impressed by a picture of Saint Martin handing half his cloak to what the child supposed to be an African. Yet a mere Africanization of pictures will no longer suffice to redress the balance. The Roman Catholic mission in Bancroft bought from the Congo a series of Stations of the Cross portraying Christ as an African; but these were rejected by the people, who said: "This is not true. You are trying to deceive us."[77]

Although the agricultural-instructional film dominated the BEKE during its second and final phase, there were exceptions, including the first production *Healthy Babies* filmed at Kenya's Kiambu hospital. While Notcutt and Latham believed the topic "too advanced" for much of East Africa, it included sequences of a pregnant woman being advised to check into a clinic, and the supervision of newborns. *Healthy Babies* reflected the broader evolution of interwar colonial thinking as European powers introduced, somewhat haltingly, bio-power institutions such as clinics, hospitals, and maternity wards. Nancy Rose Hunt has argued that in the Congo, "Medicalized childbearing was central to a historical movement that began in the 1920s" in part to "reorder reproductive hygiene" and "promote natality and stable family life."[78] It is telling that in the Congo, too, as in Anglophone colonies, visual aids were utilized to institutionalize hospitalization for birthing, thereby justifying exogenous medical practices and, by extension, the intensification of control over the bodies of the colonized. As we have seen, before World War II Belgian colonial officials displayed little interest in producing educational films,[79] but by the 1950s a paradigm shift in propaganda strategies ensured that "images of colonial maternity wards became routine in didactic material directed at Congolese: films, hygiene books, newspapers and comics."[80] As *Healthy Babies* makes clear, however, this process began earlier in British possessions, for the film sought to counter the "main errors made by native mothers," including "feeding the infant whenever it cries; feeding it on food other than milk, and lack of cleanliness."[81] In addition, the film may have been conceived in part to pique the interest of African women and increase their attendance at the shows.

Another non-agricultural film produced in the second phase was made with funds left over from the earlier allocation for Tanganyika. The Provincial Commissioner of the Lake Province suggested that, as so many films were being produced to increase agricultural efficiency, another should show "the Native working for wages." Notcutt's crew traveled to the Geita Gold Mine, near Lake Victoria, and made a film of "the very modern and efficient labour conditions there," including the "good arrangements made for housing, feeding, and the general contentment of the employees."[82]

Despite the increasing homogeneity of subject matter during the second phase, the BEKE's filming units themselves became more varied and mobile. Films were increasingly shot in locations far beyond the Vugiri studio, and the filmmakers began, however incrementally, to depart from the strictures of colonial cinema developed by William Sellers by introducing more complex shots and crosscuts.

In the three extant BEKE films, *Native Veterinary Assistants* (a.k.a. *Veterinary Training of African Natives*), *Peasant Holdings* (a.k.a. *African Peasant Farms—The Kingolwira Experiment*), and *Hookworm*, microscopic images appear for the first time, clearly going against the grain of much colonial filmmaking.[83] In the first, several strategies for improving animal husbandry are emphasized, touting hay, silage, and the benefits of breeding and branding. According to Notcutt, "There are many cases in which to explain disease it is necessary to show a microscopic view of its cause":

> As no ordinary Native has any idea of what a microscope is ... it is useless to show a highly magnified view of some object on the screen.... We endeavored to overcome this difficulty by showing one of the pupils being instructed in the use of a microscope. The instructor pulled out one of the pupil's hairs and on the screen was shown an enormous object supposed to be the tip of hair. Then a blood slide was seen being made from a diseased animal; the microscope scene was repeated and then a live trypanosome shown on the screen. This was faked by means of a plasticine model; satisfactorily so, as it deceived an expert. Our own native assistants, when we tested out the film on them, said they were clear that what they had seen was an insect in the blood too small to see with their eyes.[84]

For *Infant Malaria*, the filmmakers worked with Tanganyikan Malaria Research Officer D.B. Wilson. Notcutt had earlier prepared a storyboard underscoring the need to eliminate mosquito breeding grounds, but Wilson's knowledge of the scourge in eastern Africa led to revisions. Wilson informed Notcutt that adults had generally built up local immunities, which led to new issues the film should address: (1) how to reduce infant mortality; and (2) how to emphasize to adults that while they might not be susceptible to the disease in their own locality, they might enjoy less immunity when traveling to other districts.

Notcutt and Wilson constructed a story about an African who takes leave of his wife and newborn to visit his brother in a nearby village. Traveling through heavy rain, he complains to his brother upon arrival about the number of mosquitoes he encountered, pointing to one resting on his finger. Here the filmmakers interjected a large close-up of a mosquito. As we have seen, in other settings oversized mosquitoes were a potential source of cultural misunderstanding between colonial officials and black subjects. Notcutt, however, was happy to report that "a new device has been designed and made for taking very big pictures of insects, etc., held between the fingers so as to give an idea of scale."[85] The protagonist unfortunately catches malaria ten days later, but his brother, who works at a local apothecary, correctly diagnoses his illness. After being given a dose of quinine that promptly cures him, his brother shows him a number of children suffering from various fevers, and tells him that medicine can be obtained at a dispensary or purchased cheaply at any local post office. The protagonist then returns home only to find his own child ill from malaria. Fortunately, he had secured several doses of quinine from his brother, and his child makes a full recovery. As a way of reinforcing information imparted earlier in the film, the movie concludes with local village women coming to the family to learn more about the disease and its cure.

The films in the second phase, although restricted in subject matter, fit into the BEKE's overall objective to convey information about agricultural efficiency and Western medicine through Oldham's educational model of adaptation. Adaptation worked both ways: Western education had to be adapted to fit the needs of traditional societies, but spectators were also expected to absorb the lessons of the West, and ultimately, to adapt comfortably to the dictates of modernity. But how did the colonized respond? Did they readily serve as actors in the films? Was the content of the films taken at face value, or did viewers contest the images flickering on the outdoor screens billowing in the wind? Were there differences discernible by region, class, age, or gender? Definitive conclusions are difficult to come by, but scattered sources, while often contradictory, offer insight into how Africans responded to film propaganda, and in so doing, how the new forms of colonial beneficence and authority were negotiated by the tens of thousands of spectators who flocked to the shows.

Give Us Faida

The BEKE was subjected to African critique before production even began. In a June 1935 letter to board member Margaret Wrong, Ernest Kalibala expressed anxiety over what he saw as its inherent limitations. Kalibala, an Aggrey Memorial School instructor in Bunamwaya, Uganda, would later complete his Harvard doctorate on "The Social Structure of the Baganda Tribe of East Africa." A former member of the Church Missionary Society, Kalibala had been sent a copy of the April 1935 *Books for Africa* by Wrong, where he read a summary of the BEKE scheme just getting underway.

Kalibala's criticisms were aimed, he explained, not at the noble ambitions of "well-meaning people" for African education and uplift, but rather at what he saw as an abstract form of "superimposed education" devised in London and subsequently "transported" to the colonies. The Aggrey Memorial School, he warned, had already attempted something along the lines of visual education by "invest[ing] our money in the Cinema" in order to raise needed funds for school programs. It was the very failure of this program that worried Kalibala:

> We dealt only with East Africa Kodak Pictures of Kodak Co. USA. These pictures some of them were educational in their backgrounds, others just purely comedies. We found ourselves in a deep hole. The people won't patronize the cinema. It is not because they didn't want them but because of the regular Cinema House Cos. in the country.[86]

Kalibala found that in Kampala, both "Africans and Asiatics," while asking for "native dances to be exhibited once in a while," much preferred Charlie Chaplin and other "commercial moving pictures that talk," to films aiming at mass edification. His observations were buttressed by a visit to a nearby school, where a doctor, whose hobby it was to take local topical films of "health instruction," had provided a viewing for the school body. As the images flashed on the screen, the children only laughed. Leaving the school, Kalibala overheard several students chatting to each other: "If I knew I wouldn't have attended," one exclaimed, "there was nothing exciting."

For Kalibala, this problem pointed to a more pervasive one in colonial settings. While he did not dismiss input from missionaries concerning the project, he warned the IMC to "go slow" and advised the filmmakers that the critical issue was to ensure that "the people themselves ... be taken under consideration." Kalibala doubted seriously that the BEKE's Advisory Committee in London, due to culture bias and its physical detachment from African social life, could attain adequate knowledge of local customs to present the most positive elements of African heritage: "What the judgment of the Committee will call the best will never be the best for the Africans themselves," he declared. It is not necessary here to rehash the missionary disdain for polygamy and witchcraft, but for Kalibala, more to the point was that even simple, mundane expressions of African life found their detractors in the white community. "Certain Missionary bodies [even] object to native dances as being heathenic [sic] in everything," he complained.

Kalibala also dismissed the notion advanced by "many people in England and America" that Africans were heavily influenced by motion pictures. Reflecting the intra-racial class tensions we have seen elsewhere in this study, Kalibala claimed that "99 percent of those [Africans] attending the cinema cannot understand what it is all about. They laugh, but their laugh is just lip-deep and no more." This was even true, he believed, among the adult population for whom the experiment was primarily designed. Furthermore, he suggested that because children were largely ignored by the BEKE, the project would fail to engage large numbers of people, or, worse, would degrade into mere "routine cinema." And it was precisely this unfortunate aspect, he believed, which would lead inexorably to the end of the experiment. For as he phrased it: "Cinemas are always the very negation of the progress of the people." Proof for this assertion, he thought, could be found in the United States itself, where "the audience demands criminal cinemas or cinemas that depict the villain life of America."

Kalibala provided several suggestions for establishing a viable film experiment on the continent:

> a. That a body of trained Africans should be organised and paid by the fund to assist in the project.
> b. That certain members of the East African tribes should be called to London for consultation.
> c. That a permanent African Secretary should be established in each territory to carry out the intentions of the fund.
> d. That a certain competition program be arranged in each territory for the best dramatization of African Stories, the best one in each country to be filmed by the Fund.
> e. That a body of the so-called "old African savages in the bush" be consulted in preference to the "Professors of African culture and background residing abroad."
> f. That certain encouragement be given to these Africans who have tried to help themselves[87]

Kalibala was not the last to levy such a critique on the BEKE. Historians have invariably argued that missionary paternalism and the Colonial Office foreclosed opportunity for meaningful black contribution. To a significant extent this was true, but a closer look at the archives shows that Davis, Notcutt, and Latham were not unwilling to secure some measure of input from across the color line, however circumscribed. As we have seen, Paul Robeson actually declined an invitation to sit on the Advisory Board. Davis also sought out Estella Robeson—wife of Paul and celebrated scientist in her own right—to solicit her thoughts on the project. Following a meeting with Estella and Margaret Wrong, Davis informed Notcutt that he was impressed with the former, an "entirely new type of American negress [with] remarkable insight into the problem of the native African," who apparently provided him with advice worthy of consideration.[88]

Perhaps in response to Kalibala's criticism, when Latham arrived in East Africa in June 1935, he also made a point of eliciting opinions from select Africans on possible scenarios for the films. He first interviewed Martin Kayamba, a Christian clerk who later authored *An African in Europe* (1948) and *African Problems* (1948). Kayamba suggested Latham contact his cousin at the Bumbuli Mission (located near the BEKE headquarters), who might be able to "stage [an] Usambara initiation ceremony, using Christians who have been through the ceremony." But, Kayamba asserted, "It would have to be done secretly. Africans would object to another African showing their secrets to the uninitiated." Although Latham never made this film, his interest suggests that Kalibala's critique of missionary disdain for African cultural forms such as dancing may, in this case, have been a bit severe. But how would spectators have responded had Latham followed through with the idea of filming the secret Usambara ceremony and displaying it in public to varied audiences? No one knows for sure, but in Kayamba's opinion, "Africans would not object to seeing it on the screen—'they would just laugh and say we have discovered their secrets.'"[89]

Kayamba did, however, stress a point made by Kalibala: It was critical to secure accurate information about the "customs of each tribe of which we are making a picture." Be sure, he told Latham, to "get real African customs, dances, and plays." He made several suggestions for dances that could be shown with great effect, including the "Goma" (with 30–50 male performers) and "Bengwa" (women only) in Tanganyika, the "Lele Mama" (women only with men beating drums) in Zanzibar, a "Wayeye" snake dance, the "Kisonge" dance of the Manyema in Mombasa, and the "Warungu" devil dance of the Wabondei.

Kayamba also advised securing footage of working conditions of African laborers on sisal and coffee plantations, as well as on the mines. Perhaps as a result of this advice, the BEKE did produce, near the end of the second phase, no fewer than three films showing coffee planting and marketing techniques (*Coffee Under Banana Shade*, *High Yields from Selected Plants*, *Coffee Marketing*), as well as one on the Tanganyika mining sector (*Labour Conditions at Geita Mine*). Kayamba also warned Latham that for Uganda in particular, the Baganda would take offense if only films from neighboring territories were shown. In fact, with the exception of a short Safety First film, *Uganda Boy Scouts*, only one instructional film was produced in that territory. *Agricultural Education at Bukalasa* was made at an Agricultural Station, and explained the necessity for crop rotation to avoid soil exhaustion. In a poignant segment, the film shows a European examining a yield of cotton and finding it deficient. Calling the students together, he reads a letter from Liverpool. Notcutt then decided, again going against the grain of colonial filmmaking, to include a dissolve to a Liverpool office, where an English broker was making the decision to cease purchasing Ugandan cotton pending improvements in the grade. It is unknown how the Baganda responded to the film, or to having so few films devoted to their territory. But colonial officials there, as we will see momentarily, certainly did take offense that the BEKE had virtually bypassed Uganda in favor of the other four territories.

Latham also toured African schools to generate interest in the experiment and to ascertain what film scenarios would be most likely to capture the attention of students. At Uganda's Makerere College he organized a contest for the best story, which was to be made into a screenplay. Latham found most submissions lacking, but chose one that proposed adapting a fable about an African hare. Notcutt and Latham subsequently combined parts of several fables for the farce *The Hare and the Leopard*, with Africans starring as hares, leopards, monkeys, and rats, using spotted shirts, long tails, and makeup for costumes. Apparently, however, despite the contribution from the actors themselves (who had been given a fair amount of leeway in designing their apparel), the film failed to engage viewers either because of poor production values, or because, as one African spectator dryly commented, "The animals were merely human beings."[90]

In Kenya, Latham visited the Jeanes School following his first exhibition tour to interview indigenous teachers and "obtain their views on the present films and on what they would like to see both from Africa and elsewhere." The Jeanes School was a direct outgrowth of the Phelps-Stokes' tours of African village school in the 1920s, and reflected Oldham's effort to Africanize the curricula, train local teachers, and to "remedy the village school's failings and re-order its priorities" along the lines of a modified Tuskegeeism.[91] Given the critique of precipitant Westernization that undergirded the Jeanes School mission, it is a bit ironic, but telling, that instructors primarily expressed interest in seeing more films "of King George and his family."[92]

Some responses to the BEKE emanated from timely and volatile issues addressed by the films themselves. In May 1935, Northern Rhodesia captured the attention of the outside world when Copperbelt workers engaged in a militant strike. The "disturbance," as the riot was subsequently labeled, engulfed the mining areas of Mufulira, Nkana and Luanshya, and ended only when police fatally shot six protestors storming Luanshya's mining offices. The trigger effect for the riot had been a tax raise for mineworkers. As Charles Perrings argues, the raise constituted a strategy to push those urban Africans who were considered "surplus to the requirements of industry" back to the villages by introducing a new urban-rural differential, raising taxes on those living in the compounds by 30 percent while lowering rural rates by 25 percent.[93] But colonial officials such as Sir Alison Russell, who convened a riot commission to investigate the event, believed that more long-term, pervasive grievances festering in the colony were important contributory causes. Historian Robert Rotberg concurs, arguing that the government's refusal to allow the unionization of workers, as well as the pervasive color bar on the mines and other daily forms of discrimination, were woven into the long fuse that detonated in the uprising.[94]

The riots, of course, were not the impetus for the BEKE—the experiment had begun two months earlier—but John Merle Davis and others watched with dismay as Northern Rhodesians initiated the large-scale refusal against the industry and, indirectly, colonial domination. Davis had not explicitly predicted the strike, yet it was not entirely unexpected given his 1932 Copperbelt report declaring that industrialization in Central Africa presented Britain with pressing new problems not found elsewhere in the empire.[95] Indeed, a letter from Davis to the chief secretary of Northern Rhodesia drew the parallel:

> Our attention has been drawn to the comprehensive and discerning report of the Commission appointed to enquire into the Disturbances on the Copper Belt of Northern Rhodesia.... The Department of Social and Industrial Research of the International Missionary Council notes with much interest the fact that the findings of the Government Commission support

some of the chief findings of the Commission of Enquiry sent out by the Department in 1932 to study the effect of the Copper Mining Industry of Northern Rhodesia upon native tribal life.[96]

The riots gave Notcutt new incentive to complete the first round of films for exhibition as quickly as possible. As a putative antidote to detribalization, the BEKE would, it was hoped, help forge new social bonds bringing African elders closer to the younger generation (thus re-activating customary social controls), encourage Africans to partake willingly in the colonial enterprise, and, in the somewhat bizarre parlance of its founders, to "interpret the African to himself."[97] As a program to bolster rural development and agricultural efficiency it also sought, through less onerous means, to achieve what the new rate of taxation was designed to accomplish: to encourage "redundant" urban Africans to return to the land. In what was probably no mere coincidence, the third BEKE film, *Tax*, was in production in Tanganyika in August 1935, just a few months following the unrest. According to Latham and Notcutt, "Many Natives are under the impression that their tax goes into the pockets of local administrative officers," and thus the film showed the "old days" when a tribute to the chief was required, juxtaposed with more substantive social services provided by Britain such as medical attention, education, famine relief, and the hypothetical bonus of order and peace rendered to Africans under colonial rule.[98]

Tellingly, however, production problems surfaced the very first day of shooting when a local chief failed to fulfill his promise to provide a large force of warriors and other items for the film. Later, when Latham's unit exhibited the film, it appears to have been well received in Tanganyika, but encountered obstacles elsewhere. Notcutt and Latham fail to specify precisely which audiences responded unfavorably, but it is worthy of note that in addition to the Copperbelt, where taxation was clearly a volatile issue, colonial officials in Kenya were having difficulties of their own: in 1936, following discussions at a Provincial Commissioners' meeting, a committee was convened under Chief Native Commissioner H.R. Montgomery to investigate how best to reform the colony's antiquated hut tax system. Despite the "real increase of actual and potential wealth in the native areas of the Colony," the committee asserted that Kenya's declining tax receipts were due to a "definite reluctance on the part of a large number of natives to meet their just liabilities." Several reasons for widespread evasion can be adduced, besides the universal distaste for paying one's just liabilities, including scenarios where families were double-taxed—the father in the Location and a son on the mines or plantations—as well as indigenous opposition to the fact that non–Africans came of age at age 18, whereas Africans were obligated to pay into the system at 16.[99] Furthermore, liberal-humanitarian critics of colonial policy like Norman Leys had long argued that Kikuyu considered taxation to be little more than an outgrowth of European land expropriation: "The Government is not their government. In their view, everything it does, the tax, the labour regulations and all else, is done for the benefit of Europeans."[100]

Not surprisingly, the film, which touted in general terms the glowing benefits conferred upon local populations by colonial taxation, generally failed to persuade many spectators who flocked to the shows. In fact, even Notcutt and Latham, while suggesting that "the idea behind the film was sound," nevertheless concluded that *Tax* "was not a success," and had "[come] in for a certain amount of criticism, and was not often shown."[101]

Spectator criticism was occasionally severe enough to warrant re-shooting offending scenes. In fact, as we saw earlier, the exciting climax of the BEKE's first film, *Post Office Savings Bank*, led audiences to question the harsh punishment meted out to the thief, who suffers a fatal fall from a tree. In a survey provided to test African response, spectators suggested the thief should be arrested: "A thief does not meet his fate in such way now. He should be tried before a Native or European Court and given hard labour." Sentiment was even stronger among spectators who believed that the pursuer had pushed the thief out of the tree, leading one to argue that the man who killed the thief should himself be prosecuted. Because of the negative feedback, Notcutt filmed a new ending in which the thief survives the fall from the tree and is led off by a policeman, and the money restored to its rightful owners.[102]

Post Office Savings Bank was one of five films screened at the BEKE's London headquarters at Edinburgh House on December 19, 1935. The BFI organ *Sight and Sound* covered the event and touted the BEKE, claiming "definite evidence of increased Savings Bank deposits after showings of the film [in Africa] have reached the Unit." Whether this claim is true or not is difficult to ascertain. One pervasive problem in judging the success of the experiment at different stages is that published accounts and speeches on the BEKE often tendered glowing reports reflecting unabashed boosterism, even when reaction from the field told a different story. *Sight and Sound*, for instance, in the same article mentioned above, declared *First Farce* to be "most popular among the natives," describing it in upbeat terms as a "knockabout farce" with "infectious" acting.[103] In reality, while some audience members certainly enjoyed the film, the narrative was criticized by African elders who objected to the disrespect shown by the naughty boy to the older generation.[104] As we saw in the earlier case of *From Red Blanket to Civilization*, reports of African reaction to cinema often functioned on dual ideological registers simultaneously, making firm conclusions elusive.

Determining the BEKE's success in securing actors leads to similar issues. Jane Notcutt, who was present for much of the shooting, wrote to Davis, "As anticipated, we found little difficulty in selecting and training our actors. They take to it like a duck to water, and camera and microphone shyness is unknown to them."[105] Similarly, just prior to the experiment, a Nyasaland official reported to Cunliffe-Lister that "quite talented actors" would be found in the Protectorate. This discourse of the alleged histrionic abilities of the Other is a familiar one. African archives are replete with references to the "good" African who imitates the deportment of the civilizers, or conversely, to the "bad" African who "apes" the white man but who remains inscrutable. Tellingly, the memo above included the official's backhanded compliment to Nyasalanders' aptitude for dramaturgy: "I shall never forget investigating a native murder case in loco where the whole event was re-enacted for my benefit by the principal witnesses in a most convincing manner. The whole drama was later proved to be a tissue of lies."[106]

Despite the claim that good African actors were readily available, we have seen above that during production of *Tax*, a local chief failed to live up to his promise to bring a number of his people to act in a village scene. Other whites perceived limitations in native acting ability as well. *South African Outlook*, for example, reported on the need for short films, for "eight minutes appears to be about the average length of time that African actors can remember their lines."[107] Notcutt's attempts to overcome this obstacle were, no doubt, the reason that during the early stages of the experiment he resorted to hiring three members of a professional Zanzibar troupe. Soon, however, he found local African males to serve as cast members, his strategy being "mainly a matter of finding Natives who, in real life, approximate to the characters one wishes to portray." But for the other gender the story was different. African women were "usually intensely self-conscious and quite unreliable,"[108] and in his September 1935 Progress Report, Notcutt complained that "we have not yet discovered any female natives who have the least idea of acting."[109] In a revealing case of colonial effeminization, Notcutt actually used African boys in drag to play women's roles in comedies like *First Farce*. *Healthy Babies*, however, produced during the second stage, *did* cast females as mothers which, according to Notcutt, proved that "good native actresses can be had from institutions where native women employed under European supervision lose some of their self-consciousness."[110]

It is unclear how spectators responded to female impersonators, if indeed they suspected the deception, but a report from Northern Rhodesia shows that *First Farce* came in for other criticism from schooled Africans. In October, the BEKE crew rolled into the Universities Mission station of Mapanza, also home to St. Mark's Teachers' College, which summoned all interested villagers. Because the BEKE had commentary in Bemba and Nyanja only for Northern Rhodesia, St. Mark's assistant warden, James Mwela, narrated in Tonga for the 1,000 spectators watching the films in the College quadrangle.[111] What set Mapanza apart from other venues was the fact that the following day college students composed essays detailing their opinion of the films. Universally, they identified the principal character in *First Farce* with Kalulu (Mr. Hare) of African folk tales, known for his cunning and clever antics: "I liked Kalulu," one wrote, "because I was interested in his running. Nobody could catch him. This was peculiar in my sight."[112] But as missionary G.I. Feinnes disclosed, "There was a Puritan minority who sternly denounced Kalulu because he stole and was disobedient and played with a girl [boy!] and never stopped being bad." In addition to this "serious breach of Bantu etiquette in an African film," Feinnes noticed that some spectators thought Kalulu was more foolish than clever, and that the "picture taught nothing." Two other films, *Tea* and *Hides*, also failed to find favor among some of the discerning audience. One student found *Tea* "not interesting; I should not like to see it again"; others had little use for hide-curing films given that their own people owned no cattle.

While these comments about the films are revealing, no less so are comments various students made on scenarios they would rather see:

How the Black People used to fight.
I want to see how to fight. I think it will be good for me.
I would like to see people fighting, not many people, but two people fighting. I expected to see people fighting. That is what I like very much.
People fighting with their friends as the Abyssinians do.

As these essays make clear, even schooled Africans enjoyed barroom brawls and other crowd pleasers in commercial films at least as much as they did didactic/instructional films. But Notcutt, who was concerned about similar reactions of sophisticated audiences in areas like the Copperbelt where commercial films had been showing for years, was gratified "that the poor technical quality of our first films did not affect [the BEKE's] popularity" at Roan Antelope, Nkana and Mufulira mines.[113]

In October 1936, at the 23rd session of Brussels' International Colonial Institute, Latham outlined three promising uses of the cinema based on his experiences running the BEKE's display unit: "(a) For General Enlightenment & propaganda for better standards of living, housing, health, agriculture and animal husbandry; (b) For healthy entertainment, together with cultural development, to interpret the new world to the African and relate the new knowledge for his present condition; [and] (c) As an aid in the classroom." According to Latham, while many critics objected to intertwining the first two categories, he felt that films drawing upon both would ultimately prove most effective. Latham cited approvingly one African's comments which, from the BEKE perspective, proved the films' efficacy:

It is certainly simple to learn when you see because the things seen are not difficult to understand. The cinema such as this which could speak directly to the audience in terms and scenes well understood and realized will no doubt make a native learn something which he had been unfortunate enough to learn in the classroom.[114]

As Latham put it, "The Native rather expects, at any rate does not resent, the presence of what he calls 'faida' or profit in a picture." In Kenya in particular, he found healthy enthusiasm for the programs, including educational films. At an agricultural show in Kisii, audiences hovered around 4,000–5,000.[115] This prompted one official in Kavirondo country, who initially considered colonial cinema to be little more than "an interesting, amusing and expensive toy" whose funds would be better spent employing agricultural instructors, to grudgingly admit that it was "by no means without propaganda value."[116] Indeed, at six of the first eight Kenya exhibitions, spectators declared the film providing information on how to prevent soil run-off to be their favorite.[117]

There were, in fact, two soil-erosion films. The first had elicited significant European criticism when it was displayed to the BEKE Advisory Council in December 1935. Moreover, Notcutt admitted he had only the "vaguest idea of what soil erosion was but expected to be enlightened locally as we had not completed the part of the scenario which dealt with remedial measures. We had completed about three quarters of the film before I began to understand fully the facts about erosion and then realized that the film was directed along the wrong lines."[118] Perhaps for this reason one audience member, a former agricultural officer in Northern Rhodesia, found it "almost impossible to follow the picture," despite his expertise.[119] The filmmakers subsequently produced *Soil Erosion at Machakos* during the second BEKE stage. When this and other films were shown by the display unit, Latham marveled at the "enthusiasm of the Kenya Natives in the Reserves for educational films." While Notcutt and Latham were thrilled that the Kikuyu, Kamba and others huddled in the White Highlands appreciated the "faida" of *Soil Erosion at Machakos*, it is possible that their enthusiasm was based on economic desperation. Kikuyu and Kamba had suffered significant land alienation to white settlers and railroad projects decades before, resulting in massive overcrowding and soil depletion in the reserves. In particular, the Kamba around Machakos, where the second erosion film was produced, experienced additional privations due to cattle overstocking. Thus, their zeal for the film perhaps reflected a hope that it would help to alleviate their distress, or it may simply have been a result of seeing "their own" on the screen. What *is* clear is that the film failed to resolve the crisis. Only a few years later the government initiated a policy of compulsory de-stocking, leading the Kamba to orchestrate a campaign of passive resistance, and future Prime Minister Jomo Kenyatta, who was in London, to pen several protests in the *Manchester Guardian*. As historians Rosberg and Nottingham argue, the de-stocking plan fueled the rise of an "educated non-traditional leadership" among the Kamba, an elite group that would soon emerge as a force in the liberation struggle.[120]

As the above accounts show, while Africans often walked miles to the shows and showed appreciation for the BEKE programs, they also articulated a wide range of opinions on the project. Educated blacks expressed concerns about cultural bias and white paternalism, while many women were reticent to appear in the films at all. When action on the screen offended elders, they voiced their objections. Other groups clearly expected to be entertained, and may have been bored by instructional/propaganda films with little relevance to their own circumstances. Yet some paid close attention to these films, hoping to better their circumstances. As G.I. Feinnes put it, "The moral of the pictures which had morals were clearly grasped, but [Africans] were clearly not prepared to accept everything that was given them, and they made some unexpected criticisms."[121]

BEKE Postmortem

On May 27, 1937, the final meeting of the BEKE's Advisory Council convened at Edinburgh House to conclude the experiment. Despite the absence of heavyweights like Lugard, Oldham and Vischer, Latham and the other members present prepared a formal statement for the under secretary of state for the colonies, calling upon the Colonial Office and territorial governments to pursue the educational possibilities of the medium. Latham was also busy lobbying on his own. His "Films for the Colonies: A Call To Action," parts of which were republished in the experiment's final report, called for a central film organization in London to implement and oversee a permanent colonial film program. Based on audience response (and what he believed to be African appreciation for European imagery), new films designed for Africans should not only include educational/instructional topics along the lines of previous BEKE films, but should provide more scenes of European life. "Films making peoples of the world known to one another," Latham exhorted in a veiled reference to the rise of fascism, "showing their varied ways of living and giving a true picture of their common home-loving humanity, would do much to counteract the hate propaganda of nationalist governments."[122]

Certainly many members of the Colonial Office looked toward a continuation of the project, but the decision rested primarily in the hands of the colonial governments involved. For this reason, a June 1937 meeting of the East African Governors' Conference in Nairobi virtually sealed its fate. Northern Rhodesia "agreed unconditionally to co-operate in the scheme," but Kenya and Nyasaland adjudged the BEKE films surprisingly amateurish, prompting one official to declare, "The standard was so low in some of the films exhibited as to render them unintelligible to African audiences."[123] Uganda, in turn, expressed displeasure that the BEKE had virtually side-stepped the Protectorate, both in terms of production and exhibition, despite the colony's financial contribution to the project. Even Tanganyika, home to the experiment, refused to work toward putting the project on a more permanent footing once other East African governments backed out.[124] Colonial Agricultural Departments also expressed doubts as to the utility of having a central institution producing films with detailed instructional information. Rather, they argued, individual governments might more efficaciously do the job without "expensive professional assistance."[125]

Although Latham and Notcutt were discouraged at the cold shoulder given their proposal to extend the experiment, some BEKE cinema vans were, in fact, still in operation. Because Kenya, Uganda and Tanganyika had all contributed to the second stage of the project, nine small display units were showing the agricultural and instructional films throughout 1938. In Tanganyika alone, during this post–BEKE exhibition phase, 47 performances were given in approximately one year.[126] Renamed the "African Vernacular Cinema Experiment," the project in Tanganyika focused its energies not on production but on trying to institutionalize film-going as African cultural practice. Exhibitors showed films in cities and towns like Dar es Salaam, Moshi and Wmanza, where audiences were reportedly quite large.[127]

Although recent critics of the project have argued, in some fashion, that the BEKE mystified the intricacies of the film industry for Africans by exploiting their labor power without adequate technical training, the archives reveal that all of these nine units were operating solely through the use of African personnel.[128] As another experiment, a small entrance fee was introduced to determine whether a colonial cinema project, in competition with commercial bioscopes, could pay its own way. The relatively meager funds collected were handed over to each colony's Native Authority, but no consensus was reached as to the ability of the program to generate sufficient revenue to stand independently. In addition to trying to bolster revenue, Notcutt instituted the admission fee due to his belief that Africans "appreciate the cinema far more if they have to pay for admission, no matter how small the charge."[129]

Despite the mild successes of the post–BEKE tour, by mid–1938 Notcutt could see the end of the road and began contemplating new venues for the BEKE films. In June, he contacted the Transvaal Chamber of Mines and proposed sending them to the Witwatersrand to be included in the MCCC. The secretary of the chamber thanked Notcutt for his interest and applauded the educative potential of motion pictures. He declined Notcutt's offer, however, saying, "The Corporation's cinema shows are held primarily as a form of entertainment and relaxation for the native labourers, and the use of the motion picture in this particular circuit as an instrument of education is not the objective."[130]

Notcutt, however, did not abandon his role as filmmaker. By the end of the year he had joined L.A.W. Vickers-Haviland of the Universities' Mission in Tanganyika as cameraman and co-producer on a film version of the *Wakilindi Saga* in the Usambara Mountains. This historical epic is the tale of Mbega, a half-caste Arab child who grew up to become the ruling chief of the Wasambara people. The film was an experiment in using modern technology to capture for posterity the tribal past—to make a record, said Vickers-Haviland, of "historical and patriotic value to the tribe before the memories of the older generation fade." One of the primary goals of the filmmakers was to make the production as true to life as possible. For the sake of realism, the actors were themselves living descendants of Mbega, but as we saw with Phillips's filming of Hlambisinye Shangase, the all-too-familiar question of attire and changing social realities quickly became an issue as shooting got underway, forcing Notcutt and Vickers-Haviland to argue that it was not so much African reality with which they were concerned, but rather a more general historical truth, which allowed for a degree of poetic license:

> Mbega's father was an Arab, and it is safe to say that Arab dress has not changed much in two hundred years. But the Sambaa wore skins, and they are now unobtainable. To my regret as a budding film director seeking truth in action I had to compromise with blankets and loincloths. But here another stumbling block lay in our path—a marked disinclination by people of social standing to disclose the bare chest or head to public view. The leading actor for whom we did succeed in getting a leopard skin could only be restrained with difficulty from showing a vest, which peeped out above, and a pair of khakhi shorts which would keep disclosing their presence below his more primitive garb.[131]

By 1938, while Notcutt was busy filming in Tanganyika, the prospects for Latham and Davis to be at the forefront of colonial cinema seemed to be dwindling as the BEKE concluded and African governments declined to support a more permanent, restructured version. Indeed, in the end it was, ironically, the flow of events in Europe, and not in Africa, that revived the push for experimenting with documentary and instructional films for the colonies, in turn, leading to a further expansion of African spectatorship during the World War II era.

Conclusion

From Reel to Real: New Horizons

Colonial Cinema and the War Effort

In October 1939, the Films Division of the new British Ministry of Information (MOI) established the Colonial Film Unit (CFU) to produce films explaining the European conflict to African audiences and to build support for the war effort.[1] Latham and Sellers both applied for the position of director, showing examples of their pioneering experiments in colonial cinema to MOI officials. Although Sellers was chosen to run the CFU, Latham nevertheless offered moral support, claiming that the new experiment led by people who had the "interests of the African at heart" would serve as "an insurance against future exploitation of the cinema in Africa."[2]

It was at the MOI that Sellers met George Pearson. A heralded writer and director for such leading firms as Pathé, Samuelson, Gaumont and Welsh-Pearson, his credentials as a British filmmaker were without parallel. At age 65 Pearson joined Sellers's CFU team, and they began filming in early 1940 in Soho Square. As Pearson explained it, "Our first films were designed to tell the British wartime story to the African illiterates; simple explanations of strange inventions, the aeroplane, the tank, the barrage balloon, the searchlight, the air-raid warden, the Home Guard and the Fire Brigade."[3] Due to funding restrictions, the CFU made most of their wartime films in England, although African images were occasionally spliced in with the help of a Raw Stock scheme introduced in 1941. To appreciate the scope of the experiment, one need look no further than Arthur Champion, one of its leading mobile projectionists as well as amateur filmmaker who had taken footage for the raw stock library. Nicknamed "Bwana Cinema" by Africans throughout Kenya, Champion was on the East African circuit from July 1940 to April 1944, with his unit reportedly giving a staggering 800 performances to well over a million spectators during this period.[4] To put this figure in perspective, and to emphasize the degree to which cinema had become routinized in much of Africa by the 1940s, Champion's unit was only one of several operating during the war.

The CFU, in fact, was only one component of Britain's expanding propaganda arsenal. Another part of the equation was the program put in place by Alec Dickson, who had recently led a Nyasaland platoon of King's African Rifles. "It seemed important," Dickson said, "to devise ways of explaining what the war meant to [Africans], ways more effective than distributing Ministry of Information posters showing high-angle views of the aircraft carriers for inland tribes or landlocked territories, with injunctions in English to 'Back

Them Up.'" To his surprise, Dickson's offer to organize a Mobile Propaganda Unit for East and Central Africa found strong support within the MOI, and vans were quickly assembled and began touring the five British territories there. With soldiers from a variety of African regions to accommodate tribal cultural peculiarities, the MOI vans deployed British newsreels and other propaganda material:

> Physical training, weaponry, music, films, dancing, drama, talks, every kind of display technique was pressed into service. The resulting combination of sparkling gymnastic exercises, dramatic enactments of crisis situations, lucid educational expositions, exemplary off-duty manners and sheer fun made a profound impression on audiences over a vast area.[5]

Reports on these tours during the war show that the number of BEKE spectators, as numerous as they were, paled in comparison to Africans viewing MOI's visualization of the Allied cause in Africa. If mass black spectatorship largely originated in the interwar years, it expanded exponentially during the war with the mobilization of the CFU and MOI cinema programs. As one official phrased it in 1940, the new supply of cinema vans and films to the colonies at least eliminated "Latham's vicious circle [of] 'no projectors because no films, no films because no projectors.'"[6] Another key point can be made concerning the wartime push to explain the Allied position to Africans through a plethora of new images of the West: despite the extensive dialogue and debates that were still ongoing in the 1940s about the wisdom of showing Africans too many pictures of the white world, or their ability to understand those images, ultimately it was less ideology that would dictate the shift than it would be a politics of the pragmatic.

In order to facilitate discussion on colonial cinema techniques, audience reaction studies, mobile war propaganda units, and village cinemas, the CFU began publishing the monthly bulletin *Colonial Cinema* in 1942.[7] Although the original mandate for Sellers was to make films to bolster the war effort, by 1942 due to successful lobbying on the part of Colonial Office officials, the CFU slowly expanded its scope to include films advocating colonial development.[8] Thus, while the CFU in the early 1940s produced titles such as *The British Army* and *Guns in the Desert*, by the end of the decade films like *Better Hides and Skins* and *Baba Tunde Goes to School* were more common fare.[9]

As was the case for other programs explored in this study, viewers often subjected the CFU films to a wide range of critiques. A teacher in Northern Rhodesia complained about the presentation of the topics in the earlier films: "Show us films of actual fighting face to face, bombing towns, sinking ships, so that we may understand war; not manufacturing aeroplanes, repairing guns, inspecting troops, etc., which are mostly unintelligible and quite uninteresting to us Africans."[10] Officials also debated best practices for development initiative films, as we see in the case of one Lusaka administrator: "Like the people of any other land, Natives have a negative response to anything smacking of 'uplift.' The pill, therefore, is carefully sugared." But even this strategy failed to convince residents around the Lake Bangweulu region, who had other grievances. Here, the Government Information Department found the use of lorries untenable and had resorted to using cinema barges in the swampy areas around the lake to circulate films. But locals, reportedly mistaking European crew members for cannibals, engaged in a policy of "stoning the boat."[11]

The push to introduce Africans to "responsible" cinema proceeded along other fronts as well. In 1940, Northern Rhodesian officials established the African Film Library and Processing Committee to purchase titles from South Africa Consolidated Films, as well as sponsoring the production of documentaries by local amateurs. Organized under the auspices of Northern Rhodesia's Central Native Welfare Advisory Committee, the Film Library, which by 1949 boasted of 800 films,[12] ran its own "silent circuit" in local villages and the Copperbelt, leading one official to comment that the films "appear to be extremely well received by African audiences, many of whom have never before seen a cinematographic picture."[13] But this assessment may be an official delivering what his superiors wanted to hear, for according to a different report from the Copperbelt, viewers were apparently somewhat bored by the films which paled next to the excitement of the talkies shown by nearby mining concerns.[14]

Some 1940s films in both Central and South Africa were notable for their narratives about African labor migration—the theme that weighted so heavily on the constitution of black spectatorship itself. *Kasoma*, produced at the start of the decade, was a fictional tale about a rural villager who makes the trip to the Copperbelt in search of work. The product of an amateur filmmaker in Central Africa and bought by the Northern Rhodesian Film Library, it was shown along with native sports films and CFU war propaganda movies to migrant workers in the colony.[15] This film was followed in 1949 by *Chisoko—The African*, a 36-minute Gaumont-Instructional talkie rehashing the basic storyline of *Kasoma*, a film that similarly drove home the centrality of mining and migration in the evolution of cinema in Africa.[16] *Chisoko*, sponsored by Roan Antelope Copper Mines, Nchanga Consolidated and Rhokana Corporation, was billed as a documentary about the birth of Chisoko to a chief's daughter in 1902. Years later, Chisoko, who was "hankering for some way out of their [Africans'] monotonous, endless existence," makes the inevitable rite of passage to the Copperbelt mines, begins training, and is soon working underground. With spending cash in pocket, a satisfied Chisoko later returns to his village with his pregnant wife. After a dispute with his father over the most appropriate place for the impending childbirth, his wife soon delivers a healthy boy in the safe confines of a "white man's hospital." The commentary summing up the film is a revealing and heavy-handed piece of industrial propaganda: "Copper had brought to these primitive places more than a great industry. It had brought in the heart of a man the final break with a barbaric time, and the certain hope of an enlightened future."[17]

The theme of migration was also taken up in the first "black" South African commercial film, *African Jim* (a.k.a. *Jim Comes to Jo-Burg*, 1949), which was actually produced by white Britons Donald Swanson and Eric Rutherford, with a black cast. The film revolves around a young man who migrates to Johannesburg in search of work. While Jim has no discernible skills for manual labor and fails initially to find meaningful employment, he is soon discovered to have a mellifluous singing voice which lands him both a record deal and a beautiful town girl. Jim's romanticized rise to fame reflects the way many black South Africans tried to put a positive spin on the Transvaal's entrenched migratory system. *Jim Comes to Jo-Burg* (as the film is commonly called), which catapulted Dolly Rathebe to stardom as the female lead, was the first commercial film in South Africa to portray black migration and urbanization in a favorable light. Yet Rathebe, whose father's frequent absence due to his part-time occupation as a miner contributed to her parents' divorce,[18] was certainly aware of the often alienating realities of the Rand's labor system. Indeed, at her audition for the film, she sang her own plaintive adaptation of "Salt Lake City Blues," originally sung by Lena Horne in *Cabin in the Sky* but poignantly modified somewhat for a South African audience by Rathebe:

> Oh, I came to Jo-Burg, the Golden City
> Oh, what did I go there for?
> I should have stayed in New Orleans,
> And never gone nowhere.[19]

Black spectatorship expanded yet again in 1948, a year notable for its colonial cinema conferences in England,[20] with the inauguration of the Central African Film Unit (CAFU) by the Central African Council to integrate development schemes in Southern Rhodesia, Northern Rhodesia, and Nyasaland. In part, the postwar push for new development initiatives grew out of earlier critiques by the United States (and even the Nazis) that Britain had largely ignored its duty as trustee to stimulate economic growth in Africa.[21] Although white settlers in Southern Rhodesia were actually pushing for a high-quality, 35mm format for their own consumption, the CAFU was implemented as a 16mm project primarily targeting indigenous groups.

By mid-century, radio stations in Central Africa were also playing a part in augmenting the appeal of colonial cinema schemes in local villages. Alan Izod, for example, CAFU's first executive producer, took to the airwaves in 1950 to promote the entertainment value of CAFU's educational films with strong moral messages.[22] Similarly, Lusaka's Central African Broadcasting station advertised Northern Rhodesia's silent film library circuit: "I expect most of you," chided broadcaster Peter Young, "never think about the cinema van but hurry to the place where the films will be shown, wondering what you will see. Perhaps you say to your friend[,] 'Shall we see our favorite cowboy on his beautiful white horse?' 'Do you think there will be a British News to tell us about things in England and in the British Colonies?' 'Shall we see Charlie Chaplin? You know, he's that funny man with the very big feet and always in trouble, but always makes you laugh.'" Young went on to emphasize the need for communities to construct large, central enclosures to accommodate the film showings, or at least preparing local schoolrooms or welfare halls for the events.[23] Unlike the BEKE lorries, the mobile units in post–World War II Northern Rhodesia constituted a central means by which the news of the empire was disseminated in local villages. Radios were always incorporated into the evening programs, broadcasting music and plays between 5:30–7:30 in each village before the films started. The lorries also conveyed books published in Nyanja, Bemba, Tongo and Lozi, as well as copies of *Mutende*, the local African newspaper, for purchase by local villagers.

Old Debates and New Horizons

After 1940, even given the rash of wartime images provided for the colonized, the field of colonial film theory was still framed by the two broad and overlapping debates that had never been settled before the war. The first concerned the level of visual literacy among illiterates and other "unsophisticated" audiences, while the second questioned the efficacy of specially produced educational/instructional films for illiterates in achieving their didactic aims. The first debate involved several questions: "Can Africans even understand moving images?"

"How quickly is visual literacy obtained?"

"Is the basis for film literacy racial or cultural?"

At a 1943 Information Officers' conference in Northern Rhodesia, one official framed the debate succinctly: "One school of thought considers they should be very simple and repetive [sic] 'shots,' the other that the African can already understand an ordinary interest film, more than most people imagine." William Sellers, through his experiments beginning in the late-1920s, was the chief theorist for the former school of thought in the interwar years, and he continued his advocacy after the war despite increasing criticism from both African elites and European observers.[24]

Julian Huxley, who in 1929 had shown educational films to secondary students in Moshi, engaged Sellers in a debate during the war over precisely this issue, arguing that, in his experience, cinematic neophytes learn quickly how to read moving images, and that Sellers's film style would ultimately prove "too boring and uninteresting" to most viewers.[25] Many felt the results of the CFU's own questionnaire on audience reaction and comprehension circulating the colonies in 1943 were too inconclusive to resolve the dispute. As reported in *Colonial Cinema*, "The replies reveal valuable info but even more they reveal the need for further research and the inadequacy of the method employed. Replies from different territories often contradicted each other, are inconsistent in themselves, and lack a common, systematic approach."[26] By the early 1950s, however, studies in culturally diverse regions of Tanganyika and Nigeria were revealing that moving images, as well as complex editing techniques such as dissolves, mixes and fades, were capable of being understood rather quickly by all audiences, if indeed they had ever been misinterpreted at all.[27]

Those engaged in the second debate assumed that Africans were capable of decoding moving images, but questioned whether they did, in fact, derive "faida" from the pictures. This debate, of course, was not new. Some Europeans had earlier criticized the notion that Africans could be educated at all by simply sitting through a movie. One white observer of the BEKE audiences complained, "I must say no one has grasped the educational aim of them. As I told you, they cannot judge at all by seeing films once. They just fill their eyes, nothing gets to the mind."[28] And after the war, even MOI propagandist Alec Dickson expressed doubts regarding his own efforts to deploy cinema didactically in West Africa: "No matter what the 'might-have-beens' and the future possibilities of the cinema in theory—this 'squirting pictures at them in the dark' is to-day in practice useless as a vehicle for Mass Education.... Adult Education, we know, needs not only a book, but a tutor and a theme."[29] And in 1951, the Gold Coast's chief social development officer complained that "crowds turn out to see [British] films and it is common to meet an audience of a thousand people gathered around a mobile cinema. The wonder and magic of the cinema is fully appreciated, yet from an instructional point of view little or nothing may be learned."[30]

These issues would never be resolved conclusively, but rather continued to fester with the expansion of black spectatorship in the postwar years. Opportunities for Africans across the continent to view films increased dramatically as colonial cinema programs expanded, some segregation laws were rescinded, and as more black cinemas opened.[31] In fact, cinemas sometimes played a part in the agenda to break down entrenched patterns of racial exclusion in the colonial sphere. In May 1959, Northern Rhodesia's African National Congress provincial president D.C. Mwansa declared that activists planned to converge upon "the Lusaka swimming bath, the Cinemas and the churches" on the weekend to call for greater access to white facilities.[32] Even after integration was accomplished the following year, the issue of racial mixing proved to be a flashpoint for racial violence. On the Copperbelt at the beginning of September 1960, a new law opening up formerly all-white cinemas, hotels and restaurants to all races led to two days of pitched battles in the towns of Kitwe and Ndola. In the latter a racial altercation between blacks and whites emerging from a cocktail bar and a hotel quickly escalated to a full street battle. Oddly, according to one report, "A lone African [who] stood in the middle of the street delivering a speech on the elimination of the color bar ... was unmolested."[33]

By the 1950s, then, on the eve of independence for many African colonies, cinema had become entrenched in Black Africa. Wading through six decades of the now-maligned cinematic oeuvre of, among others, explorers, adventurers, ethnologists, missionaries, colonial officials and corporate interests, African audiences in conjunction with a burgeoning corps of indigenous filmmakers would begin, incrementally, to set their own cultural agenda. The transfer of political power would lead to flag-lowering ceremonies and the final fade-out for colonial cinema, yet in many ways African Cinema had just begun. For as Ngugi Wa Thiong'o affirms, "There have to be films made by Africans on the African condition before we can talk about African cinema."[34]

Chapter Notes

Preface

1. This topic has been the subject of debate due to Nollywood's popularity. See Laura Fair, "Songs, Stories, Action! Audience Preferences in Tanzania, 1950s-1980s," in Mahir Şaul and Ralph A. Austen (eds.), *Viewing African Cinema in the Twenty First Century: Art Films and the Nollywood Video Revolution* (Athens: Ohio University Press, 2010), 108–111.

Introduction

1. Fernando Solanas and Octavio Getino, "Towards a Third Cinema," in Bill Nichols (ed.), *Movies and Methods: An Anthology* (Berkeley: University of California Press, 1976), 44–64.
2. James Genova, *Cinema and Development in West Africa* (Bloomington: Indiana University Press, 2013), 4.
3. Samba Diop, *African Francophone Cinema* (New Orleans: University Press of the South, 2004), 1.
4. Matthew G. Stanard, *Selling the Congo: A History of European Pro-Empire Propaganda and the Making of Belgian Imperialism* (Lincoln: University of Nebraska Press, 2011), 220.
5. Wes Felton, "Caught in the Undertow: African Francophone Cinema in the French New Wave," *Senses of Cinema*, 57, December 2010, @ http://sensesofcinema.com/2010/feature-articles/caught-in-the-undertow-african-francophone-cinema-in-the-french-new-wave/, accessed February 3, 2013.
6. For more on FEPACI, see http://www.fepaci.org/aboutus.htm.
7. Martin Botha, *South African Cinema 1896–2003* (Bristol: Intellect, 2012), 37–38.
8. Alison Griffiths, *Wondrous Difference: Cinema, Anthropology & Turn-of-the-Century Visual Culture* (New York: Columbia University Press, 2002), 199.
9. Paulin Soumanou Vieyra, *Le Cinema Africain: Des origines à 1973* (Paris: Présence Africaine, 1975), 25.
10. Kedmon Nyasha Hungwe interview with Michael Raeburn (Harare, 2001), @ http://www.ed.mtu.edu/~khungwe/afrika/kedmon-hungwe/michael-raeburn.html, accessed February 2, 2014.
11. Samba Gadjigo, *Ousmane Sembène: The Making of a Militant Artist* (Bloomington: Indiana University Press, 2010).
12. For an analysis of *Emitai*, see John D.H. Downing, "Post-Tricolor African Cinema: Toward a Richer Vision," in Dina Sherzer (ed.), *Cinema, Colonialism, Postcolonialism: Perspectives from the French and Francophone Worlds* (Austin: University of Texas Press, 1996), 194–196.
13. See Mbye Cham, "Reconfiguration of the Past in the Films of Ousmane Sembène," in Marcia Landy (ed.), *The Historical Film: History and Memory in Media* (New Brunswick: Rutgers University Press, 2000), 261–266.
14. Françoise Balogun, *The Cinema in Nigeria* (Enugu, Nigeria: Delta Publications, 1987), 23–4.
15. Andrew Rice, "A Scorcese in Lagos: The Making of Nigeria's Film Industry," *The New York Times Magazine* (February 23, 2012), 2. By circumventing standard funding/distribution patterns, Nollywood may be re-writing the story of African Cinema. For a discussion of cultural elitism among African film scholars, see Onookome Okome, "Nollywood and its Critics," in Şaul and Austen (eds.), *Viewing African Cinema in the Twenty First Century*, 26–41.
16. Françoise Balogun, "Booming Videoeconomy: The Case of Nigeria," in Françoise Pfaff (ed.), *Focus on African Films* (Bloomington: Indiana University Press, 2004), 173–181.
17. Kristin Alexandra Rasmussen, "Kinna-Uganda: A Review of Uganda's National Cinema" (Master's Thesis, San Jose State University, 2010), 84.
18. The DVD release reflects the struggle of African filmmakers to break through the barrier with the American public and compete with Hollywood: "An Oedipal story mixed with magic, *Yeelen* is as visually stunning as anything from Hollywood." *Yeelen*, King Video, DVD (2002).
19. Francoise Pfaff, *Twenty-five Black African Filmmakers: A Critical Study, with Filmography and Bio-bibliography* (Westport, CT: Greenwood Press, 1988).
20. David Murphy, "Africans filming Africa: questioning theories of an authentic African cinema," *Journal of African Cultural Studies* 13, 2 (December 2000), 239–249. Ikechukwu Obiaya, "A Break with the Past: The Nigerian Video-film Industry in the Context of Colonial Filmmaking," *Film History* 23, 2 (2011), 129–146.

21. Nwachukwu Frank Ukadike, *Black African Cinema*, 31.

22. Ntongela Masilela, "Come Back Africa and South African film history," *Jumpcut* 36 (May 1991), 61–65.

23. Hyginus Ekwuazi, "Towards the Decolonization of African Film," *Africa Media Review* 5, 2 (1991), 99.

24. Rex Stevenson, "Cinemas and Censorship in Colonial Malaya," *Journal of Southeast Asian Studies* 5, 2 (September 1974). Seth Feldman, "Viewer, Viewing, Viewed: A Critique of Subject-Generated Documentary," *Journal of the University Film Association* 29, 1 (1977). Rosaleen Smyth, "The Development of British Colonial Film Policy, 1927–1939, with Special Reference to East and Central Africa," *Journal of African History* 20, 3 (1979). Rosaleen Smyth, "The Development of Government Propaganda in Northern Rhodesia up to 1953" (PhD diss., University of London, 1983). Guido Convents, *A la recherché des images oubliées: Préhistoiree de cinema en Afrique, 1897–1918* (Bruxelles: OCIC, 1986).

25. Richard Maynard, *Africa on Film: Myth and Reality* (Rochelle Park, NJ: Hayden Book, 1974). Keyan Tomaselli, *Myth, Race and Power: South Africans Imaged on Film and TV* (Bellville, South Africa: Anthropos, 1986). Keyan Tomaselli, *The Cinema of Apartheid: Race and Class in South Africa Film* (New York: Athens Printing Corporation, 1988). Donald Bogle, *Toms, Coons, Mammies & Bucks* (New York: Continuum, 1989). Mark Reid, *Redefining Black Film* (Berkeley: University of California Press, 1993). Thomas Cripps, *Slow Fade to Black: The Negro in American Film, 1900–42* (London: Oxford University Press, 1993). Kenneth Cameron, *Africa on Film: Beyond Black and White* (New York: Continuum, 1994). Peter Davis, *In Darkest Hollywood: Exploring the Jungle's of Cinema's South Africa* (Athens: Ohio University Press, 1996).

26. Gregory A. Waller, *Main Street Amusements: Movies and Commercial Entertainment in a Southern City, 1896–1930* (Washington, D.C.: Smithsonian Institution Press, 1995). bell hooks, "The Oppositional Gaze: Black Female Spectators," in John Belton (ed.), *Movies and Mass Culture* (New Brunswick: Rutgers University Press, 1996). Daniel Bernardi (ed.), *The Birth of Whiteness: Race and the Emergence of U.S. Cinema* (New Brunswick: Rutgers University Press, 1996). Melvyn Stokes & Richard Maltby (eds.), *American Movie Audiences, from the Turn of the Century to the Early Sound Era* (London: BFI, 1999).

27. Judith Mayne, *Cinema and Spectatorship* (London: Routledge, 1993).

28. Paul Landau, "Empires of the Visual: Photography and Colonial Administration in Africa," in Landau and Kaspin (eds.), *Images and Empires*, 149. See also David Giltrow, "Young Tanzanians and the Cinema" (PhD diss., Syracuse University, 1973).

29. Thelma Gutsche, "Films and the African," 2.

30. Melvyn Stokes and Richard Maltby (eds.), *Hollywood Abroad: Audiences and Cultural Exchange* (London: BFI, 2007).

31. Charles Ambler, "Popular Films and Colonial Audiences: The Movies in Northern Rhodesia," *American Historical Review* 106, 1 (February 2001), 81–105. Andrew Burton, "Urchins, Loafers and the Cult of the Cowboy: Urbanization and Delinquency in Dar es Salaam, 1919–61," *Journal of African History* 42, 2 (2001), 199–216. Marissa Moorman, "Of Westerns, Women and War: Resituating Angolan Cinema and the Nation," *Research in African Literatures* 32 (2001), 103–22.

32. James Burns, "John Wayne on the Zambezi: Cinema, Empire, and the American Western in British Central Africa," *International Journal of African Historical Studies* 35, 1 (2002), 103–117. James Burns, "The African Bioscope—Movie House Culture in British Colonial Africa," *Afrique & Histoire* 1, 5 (2006), 65–80. James Burns, "Cape Town Bioscope Culture and *The Rose of Rhodesia*" in *Screening the Past*, Issue 25: Special Issue: Colonial Africa on the Silent Screen: Recovering *The Rose of Rhodesia* (September 2009), http://www.latrobe.edu.au/screeningthepast/25/rose-of-rhodesia/rose-of-rhodesia.html.

33. Marcus Power, "Post-colonial Cinema and the Reconfiguration of Moçambicanidade," *Lusotopie* 11 (2004), 261–78.

34. Martin Botha, *South African Cinema: 1896–2010*, 12.

35. Thelma Gutsche, "Films and the African," University of Cape Town archives (hereafter UCT), Thelma Gutsche papers, BC 703, F1, unpublished mss, 1950, 2. See also L. van Bever, "Le Cinema pour Africains" (Brussels: G. van Campenhout, 1952).

36. Phyllis Martin, *Leisure and Society in Colonial Brazzaville* (Cambridge: Cambridge University Press, 2002), 88.

37. James Burns, *Flickering Shadows* (Athens: Ohio University Press, 2002), xviii.

38. See FilmAid website @ http://www.filmaid.org/about-us/overview.

39. Clyde Taylor, "Africa: The Last Cinema," in William Luhr (ed.), *World Cinema Since 1945* (New York: Ungar Publishing, 1987), 2.

40. This issue has absorbed American film scholars researching the demographics of early film spectatorship. Miriam Hansen, "Early Silent Cinema: Whose Public Sphere?," *New German Critique*¬ 29 (Spring-Summer 1983), 147–184.

41. Tafatoana Mahoso, "Unwinding the African Dream on African Ground," in June Givanni (ed.), *Symbolic Narratives/African Cinema: Audiences, Theory and Moving Image* (London: BFI, 2000), 199.

42. Ian Phimister and Charles van Onselen, "The Political Economy of Tribal Animosity: A Case Study of the 1929 Bulawayo Location Faction Fight," *Journal of Southern African Studies* 6, 1 (October 1979), 1–43.

Chapter 1

1. Elizabeth Heath, "Cinema, African," in Kwame Anthony Appiah and Henry Louis Gates (eds.), *Africana: The Encyclopedia of the African and African American Experience* (New York: Basic Books, 1999), 436-7. Edward Horatio-Jones, "Historical Review of the Cinema in West Africa and Black World and Its Implications for a Film Industry in Nigeria," 74, cited in Ukadike, *Black African Cinema*, 31.

2. Gordon Hendricks, *The Kinetoscope: America's First Commercially Successful Motion Picture Exhibitor* (New York: Theodore Gaus' Sons, 1966).
3. Cited in Gutsche, *The History and Social Significance of Motion Pictures in South Africa*, 8.
4. Stephen Brockmann, *A Critical History of German Film* (Rochester: Camden House, 2010), 13.
5. Thomas Prasch, "Introduction," *The American Historical Review* 100, 4 (October 1995), 1190–1193.
6. Gutsche, *The History and Social Significance of Motion Pictures in South Africa*, 12. Neil Parsons, Botswana Cinema and Film Studies, 1st edition, http://ubh.tripod.com/cinema/bots-cinema-studies.htm, March 2004, accessed September 3, 2011.
7. Cited in "Alexandria, Why? II. The Beginnings of the Cinema Industry in Alexandria," http://www.bibalex.org/AlexCinema/historical/beginnings.htm, accessed October 22, 2011.
8. Viola Shafik, *Arab Cinema: History and Cultural Identity* (Cairo: American University in Cairo Press, 2007), 10.
9. Roy Armes, *African Filmmaking: North and South of the Sahara* (Bloomington: Indiana University Press, 2006), 24–25.
10. Jean Rouch, "The Awakening of African Cinema," *The Unesco Courier* 3 (1962), 10.
11. Manthia Diawara, *African Cinema: Politics and Culture* (Bloomington: Indiana University Press, 1992), 52.
12. Luke McKernan, *Charles Urban: Pioneering the Non-Fiction Film in Britain and America, 1897–1925* (Exeter: University of Exeter Press, 2013).
13. Gutsche, *The History and Social Significance of Motion Pictures in South Africa*, 29.
14. Charles Musser, *High-Class Moving Pictures: Lyman H. Howe and the Forgotten Era of Traveling Exhibition, 1880–1920* (Princeton: Princeton University Press, 1991).
15. Raphaëlle Costa de Beauregard and Melvyn Stokes, "The Reception of American Films in France, c. 1910–20," in Maltby and Stokes (eds.), *Hollywood Abroad*, 22.
16. For this and the following section on bioscopes, see Gutsche, *The History and Social Significance of the Motion Pictures in South Africa*, 95–103.
17. Natalie Barkas, *Thirty Thousand Miles for the Films* (London: Blackie and Sons, 1937), 184.
18. Aloha Baker, *Call to Adventure!* (New York: Robert M. McBride, 1939), 199–200.
19. Mohamed Awad & Sahar Hamouda, *The Birth of the Seventh Art in Alexandria* (Alexandria: Bibliotheca Alexandrina, 2007), "The Cinema Industry," 3–7.
20. James Genova, *Cinema and Development in West Africa*, 24.
21. James Burns, "Cape Town Bioscope Culture and The Rose of Rhodesia."
22. Denver Museum of Natural History, Special Collections, Paul Hoefler, "A Cinematographer in Africa" (unpublished manuscript, n.d.), 18.
23. Robert J. Gordon, "The Battle for the Bioscope in Namibia," *African Identities* 3, 1 (2005), 38.
24. Marcus Power, "Post-Colonial Cinema and the reconfiguration of Moçambicanidade," *Lusotopie* (2004), 265.
25. Guido Convents, *Os Moçambicanos perante o cinema e o audiovisual* (Maputo: Imagens & Realidade, 2011), 59.
26. James Brennan, "Democratizing Cinema and Censorship in Tanzania, 1920–1980," *The International Journal of African Historical Studies* 38, 3 (2005), 484–85. David Henry Anthony III, "Culture and Society in a Town in Transition: A People's History of Dar es Salaam, 1865–1939" (PhD diss., University of Wisconsin-Madison, 1983), 148.
27. Cited in Brennan, "Democratizing Cinema," 488.
28. Ibid., 492.
29. Andrew Burton, "Urchins, Loafers and the Cult of the Cowboy: Urbanization and Delinquency in Dar es Salaam, 1919–61," *Journal of African History* 42 (2001), 206.
30. Email correspondence with Brigitte Reinwald, June 4, 2012. Brigitte Reinwald, "'Tonight at the Empire': Cinema and urbanity in Zanzibar, 1920s to 1960s," *Afrique & histoire* 1, 5 (2006), http://www.cairn.info/article.php?ID_ARTICLE=AFHI_005_109, accessed March 1, 2012.
31. Quoted in Ibid.
32. John McKendree Springer, *Pioneering in the Congo* (New York: Katanga Press, 1916), xv.
33. Philip Mosley, *Split Screen: Belgian Cinema and Cultural Identity* (Albany: State University of New York Press, 2001), 42.
34. A. Cameron Gilg (ed. Barry Cockcroft), *Turn Left—The Riffs Have Risen: From England to Cape Town in a Baby Car* (London: RAF Publishing, 1981), 93.
35. James Burns, "The African Bioscope." Birgit Meyer, "Ghanaian Popular Cinema and the Magic in and of Film," in Birgit Meyer and Peter Pels (eds.), *Magic and Modernity: Interfaces of Revelation and Concealment* (Stanford: Stanford University Press, 2003), 204.
36. Cited in Phyllis Martin, *Leisure and Society in Colonial Brazzaville*, 86.
37. Ruth Mayer, *Artificial Africas: Colonial Images in the Times of Globalization* (Hanover, NH: University of New England Press, 2002), 27–40.
38. Brian Larkin, *Signal and Noise: Media, Infrastructure, and Urban Culture in Nigeria* (Durham: Duke University Press, 2008), 116.
39. Heike Behrend, *Alice Lakwena & the Holy Spirits* (Oxford: James Currey, 1999), 114.
40. Rosita Forbes, *From Red Sea to Blue Nile* (Middlesex, England: Penguin, 1939), 199.
41. Ibid., 101.
42. Human Studies Film Archives (hereafter HSFA), 97.7, William O. Field collection, North Africa Trip: Notes, February 28, 1928, 4.
43. HSFA has archived *Frederick Wulsin's Travel Footage of Africa* (1927), including shots of the White Nile, Mbuti, a Catholic mission, and Muslim chiefs in French Equatorial Africa. HSFA, AF-82.1.1.
44. Ruth Ben-Ghiat, "The Italian Colonial Cinema: Agendas and Audiences," in Ruth Ben-Ghiat and Mia Fuller (eds.), *Italian Colonialism* (New York: Palgrave Macmillan, 2008), 184.
45. Robert J. Gordon, "'Captured on Film': Bushmen and the Claptrap of Performative Primitives," in Landau and Kaspin (eds.), *Images and Empires*, 220.

46. John Brom, *The Pitiless Jungle* (New York: David McKay, 1955), 138.
47. W.S. Van Dyke, "Diary of a Film: Governor of Uganda visits American Company producing 'Trader Horn,'" *New York Times*, September 22, 1929, X8.
48. Son Excellence Amadou Hampaté Ba, "Le dit di cinema Africain." In *Film Ethnographiques sur l'Afrique noire* (Paris: UNESCO, 1967), 9–11.
49. Dorothy L. Pond, "If Women Have Courage. Among Shepherds, Shieks [sic] & Scientists in Algeria," unpublished manuscript, HSFA, 82.5, Beloit/Logan Museum Collection, Supplemental Files, 37.
50. Manthia Diarwara, "Black Spectatorship: Problems of Identification and Resistance," *Screen* 29, 4 (Fall 1988), 66–79.
51. Meg Gehrts, *A Camera Actress in the Wilds of Togoland; the adventures, observations and experiences of a cinematograph actress in West African forests whilst collecting films depicting native life and when posing as the white woman in Anglo-African cinematograph films* (Philadelphia: J.B. Lippincott, 1915), 33.
52. Gutsche, "Films and the African," 2–3.
53. Gordon, "'Captured on Film,'" 220.
54. Anthony Sampson, *Drum: A Venture into the New Africa* (London: Collins, 1956), 121.
55. J. Koyinde Vaughan, "Africa and the Cinema," in Langston Hughes (ed.), *An African Treasury* (New York: Crown, 1960), 90.
56. Andre Gide, *Travels in the Congo* (New York: Modern Age Books, 1937), 2.
57. Philip Mosley, *Split Screen*, 34.
58. *The Lagos Standard*, August 12, 1903, 2. See also *The Lagos Standard*, August 19, 1903, 2.
59. *Lagos Weekly Record*, August 22, 1903, 4; *Lagos Weekly Record*, August 29, 1903, 4; *The Lagos Standard*, August 26, 1903, 2.
60. Janice A. Petterchak, *Lone Scout: W.D. Boyce and American Boy Scouting* (Kingston, ON: Legacy Press, 2010), 57.
61. See James Burns, *Cinema and Society in the British Empire, 1895–1940* (New York: Palgrave Macmillan, 2013), 195, n. 69.
62. *The Lagos Standard*, "News, Notes and Comments," June 24, 1914.
63. Erick Berry, "Charlie Captures Africa's Gold Coast," *New York Times*, July 5, 1925, SM16.
64. Stephen Wattskano, "On the African Movie Menus," *New York Times*, April 36, 1953, X4.
65. Berry, "Charlie Captures Africa's Gold Coast."
66. Onookome Okome, "The Context of Film Production in Nigeria: The Colonial Heritage," in Okome and Haynes, *Cinema and Social Change in West Africa*, 29.
67. L.M. Ross, "Africans and Propaganda Films," *United Empire* XXXI, 2 (February 1940), 3–5.
68. Oladipo O. Olubomehin, "Cinema Business in Lagos, Nigeria since 1903," *Historical Research Letter* 3 (2012), 1–2.
69. C.T.C. Taylor, *A History of Rhodesian Entertainment, 1890–1930* (Salisbury: Collins, 1968), 106–7.
70. Public Record Office (PRO), Colonial Office (hereafter CO), 323/1356/4, Minutes of 68th Meeting of the Advisory Committee on Education in the Colonies, May 28, 1936, announcement by Vischer.
71. Yale Divinity, International Missionary Council archives (IMC), 26.31.29, fiche #1, Diary of G.C. Latham, "Bantu Educational Kinema Experiment," June 29, 1935, 9.
72. Genova, *Cinema and Development in West Africa*, 26.
73. A.H. Weiler, "M-G-M takes 'Greatest Ride in Town'-Report from Togoland-Addenda," *New York Times*, September 2, 1956, X5.
74. PRO, CO 323/1316/5, Memo #64, Colonial Official at Government House, Zomba, Nyasaland, to Secretary of State for the Colonies Cunliffe-Lister, February 2, 1935.
75. Gordon, "The Battle for the Bioscope in Namibia," 43.
76. Ibid., 43. Gordon, "'Captured on Film,'" 218.
77. Interview with John Brom's widow, Olga Brom Spencer, November 10, 2012. See also Glenn Reynolds (ed.), *Africa's Last Romantic: The Films, Books and Expeditions of John L. Brom* (New York: Peter Lang, 2014), Ch. 16.
78. Martin, *Leisure and Society in Colonial Brazzaville*, 87.
79. Manthia Diawara, *African Cinema*, 22.
80. Martin, *Leisure and Society in Colonial Brazzaville*, 87–9.
81. Cited in James Genova, "Cinema and the Struggle to (De)colonize the Mind in French/Francophone West Africa (1950s-1960s)," *The Journal of the Midwest Modern Language Association* 39, 1 (Spring 2006), 50–62.
82. David Henry Anthony III, "Culture and Society in a Town in Transition: A People's History of Dar es Salaam, 1865–1939," 148–9.
83. Olubomchin, "Cinema Business in Lagos, Nigeria since 1903," 2.
84. Brian Willan, *Sol Plaatje: South African Nationalist 1876–1932* (Berkeley: University of California Press, 1984), 303. Ntongela Masilela, "The New African Movement and the Beginnings of Film Culture in South Africa," in Balseiro and Masilela (eds.), *To Change Reels*, 19–20.
85. Martin Johnson, *Congorilla: Adventures with Pygmies and Gorillas in Africa* (New York: Harcourt, Brace, 1931), 86–7. Pascal James Imperato and Eleanor M. Imperato, *They Married Adventure: The Wandering Lives of Martin and Osa Johnson* (New Brunswick: Rutgers University Press, 1992), 142.
86. University of New Hampshire, Dimond Library, Milne Special Collections, Margaret Carson Hubbard papers (hereafter MCH), MC 17, Box 14, Margaret Carson Hubbard Scrapbook, "Those Barotse," *Natural History*, Feb. 1950, 57–8. See also Margaret Carson Hubbard, *No One to Blame: An African Adventure* (New York: Minton, Balch, 1934), 192, 198–99.
87. Neil Parsons, "A History of Botswana Cinema, Part I," http://www.mmegi.bw/index.php?sid=6&aid=54&dir=2007/September/Friday21, accessed April 11, 2011.
88. L.A. Notcutt and G.C. Latham, *The African and the Cinema: An Account of the work of the Bantu Educational Cinema Experiment during the period March 1935 to May 1937* (London: Edinburgh House Press, 1937), 94.

89. Awad & Hamouda, *The Birth of the Seventh Art in Alexandria*, "Mohamed Bayoumi."
90. Hassoldt Davis, *Sorcerer's Village* (New York: Duell, Sloan and Pearce, 1955), 11.
91. Ibid., 74.

Chapter 2

1. Thomas J. Bassett, "Cartography and Empire Building in Nineteenth Century West Africa," *Geographical Review* 84, 3 (July 1994), 316.
2. James R. Ryan, *Picturing Empire: Photography and the Visualization of the British Empire* (Chicago: University of Chicago Press, 1997), 29–34.
3. Lantern slides were popular among missionaries. Stereographs were an early form of 3-D technology, while *cartes postales* offered images of Africa produced in abundance. Georges Meurillon, *Cartes postales d'Afrique de l'ouest* (Paris: ICG Mémoire directe), CD-Rom atlas du patrimoine, no. 4 (1998?).
4. Ryan, *Picturing Empire*, 143.
5. John Phillip Short, *Magic Lantern Empire: Colonialism and Society in Germany* (Ithaca: Cornell University Press, 2012), 82.
6. Jeff Bowersox, *Raising Germans in the Age of Empire: Youth and Colonial Culture, 1871–1914* (Oxford: Oxford University Press, 2013), 9.
7. Guido Convents, "Film and German Colonial Propaganda for the Black African Territories to 1918," in Paolo Cherchi Usai and Lorenzo Codelli (eds.), *Before Caligari: German Cinema, 1895–1920* (Madison: University of Wisconsin Press, 1991), 58–76.
8. Wolfgang Fuhrmann, "Patriotism, Spectacle, and Reverie," in Volker Langbehn (ed.), *German Colonialism, Visual Culture and Modern Memory* (New York: Routledge, 2012), 150.
9. Peter Bondanella, *A History of Italian Cinema* (New York: Bloomsbury Academic, 2009), 8.
10. Ruth Ben-Ghiat, "The Italian Colonial Cinema: Agendas and Audiences," in Ruth Ben-Ghiat and Mia Fuller (eds.) *Italian Colonialism* (New York: Palgrave Macmillan, 2005), 180.
11. Roberta di Carmine, *Italy Meets Africa: Colonial Discourses in Italian Cinema* (New York: Peter Lang, 2011), 33.
12. Cecilia Boggio, "Black Shirts / Black Skins: Fascist Italy's Colonial Anxieties and Lo Squadrone Bianco," in Patrizio Palumbo & Angelo del Boca (eds.), *A Place in the Sun: Africa in Italian Colonial Culture from Post-Unification to the Present* (Berkeley: University of California Press, 2003), 280–83.
13. David Henry Slavin, "French Cinema's Other First Wave: Political and Racial Economies of Cinéma colonial, 1918 to 1934," *Cinema Journal* 37, 1 (Fall 1997), 24.
14. Alice Conklin, *A Mission to Civilize: The Republican Idea of Empire in France and West Africa, 1895–1930* (Stanford: Stanford University Press, 1997), 41.
15. Gary Wilder, *The French Imperial Nation-State: Negritude and Colonial Humanism between the Two World Wars* (Chicago: University of Chicago Press, 2005), 30.
16. Peter Bloom, *French Colonial Documentary: Mythologies of Humanitarianism* (Minneapolis: University of Minnesota Press, 2008), 128.
17. Dominic Thomas, *Africa and France: Postcolonial Cultures, Migration and Racism* (Bloomington: Indiana University Press, 2013), 110.
18. Alice J. Smith, "Rene Maran's *Batouala* and the Prix-Goncourt," *Contributions in Black Studies: A Journal of African and African American Studies* 4 (August 2008).
19. A. Cameron Gilg (Barry Cockcroft, ed.), *Turn Left—The Riffs Have Risen*, 33–36.
20. Ruth Ginio, "Vichy Rule in French West Africa: Prelude to Decolonization?," *French Colonial History* 4 (2003), 206.
21. Cited in James Genova, "Cinema and the Struggle to (De)Colonize the Mind," 52.
22. Fernando Arenas, *Lusophone Africa* (Minneapolis: University of Minnesota Press, 2011), 106–07.
23. See Mosley, *Split Screen*, 33. Leen Engelen, "Congo Made in Belgium," @ http://www.rektoverso.be/artikel/congo-made-belgium, accessed September 21, 2013. Stannard, *Selling the Congo*, 207–40.
24. Royal Belgian Film Archive, *Belgisch Congo Belge: Filmed by Gérard de Boe, André Cauvin & Ernest Genval* (Tervuren, Cinematek, n.d.), 2 DVDs.
25. L. Van Bever, *Le Cinéma pour Africain* (Brussels: G. Van Campenhout, 1952), 23.
26. Luke McKernan, "Jean Alexandre Louis Promio," Who's Who of Victorian Cinema, @ http://www.victorian-cinema.net/promio.htm, accessed November 10, 2011.
27. Michael Allan, "Deserted histories," 159.
28. Andrew Roberts, "Africa on Film to 1940," *History in Africa* 14 (1987), 191.
29. Cited in http://www.colonialfilms.org.uk/node/1186, "Landing of Savage South Africa at Southampton," BFI ID#403239, accessed December 7, 2011.
30. Cited in http://www.colonialfilm.org.uk/node/57, accessed January 4, 2012.
31. Cited in http://www.colonialfilm.org.uk/node/57, accessed February 19, 2012.
32. Arch R. Wiggins and Robert Sandall, *The History of the Salvation Army*, Vol. V (London: Thomas Nelson and Sons, 1968), 203.
33. Roberts, *Africa on Film*, 192.
34. Nicholas Pronay, "British Newsreels in the 1930s: Their policies and impact," *History* 57, #189 (February 1972), 63.
35. John McDonald, "Press, Radio, Films," *Public Opinion Quarterly* (September 1940), 520.
36. U.S. National Archives, Records of the Office of Strategic Services (OSS), Record Group 226.3.11: Records of the Field Photographic Branch (34 reels on North Africa, and Italy). See also Darryl F. Zanuck, *Tunis Expedition* (New York: Random House, 1943), 83.
37. "At the Paramount," *New York Times*, October 12, 1935, 12.
38. "Travel film series will set high standard," *Salt Lake Telegram*, August 26, 1916.
39. "Chester entertains Federated Folk," *New York Morning Telegraph*, February 20, 1921.
40. Jean Hartley, *Africa's Big Five and other Wildlife*

Filmmakers (Nairobi: Twaweza Communications, 2010), 26.

41. Mordaunt Hall, "Tales of Adventure: Six explorer give lectures with film scenes," *New York Times,* December 20, 1931, X4.

42. American Museum of Natural History (hereafter AMNH), FC2, *Adventures on the Upper Nile,* O'Donnell-Clark African Expedition.

43. George E. Duck, "Carl von Hoffman—Archival Notes," *Explorers Journal: Official Quarterly of the Explorers Club* 60, 2 (June 1982), 51.

44. Carl von Hoffman, *Jungle Gods* (New York: Henry Holt, 1929). Carl von Hoffman, *Jerry on Safari* (London: J.B. Lippincott, 1936).

45. "Gleanings from the Screen," *New York Times,* December 11, 1927, X6.

46. Forbes, *From Red Sea to Blue Nile,* 278.

47. Privately held archival letter: Rosita Forbes to James B. Pond, January 27, 1925.

48. Crossley Motor Archives, F.N. Redhead, *Major Court Treatt's 12,732 Miles Motor Adventure "Cape to Cairo": The film record of an historic motor journey* (Publicity Programme: Crossley Register, n.d.). Stella Court Treatt, *Cape to Cairo: The Record of a Historic Motor Journey* (Boston: Little, Brown, 1927), 14.

49. Captain Angus Buchanan, *Sahara* (London: John Murray, 1926).

50. Redhead, *Major Court Treatt's 12,732 Miles Motor Adventure,* 12.

51. Treatt, *Cape to Cairo,* 211.

52. "Capetown to Cairo by motor: A British Expedition," *Brisbane Courier,* August 29, 1924, 14.

53. Aloha Baker, *Call to Adventure,* 19. Her reputation is actively promoted, see http://www.alohawanderwell.com/biography.html.

54. Baker, *Call to Adventure,* 161.

55. Ibid., 271.

56. HSFA, AF-93.29.1: *Car and Camera around the World* (1929).

57. "Miss Leila Roosevelt to marry today: Kin of Late President to wed Armand G. Denis at home of E.R. Merritt, Oyster Bay," *New York Times,* July 8, 1926, 29.

58. Hassoldt Davis once claimed that producers "ruined" the American version of *Goona Goona.* See MCH, Box 1, f.8, letter from Hassoldt Davis to Margaret Carson Hubbard, October 24, 1937.

59. "Desert Auto trip thrills Mrs. Denis," *New York Times,* November 30, 1933, 29.

60. "Roosevelt Kin off to make film thriller starring Mr. Gorilla," part of promotional flyer or newspaper clipping, Chrysler Historical Services, Detroit, Michigan.

61. "The Belgian Congo: The Denis-Roosevelt Expedition Films—Its Giants and Pygmies, Its Customs and Ceremonies, Its Animals and Atmosphere," *LIFE* 4, 25 (June 20, 1938), 45.

62. "Dodge Presents Ten Films," *Business Screen: The Magazine of Commercial and Educational Films* 3, 1 (1940), 17–20.

63. *De Touggourt a Tozeur par le desert,* Renault publicity brochure, 1924(?).

64. *A Sahara Sunset: Burning Up the World,* French Line Cruise publicity brochure, 1929.

65. See Alison Murray Levine, "Film and Colonial Memory: La Croisiere Noire 1924–2004," in Alex Hargreaves (ed.), *Memory, Empire and Postcolonialism: Legacies of French Colonialism* (Lanham, MD: Lexington Press, 2005), 81–97.

66. Georges-Marie Haardt & Louis Audouin-Dubreuil, *The Black Journey: Across Central Africa with the Citroën Expedition* (New York: Negro Universities Press, 1969), 9.

67. Bloom, *French Colonial Documentary,* 78–9.

68. W.D. Hambly, "Racial Conflict in Africa," *The Journal of Negro History* 12, 4 (October 1927), 579–80.

69. Bloom, *French Colonial Documentary,* 70.

70. H.E. Symons, *Two Roads to Africa* (London: John Gifford, 1939).

71. Richard Pape, *From Cape Cold to Cape Hot* (London: Greenberg, 1955). "Obituary: Richard Pape," *The Independent* (July 12, 1995). Bent Horsington, "Pape-shape but not so Longbridge fashion," *Austin Times: A Newsletter for Enthusiasts of Austin pre–1955,* 2, 3 (August/September 2004).

72. Author's interview with Olga Spencer, June 11, 2012. See also Reynolds (ed.), *Africa's Last Romantic,* Chapters 5–10. John L. Brom, *20,000 Miles through the African Jungle* (London: Victor Gollancz, 1958).

73. Hand-bound publicity folio, *African Odyssey: Created by John Brom* (n.p., n.d.), author's possession. Although titles appear to have changed occasionally, the six 30-minute segments listed include *Dr. Livingstone, I presume; Africa Sings and Dances; On the Traces of the Slave-Traders; In the Land of Mirages; The Sahara was Green;* and *The Black Moslem.* These films are preserved at the Human Studies Film Archives.

74. Roderick P. Neumann, *Imposing Wilderness: Struggles over Livelihood and Nature Preservation in Africa* (Berkeley: University of California Press, 1998). Dan Brockington, *Fortress Conservation: The Preservation of the Mkomazi Game Reserve, Tanzania* (Bloomington: Indiana University Press, 2002).

75. Palle B. Petterson, *Cameras into the Wild: A History of Early Wildlife and Expedition Filmmaking, 1895–1928* (Jefferson, NC: McFarland, 2011), 188. Petterson cannot locate his source for this film (author correspondence with Petterson, November 7, 2013), but a member of the Brocklehurst family who has spent decades on genealogical research has no record of Philip Brocklehurst, Sr. ever going to Africa, or directing any films (author correspondence with Frank Brocklehurst, November 5, 2013).

76. C.G. Schillings, *With Flashlight and Rifle* (New York: Harper and Brothers, 1905). C.G. Schillings, *In Wildest Africa* (New York: Harper and Brothers, 1907).

77. Cynthia Chris, *Watching Wildlife* (Minneapolis: University of Minnesota Press, 2006), 9.

78. Petterson, *Cameras into the Wild,* 94–95.

79. James Lippitt Clark, "By Motor from Nairobi to the Nile," *Natural History* XXIX, 3 (May–June), 262.

80. Brian Herne, *White Hunters: The Golden Age of African Safaris* (New York: Henry Holt, 1999), 79.

81. Derek Bousé, *Wildlife Films* (Philadelphia: University of Pennsylvania Press, 2000), 48.

82. Petterson, *Cameras into the Wild,* 101.

83. Petterchak, *Lone Scout,* 58.

84. Imperato and Imperato, *They Married Adventure,* 178.

85. "On the Cinema Horizon," *New York Times*, February 8, 1931, 111.
86. "Films from the Air," *Flight: The Aircraft Engineer and Airships* XXIV, 2 (January 8, 1932), 42.
87. "Woman to Explore River of Mystery: Lady Mackenzie Plans Trip of Discovery on Tana, in Jungles of East Africa," *New York Times*, October 12, 1919.
88. Anonymous, privately held archival material: Paul Lieberenz—letters, dossiers and film scripts.
89. Imperato and Imperato, *They Married Adventure*, 110–111.
90. Universal Pictures Publicity cards, *Hunting Big Game in Africa with Gun and Camera*, set of 12 (1922), author's possession.
91. Jeannette Eileen Jones, *In Search of Brightest Africa: Reimagining the Dark Continent in American Culture, 1884–1936* (Athens: University of Georgia Press, 2010), 186–87.
92. Imperato and Imperato, *They Married Adventure*, 116–17.
93. Christine Nicholls, *Red Strangers: The White Tribe of Kenya* (Middlesex: Timewell Press, 2005), 67–8.
94. MCH, MC 17, Box 2 f.1, MCH Vita.
95. MCH, MC 17, Box 1, f.2, letter from R.W. Perkins to MCH, March 17, 1936. Margaret Carson Hubbard, *African Gamble* (New York: G.P. Putnam's Sons), 10–11.
96. MCH, MC 17, Box 2, f.16, Hubbard, "Africa for Actors: the leopard obliged, so did the buffalo—but the lion and the crocodile proved coy," *Esquire* (Autumn 1933), 71, 77.
97. Hubbard, *African Gamble*, 189.
98. MCH, MC 17, Box 1, f.2, letter from MCH to "Ted," March 16, 1958.
99. MCH, MC 17, Box 1, f.7, November 13, 1967, letter from Hubbard to Dolkart, MCH, MC 17, Box 1, f.10, screenplay for *Gold*. The film is archived at UCLA, Powell Library, Archive Research and Study Center, M12056.
100. Souvenir expedition postcard from Lewis Cotlow to Andrew Baird (1937), author's possession.
101. Cited in Amy Staples, "'The Last of the Great (Foot-Slogging) Explorers': Lewis Cotlow and the Ethnographic Imaginary in Popular Travel Film," in Ruoff (ed.), *Virtual Voyages*, 202.
102. Alice L. Conklin, *In the Museum of Man: Race, Anthropology, and Empire in France, 1850–1950* (Ithaca: Cornell University Press, 2013), 92–3; 203.
103. Ruth Larson, "Ethnography, Thievery, and Cultural Identity: A Rereading of Michel Leiris's L'Afrique fantôme," *PMLA* 112, 2 (March 1997), 231.
104. Ibid., 207, n. 45.
105. HSFA, AF-82.1.1: *Frederick Wulsin's Travel Footage of Africa*.
106. HSFA, William O. Field papers, William O. Field to Diana Field, May 12, 1993. See also HSFA, 97.7.1: *Up the Nile to Central Africa*.
107. HSFA, William O. Field papers, "Titles" for *Up the Nile to Central Africa*, #29, #52, #45.
108. *Annual Report of the Board of Regents of The Smithsonian Institution, 1926* (Washington, D.C.: U.S. Government Printing Office, 1927), 106–07.
109. Elizabeth Eastman, *George Eastman: A Biography* (Rochester: University of Rochester Press, 2006), 497.
110. George Eastman, *Chronicles of an African Trip* (Rochester: John P. Smith, 1927), 53, 57.
111. Ibid., 54–55.
112. Ibid., 65.
113. Ibid., 70–71.
114. Suydam Cutting, *The Fire Ox and Other Years* (New York: Scribner's, 1940), 335.
115. Ibid., 340.
116. Ibid., 347.
117. AMNH, FC163: *Abyssinia* (1936).
118. HSFA, 82.5: Beloit College, Logan Museum, Box 2, folder 5, newspaper clipping, "His Work in Journal gets him job in Africa," *Milwaukee Journal*, January 2, 1930, 3.
119. HSFA, 82.5: Beloit College, Logan Museum, Box 2, folder 5, newspaper clipping, "Algerian Movies to be shown by Pond here," *The Round Table*, November 1, 1930, 1.
120. HSFA, 82.5: Beloit College, Logan Museum, Box 2, folder 5, Pond to Whiteford, March 28, 1945.
121. HSFA, 82.5: Beloit College, Logan Museum, Box 2, folder 5, Pond to Eastman Teaching Films, February 2, 1934; Edwards to Pond, March 23, 1934.
122. Harvard University, Harvard Medical Library, Richard P. Strong papers, 182–1948, *Harvard African Expedition of 1934*.
123. I.C. Jarvie, "The Problem of the Ethnographic Real," *Current Anthropology* 24, 3 (June 1983), 313.
124. Marta Braun, *Picturing Time: The Work of Etienne-Jules Marey* (Chicago: University of Chicago Press, 1995), 109.
125. Bloom, *French Colonial Documentary*, 20–21.
126. Assenka Oksiloff, *Picturing the Primitive* (New York: Palgrave, 2001), 1.
127. Marcel Fournier and Jane Marie Todd, *Marcel Mauss: A Biography* (Princeton: Princeton University Press, 2005), 277.
128. Adolf Friedrich, *From the Congo to the Niger and the Nile: An Account of the German Central African Expedition of 1910-11, Vol. I* (Philadelphia: John Winston, 1914), 236.
129. Gehrts, *A Camera Actress in the Wilds of Togoland*, 20.
130. Karl Weule (trans. Alice Werner), *Native Life in East Africa: The Results of an Ethnological Research Expedition* (London: Sir Isaac Pitman & Sons, 1909), 385.
131. Cited in Oksiloff, *Picturing the Primitive*, 46.
132. Robert Gordon, *Picturing Bushmen: The Denver African Expedition of 1925* (Athens: Ohio University Press, 1997), 27.
133. Will J. Cameron, *Ethnology of the Kalahari Bushmen* (Chicago, 1929), 1.
134. Will J. Cameron, "From Capetown to the Belgian Congo," *The Executives' Club News* (Christmas 1929), 3–5.
135. Jennifer Peterson, cited in Alison Griffiths, *Wondrous Difference*, 285.
136. A. Hrdlička, James Mooney and W.D.W., "Anthropologic Miscellanea," *American Anthropologist*, New Series 14, 4 (October–December 1912), 697.
137. Paul Hoefler, *Africa Speaks: A Story of Adventure* (Philadelphia: John C. Winston, 1931), 149.

138. Glenn Reynolds (ed.), *Africa's Last Romantic*, 73.
139. HSFA, 77.1.1.1, 1–4: *Melville Herskovits' Film Study of West Africa, 1931.*
140. Walter Goldschmidt, "Ethnographic Film: Definition and Exegesis," PIEF Newsletter 3, 2 (1972), 1.
141. Donald Ker, *African Adventure* (Harrisburg: Stackpole, 1957), 134.
142. Hoffman, "Carl von Hoffman—Archival Notes," 51.
143. Hoffman, "Pagans Look Upon Photographer's Apparatus as Medicine Box—Bride Doesn't Like Being Photographed," *New York Times*, October 9, 1927, X7.
144. Brooklyn Museum Archives, Delia Akeley Diary, April 18, 1925.
145. HSFA, 82.5.1, *Logan African Expedition Beloit College* (1930). "Pond's Photo Expert Back," *The Milwaukee Journal*, July 15, 1930, extract in HSFA, 82.5, Beloit College, Box 2, folder 5.
146. Natalie Barkas, *Thirty Thousand Miles for the Films*, 169.
147. MCH, MC 17, Box 14, Scrapbook, "For Immediate Release," University of California-Berkeley, April 17, 1973.
148. Author's interview with Olga Spencer, October 4, 2013.
149. Osa Johnson, *Four Years in Paradise* (Garden City: Garden City Publishing, 1941), 44–5.
150. Friedrich, *From the Congo to the Niger and the Nile*, 235.
151. Gehrts, *A Camera Actress in the Wilds of Togoland*, 49–51.
152. "The Pope and the Cinema," *Catholic Herald*, July 24, 1936, 5. Robert Molhant, *Catholics in the Cinema: A Strange History of Belief and Passion* (Brussels: OCIC, 2000).
153. HSFA, 9998.23 Missionaries of Africa collection, Dorothy Stockbridge, "Africa Priest's Mission for 20 Years," *Sarasota Journal* (June 16, 1976), D.
154. *The Buffaloes: A Story of Maryknoll Society's First Fifty Years in Tanzania*, unpublished manuscript, Maryknoll Society archives, Ossining, NY, n.d., 78.
155. These films are archived at Maryknoll.
156. James Horne Morrison, *The Missionary Heroes of Africa* (New York: George H. Doran, 1922), 53–58.
157. Email correspondence with Neil Parsons, December 5, 2011.
158. Birmingham Library, Special Collections, Church Missionary Society archives (hereafter CMS), "The Missionary Film Committee: Its Policy and Work," 1–3.
159. CMS, "Report on Co-operative Film Work," June 25, 1930.
160. CMS, CMS Home Secretary to Britton, July 9, 1930.
161. CMS, Extract from the Minutes of the Missionary Film Committee, November 13, 1930.
162. Glenn Reynolds (ed.), *Images Out of Africa: The Virginia Garner Diaries of the Africa Motion Picture Project* (Lanham, MD: University Press of America, 2011).
163. National Archives and Record Administration, Harmon Foundation, How an African Tribe Is Ruled under Colonial Government, Program Material, 4.
164. Shiori Hasegawa, "Sensational Africa: Roosevelt's Cultural Politics and Expeditionary Filmmaking, 1909–1910," vol. 1 (2010) @ https://journal.hass.tsukuba.ac.jp/interfaculty/article/view/8/10, accessed November 13, 2011.
165. Hoefler, *Africa Speaks*, 4.
166. Edward Bernds, *Mr. Bernds Goes to Hollywood* (Lanham, MD: Scarecrow Press, 1999), Ch. 5.
167. Quoted in "Stampede (1930)," in BFI's Screenonline @ http://screenonline.org.uk/film/id/1401935/index.html, accessed December 1, 2011. Stella Court Treatt, *Sudan Sand: Filming the Baggara Natives* (London: George Harrap, 1930).
168. Mordaunt Hall, review of *Stampede*, *New York Times*, April 28, 1930.
169. *Patterson v. Century Productions, Inc.*, District Court, New York, March 25, 1937.

Chapter 3

1. "Rushes," *Movie Makers: Magazine of the Amateur Cinema League, Inc.* 4, 10 (October 1929), 676.
2. Cited in Frederick Bridgman, "Social Conditions in Johannesburg," *International Review of Missions* 15 (1926), 569.
3. Harvard University, Houghton Library, American Board of Commissioners for Foreign Missions papers (hereafter ABCFM), reel 207, #419.
4. Clifford H. Scott, "American Missionaries in Darkest Africa, 1890–1940," in Hamilton Craven (ed.), *Ideas in American Cultures* (Ames: Iowa State University Press, 1982), 74.
5. "James Dexter Taylor," *Missionary Herald* (Dec. 1899).
6. Ray Phillips, "The Missionary as Interracial Interpreter, or American Influence in African Race Relations," *Drums in the Darkness*, Wits, SAIRR, p. 1. R.V. Selope Thema, "The Establishment of Joint Councils and a Federal Council," Wits, Joint Councils papers, AC 3.3.1, 5. Tim Couzens, "Moralizing Leisure Time: The Transatlantic connection and black Johannesburg, 1918–1936," in Shula Marks and Richard Rathbone (eds.), *Industrialization and Social Change in South Africa* (New York: Longman Group, 1982), 314–337.
7. In *White Power and the Liberal Conscience*, Paul Rich suggests incorrectly that "the centre began to establish itself from the end of 1920" (p. 16). However, Alan Cobley in *Class and Consciousness*, notes that the BMSC opened in 1924 (p. 81).
8. Phillips, ABCFM, reel #211.
9. Rich, *White Power*, 15.
10. Ray Phillips, "Religion and Recreation," Wits, Joint Councils papers, AC 3.3.3., n.d. For Phillips discussing his role as social engineer, see Phillips, "The Missionary as Interracial Interpreter," 13.
11. Phillips, *The Bantu Are Coming*, 44.
12. ABCFM, reel #211.
13. R.V. Selope Thema, "Social Conditions of the Africans," in Taylor, *Christianity and the Natives of South Africa*, 50.

14. Duke University, J. Walter Thompson papers, Staff Meeting Minutes, Box 3, folder 7, Mr. McArdle, May 26, 1931.
15. Philip and Iona Mayer, *Townsmen or Tribesmen* (London: Oxford University Press, 1974), 16.
16. ABCFM, reel #211.
17. Modikwe Dikobe, *The Marabi Dance* (London: Heinemann International, 1973), 71–2.
18. "BMSC Annual Report," *Umteteli wa Bantu*, March 23, 1935.
19. The Employment Bureau of Africa archives (hereafter TEBA) Phillips, Box #224: American Board of Missions (hereafter ABM); folder: American Board of Missions (ABM), A4, *Phillips News #5*, December 25, 1925.
20. Phillips, *Drums in the Darkness*, 4.
21. TEBA, *Phillips News #5*, December 25, 1920. Ray Phillips, "Looking Back on our Furlough," *Missionary Review of the World* 61 (1938), 363–4. Ray Phillips, "Why Africa Turns from the Gospel," *The Christian Century* 47 (January 15, 1930), 80–2. By the mid-1930s, both black workers and the black *petit-bourgeoisie* were becoming disenchanted with Phillips and white liberals for their accommodation to black voter disenfranchisement. Gail Gerhardt, *Black Power in South Africa* (Berkeley: University of California Press, 1978), 36–7.
22. Dating Phillips' program has been difficult to track down with precision. My dating is based on "City Deep Cinema," a February 28, 1921, article in *The Star*, Johannesburg's leading daily, stating that the Phillips had been engaged for "nine months past" on his film exhibition experiment. If correct, this would make May or June 1920 the most likely launch date.
23. Phillips, ABCFM, reel #211.
24. TEBA, *Phillips News*, December 20, 1920.
25. "News From Filmland," *The Star*, July 12, 1922.
26. TEBA, Box #224: ABM; Folder: ABM, A4, Rand Mines Secretary to Mine managers re: Native Bioscope Shows, November 24, 1920.
27. An exception was the manager of Village Deep, Ltd., who thought "a bioscope show in the compound would be an exceedingly good thing, and would tend to popularize mine work amongst natives." TEBA, Box #224: ABM; Folder: ABM, A4: Manager of Village Deep, Ltd., to Rand Mines Secretary, November 27, 1920.
28. Phillips, *The Bantu in the City*, 142–45.
29. TEBA, Box #224: ABM; Folder: ABM, A4: Manager of Robinson Deep Gold Mining Companies to Rand Mines Secretary, December 1, 1920. Manager of New Modderfontein Gold Mining Company, Ltd, to Rand Mines Secretary, December 8, 1920. See also Burns, *Flickering Shadows*, Ch. 2.
30. TEBA, Box #224: ABM; Folder: ABM, A4, Manager of Modderfontein B. Gold Mines, Ltd, to Rand Mine Secretary, December 8, 1920. A.J. Walton, General Manager of Crown Mines, Ltd, to Rand Mines Secretary, December 3, 1920.
31. TEBA, Box #224: ABM; Folder: ABM, A4: Manager of New Modderfontein Gold Mining Co. to Rand Mines Secretary, January 11, 1921. See also Rand Mines Secretary to managers of The Central Mining and Investment Corp., January 25, 1921, who reported that after a showing at New Modderfontein, Mr. Sharp declared that Phillips' shows were "excellent and provided suitable films are selected would tend to popularize a compound. The natives all wish to know when the next show is going to take place."
32. Cited in Phillips, *The Bantu Are Coming*, 141.
33. TEBA, Box #224: ABM; Folder: ABM, A4, Manager of Knight Central, Ltd., to Rand Mines Secretary, December 8, 1920; Manager of Crown Mines Ltd., to Rand Mines Secretary, December 3, 1920; Manager of Ferreira Deep Ltd. to Rand Mines Secretary, November 26, 1920.
34. Phillips, *The Bantu Are Coming*, 141.
35. A.P. Cartwright, *Golden Age: The Story of the Industrialization of South Africa and the Part Played in It by the Corner House Group of Companies 1910–1967* (Cape Town: Purnell and Sons, 1968), 65.
36. TEBA, Box #224: AMB; Folder: ABM, A4, Edward Grant, Manager of East Rand Proprietary Mines, Ltd, to Rand Mines Secretary, November 27, 1920.
37. Robert R. Edgar (ed.), *The Travel Notes of Ralph Bunche, 28 Sept. 1937–1 Jan. 1938* (Athens: Ohio University Press, 1992), 172.
38. TEBA, Box #224: ABM; Folder: ABM, A4, Acting Secretary of NRC to All Mine Managers, Circular Letter No. 348, March 10, 1921.
39. TEBA, Box #224; ABM; Folder: ABM, A4, Phillips to NRC Chairman Charles W. Villiers, March 19, 1921.
40. Wits, SAIRR, Box: "Broadcasting and Films," B61.3, Supervisor, Mines Compound Cinema Circuit [Hallendorff], to SAIRR official [J.D. Rheinallt-Jones?], n.d. [1936].
41. TEBA, Box #224: ABM; Folder: ABM, A4, Phillips to NRC, June 2, 1921. Concerning the issue of chest colds, Dr. A. Dodds, Medical Officer for Rose Deep, reported a "considerable increase in the number of chest cases admitted to Hospital," TEBA, Box #224: ABM; Folder: ABM, A4, Manager of Rose Deep to Secretary of NRC, May 28, 1921. Other managers ridiculed the idea and opposed restricting the shows. TEBA, Phillips to Secretary of NRC, June 7, 1921. Many mines did, however, cease showings a few months later between June and August 1921.
42. Charles Ambler, "Popular Films and Colonial Audiences," 95.
43. TEBA, Box #224: ABM; Folder: ABM, A4, Phillips to NRC, June 2, 1921.
44. Phillips, *The Bantu Are Coming*, 146 (emphasis in original).
45. Eslanda Goode Robeson, *African Journey* (New York: John Day, 1945), 137.
46. TEBA, Box #224: ABM, Folder: ABM, A4, Phillips to Rand Mines Secretary, October 4, 1921; Phillips to Rand Mines Secretary, December 3, 1921.
47. TEBA, Box #224: ABM, Folder: ABM, A4, Anonymous to Managing Director J. Andrew Cohen, Luipardsvlei, November 7, 1921.
48. Charles van Onselen, *Chibaro* (London: Pluto Press, 1976), 34–8.
49. C.T.C. Taylor, *A History of Rhodesian Entertainment 1890–1930* (Salisbury: Collins [Pvt] Ltd., 1968), 75, 87. See also Burns, *Flickering Shadows*, 8.
50. van Onselen, *Chibaro*, 192.

51. National Archives of Zambia (hereafter NAZ), RC85, D.C. J. Moffat Thomson to Hamilton, CID and Head of Censorship Board: "Censorship of Cinematograph Films," April 28, 1927. See also NAZ, RC85, #4, March 10, 1927; Northern Rhodesian Police Lieutenant Hamilton to the Honourable Acting Chief Secretary of Livingstone, March 10, 1927.

52. University of Cape Town (hereafter UCT), Monica and Godfrey Wilson papers, BC 880, E9.4, H. Franklin, "Report on Welfare Work Amongst Urbanised Natives at Broken Hill," Section II, #6: Native Cinema.

53. John Merle Davis, "The Problem for Missions," in John Merle Davis (ed.), *Modern Industry and the African* (London: Macmillan, 1933), 307.

54. See Hortense Powdermaker, *Copper Town: Changing Africa* (New York: Harper & Row, 1962), 255, who dates Copperbelt shows to 1928. Also see Charles Coulter, "The Sociological Problem," in Davis, *Modern Industry and the African* (p. 72), who asserts that Roan Antelope was the first mine to introduce movies for miners on the Copperbelt.

55. Robert Retamal, "Great North Road—Nkana in the Thirties and Forties," Cinema, http://www.greatnorthroad.org/livingstone/nkana.shtml, accessed January 4, 2005.

56. Zambian Consolidated Copper Mines archives (hereafter ZCCM), Ndola, Zambia, 16.2.7C: "Cinema Hall, European, Construction and Operating," June 1933–February 1952. See also "A Magnificent Hall Presented," *Bulawayo Chronicle*, May 13, 1935.

57. Phillips, *The Bantu in the City*, 191.
58. van Onselen, *Chibaro*, 192.
59. *Rand Daily Mail*, January 7, 1922.
60. Phillips, *The Bantu Are Coming*, 147.
61. *South African Pictorial: Stage and Screen*, January 21, 1922.
62. "Natives Quietly Happy," *Rand Daily Mail*, January 13, 1922.
63. "Exemplary Behaviour in Crisis," *Rand Daily Mail*, February 14, 1922.
64. Phillips, *The Bantu Are Coming*, 148.
65. Roux, *Time Longer Than Rope*, 150.
66. Phillips, *The Bantu Are Coming*, 148.
67. Ibid., 150.
68. TEBA, Binder #70, Folder: "1922 Strike, Correspondence and Circulars," Memo #32186, Rand Mines Secretary to the General Officer Commanding, March 10, 1922.
69. TEBA, Box #224: ABM; Folder: AMB, A4, Memo #32197, Rand Mines Secretary to General Officer Commanding, March 10, 1922.
70. See A. Nzula's review of Phillips, *The Bantu Are Coming* in *Umsebenzi*, December 9, 1930.
71. Edgar, *The Travel Notes of Ralphe Bunche*, 205.
72. "Bantu Men's Social Centre," *Umteteli wa Bantu*, March 6, 1926, 4.
73. Cited in Brian Kennedy, "Missionaries, Black Converts, and Separatists on the Rand, 1886–1910: From Accommodation to Resistance," *Journal of Imperial and Commonwealth History* 20, 2 (May 1991), 205.
74. Jeeves, *Migrant Labour in South Africa's Mining Economy*, 25.
75. UCT, A.B. Xuma papers, BC2B, 78/63, #2, 3101531–310630a.
76. G.G. Ndzotyana, "The Problems of Native Townships," *The Bantu Mirror*, February 5, 1938.
77. TEBA, Box #224: ABM; Folder: ABM, A4, Phillips to NRC Secretary, December 3, 1921.
78. van Onselen, *Chibaro*, 192.
79. Phillips, *The Bantu in the City*, 292.
80. Ray Phillips, *African Youth and Sexual Hygiene* (Durban: American Board Mission in South Africa, 1935), 30.
81. PRO, CO 859/624, Ravemcco Study, 1953.
82. Phillips, *Drums in the Darkness*, 2.
83. Ibid., 1.
84. ABCFM, reel #211.
85. William Muraskin, "The Social-Control Theory in American History: A Critique," *Journal of Social History* 9 (1976), 559–69.
86. *South African Outlook*, January 2, 1931, 4.
87. Gutsche, *The History and Significance of Motion Pictures in South Africa*, 294, n. 32.
88. NAZ, RC85, Joseph Brundell, Chief Superintendent, CID, B.S.A. Southern Rhodesia Police, to Officer in Charge, CIC, Livingstone, June 7, 1927.
89. Wits, SAIRR, Education Box, Kb12, file #2, J.D. Rheinallt-Jones to Mrs. U.S. Potter, August 28, 1937. Phillips, *The Bantu in the City*, 316–17.
90. Gutsche, *The History and Significance of Motion Pictures in South Africa*, 300–301.
91. FPB: Documents and Legislation, "From Censorship to Classification," http://www.fpb.gov.za/documents/history.htm, accessed April 15, 2004.
92. Gutsche, *The History and Significance of Motion Pictures in South Africa*, 299–300.
93. Burns, *Flickering Shadows*, 13.
94. Ibid., 17–18.
95. NAZ, RC85, #24, "Minute by His Excellency."
96. NAZ, RC85, #6, March 1927, Hamilton of CID, Northern Rhodesia, to Honourable Acting Chief Secretary. NAZ, RC85, April 1927, T. Hamilton to District Commissioner of Broken Hill. For the 1950s debate over the suitability of the cowboy film in Northern Rhodesia, see NAZ, SEC5/16, vol. I, #93, S. Taylor, Northern Rhodesian Chamber of Mines, to Chief Secretary, Northern Rhodesian Government, August 16, 1956.
97. NAZ, RC85, #22, Latham, Northern Rhodesian Director of Native Education, to Secretary of Native Affairs, Livingstone, June 29, 1927.
98. Secretary of State for the Colonies, Colonial Office Conference, 1927: Summary of Proceedings. Cmd. 2883 (London: His Majesty's Stationery Office, June 1927), Appendix XVIII, "Cinematograph Films," 246.
99. Rob Skinner, "'Natives are not critical of photographic quality.'"
100. *Colonial Office Conference, 1927, Summary of Proceedings*, 245.
101. Poonam Arora, "Imperiling the Prestige of the White Woman: Colonial Anxiety and Film Censorship in British India," *Visual Anthropology Review* 11, 2 (1995).
102. Commission on Educational and Cultural Films, *The Film in National Life: Being the Report of an*

Inquiry Conducted by the Commission on Educational and Cultural Films into the Service which the Cinematograph may Render to Education and Social Progress (London: George Allen and Unwin, 1932), 133.

103. Phillips, *The Bantu in the City*, 324–5.
104. Wits, SAIRR, Part I, Box B56, 1–7, "Military Affairs and Others," 56.4.2, Conference on Native Juvenile Delinquency; Ray Phillips, "A Survey of the Situation on the Witwatersrand," n.d. [1938?], 8.
105. NAZ, RC85, Joseph Brundell, Chief Superintendent, CID, B.S.A. Southern Rhodesian Police, to Officer in Charge, CIC Livingstone, June 7, 1927. NAZ, RC85, #20, Hamilton, Head of Northern Rhodesian Censor Board to Acting Chief Secretary, June 16, 1927.
106. *The Film in National Life*, 134.
107. NAZ, SEC. 2/1122, #285, letter from J.G.P. to Information Officer, February 5, 1946.
108. *Rand Daily Mail*, February 11, 1956. Another example of inconsistent enforcement occurred a few years later, when theaters in Durban prohibited Africans from seeing *Bravados* and *Ocean's Eleven*, while Johannesburg theaters approved these films for all audiences. By 1947, films were apparently only going through two stages of censorship in South Africa, the first by the official Board of Censors and a second by a Board appointed by the NRC. See J.D. Rheinallt-Jones, "A Study of Leisure Time Activities for Native Mine Workers," Wits, J.D. Rheinallt-Jones papers, G2/16, Box G1-G2, "Printed Items," 11.
109. Mabel Carney, *African Letters* (S.L.: s.n., 1926), 17.
110. Ray Phillips, "Social Work in South Africa," in *Christianity and the Natives of South Africa: A Year Book of South African Missions*, no author (Lovedale Press, 1929), 148.
111. Phillips, *The Bantu in the City*, 315.
112. James Dexter Taylor, "Relations between Black and White Races in South Africa," in *Jerusalem meeting of the International Missionary Council, 24 March–8 April 1928* (London: International Missionary Council, 1928), 31.
113. Wits, SAIRR, B61.3, Broadcasting and Films folder, A.W. Wilkie to Rheinallt-Jones, August 3, 1936.
114. Ray Phillips, "Religion and Recreation," Joint Councils papers, Wits, Ac3.3.3, 4.
115. Ibid., 6.
116. Ibid. See also Phillips, "Social Work in South Africa," 148.
117. TEBA, Box #224: ABM; Folder: ABM, A4, Memo #20781, Transvaal Secretary of Mines to Phillips, January 18, 1929.
118. *Rand Daily Mail*, December 10, 1936.
119. Wits, SAIRR, B73.7, Films—Advisory Board file, letter from Robertson, Hon. Secretary of the Pretoria Native Welfare Association, to Lynn Saffery, Hon. Secretary, Consultative Committee of Joint Councils, Johannesburg, November 25, 1936.
120. *Rand Daily Mail*, April 18, 1936.
121. TEBA, Box #224: ABM; Folder: AMB, January 18, 1933.
122. Archie Crawford, "Riding into the African Sunset with 'Lo-Jack,'" *Teba Times* 5, 3 (1985).
123. "Talkie Cinema at Marabastad," *Umteteli wa Bantu*, June 1, 1935.
124. "Location Bioscope," *Bantu World*, September 13, 1941.
125. TEBA, Box #224: ABM; Folder: ABM, Phillips to The General Manager, NRC, February 18, 1935.
126. TEBA, Box #457; Folder: Mines Compound Cinema Circuit, Monthly Reports.
127. Phillips, *The Bantu in the City*, Appendix G: "Films Exhibited on the Mission Circuit," 424–5.
128. Eileen Bowser, *The Transformation of Cinema: 1907-1915* (Berkeley: University of California Press, 1994), 133.
129. "Jesus in Moving Pictures," *New York Times*, October 27, 1912, C3.
130. Cited in Gutsche, *The History and Social Significance of Motion Pictures in South Africa*, 228, n. 17. See also Thelma Gutsche, "From Manger to Cross: A Great Revival," UCT, Gutsche papers, BC703, F1.
131. *From Manger to the Cross*, United States Library of Congress, Madison Building, Motion Picture/TV Reading Room, LC#90716856.
132. ABCFM, reel #211, "Native Leisure Hours."
133. Gutsche, "From Manger to Cross," 1.
134. Wits, SAIRR, 73.1.1–5, BMSC, March–April Bulletin, "Monthly Thoughts," 1938, 1.
135. Burns, *Flickering Shadows*, 37–8.
136. TEBA, Box #224: ABM; Folder: ABM, A4, Phillips to General Manager [Gemmill], Native Recruiting Corporation, December 12, 1924.
137. D.P. Cushing, News Editor, ABCFM, "Christianity versus African Heathenism: Ray Phillips' Social Work."
138. TEBA, Box #224: ABM; Folder: ABM, A4, Phillips to General Manager [Gemmill], Native Recruiting Corporation, December 12, 1924.
139. Cited in van Onselen, *Chibaro*, 193.
140. James R. Brennan, "Democratizing Cinema and Censorship in Tanzania, 1920–1940," 494, n. 71.
141. A. Adu Boahen (ed.), *Africa Under Colonial Domination: 1880–1935*, Vol. VII (Berkeley: University of California Press, 1990), 234.
142. "Charlie Chaplin Films," *Colonial Cinema* 1, 2 (December 1942).
143. "One of the World's Strangest Cinema Circuits," *The Star*, December 29, 1947.
144. Powdermaker, *Copper Town*, 265.
145. J. Koyinde Vaughan, "Africa and the Cinema," in Langston Hughes (ed.), *An African Treasury* (New York: Crown, 1960), 92.
146. Wits, SAIRR, Part I, B73.5, folder: Black Recreational Facilities, 1947, par. 79–82: J.D. Rheinallt-Jones, "The Film."
147. Phillips, *The Bantu Are Coming*, 149.
148. Powdermaker, *Copper Town*, 265–6.
149. David Kerr, "The Best of Both Worlds? Colonial Film Policy and Practice in Northern Rhodesia and Nyasaland," 1–2.
150. Manthia Diawara, *African Cinema*, 1.
151. Erick Berry, "Charlie Captures Africa's Gold Coast," *New York Times*, July 5, 1925, SM16.
152. TEBA, Box #224: ABM; Folder: ABM, Phillips to The Secretaries, Transvaal Chamber of Mines, Memo #45957, December 15, 1932, 1.
153. Ibid., 3.
154. TEBA, Box #224: ABM; Folder: ABM, A4,

Phillips to General Manager [Gemmill], Native Recruiting Corporation, December 12, 1924, 2.
155. TEBA, Box #224: ABM; Folder: ABM, A4, "Report of Compound Welfare Worker," May 10–June 1, 1929, 1.
156. Philip and Iona Mayer, *Townsmen or Tribesmen*, viii-ix.
157. Ibid., 79–80.
158. Yale University, Loram papers, C.T. Loram, "Memorandum on 'Research and Training in the Introduction of Western Civilization to Non-Western Peoples,'" n.d., Box #2, #78.
159. E.R. Kellersberger, "An African Witchdoctor and the Great Physician," *Congo Mission News* (July 1935).
160. Wits, Rheinallt-Jones papers, Box #G1-G2, "Summary of DFR's Presidential Address on the Development of Central and Southern Africa."
161. Phillips, *The Bantu Are Coming*, 153–4.
162. Ibid., 155.
163. Cited in Richard Hall, *Zambia* (London: Frederick A. Praeger, 1967), 36.
164. Walter Benjamin, "The Work of Art in the Age of Mechanical Reproduction," in Benjamin, *Illuminations* (New York: Schocken Books, 1978), 221.
165. Allison James and Jo Booth, *Anthropology Meets Photography on the Internet*, http:xxx.intergraphjournal.com/enhanced/article2/phototxt.htm, accessed September 12, 2004, 6.
166. Martine Astier Loutfi, "Film Industry and Colonial Representation," in Dina Sherzer (ed.), *Cinema, Colonialism, Postcolonialism*, 21. I explore this issue in my introduction to the Africa Motion Picture Project. Glenn Reynolds (ed.), *Images Out of Africa*.
167. Phillips, *The Bantu Are Coming*, 155–6.
168. Slavin, *Colonial Cinema and Imperial France*, 19.
169. Presumably it did not, although there are no known extant copies.
170. Phillips, *The Bantu Are Coming*, 156–8.
171. ABCFM, reel #211, Phillips to Enoch Bell, June 8, 1924.

Chapter 4

1. Yekutiel Gershoni, *Africans on African-Americans*, 5.
2. Jonathan Haynes, "Nigerian Cinema: Structural Adjustments," in Jonathan Haynes & Onookome Okome (eds.), *Cinema and Social Change in West Africa*, 8.
3. An exception was Katanga's stabilization policy.
4. Burns, *Flickering Shadows*, 157.
5. Homi Bhabha, "Of Mimicry and Man," in Bhabha, *The Location of Culture* (New York: Routledge, 1995), 86.
6. Neil Smith, "In the Beginning…," *Cinema* 4, 4 (Winter 1964: Johannesburg Film Society and the Federation of Film Societies of Southern and Central Africa), 33. Thelma Gutsche, "How the Cinema Came to South Africa," UCT, Gutsche papers, BC703, C28, unpublished mss, n.d. [1945?].
7. Gutsche, *The History and Social Significance of Motion Pictures in South Africa*, esp. Ch. I-VIII. Gutsche, "How the Cinema Came to South Africa." C.T.C. Taylor, *The History of Rhodesian Entertainment, 1890–1930*.
8. Es'kia Mphalele, *Down Second Avenue* (Berlin: Seven Sea Books, 1962), 95.
9. Absalom Vilakazi, *Zulu Transformations* (Pietermaritzburg: University of Natal Press, 1965), 76. Clive Glaser, *Bo-Tsotsi: The Youth Gangs of Soweto, 1935–1976* (Cape Town: David Phillip, 2000), 48–9.
10. IMC 26.31.30, W.E. Tabb to John Merle Davis, September 1, 1935.
11. Paul Landau, "Introduction: An Amazing Distance: Pictures and People in Africa," in Landau & Kaspin (eds.), *Images and Empires*, 24. Didier Gondola, "Tropical Cowboys: Westerns, Violence, and Masculinity among the Young Bills of Kinshasa," *Afrique & Histoire* 7, 1 (2009), 75–98.
12. Bridgman noted the stresses as Africans crowded from "open country" to the cramped towns. Frederick Bridgman, "Social Conditions in Johannesburg," *International Review of Missions* 15 (1926), 569–70.
13. Mark Beittel, "'Mapantsula': Cinema, Crime and Politics on the Witwatersrand," *Journal of Southern African Studies* 16, 4 (December 1990), 754.
14. The popularity of cowboy films throughout the African Diaspora has itself informed cinematic narratives. In *The Harder They Come* (1971) starring reggae artist Jimmy Cliff, Jamaican ghetto youth attend Wild West films and cheer the white protagonist.
15. TEBA, Box 317: Propaganda-Cinematograph; Folder 2, Transvaal Chamber of Mines Secretary to L.A. Notcutt, Memo #85966, June 24, 1938, "Extract from Report by Cinema Circuit Supervisor."
16. Marissa Moorman, "Of Westerns, Women and War: Re-Situating Angolan Cinema and the Nation," 104.
17. Ibid., 108.
18. Archie Crawford, "Riding Into the African Sunset with 'Lo-Jack,'" *TEBA Times* 5, 3, p. 4.
19. TEBA, Box 224: ABM; Folder: AMB, J.D. Morton, Secretary, to the Rhodesia Chamber of Mines, Bulawayo, September 17, 1935.
20. The exact chronology of the introduction of film into the Rhodesias is difficult to trace. But see ZNA, May 3, 1927, letter from Hamilton to Livingstone's Acting Chief Secretary, stating that MCCC films had been imported "four years earlier."
21. By 1932, 85 percent of Wankie's miners had three years' service. John Merle Davis, *Modern Industry and the African* (London: Macmillan, 1933), 72. Richard Hall, *Zambia*, 252.
22. Davis, *Modern Industry and the African*, 72.
23. David Kerr, "The Best of Both Worlds? Colonial Film Policy and Practice in Northern Rhodesia and Nyasaland," *Critical Arts* 7, 1-2 (1993).
24. Rosaleen Smyth, "The Development of Government Propaganda in Northern Rhodesia," (Ph.D. diss., University of London, 1983). Powdermaker, *Copper Town*, 255.
25. "The Cinema in Northern Rhodesia," *Colonial Cinema* (June 1944), 22.

26. F. Spearpoint, "The African Native and the Rhodesian Copper Mines," Supplement to the *Journal of the Royal African Society* XXXVI, CXLIV (July 1937), 42–3.
27. Cited in Burns, *Flickering Shadows*, 158.
28. Wits, SAIRR, Part I, Box B56, 1–7; Folder: Military Affairs and Others, 56.4.2, n.d., Ray Phillips, "A Survey of the Situation on the Witwatersrand."
29. TEBA, Box 224: ABM; Folder: AMB, Phillips to Gemmill, September 22, 1935.
30. Colin Beale, "The Commercial Entertainment Film and Its Effect on Colonial Peoples," in *The Film in Colonial Development: A Report of a Conference* (London: British Film Institute, 1948), 17. See also Woody S. Manqupu, "Non-Europeans are flocking to Cinemas," *The Star*, March 23, 1962.
31. Wits, Rheinallt-Jones papers, G2/16, Box G1-G2, "Printed Items," J.D. Rheinallt-Jones, "A Study of Leisure-Time Activities for Native Mine Workers," 12.
32. Wits, SAIRR, 73.7, Films, Advisory Board, E.G. Malherbe to G.C. Latham, "Films for Natives," January 11, 1936.
33. Colin Beale, "The Commercial Entertainment Film," 17.
34. Harry Franklin, "The Central African Screen," *Colonial Cinema* (December 1950), 85.
35. Louis Nell, *Images of Yesteryear: Filmmaking in Central Africa* (Harare: HarperCollins, 1998), 140.
36. Spearpoint, "The African Native," 42. Franklin, "The Central African Screen," 85.
37. Examples include *Gold* (1932, as Jack Tarrant) and *A Six Shootin' Romance* (1926, as "Lightnin'" Jack).
38. Richard Slotkin, "Buffalo Bill's 'Wild West' and the Mythologization of the American Empire," in Amy Kaplan & Donald Pease (eds.), *Cultures of United States Imperialism* (Durham: Duke University Press, 1993), 164–81. Will Wright, *The Wild West* (London: Sage, 2001), esp. "The Popular Cowboy," 8–11.
39. Michael Taussig, *Mimesis and Alterity* (New York: Routledge, 1993). Paul Stoller, *Embodying Colonial Memories* (New York: Routledge, 1995). Graham Huggan, "(Post)Colonialism, Anthropology, and the Magic of Mimesis," *Culture Critique* 38 (Winter 1997–8). Fritz Kramer, *The Red Fez: Art and Spirit Possession in Africa* (New York: Verso, 1993).
40. Taussig, *Mimesis and Alterity*. See also Herbert Cole, *Mbari* (Bloomington: Indiana University Press, 1982).
41. Stoller, *Embodying Colonial Memories*, 21–2, 76.
42. Ibid.
43. Taussig, *Mimesis and Alterity*, 47–8.
44. See Julius Lips, *The Savage Hits Back* (New York: University Books, 1966 [1937]), who collected examples of the reverse "colonial gaze."
45. ZNA, Sec 5/16, vol. 1, no. 8, Allanson to Director of Department of Information, Lusaka, January 27, 1956.
46. Vilakazi, *Zulu Transformations*, 76.
47. For a similar discussion of how the body is imbricated within social collectivities, see Jean Comaroff, *Body of Power, Spirit of Resistance: The Culture and History of a South African People* (Chicago: University of Chicago Press, 1985), 6–9.
48. Eric Gable, "Bad Copies: The Colonial Aesthetic and the Manjaco-Portuguese Encounter," in Landau & Kaspin, *Images and Empires*, 319, n. 39.
49. Huggan, "(Post)Colonialism, Anthropology, and the Magic of Mimesis," 94–5.
50. Stoller, *Embodying Colonial Memories*, 195–6, my emphasis.
51. Monica Hunter, *Reaction to Conquest* (London: Oxford University Press, 1961), 435.
52. Jean Baudrillard, *For a Critique of the Political Economy of the Sign* (St. Louis: Telos Press, 1981), 49.
53. *The Natal Mercury*, October 31, 1947, Letter to the Editor ("Daily Forum" column).
54. Burns, *Flickering Shadows*, 151.
55. ZNA, Sec 2/1280, #249 A-B, Extract from African Provincial Council, Western Province, 6th Meeting at Luanshya, July 9–10, 1947.
56. ZNA, Sec 2/1211, no. 346/1, "Rex vs. John Kanda and Five Other Africans," Mufulira Monthly Report, 1947.
57. Beittel, "Mapantsula," 755. Likewise, in 1955 the Senior Welfare Officer of the Livingstone Municipality, Northern Rhodesia, declared, "I have on a number of occasions complained to African Consolidated Films, Ltd. about the poor quality of films supplied to African audiences." ZNA, Sec 5/16, vol. 1, October 25, 1955, Senior Welfare Officer of Livingstone to the Secretary, African Censorship Board.
58. Onookome Okome, "The Context of Film Production in Nigeria: the Colonial Heritage," in Okome & Haynes (eds.), *Cinema and Social Change in West Africa*, 39, n. 3.
59. Ibid., 33.
60. Elliot P. Skinner, *African Urban Life: The Transformation of Ouagadougou* (Princeton: Princeton University Press, 1974), 285–6.
61. Kwame Nkrumah, *Neo-Colonialism: The Last Stage of Imperialism* (New York: International Publishers, 1965), 246.
62. Rosaleen Smyth, "The British Colonial Film Unit and Sub-Saharan Africa, 1939–45."
63. Okome, "The Context of Film Production in Nigeria," 33–4.
64. Nwachukwu Frank Ukadike, *Black African Cinema*, 31.
65. Cited in Robert Stam and Louise Spence, "Colonialism, Racism and Representation—An Introduction," *Screen* 24, 2 (March 1983), 12.
66. Diawara, "Black Spectatorship."
67. For the power of the gaze in European travel writing, see Pratt, *Imperial Eyes: Travel Writing and Transculturation*.
68. Rob Nixon, *Homelands, Harlem and Hollywood*, 35.
69. Anthony Sampson, *Drum: An Adventure into the New Africa* (London: Collins, 1956), 106–7.
70. See also Mac Fenwick, "'Tough Guy, eh?': The Gangster-Figure in Drum," *Journal of Southern African Studies* 22, 4 (December 1996), 621, 629.
71. Fenwick, "'Tough Guy, eh?,'" 629.
72. Crawford, "Riding into the African Sunset with 'Lo-Jack,'" 5.
73. Wits, Rheinallt-Jones, "A Study of Leisure Time Activities for Native Mine Workers," 12. Projectionists

like William Orr agreed with Rheinallt-Jones: "Cowboy films were always the most popular [among miners]." William Orr, "William Orr—Teba's Movie Man," *Times* (*Teba Quarterly*) 7, 1 (First quarter 1987), 5.

74. Lewis Nkosi, cited in Rob Nixon, *Homelands, Harlem and Hollywood*, 35.

75. See Tehar Cheriaa, "Weapons of Resistance," in June Givanni (ed.), *Symbolic Narratives / African Cinema: Audiences*, 238: "This war has simultaneously changed in an astonishing manner in its weapons and military tactics.... It has really become a war of images."

76. Powdermaker, *Copper Town*, 262.

77. Stuart Hall, "Cultural Identity and Cinematic Representation," *Framework* 36 (1989), 68.

78. Elihu Katz and Tamar Liebes, "Mutual Aid in the Decodin of Dallas: Preliminary Notes from a Cross-Cultural Study," in Phillip Drummond & Richard Paterson (eds.), *Television in Transition: Papers from the 1st International Television Studies Conference* (London: BFI, 1985), 189.

79. Ibid., 188.

80. Powdermaker, *Copper Town*, 158.

81. Ibid., 263.

82. J.A.K. Leslie, *A Survey of Dar Es Salaam* (London: Oxford University Press, 1963), 109.

83. *Tribal Dancing on the Gold Mines* (Johannesburg: Chamber of Mines, P.R.D. Series no. 129, Cygnet Print Limited, n.a., n.d. [1970?]), 13.

84. A.L. Epstein, *Politics in an Urban African Community* (Manchester: Manchester University Press, 1958), 10.

85. ZNA, Sec 5/16, vol. 1, #52, P.G.D. Clark, Acting Chief Information Officer to Films Officer, Lusaka, February 7, 1954.

86. ZNA, Sec 5/16, vol. 1, #77, J.G. Phillips, Acting Chief Information Officer to Provincial Commissioner, Kasama, October 17, 1955.

87. Franklin, "The Central African Screen," 85.

88. Author's interview with anonymous art collector, November 2, 2011.

89. Okome, "The Context of Film Production in Nigeria," 27.

90. Virginia Wright Wexman, "The Family on the Land," in Daniel Bernardi (ed.), *The Birth of Whiteness: Race and the Emergence of U.S. Cinema* (New Brunswick: Rutgers University Press, 1996), 129–69.

91. E.J. Hobsbawm, *The Age of Capital, 1848–1875* (New York: Scribner's, 1975), 140.

92. Cited in Louise Bourgault, *Mass Media in Sub-Saharan Africa* (Bloomington: Indiana University Press, 1995), 13.

93. Powdermaker, *Copper Town*, 261–2.

94. Phillips, *The Bantu in the City*, 424.

95. Charles Tilly, *The Politics of Collective Violence* (New York: Cambridge University Press, 2003), 1.

96. Avtar Brah & Annie E. Coombs (eds.), Introduction to *Hybridity and Its Discontents* (New York: Routledge, 2000), 1.

97. Cited in Aletta J. Norval, "Rethinking Ethnicity: Identification, Hybridity and Democracy," in Paris Yeros (ed.), *Ethnicity and Nationalism in Africa* (New York: St. Martin's Press, 1999), 89.

98. Cited in Bernard Magubane, Introduction to Don Mattera, *Sophiatown: Coming of Age in South Africa* (Boston: Beacon Press, 1987), xvii.

99. Mattera, *Sophiatown*, 64.

100. Homi Bhabha, "The Other Question," in Bhabha, *The Location of Culture* (New York: Routledge, 1994), 70.

101. Ibid., 69.

102. Blacks were present on the American frontier. Monroe L. Billington & Roger D. Hardaway, *African Americans on the Western Frontier* (Boulder: University Press of Colorado, 2001).

103. Frederick Jackson Turner, "The Significance of the Frontier in American History," *Annual Report of the American Historical Association for the Year 1893* (Washington, D.C.: AHA, 1894). Richard Hofstadter, *The Progressive Historians: Turner, Beard, Parrington* (Chicago: University of Chicago Press, 1968), 84.

Chapter 5

1. An exception is T. Dunbar Moodie, *Going for Gold* (Berkeley: University of California Press, 1994).

2. X.C. Birkenbach & Roux van der Merwe, "Black Employees' Perceptions of Organizational Pay Practices: The Development and Application of an Instrument," *Psychologia Africana* 18, 47 (1979), 47.

3. Norman Levy, *The Foundations of the South African Cheap Labour System* (London: Routledge and Kegan Paul, 1982), 61–2.

4. Charles van Onselen, "Reactions to Rinderpest in Southern Africa, 1896–97," *Journal of African History* 13, 3 (1972), 486.

5. Basil Davidson, *The African Slave Trade* (Boston: Little, Brown, 1980), 126.

6. Jeeves, *Migrant Labour in South Africa's Mining Economy*, 5. Francis Wilson, *Labour in the South African Gold Mines, 1911–1969* (Cambridge: Cambridge University Press, 1972). F.A. Johnstone, *Class, Race and Gold* (London: Routledge & Kegan Paul, 1976). Rob Davies, *Capital, State and White Labour in South Africa, 1900–1960* (Brighton: Harvester Press, 1979).

7. I. Schapera, *Migrant Labour and Tribal Life* (London: Oxford University Press, 1947), 145–46. I. Schapera, "Labour Migration from a Bechuanaland Native Reserve," *Journal of the African Society* 32 (1933), 386–97.

8. van der Horst, *Native Labour in South Africa*, 133.

9. Jeeves, *Migrant Labour in South Africa's Mining Economy*, 90.

10. William Beinart, "Joyini Inkomo: Cattle Advances and the Origins of Migrancy from Pondoland," *Journal of Southern African Studies* 5 (1979), 199–219.

11. Wits, SAIRR, Part I, "Mining Industry Board, Memorandum by Joint Council of Europeans and Natives. Constitution and Membership," Box B36: Native Labour in the Mines, 36.1.1, p. 3.

12. Les Switzer, *Power and Resistance in an African Society: The Ciskei Xhosa and the Making of South Africa* (Madison: University of Wisconsin Press), 95.

13. Elliot Skinner, "Labor Migration and National Development in Africa," in Beverly Lindsay (ed.),

African Migration and National Development (University Park: Penn State University, 1985), 29.

14. van Onselen, *Chibaro*, 65.

15. Jeeves, *Migrant Labour in South Africa's Mining Economy*, 90.

16. Ibid., 79.

17. Wits, SAIRR, Part I, Box B36: Native Labour in the Mines, 36.1.1., "Native Recruiting Corporation, Ltd. Statement of Evidence for the Mining Industry Board," 4.

18. Ibid., 1–2.

19. John Lang, *Bullion Johannesburg* (Johannesburg: Jonathan Ball Publishing, 1986), 234.

20. "About Teba," http://home.intekom.com/teba/www/about.html, accessed March 3, 2005.

21. van der Horst, *Native Labour in South Africa*, 187.

22. Wits, SAIRR, Part I, Box B36: Native Labour in the Mines, 36.1.1, "Statement made by Mr. H.M. Taberer to Mining Industry Board," 1.

23. Gutsche, *The History and Social Significance of Motion Pictures in South Africa*, 101.

24. Ibid., 311–312.

25. TEBA, Box 253: Propaganda; Folder: Red Blanket to Civilization, Memo #4637, Gemmill to Messrs Webber, Wentzel, Solomon & Friel, March 21, 1925.

26. Joel Gregory & Victor Piche, "Migrants and Proletarians," in Chris Allen (ed.), *Sub-Saharan Africa* (New York: Monthly Review Press, 1982), 27.

27. TEBA, Box 253: Propaganda; Folder: Red Blanket to Civilization; "Memorandum re: Native Life Film," April 7, 1925.

28. Gutsche, *The History and Social Significance of Motion Pictures in South Africa*, 355.

29. TEBA, Box 317: Propaganda-Cinematograph; Folder 1, Taberer to Gemmill, October 6, 1931.

30. J. Gregory & V. Piche, "Migrants and Proletarians," in Chris Allen (ed.), *Sub-Saharan Africa* (New York, Monthly Review Press, 1982), 27.

31. See also Rita Schafer, "Men's Migrant Labor and its Effect on Gender Relations in Rural Zimbabwe," in Jacqueline Knorr & Barbara Meier (eds.), *Women and Migration* (New York: St. Martin's Press, 2000).

32. Population figures are from Ibid., 74, and Colin Bundy, *The Rise and Fall of the South African Peasantry* (Berkeley: University of California Press, 1979), 127.

33. de Kiewiet, *A History of South Africa*, 200.

34. Bundy, *The Rise and Fall of the South African Peasantry*, 131.

35. van der Horst, *Native Labour in South Africa*, 306.

36. UCT, Margaret Ballinger papers, BC 347, #2.IV.10, n.d. William Ballinger, "Migrant Labour. Trek." See also Wits, SAIRR, Part I, Box B36: Native Labour in Mines; Folder B36.1, n.d., "Witwatersrand Mine Native Wages Commission. Gold Producers' Committees Case Summing Up and Argument."

37. Ibid., 355. Phillips, *The Bantu in the City*, Appendix G, 425. Alan Jeeves, Jonathan Crush & David Yudelman, *South Africa's Labour Empire: A History of Black Migrancy to the Gold Mines* (Boulder: Westview Press, 1991), 64.

38. Gutsche, *The History and Social Significance of Motion Pictures in South Africa*, 322.

39. Phillips, *The Bantu in the City*, Appendix G, 425.

40. Gutsche, *The History and Social Significance of Motion Pictures in South Africa*, 322.

41. TEBA, Box 317: Propaganda-Cinematograph; Folder 1, Memo #30768, Gemmill to District Manager at Zoekmakaar, September 25, 1930.

42. van der Horst, *Native Labour in South Africa*, 202.

43. Rich, *White Power and the Liberal Conscience*, 34.

44. TEBA, Box 317: Propaganda-Cinematograph; Folder 1, Memo E 7/15693, Thompson to Gemmill, October 2, 1930.

45. TEBA, Box 217: Propaganda-Cinematograph; Folder 1, Stubbs to Gemmill, October 8, 1930.

46. William Sellers, "Films for Primitive People," *Documentary Newsletter* (September 1941).

47. TEBA, Box 317: Propaganda-Cinematograph; Folder 1, Zoekmakaar Superintendent to Gemmill, October 2, 1930.

48. Burns, *Flickering Shadows*, 38. See also *The Film in Colonial Development: A Report of a Conference* (London: British Film Institute, 1948).

49. *De Voortrekkers* (1916) resonated with D.W. Griffith's *The Birth of a Nation* (1915).

50. TEBA, Box 317: Propaganda-Cinematograph; Folder 1, Letcher to Gemmill, November 17, 1930.

51. TEBA, Box 317: Propaganda-Cinematograph; Folder 1, Pietermaritzburg District Superintendent to Gemmill, October 14, 1930.

52. TEBA, Box 317: Propaganda-Cinematograph; Folder 1, Stubbs to Gemmill, October 10, 1930.

53. TEBA, Box 317: Propaganda-Cinematograph; Folder 1, Thompson to Gemmill, October 2, 1930.

54. TEBA, Box 317: Propaganda-Cinematograph; Folder 1, Gemmill to Taberer, February 17, 1931.

55. Diawara, *African Cinema: Politics & Culture*, 17.

56. L. Doob, *Communication in Africa: A Search for Boundaries* (New Haven: Yale University Press, 1961), 158.

57. TEBA, Box 317: Propaganda-Cinematograph; Folder 1, Taberer to Gemmill, July 10, 1931.

58. TEBA, Box 317: Propaganda-Cinematograph; Folder 1, Wellbeloved to Gemmill, March 30, 1933.

59. TEBA, Box 317: Propaganda-Cinematograph; Folder 1, Wellbeloved to Gemmill, March 12, 1935. The Ciskei was not on the original list of seven tribal films; it is unclear when it was added.

60. TEBA, Box 317: Propaganda-Cinematograph; Folder 1, Wellbeloved to Gemmill, March 30, 1933.

61. TEBA, Box 317: Propaganda-Cinematograph; Folder 1, Wellbeloved to Gemmill, June 28, 1935.

62. TEBA, Box 317: Propaganda-Cinematograph; Folder 1, "Native Recruiting," untitled newspaper clipping.

63. "'Movie' of Natives on Mines," *Queenstown Daily Reporter*, June 6, 1937.

64. TEBA, Box 317: Propaganda-Cinematograph; Folder 2, L.B. Koza to "Dear Sir of the W.N.L.A.," July 29, 1939.

65. Gutsche, *The History and Social Significance of Motion Pictures in South Africa*, 379.
66. Bill Larkin, *Teba Times* 14 (July 1980), 5.
67. ABCFM, D.P. Cushing, "Christianity versus African Heathenism: Ray Phillips' Social Service Work," in Wits, either SAIRR papers or Joint Councils papers, 1930, 3.
68. TEBA, Binder B339; Folder: Bechuanaland Monthly Reports, District Superintendent to General Manager of NRC, April 16, 1951.
69. TEBA, Box 317: Propaganda-Cinematograph; Folder 1, Butterworth District Superintendent to Gemmill, August 17, 1937.
70. TEBA, Box 317: Propaganda-Cinematograph; Folder 1, Pietermaritzburg District Superintendent to Gemmill, April 2, 1937.
71. TEBA, Box 317: Propaganda-Cinematograph; Folder 1, R. Montgomery to Gemmill, October 14, 1937. See also Queenstown Superintendent to Gemmill, June 29, 1937, who noted, "It is easy with the help of loudspeakers to get large audiences."
72. TEBA, Binder B104, Umtata Monthly Report for April, E.3/35290, Umtata District Superintendent to Gemmill, April 30, 1938.
73. TEBA, Box 317: Propaganda-Cinematograph; Folder 2, Swaziland recruiting agent to the General Manager, NRC, no. 5972/N8/5, October 2, 1939.
74. TEBA, Box 317: Propaganda-Cinematograph; Folder 1, Queenstown District Superintendent to Gemmill, June 29, 1937.
75. Jacobson, *Barbarian Virtues* (New York: Hill & Wang, 2000), 54.
76. Jeeves, *Migrant Labour in South Africa's Mining Economy*, 141.
77. TEBA, Box 317: Propaganda-Cinematograph; Folder 1, Pietermaritzburg District Superintendent to Gemmill, April 2, 1937.
78. TEBA, Box 317: Propaganda-Cinematograph; Folder 1, Butterworth District Superintendent to Gemmill, August 17, 1937.
79. Eslanda Robeson, *African Journey*, 67.
80. Julie Baker, "The Silent Crisis: Black Labour, Disease and the Sociology and Politics of Health in the South African Gold Mines, 1902–30," PhD diss., Queens University, Kingston, 1989.
81. Irma Watkins-Owens, *Blood Relations: Caribbean Immigrants and the Harlem Community* (Bloomington: Indiana University Press, 1996), 14.
82. Shula Marks, "The Gender Dilemma in Nursing History: The Case of the South African Mine Hospitals," seminar paper delivered December 2000 at Oxford Brookes University, http://www.qmuc.ac.uk/hn/history/seminars00.html, p. 4, accessed December 27, 2004.
83. A.P. Cartwright, *Golden Age: The Story of the Industrialization of South Africa and the part played in it by the Corner House group of Companies* (Cape Town: Purnell & Sons, 1968), 171.
84. TEBA, WNLA; Folder: Bioscope Films, Circular No. 12/21, Letter from E.L.R. Kelsey, February 3, 1921.
85. Gutsche, *The History and Social Significance of Motion Pictures in South Africa*, 321.
86. TEBA, Box 224, ABM: Folder: ABM, A4, Compound Managers' Association to Secretary of NRC, January 26, 1923. Also Phillips to Secretary of NRC, January 31, 1923.
87. Burns, *Flickering Shadows*, 79–80.
88. Gutsche, *The History and Social Significance of Motion Pictures in South Africa*, 380.
89. "Mobile Cinema Units," *Books for Africa* (April 1942).
90. Alan Jeeves, "The State, The Cinema, and Health Propaganda for Africans in Pre-Apartheid South Africa, 1932–48," *South African Historical Journal* 48 (May 2003), 117.
91. Gutsche, *The History and Social Significance of Motion Pictures in South Africa*, 374. See also Jeeves, "The State, The Cinema, and Health Propaganda for Africans," 120, n. 46.
92. Ibid., 120. For instance, *The End of the Road* (1919), a film authorized by the U.S. Public Health Services about syphilis.
93. W.V. Brelsford, "Analysis of African Reaction to Propaganda Film," *NADA*, The Southern Rhodesian Native Affairs Department, Annual #24 (1947), 7.
94. Megan Vaughan, *Curing Their Ills: Colonial Power and African Illness* (Stanford: Stanford University Press, 1991), 180–88; Brelsford, "Analysis of African Reaction to Propaganda Film," 7–8; Jeeves, "The State, The Cinema, and Health Propaganda for Africans in Pre-Apartheid South Africa, 1932–48," 122–6.
95. TEBA, Box 224: ABM; Folder: ABM Compound Cinema Circuit, Phillips to General Manager, NRC, July 14, 1940.
96. Karen Jochelson, *The Colour of Disease: Syphilis and Racism in South Africa* (New York: Palgrave/Oxford, 2001).
97. R. Cancel, "'Come Back South Africa': Cinematic Representations of Apartheid over Three Eras of Resistance," in Pfaff (ed.), *Focus on African Films*, 17–19.
98. Jeeves, "The State, The Cinema, and Health Propaganda for Africans," 122.
99. Gutsche, *The History and Social Significance of Motion Pictures in South Africa*, 380.
100. TEBA, Box 224: ABM; Folder ABM Compound Cinema Circuit, Phillips to General Manager, NRC, July 14, 1940.
101. Brelsford, "Analysis of African Reaction to Propaganda Film," 10, 15.
102. Ibid., 21.
103. Ibid., 8, 13.
104. Ibid., 7.
105. Eerily similar problems surface today. Note the reception in Uganda to *Kony 2012*: "The film was projected onto an ersatz cinema screen fashioned from a white sheet.... The reaction? Puzzlement, then anger, which boiled over into scuffles and stone-throwing that sent organizers fleeing for cover." "Appalled Ugandans riot at Kony 2012 screening," *Mail & Guardian* online, March 15, 2012, http://mg.co.za/article/2012-03-15-outrage-violence-greets-Kony-2012-video-in-Uganda/.
106. Brelsford, "Analysis of African Reaction to Propaganda Film," 21.

Chapter 6

1. Nicholas Reeves, *The Power of Film Propaganda* (London: Cassell, 1999), 43–82.
2. PRO, CO859/624.
3. Thelma Gutsche, "Failure of Omission: Britain's Film Propaganda," UCT, Thelma Gutsche papers, BC703, F2, July 8, 1940.
4. PRO, CO859/624. After World War I, the Ministry of Agriculture, Fisheries and Food continued to use propaganda aids such as film, press, and radio.
5. Sir James Marchant (ed.), *The Cinema In Education: Being the Report of the Psychological Investigation Conducted by Special Subcommittees Appointed by the Cinema Commission of Enquiry Established by the National Council of Public Morals* (London: George Allen & Unwin, 1925).
6. Colonial Office Conference, 1927, Summary of Proceedings, Cmd. 2883, Annex I. *The Educational Use of Cinematograph Films* (London: His Majesty's Stationery Office), 252.
7. "Work of the Imperial Institute," *The Times*, April 24, 1929.
8. L.A. Notcutt & G.C. Latham, *The African and the Cinema: An account of the work of the Bantu Educational Kinema Experiment during the period March 1935 to May 1937*, 11.
9. House of Commons Debates, March 16, 1927, 2040, 2044.
10. Rob Skinner, "'Natives are not critical of photographic quality,'" 1.
11. Rosaleen Smyth, "The Development of British Colonial Film Policy, 1927–1939, with special reference to East and Central Africa," 438.
12. *Colonial Office Conference, 1927, Conference of Proceedings*, 71.
13. Sir Robert Donald, "Films and the Empire," *The Nineteenth Century—And After* vol. C, 596 (October 1926), 499.
14. Michael Havinden and David Meredith, *Colonialism and Development: Britain and its Tropical Colonies, 1850–1960* (New York: Routledge, 1993), 150.
15. John Grierson, "The E.M.B. Film Unit," *Cinema Quarterly* 1, 4 (Summer 1933), 203. Andrew Higson, "Britain's Outstanding Contribution to the Film," in Charles Baar (ed.), *All Our Yesterdays* (London: BFI Publishing, 1986).
16. Stuart Hood, "John Grierson and the Documentary Film Movement," in James Curran and Vincent Porter (eds.), *British Film History* (Totowa, NJ: Barnes & Noble, 1983), 101.
17. Hood, "John Grierson and the Documentary Film Movement," 104.
18. Grierson, "The E.M.B. Film Unit," 204.
19. Ibid., 205.
20. Stephen Constantine, "'Bringing the Empire Alive': The Empire Marketing Board and Imperial Propaganda, 1926–33," in John Mackenzie (ed.), *Imperialism and Popular Culture* (Manchester: Manchester University Press, 1986), 200.
21. *Colonial Office Conference, 1927, Summary of Proceedings*, 251.
22. *The Film in National Life*, 132.
23. "The Report of the Colonial Films Committee," *Western Equatorial Africa Church Magazine* 36, 440 (February 1931), 37.
24. David Meredith, "the British Government and Colonial Economic Policy, 1919–39," *The Economic History Review*, 2nd Series, 28, 3 (1975), 486.
25. PRO, CO 323/1126/15: Lord Passfield's Circular to Colonial Governments in Africa, August 18, 1930.
26. *The Film in National Life*, 132–3.
27. Ibid. For cinema in Malaya, see Rex Stevenson, "Cinemas and Censorship in Colonial Malaya," *Journal of Southeast Asian Studies* V, 2 (September 1974).
28. Stephen P. Hughes, "the Pre-Phalke Era in South India: Reflections on the Formation of Film Audiences in Madras," *South Indian Cinema Studies* 2 (July–December 1996), 161–2. Stephen P. Hughes, "Policing Silent Film Exhibition in Colonial South India," in Ravi S. Vasudevan (ed.), *Making Meaning in Indian Cinema* (New Delhi: Oxford University Press, 2000), 39–64.
29. Hughes, "The Pre-Phalke Era in South India," 167–72.
30. "Motion Pictures in India," U.S. Department of Commerce, Trade Information Bulletin #614 (Washington, D.C.: Government Printing Office, 1929), 1.
31. For cinema and the working class in Bombay, see Kunj Patel, *Rural Labour in Industrial Bombay* (Bombay: Popular Prakashan, 1963), Ch. 10.
32. Oriental and India Office (hereafter OIO) archives, British Library, L/PJ/6/174/7: *Report of the Indian Cinematograph Committee, 1927–8* (Calcutta: Government of India Central Publication), 21.
33. Dewan Sharar, "The Cinema in India: Its Scope and Possibilities," *The Asiatic Review* 33 (July 1937), 479.
34. Philip Woods, "Film Propaganda in India, 1914–23," *Historical Journal of Film, Radio and Television* 15, 4 (1995), 543–553.
35. Edward Thompson, "Notes on the Way," *Time and Tide*, April 24, 1937.
36. Prem Chowdhry, *Colonial India and the Making of Empire Cinema: Image, Ideology and Identity* (New York: Manchester University Press, 2001), 19.
37. William Marston Seabury, *Motion Picture Problems* (New York: Avondale Press, 1929), 398–9. OIO, L/PJ/6/1747, "Subject: The Censorship of Cinematograph Films in India."
38. "Cinema Problems," *The Guardian*, June 20, 1935.
39. "Censorship of Films," *The Englishman*, October 22, 1925, in OIO, L/PJ/6/174/7.
40. *Report of the Indian Cinematograph Committee*, 4–5.
41. Constance Bromley, "Films that Lower Our Prestige in India," *Leeds Mercury*, August 20, 1926, in OIO, L/PJ/6/174/7.
42. Sir Hesketh Bell, "The Cinema in the East: Factor in Spread of Communism," *The Times*, September 18, 1926.
43. "Film in India: Educating the Masses," *London Times Educational Supplement*, March 30, 1929.
44. OIO, L/PJ/8/127, Hando to Peel, February 18, 1937.

45. Chowdhry, *Colonial India and the Making of Empire Cinema*, 57, 96.
46. Hesketh Bell, "Cinema in Africa: Perverted Views of European Life," *The Times*, October 4, 1926.
47. Edward H. Berman (ed.), *African Reactions to Missionary Education* (New York: Teachers' College Press, 1975), xii.
48. David B. Abernathy, *The Political Dilemma of Popular Education: An African Case* (Stamford: Stamford University Press, 1969), 79.
49. Mabel Carney, Introduction to Albert Helser, *Education of Primitive People* (New York: Flem H. Revels, 1934), 7.
50. *British Tropical Africa: The Place of the Vernacular in Native Education*, Memorandum by the Advisory Committee on Native Education in Tropical Africa, African No. 1110 (Colonial Office, May 1927).
51. Richard Gray, *The Two Nations* (London: Oxford University Press, 1960), 130.
52. Kenneth King, *Pan-Africanism and Education* (Oxford: Clarendon Press, 1971), 15–16.
53. Gershoni, *Africans on African-Americans*, 28.
54. A. Victor Murray, "Education Under Indirect Rule," *Journal of the Royal African Society* 34 (July 1935), 227–68. William Malcolm Hailey, "An African Survey," in Robert O. Collins (ed.), *Historical Problems of Imperial Africa* (Princeton: Markus Wiener Publishers, 1996), 201.
55. *Higher Education in East Africa: Report of the Commission appointed by the Secretary of State for the Colonies*, Colonial No. 142 (London: Her Majesty's Stationery Office, September 1937), 41–2.
56. Charles T. Loram, *Education of the South African Native* (London: Longmans, Green, 1917). Thomas Jesse Jones, *Negro Education: A Study of the Private and Higher Schools for Coloured People in the United States*, Volume I & II (Washington, D.C.: Government Printing Office, 1917).
57. "In Memorium: Thomas Jesse Jones 1873–1950," Nashville, Emory Ross papers, Disciples of Christ (hereafter DOC), Box 4: Writings. See also E.H. Berman, "Education in Africa and America: A History of the Phelps-Stokes Fund," Columbia University Ed.D dissertation.
58. John W. Cell (ed.), *By Kenya Possessed: The Correspondence of Norman Leys and J.H. Oldham 1918–1926* (Chicago: University of Chicago Press, 1976), 37–8. King, *Pan-Africanism and Education*, 52. Joseph Oldham, "Christian Missions and the Education of the Negro," *International Review of Missions* VII (1918), 242–47. Roland Oliver, *The Missionary Factor in East Africa* (London: Longmans, Green, 1969), 250–3.
59. Edwin W. Smith, *Aggrey of Africa: A Study in Black and White* (Great Britain: Garden City Press, 1932), 144–5.
60. ABCFM, reel 211, J.D. Rheinallt-Jones to Miss Ida A. Tourtellot of Phelps-Stokes Fund, May 18, 1921.
61. Thomas Jesse Jones, *Phelps-Stokes Commission on Education in Africa* (New York: Phelps-Stokes Fund, 1922), 216.
62. "Notes and Comments," *The Colonial Review* IV, 2 (June 1945).
63. King, *Pan-Africanism and Education*, 178.
64. DOC, "In Memoriam: T.J. Jones."
65. Hanns Vischer, "The Educational Use of Cinematograph Films," Colonial Office Conference, 28.
66. *Education Policy in British Tropical Africa*, Memorandum submitted to the Secretary of State for the Colonies by the Advisory Committee on Native Education in the British Tropical African Dependencies, Cmd. 2374 (London: His Majesty's Stationery Office, March 1925).
67. Mackenzie, Fraser, Bridgman, and Oldham, *Friends of Africa*, 174.
68. Louis, *In the Name of God, Go!*, 97–8.
69. IMC, RG85, 261.001. See also Robert G. Gregory, *Sidney Webb and East Africa: Labour's Experiment with the Doctrine of Native Paramountcy* (Berkeley: University of California's Publications in History, vol. 72, 1962), 5–45.
70. J.H. Oldham and B.D. Gibson, *The Remaking of Man in Africa* (London: Oxford University Press, 1931), 64.
71. William Sellers, "The Production of Films for Primitive People," *Overseas Education* XIII, 1 (October 1941), 221–2. C.Y. Carstairs, "The Colonial Cinema," *Corona* (January 1953), 53–5.
72. William Sellers, "Making Films in and for the Colonies," *Royal Society of the Arts*, October 16, 1953, speaks of producing the film in 1926. However, James Burns, Rosaleen Smyth and Colonial Office memos suggest the film dates to 1929; but this calls into question why Sellers would observe reactions of Africans to British documentaries for three years before making a film, given that it was designed to combat plague. If the 1929 dating is correct, then Paterson's *Hookworm Campaign on the Kenya Coast* (1926) predates it by a few years.
73. Sellers, "Making Films in and for the Colonies," 830–1. Sellers, "The Production of Films for Primitive People," 222.
74. Author's interview with anonymous CAFU cameraman at the First International African Film and History Conference, Cape Town, South Africa, July 2002.
75. Sellers, "The Production of Films for Primitive People," 222–3.
76. *Colonial Cinema* 3, 4 (December 1945).
77. *Colonial Cinema* 5, 2 (June 1947). Rosaleen Smyth, "The film as an instrument of modernization and social change in Africa; the long view," paper delivered at Revisiting Modernization Conference, University of Ghana, Legon, July 27–31, 2009, 2.
78. Megan Vaughan, *Curing Their Ills*, 189.
79. Ibid., 223.
80. Sellers, "Making Films in and for the Colonies," 831.
81. Timothy Burke, "'Our Mosquitoes Are Not So Big': Images and Modernity in Zimbabwe," in Landau and Kaplan (eds.), *Images and Empires*, 41.
82. James Clifford, "On Ethnographic Allegory," in James Clifford and George E. Marcus (eds.), *Writing Culture: The Poetics and Politics of Ethnography* (Berkeley: University of California Press, 1986), 102–3.
83. PRO, CO 323/1252/15: Julian Huxley, "Report

on the Use of Film for Education Purposes in East Africa." See also Huxley, *Africa View* (New York: Harper & Brothers, 1931), 58–9.

84. Huxley, *Africa View*, 59–60.

85. PRO, CO 3231252/15, Huxley, "Report on the Use of Film for Education Purposes in East Africa" (emphasis in original), 2.

86. Huxley, *Africa View*, 60–1.

87. PRO, CO 3231252/15, Huxley, "Report," 4.

88. Ibid.

89. Julian Huxley, "More Aspects of Africa, III: Educating the Native, The Better Way," *The Times*, March 12, 1930, 16. Huxley, *Africa View*, 167–8. PRO, CO 323/1252/15, Huxley, "Report," 3.

90. Huxley, *Africa View*, 168.

91. Smyth, "The film as an instrument of modernization," 2.

92. Huxley, *Africa View*, 168. *The Film in National Life*, 137. Smyth, "The Development of British Colonial Film Policy, 1927–1939," 437–50. Smyth, "The Development of Government Propaganda in Northern Rhodesia up to 1953," 110.

93. PRO, CO 323/1252/15, Orr to Vernon, April 24, 1931.

94. Rob Skinner, "'Natives are not critical,'" 3.

95. R.V. Vernon, PRO, CO 3231253/5. For Passfield and the EMB, see Constantine, "Bringing the Empire Alive," 198–9.

96. *The Film in National Life*, 1.

97. "Proposal: Production of Propaganda, Interest and Cultural Film for His Majesty's East African Dependencies," 1930, PRO, CO 323/1113/8.

98. King, *Pan-Africanism and Education*, 103–4. *Report of the Education Commission of the East African Protectorate* (Nairobi: Swift Press, 1919).

99. James Russell Orr, "The Use of the Kinema in the Guidance of Backward Races," *Journal of the Royal African Society* 30 (1931), 243.

100. Colonial Office memo sent to Rockefeller Foundation, PRO, CO 323/1122/16, July 30, 1931.

101. Ibid. Also see Minutes of January 30, 1931, meeting discussing Vernon's "Proposed Enquiry into the Effect of Films on Backward Races in a Selected British Dependency"; and PRO, CO 323/112615, Orr to Vernon, April 24, 1931.

102. PRO, CO 554/92/15, Beresford Gale to Hanns Vischer, November 1932.

103. Thomas P. Ofcansky and Britt L. Ehrhardt, "Man with a Mission: Early Physicians in British East Africa," *Wellcome History* 41 (Summer 2009), 3. Rosaleen Smyth, "Movies and Mandarins: the Official Film and British Colonial Africa," in James Curran & Vincent Porter (eds.), *British Cinema History* (Totowa, NJ: Barnes & Noble, 1983), 130.

104. A.R. Paterson, *The Book of Civilization: Part I* (London: Longmans, Green, 1934), x.

105. A.R. Paterson, *The Book of Civilization: Part II* (London: Longmans, Green, 1935).

106. PRO, CO 323/1252/16, A.R. Paterson, "Suggestions with Regard to the Production of Educational Films for East African Natives," 5–6.

107. Ibid., 6.

108. Wits, SAIRR, B 61.3, Broadcasting and Films; Dr. Luciano de Feo, Director of International Educational Cinematographe Institute to Rheinallt-Jones, March 8, 1933.

Chapter 7

1. John Tomlinson, *Cultural Imperialism: A Critical Introduction* (Baltimore: Continuum International Publishing Group, 1991).

2. Rosaleen Smyth, "The British Colonial Film Unit and Sub-Saharan Africa, 1939–1945," *Historical Journal of Film, Radio and Television* 8, 3 (1988), 285–298. Alec Dickson (Mora Dickson, ed.), *A Chance to Serve* (London: Dobson Books, 1976), 27–30. George Pearson, *Flashback: An Autobiography of a British Film Maker* (London: G. Allen & Unwin, 1957), 202–212.

3. Rosaleen Smyth, "The Development of British Colonial Film Policy, 1927–1939, with Special Reference to East and Central Africa," *Journal of African History* 20, 3 (1979). Mike Ssali, "The Development and Role of an African Film Industry in East Africa with Special Reference to Tanzania, 1922–1983," Ph.D. diss., University of California at Los Angeles, 1988. David Kerr, "'The Best of Both Worlds?' Colonial Film Policy and Practice in Northern Rhodesia and Nyasaland," *Critical Arts* 7, 1–2 (1993). Rob Skinner, "'Natives are not critical of photographic quality,' – Censorship, Education and Film in African Colonies Between the Wars," *University of Sussex Journal of Contemporary History* 2 (April 2001). See also "'Seeing is Believing,' Colonial Health Education Films and the Question of Identity," in Megan Vaughan, *Curing Their Ills: Colonial Power and African Illness* (Stanford, 1991), Ch. 8, 180–99. Andrew M. Ivaska, "Negotiating 'culture' in a cosmopolitan capital: Urban style and the Tanzanian state in colonial and post-colonial Dar es Salaam," Ph.D. diss., University of Michigan, 2003, Ch. 2.

4. A.B. MacLean, "Formation of the British South Africa Company—Occupation of Rhodesia, and the Granting of Several Mining Concessions." See also ZCCM, 10.8.5a: "Roan Antelope Mine—History of the Copperbelt," unpublished mss., n.d. [1949?].

5. Hall, *Zambia*, 251.

6. "Collier's Story of his discover of the Roan and Rietbok Claims," *Bulawayo Chronicle*, March 28, 1934.

7. Marcia Muldrow Burdette, *Zambia, Between Two Worlds* (Boulder, CO: Westview Press, 1988), 16.

8. Isaac F. Marcosson, *Anaconda* (New York: Dodd, Mead, 1957). John Higginson, *A Working Class in the Making: Belgian Colonial Labor Policy, Private Enterprise, and the African Mineworker, 1907–1951* (Madison: University of Wisconsin Press, 1989).

9. See *James Moir, Prospector* (16 min, B&W): Steven Ohrn and Rebecca Riley, *Africa from Real to Reel: An African Filmography* (Waltham, MA: African Studies Association, 1976), 51.

10. R.H. Tawney, "The Bearing of Christianity on Social and Industrial Questions," in *Christianity and the Growth of Industrialism in Asia, Africa and South America, Vol. V: Report of the Jerusalem Meeting of the International Missionary Council, March 24th–April 8th, 1928* (London: Oxford University Press, 1928), 159.

11. IMC/CBMS, BH2005, Box 1212, #48, Jamieson to Oldham, November 21, 1930.
12. Ibid.
13. IMC/CBMS, BH2005, Box 1212, #48, Oldham to Jamieson, October 22, 1930. Davis, *An Autobiography* (self published, n.d.), 128.
14. Davis, *An Autobiography*, 5–10.
15. Taylor, *Frederick Brainerd Bridgman*, 13.
16. IMC/CBMS, BH2005, Box 1212, #48, Oldham to Rheinallt-Jones, October 15, 1930.
17. IMC/CMBS, BH2005, Box 1212, #47, Joseph Oldham, "The Mining Problem of Rhodesia, South Africa and the Belgian Congo," Confidential memorandum, n.d. [1930 or 1931].
18. IMC/CBMS, BH2005, Box #1212, #47, 7 Sept. 1930. BH2005, Box #1212, #47, B.D. Gibson to Wilson, September 25, 1930.
19. IMC/CBMS, BH2005, Box #1212, #47, Phillips to Oldham, November 19, 1930.
20. Wits, SAIRR, B93.1.3, IMC, "Report on Africa Tour," John Merle Davis to Thomas Jesse Jones, January 13, 1931. Yale Divinity (hereafter YD), John R. Mott papers, "Report on Africa Tour," J. Merle Davis to John R. Mott, December 24, 1931.
21. Columbia Rare Book and Manuscript Room, Carnegie Corporation Grant Files (hereafter CCG), Box 186, Folder: "International Missionary Council—Study of Native Conditions in Mining Areas," by Joseph Oldham, 3.
22. Frederick Cooper, *Decolonization and African Society* (Cambridge: Cambridge University Press, 1996), 52–3.
23. Davis, *Modern Industry and the African*, 376–82.
24. IMC/CBMS, BH2005, Box #1212, #47, "Notes of Africa Group" meeting, June 9, 1933.
25. TEBA, Box 224: ABM; Folder, ABM, "Cinema Circuit—Your M. 45952," Ray Phillips to The Secretaries, Transvaal Chamber of Mines, December 15, 1932. See also "IMC—Survey of Native Conditions in Mining Areas," 19.
26. Davis, *Modern Industry and the African*, 325.
27. Ibid., 324.
28. CCG, Box 186, Folder: IMC/Study of Cinema, "An International Study of the Cinema." Submitted by J. Merle Davis, International Missionary Council.
29. Major L.A. Notcutt, "Sisal Economics," in *Tropical Life* (London: John Bale, Sons & Danielsson, 1923).
30. IMC 26.31.29, #3–10, "Notes for Latham: Origin and Aims of Experiment." See also PRO, CO 323/1253/5, John Merle Davis, Outline of experimental production of cinema films: VIII: "Staff and Personnel," 8.
31. Frank Melland and Cullen Young, *African Dilemma* (London: The United Society for Christian Literature, 1937), 140.
32. PRO, CO 323/1253/5.
33. IMC 26.31.30, Henry Turner to Notcutt, September 17, 1936.
34. Davis, "An International Study of the Cinema," 2.
35. T.H. Baxter, *A Dash Through Africa* (London: Missionary Film Committee, 1928), 2.
36. Ibid., 37–8.

37. CO, 323/1253/5, R.V. Vernon on the background for the BEKE, November 20, 1934.
38. Cited in Smyth, "The Development of British Colonial Film Policy, 1927–1939," 442.
39. A'Lelia Bundles, *On Her Own Ground: The Life and Times of Madam C.J. Walker* (New York: Washington Square Press, 1901), 97.
40. Frederick P. Keppel, "A Comment on Christian Missions in Africa," *IRM* 18 (1929), 503.
41. Wits, Joint Councils papers, Cj 2.1.6C, James Dexter Taylor to Dr. F.P. Keppel, August 5, 1926.
42. Michael Law, "Into 'Terra Incognita': Considerations on the 'Timeliness' and 'Importance' of the Carnegie Corporation's Early Involvement in Adult Education," *New Horizons in Adult Education* 2, no. 11/21/88 (Fall 1988), 33.
43. Davis, "An International Study of the Cinema," 3. In *The African and the Cinema*, Notcutt and Latham state that it was Keppel who suggested limiting the scope of the experiment to an East African territory (p. 10).
44. PRO, CO 323/1253/5, Proposal for BEKE, attachment to J. Merle Davis memo to R.V. Vernon, October 10, 1934.
45. PRO, CO 323/1253/5, Davis to Vernon, November 9, 1934; Vernon to Davis, November 13, 1934; Davis to Vernon, November 23, 1934. See also IMC 26.31.29, no. 3–10, A.L. Notcutt, "Notes for Latham: History of the Experiment."
46. "Native Kinemas in East Africa," *Kinematograph Weekly*, July 18, 1935, 23.
47. For correspondence between the BFI and Vernon, and a list of proposed Advisory Board members, see PRO, CO 323/1316/5, BFI General Manager to Vernon, March 6, 1935, and "Suggested Council for Bantu Film Experiment." For a list of actual members, see Notcutt and Latham, *The African and the Cinema*, Appendix A, 209–10.
48. IMC, 26.31.30, Hoernle to Davis, November 8, 1934. Davis to Phillips, September 28, 1934. Davis to Schapera, April 17, 1935. Davis to Robeson, June 25, 1935.
49. IMC, 26.00.25, Davis to Franklin, November 1935; Davis to Jains, December 6, 1935; Madras Film Appraisal Committee: Report for 1934–5, 3.
50. PRO, CO 325/1253/5, P. Cunliffe-Lister to East African Governments, December 7, 1934. See also Kenya National Archives (KNA), N.I.T.D. and Artisans, DC/KAPT/1/4/14, #1–2: Circular letter re: BEKE, From the Secretariat, May 20, 1935. See also IMC 26.31.30, J.M. Davis to Robert Caldwell, Esq., Northern Rhodesian Department of Education, October 4, 1934.
51. See W.D. Reynolds, "A Missionary Education: A Study in Cooperation," *Congo Mission News* (July 1937), 14.
52. British Film Institute (hereafter BFI), Bantu Educational Kinema Experiment papers, "Origin and History."
53. Ibid., 2.
54. PRO, CO 323/1316/5, "Minutes of the First Meeting of the Advisory Council of the Bantu Educational Kinema Experiment," 5.
55. PRO, CO 325/1316/5, "A Bantu Educational

Cinema Experiment": "1) Importance of the Experiment."

56. PRO, CO 325/1316/5, Acting Governor of Kenya to Sir Philip Cunliffe-Lister, Secretary of State for the Colonies, March 27, 1935.

57. IMC 26.31.28, Messrs Hogg, Robinson & Capel-Cure Ltd. to J. Merle Davis, August 30, 1935.

58. *IRM* 24,46 (1935), ii-iii; *IRM* 24, 47 (1935), vii; *IRM* 25, 49 (1936), vi; *IRM* 25, 51 (1936), ii. *Sight and Sound* 4, 14 (Summer 1935), 92. *East Africa* (March 28, 1935); *Crown Colonist* (May 1935). *Congo Mission News* (July 1935), 32. See also *Oversea Education* VI, 4 (July 1935), 189–90; *Rand Daily Mail*, October 18, 1935.

59. "Natives and Talkies," *Cape Argus*, April 11, 1936. "London Sees Bantu 'Charlie Chaplin,'" *Rand Daily Mail*, January 15, 1936.

60. IMC 26.31.28, Notcutt to Latham, April 23, 1935; "Synopsis for Introductory Film."

61. PRO, CO 323/1316/5, Zanzibar British Resident to Malcolm McDonald, August 14, 1935.

62. IMC 26.31.30, John Merle Davis to Ruth Rouse, April 16, 1936. For a history of the Student Christian Federation, see Ruth Rouse, *The World's Student Christian Federation* (London: S.C.M. Press, 1948).

63. IMC 26.31.29, "Bantu Educational Kinema Experiment," Diary of G.C. Latham, entry for 27 June 1935.

64. Ibid., 36–8.

65. Ibid., 39.

66. IMC 26.31.30, J. Merle Davis to the Reverend A.J. Cross, Ndola, Northern Rhodesia, November 22, 1935.

67. IMC 26.31.28, Notcutt to J. Merle Davis, August 1, 1935.

68. Seth Feldman was able to look at this material before it was misplaced. Seth Feldman, "Viewer, Viewing, Viewed: A Critique of Subject-Generated Documentary," *Journal of the University Film Association* 29, 1, 23–36. See also Rosaleen Smyth, "The Development of British Colonial Film Policy, 1927–1939," note #46.

69. Feldman states, in "Viewer, Viewing, Viewed…" (note #5), that Notcutt and Latham failed in their published report to mention the inclusion of *White People* in the BEKE's first tour. While the film is downplayed in *The African and the Cinema*, it is referenced as a "composite film" on p. 75. See also PRO, CO 323/1316/5, Davis to Vernon, November 5, 1935, 2. On four films of the king, see IMC 26.31.28, Notcutt to Davis, May 7, 1935.

70. Notcutt and Latham, *The African and the Cinema*, 41–7.

71. PRO, CO 323/1365/5, Davis to Vernon, November 5, 1935.

72. PRO, CO 323/1356/4, Minutes of 3rd Advisory Council, July 30, 1936; emphasis in original.

73. PRO, CO 323/1356/4, Section II, Summary of Observers' Views.

74. John V. Taylor & Dorothea Lehmann, *Christians of the Copperbelt* (London: SCM Press, 1961), 18.

75. IMC 26.31.30, J. Merle Davis to L.A. Notcutt, March 7, 1936.

76. IMC 26.31.30, J. Merle Davis to Benjamin Gregory of London's *Methodist Times and Leader*, n.d.

77. Taylor & Lehmann, *Christians of the Copperbelt*, 189–90.

78. Nancy Rose Hunt, *A Colonial Lexicon of Birth Ritual, Medicalization and Mobility in the Congo* (Durham: Duke University Press, 1999), 268.

79. See Heath, "Cinema, African," 436, column 1.

80. Hunt, *A Colonial Lexicon*, 270.

81. Notcutt and Latham, *The African and the Cinema*, 51–2. For a discussion of the limitations of extending Foucault's power/knowledge nexus to Africa, see Megan Vaughan, *Curing Their Ills*, 8–12.

82. Notcutt and Latham, *The African and the Cinema*, 68–9.

83. These three films were viewed at the BFI, London, where they are stored with a small amount of archival material.

84. Notcutt and Latham, *The African and the Cinema*, 58.

85. IMC 26.31.29, "B.E.K.E., Progress Report—September 1936."

86. IMC 26.31.30, Kalibala to Wrong, June 26, 1935.

87. Ibid.

88. IMC 26.31.30, J. Merle Davis to Notcutt, July 2, 1935. Unfortunately the details of the meeting were not put to paper.

89. IMC 26.31.29, fiche #1, "Bantu Educational Kinema Experiment," Diary of G.C. Latham, June 14, 1935.

90. Notcutt and Latham, *The African and the Cinema*, 47–8.

91. King, *Pan-Africanism and Education*, 150.

92. BFI, BEKE papers, G.C. Latham's diary from October 7–November 31, 1935, Item #4.

93. Charles Perrings, *Black Mineworkers in Central Africa* (New York: Africana Publishing Corporation, 1979), 208–9.

94. *Report of the Commission appointed to enquire into the Disturbances in the Copperbelt, Northern Rhodesia, July 1940* (Lusaka, Government Printing Office), 8–9. Robert Rotberg, *The Rise of Nationalism in Central Africa* (Cambridge: Harvard University Press, 1971), 160–7.

95. Richard Brown, "Anthropology and Colonial Rule: The Case of Godfrey Wilson and the Rhodes-Livingstone Institute, Northern Rhodesia," in Talal Asad (ed.), *Anthropology and the Colonial Encounter*, 180.

96. IMC 26.31.30, J. Merle Davis to Chief Secretary, Northern Rhodesia, December 3, 1935.

97. IMC 323/1316/5, 1st Meeting of the BEKE Advisory Council, March 29, 1935.

98. Notcutt and Latham, *The African and the Cinema*, 35.

99. G. Walsh & H.R. Montgomery, "Report on Native Taxation" (Nairobi: Government Printer, 1936), 13–14 (#49 and #52), 34 (#105), 49 (#168).

100. Cited in Bruce Berman and John Lonsdale, *Unhappy Valley: Conflict in Kenya and Africa* (Athens: Ohio University Press, 1992), 83.

101. Notcutt and Latham, *The African and the Cinema*, 35.

102. Ibid., 31–4.
103. "Bantu Experiment Films," *Sight and Sound* 4, 16 (Winter 1935–6), 192.
104. Notcutt and Latham, *The African and the Cinema*, 39.
105. IMC 26.31.28, Jane Notcutt to John Merle Davis, October 6, 1935.
106. PRO, CO 323/1316/5, Nyasaland official to Cunliffe-Lister, February 2, 1935, emphasis in original.
107. Clipping in CCG, BEKE Grant Files, Box 186, Study of Cinema folder, *South African Outlook*, May 4, 1936.
108. Notcutt and Latham, *The African and the Cinema*, 144.
109. IMC 26.31.29, "Bantu Educational Kinema Experiment, Progress Report for August 1935 Received from the Field Director, Major L. Notcutt at Vugiri, Tanganyika Territory," 3.
110. Notcutt and Latham, *The African and the Cinema*, 52.
111. Ibid., 82.
112. G.I. Fiennes, "That Moving and Telling Picture," *Central Africa* LIV, 638 (February 1936), 29–32.
113. Notcutt and Latham, *The African and the Cinema*, 81.
114. *Sight and Sound* 5, 20 (Winter 1936–7), extract from a paper at the 23rd session of the International Colonial Institute (Brussels), held in London, October 1936.
115. Notcutt and Latham, *The African and the Cinema*, 96.
116. KNA, PC/NZA/3/15/157, #43: BEKE, District Commissioner of South Kavirondo to Provincial Commissioner, September 24, 1938.
117. PRO, CO 323/1356/4, Minutes of the 70th Meeting of the Advisory Committee on Education in the Colonies, July 23, 1936.
118. Onyero Mgbejume, *Film In Nigeria ... Development, Problems and Promise* (Nairobi: African Council on Communication Education, 1989), 10–11.
119. IMC 26.31.30, J. Merle Davis to Notcutt, December 14, 1935.
120. Carl Rosberg Jr. and John Nottingham, *The Myth of "Mau Mau": Nationalism in Kenya* (Nairobi: Transafrica Press, 1985), 164–74.
121. G.I. Fiennes, "That Moving and Telling Picture," 31.
122. PRO, CO 323/1535/2, G.C. Latham, "Films for the Colonies: A Call to Action," #5.
123. PRO, CO 323/1535/2, Copy of Minute by the Director of Education E. Travers Lacey, Enclosure no. 1 (Nyasaland no. 107), February 23, 1938. See also PRO, CO 323/1535/2, memo by Bowyer of Colonial Office, May 8, 1938.
124. PRO, CO 323/1421/10, Conference of Governors of British East African Territories, June 1937: Bantu Educational Kinema Experiment, Memorandum by Government of Tanganyika. Smyth, "The Development of British Colonial Film Policy, 1927–1939," 445.
125. PRO, CO 323/1535/2, memo by Bowyer of Colonial Office, May 8, 1938.
126. PRO, CO 323/1421/10: "Suggestions for Use of Cinema Units and Films Supplied to Kenya Government," #5.
127. David Henry Anthony III, "Culture and Society in a Town in Transition," 151.
128. TEBA, Box 317, Propaganda-Cinematograph; Folder 2, Notcutt to General Manager of Native Recruiting Corporation, June 8, 1938. Notcutt also drew up a list of "Suggestions for Use of Cinema Units and Films Supplied to Kenya Government," in PRO, CO 323/1421/10. For an interpretations of the BEKE's putative "techno-paternalism," see Manthia Diawara, *African Cinema*, 10–11.
129. TEBA, Box 317, Propaganda-Cinematograph; Folder 1, Notcutt to General Manager, South African Native Recruiting Corporation, May 18, 1938.
130. TEBA, Box 317, Propaganda-Cinematograph; Folder 2, Transvaal Chamber of Mines Secretary to Notcutt, June 24, 1938.
131. L.A.W. Vickers-Haviland, "The Making of an African Historical Film," *Tanganyika Notes and Records* VI (1938), 82–6.

Conclusion

1. "Colonial Cinema," *Colonial Cinema* 1, 1 (November 1942), 1. See also Smyth, "The Development of British Colonial Film Policy, 1927–1939," 450.
2. NAZ, Sec. 2/1280, #1/8, Latham to Sandford, August 30, 1939.
3. George Pearson, *Flashback* (London: George Allen & Unwin, 1957), 204.
4. "'Bwana Cinema' Retires after Useful Sojourn," *East African Standard*, April 10, 1944.
5. Alec Dickson (ed. by Mora Dickson), *A Chance to Serve* (London: Dobson Books, 1976), 28.
6. NAZ, Sec. 2/1280, #1/5, C. Eastwood to Sandford, February 14, 1940.
7. See the inaugural issue of *Colonial Cinema* 1, 1 (November 1942).
8. Smyth, "The Development of Government Propaganda in Northern Rhodesia Up to 1953," 230.
9. *Colonial Cinema* 1, 1 (November 1942), 2. "Films for the Colonies," *Corona* 1, 5 (June 1949), 20–21.
10. Cited in David Kerr, "The Best of Both Worlds: Colonial Film Policy and Practice in Northern Rhodesia and Nyasaland," 9.
11. "One of World's Strangest Cinema Circuits: Films Used to Enlighten Northern Rhodesia's Natives," *The Star*, December 29, 1947.
12. NAZ, Sec. 2/1122, #14/1, Minutes of 1st Meeting of the Film Library and Purchasing Committee, held at Nkana, November 7, 1940. See also NAZ, Sec. 2/1122, #84/1: list of films purchased by the African Film Library. NAZ, Sec. 2/1122, #97, 1942, Films for African betterment.
13. NAZ Sec. 2, 1122, #41/2: African Film Library, "Films for Africans," July 9, 1941.
14. For the Northern Rhodesian Film Library, see Smyth, "The Development of Government Propaganda in Northern Rhodesia up to 1953," 235–9.
15. NAZ, Sec. 2/1122, #84/1, purchased around 1942 by the Film Library.

16. ZCCM, 18.1.7D: Propaganda Films Distribution.

17. *Chisoko—The African*, BFI Colonial Films @ http://www.colonialfilm.org.uk/node/46, accessed March 12, 2012.

18. Shola Adenekan, "Dolly Rathebe: South Africa's first internationally renowned black diva," *The Guardian* obituary, September 28, 2004.

19. Cited in Peter Davis, *In Darkest Hollywood*, online as "That's Dolly" @ http://www.witness.co.za/content/2004_09/27372.htm, accessed January 4, 2005.

20. For instance, the BFI organized a London conference in Jan. 1948 with the support of the Colonial Office. See *The Film in Colonial Development* (London: BFI, 1948). Also, the International Committee of the Scientific Film Association, in conjunction with British Documentary, established the Colonial Film Committee, and met in September 1948. See Dr. K.L. Little, "The Sociological Implications of the Film in Colonial Areas," *Colonial Review* (March 1949), 15–16.

21. Kedmon Hungwe, "Fifty Years of Film-making in Zimbabwe," http://www.szs.net/kedmon-hungwe/film-making-in-zimbabwe.html, accessed June 25, 2004.

22. Ibid.

23. Wits, SAIRR, B73.7, Films—Advisory Board, Peter U. Young, "The Central African Broadcasting Station, Lusaka. The Work of the Cinema Section in Northern Rhodesia," broadcast in English, June 9, 1949.

24. This debate has been covered by Burns, *Flickering Shadows*, 51–59.

25. Cited in Smyth, "The British Colonial Film Unit and sub–Saharan Africa, 1939–1945," 287. There seemed to be increasing doubt about the ability of film alone to convey the desired message. One CFU report emphasized that "during the training of the mass education team it was discovered that [*Amenu's Child*] was far more effective as a medium of instruction if the story was first told to the audience, using stills from the film and stressing certain points. Immediately afterwards the film would be screened and ... a discussion would follow once again stressing the desired points." PRO, CO 859/624.

26. Questionnaire in *Colonial Cinema* V, 3 (September 1947).

27. P. Morton-Williams, *Cinema in Rural Nigeria*, 335–40. Burns, *Flickering Shadows*, 54–59. Mike Ssali, "The Development and Role of an African Film Industry in East Africa with Special Reference to Tanzania, 1922–1984," 87–88.

28. PRO, CO 323/1356/4, BEKE Interim Report, Section II, Summary of Observers—Views, N1.

29. A.G. Dickson, "Mass Education in Togoland," *African Affairs* 49 (1950), 146–7.

30. A.R.G. Prosser, Chief Social Development Officer, Gold Coast, "An Experiment in Community Development" 2, 3 (June 1951), 52.

31. In South Africa, these included *Goldberg's, Odin*, and *Balansky's*.

32. "Africans to step up drive on color bar," *New York Times*, May 8, 1959, p. 2.

33. "Rhodesia police act to bar riots," *New York Times*, September 4, 1960, p. 3.

34. Ngugi Wa Thiong'o, "Is the Decolonisation of the Mind a Prerequisite for the Independence of Thought and the Creative Practice of African Cinema?," in June Givanni (ed.), *Symbolic Narratives / African Cinema: Audiences, Theory and the Moving Image* (London: BFI Publishing, 2000), 93.

Bibliography

Ambler, Charles. "Popular Films and Colonial Audiences: The Movies in Northern Rhodesia." *American Historical Review* 106, no. 1 (2001): 81–105.

Anthony, David Henry III. "Culture and Society in a Town in Transition: A People's History of Dar es Salaam, 1865-1939." PhD diss., University of Wisconsin-Madison, 1983.

Baker, Aloha. *Call to Adventure!* New York, 1939.

Balogun, Françoise. *The Cinema in Nigeria*. Enugu, 1987.

Balseiro, Isabel, and Ntongela Masilela. *To Change Reels: Film and Film Culture in South Africa*. Detroit, 2003.

Barkas, Natalie. *Thirty Thousand Miles for the films*. London, 1937.

Ben-Ghiat, Ruth, and Mia Fuller, eds. *Italian Colonialism*. New York, 2008.

Bever, L. van. *Le Cinéma pour Africains*. Brussels, 1952.

Bloom, Peter. *French Colonial Documentary: Mythologies of Humanitarianism*. Minneapolis, 2008.

Botha, Martin. *South African Cinema 1896-2003*. Bristol, 2012.

Brennan, James. "Democratizing Cinema and Censorship in Tanzania, 1920-1980," *The International Journal of African Historical Studies* 38, no. 3 (2005): 484–485.

Brom, John. *The Pitiless Jungle*. New York, 1955.

———. *20,000 Miles in the African Jungle*. London, 1958.

Burns, James. "The African Bioscope—Movie House Culture in British Colonial Africa," *Afrique & Histoire* 1, no. 5 (2006): 65–80.

———. *Cinema and Society in the British Empire, 1895-1940*. New York, 2013.

———. *Flickering Shadows: Cinema and Identity in Colonial Zimbabwe*. Athens, 2002.

———. "John Wayne on the Zambezi: Cinema, Empire, and the American Western in British Central Africa." *International Journal of African Historical Studies* 35, no. 1 (2002): 103–117.

Burton, Andrew. "Urchins, Loafers and the Cult of the Cowboy: Urbanization and Delinquency in Dar es Salaam, 1919–61." *Journal of African History* 42, no. 2 (2001): 199–216.

Cameron, Kenneth. *Africa on Film: Beyond Black and White*. New York, 1994.

Cham, Mbye. "Reconfiguration of the Past in the Films of Ousmane Sembène." In *The Historical Film: History and Memory in Media*, ed. Marcia Landy, 261–266. New Brunswick, 2000.

Chowdry, Prem. *Colonial India and the Making of Empire Cinema: Image, Ideology and Identity*. Manchester, 2000.

Convents, Guido. "Film and German Colonial Propaganda for the Black African Territories to 1918." In *Before Caligari: German Cinema, 1895-1920*. eds. Paolo Cherchi Usai and Lorenzo Codelli. Madison. 1991, 58–76.

———. *Os Moçambicanos perante o cinema e o audiovisual*. Maputo, 2011.

Davis, J. Merle. *Modern Industry and the African*. London, 1933.

Davis, Peter. *In Darkest Hollywood: Exploring the Jungle's of Cinema's South Africa*. Athens, 1996.

Diawara, Manthia. *African Cinema: Politics and Culture*. Bloomington, 1992.

———. "Black Spectatorship: Problems of Identification and Resistance." In *Black American Cinema*, ed. Manthia Diawara, 211–220. New York, 1993.

Diop, Samba. *African Francophone Cinema*. New Orleans, 2004.

Ekwuazi, Hyginus. "Towards the Decolonization of African Film." *Africa Media Review* 5, no. 2 (1991): 95–106.

Feldman, Seth. "Viewer, Viewing, Viewed: A Critique of Subject-Generated Documentary." *Journal of the University Film Association* 29, no. 1 (Fall 1977): 23–26, 35–36.

Forbes, Rosita. *From Red Sea to Blue Nile*. Middlesex, 1939.

Fuhrmann, Wolfgang. "Patriotism, Spectacle, and Reverie." In *German Colonialism, Visual Culture and Modern Memory*, ed. Volker Langbehn. New York, 2012.

Gadjigo, Samba. *Ousmane Sembène: The Making of a Militant Artist*. Bloomington, 2010.

Gehrts, Meg. *A Camera Actress in the Wilds of Togoland; the adventures, observations and experiences of a cinematograph actress in West African forests whilst collecting films depicting native life and when posing as the white woman in Anglo-African cinematograph films*. Philadelphia, 1915.

Genova, James. *Cinema and Development in West Africa*. Bloomington, 2013.

Gilg, A. Cameron, *Turn Left—The Riffs Have Risen: From England to Cape Town in a Baby Car*, ed. Barry Cockcroft. London, 1981.

Giltrow, David. "Young Tanzanians and the Cinema." PhD diss., Syracuse University, 1973.

Givanni, June, and Imruh Bakari, eds. *Symbolic Narratives/African Cinema: Audiences, Theory and the Moving Image*. London, 2000.

Gordon, Robert. *Picturing Bushmen: The Denver African Expedition of 1925*. Athens, 1997.

Gordon, Robert J. "The Battle for the Bioscope in Namibia," *African Identities* 3, no. 1 (2005). 37–50.

Griffiths, Alison. *Wondrous Difference: Cinema, Anthropology & Turn-of-the-Century Visual Culture*. New York, 2002.

Gugler, Josef. *African Cinema: Re-Imagining a Continent*. Bloomington, 2003.

Gutsche, Thelma. *The History and Social Significance of the Motion Pictures in South Africa*. Cape Town, 1972.

hooks, bell. "The Oppositional Gaze: Black Female Spectators." In *Movies and Mass Culture*, ed. John Belton, 247–264. New Brunswick, 1996.

Johnson, Martin. *Congorilla: Adventures with Pygmies and Gorillas in Africa* (New York: Harcourt, Brace, 1931.

Johnson, Osa. *Four Years in Paradise*. Garden City, 1941.

Kerr, David. "'The Best of Both Worlds?' Colonial Film Policy and Practice in Northern Rhodesia and Nysasaland." *Critical Arts* 7, no. 1–2 (1993): 11–42.

Landau, Paul, and Deborah Kaspin, eds. *Images and Empires*, Berkeley, 2002.

Larkin, Brian. *Signal and Noise: Media, Infrastructure and Urban Culture in Nigeria*. Durham, 2008.

Luhr, William, ed. *World Cinema Since 1945*. New York, 1987.

Malkmus, Lizbeth, and Roy Armes. *Arab and African Filmmaking*. Atlantic Highlands, 1991.

Martin, Phyllis. *Leisure and Society in Colonial Brazzaville*. Cambridge, 2002.

Masilela, Ntongela. "Come Back Africa and South African film history." *Jumpcut* 36 (1991): 61–65.

Mayer, Ruth. *Artificial Africas: Colonial Images in the Times of Globalization*. Lebanon, 2002.

Maynard, Richard. *Africa on Film: Myth and Reality*. Rochelle Park, 1974.

Mgbejume, Onyero. *Film in Nigeria: Development, Problems and Promise*. Nairobi, 1981.

Moorman, Marissa. "Of Westerns, Women and War: Resituating Angolan Cinema and the Nation." *Research in African Literatures* 32 (2001): 103–122.

Mosley, Philip. *Split Screen: Belgian Cinema and Cultural Identity*. Albany, 2001.

Nixon, Rob. *Homelands, Harlem and Hollywood*. New York, 1994.

Notcutt, L.A., and G.C. Latham. *The African and the Cinema: An Account of the work of the Bantu Educational Cinema Experiment during the period March 1935 to May 1937*. London, 1937.

Okome, Onookome, and Jonathan Haynes. *Cinema and Social Change in West Africa*. Jos, 1997.

Oksiloff, Assenka. *Picturing the Primitive*. New York, 2001.

Olubomehin, Oladipo O. "Cinema Business in Lagos, Nigeria since 1903," *Historical Research Letter* 3 (2012), 1–10.

Pfaff, Françoise. *Twenty-five Black African Filmmakers: A Critical Study, with Filmography and Biobibliography*. Westport, 1988.

Phillips, Ray. *The Bantu Are Coming: Phases of South Africa's Race Problem*. London, 1930.

_____. *The Bantu in the City*. London, 1937.

Phimister, Ian, and Charles van Onselen. "The Political Economy of Tribal Animosity: A Case Study of the 1929 Bulawayo Location Faction Fight." *Journal of Southern African Studies* 6, no. 1 (1979): 1–43.

Powdermaker, Hortense. *Copper Town: Changing Africa*. New York, 1962.

Power, Marcus. "Post-colonial Cinema and the Reconfiguration of Moçambicanidade." *Lusotopie* 11 (2004): 261–78.

Rasmussen, Kristin Alexandra. "Kinna-Uganda: A Review of Uganda's National Cinema." Master's thesis, San Jose State University, 2010.

Reinwald, Brigitte. "'Tonight at the Empire': Cinema and Urbanity in Zanzibar, 1920s to 1960s." *Afrique & histoire* 1, no. 5 (2006): 81–109.

Reynolds, Glenn, ed. *Africa's Last Romantic: The Films, Books and Explorations of John Brom*. New York, 2014.

_____, ed. *Images Out of Africa: The Virginia Garner Diaries of the Africa Motion Picture Project*. Lanham, 2011.

Rony, Fatimah Tobing. *The Third Eye: Race, Cinema, and the Ethnographic Spectacle*. Durham, 1996.

Ross, L.M. "Africans and Propaganda Films." *United Empire* XXXI, no. 2 (1940), 3–5.

Şaul, Mahir, and Ralph A., eds. *Viewing African Cinema in the Twenty First Century: Art Films and the Nollywood Video Revolution*. Athens, 2010.

Sherzer, Dina, ed. *Cinema, Colonialism, Postcolonialism: Perspectives from the French and Francophone Worlds*. Austin, 1996.

Skinner, Rob. "Making Films for Illiterates in Africa: The Instructional Film in British Africa, 1927–1955." Master's thesis, University of Sussex, 1999.

_____. "'Natives are not critical of photographic quality'—Censorship, Education and Films in African Colonies Between the Wars." *University of Sussex Journal of Contemporary History* 2 (2001): 1–9.

Slavin, David Henry. *Colonial Cinema and Imperial France, 1919-1939: White Blind Spots, Male Fantasies, Settler Myths.* Baltimore, 2001.

———. "French Cinema's Other First Wave: Political and Racial Economies of Cinéma colonial, 1918 to 1934." *Cinema Journal* 37, no. 1 (1997).

Smyth, Rosaleen. "Britain's African Colonies and British Propaganda during the Second World War." *Journal of Imperial and Commonwealth History* 14, no. 1 (1985): 65-82.

———. "The Central African Film Unit's Images of Empire, 1948-1963." *Historical Journal of Film, Radio and Television* 3, no. 2 (1983).

———. "The Development of British Colonial Film Policy, 1927-1939, with Special Reference to East and Central Africa." *Journal of African History* 20, no. 3 (1979): 437-450.

———. "The Development of Government Propaganda in Northern Rhodesia up to 1953." PhD diss., University of London, 1983.

———. "Movies and Mandarins: The Official Film and British Colonial Africa." In *British Cinema History*, ed. James Curran and Vincent Porter. Totowa, 1983.

———. "The Post-War Career of the Colonial Film Unit in Africa: 1946-1955." *Historical Journal of Film, Radio and Television* 12, no. 2 (1992): 163-177.

Ssali, Mike. "The Development and Role of an African Film Industry in East Africa with Special Reference to Tanzania, 1922-1984." PhD diss., University of California at Los Angeles, 1988.

Stam, Robert, and Louise Spence. "Colonialism, Racism, and Representation—An Introduction." *Screen* 24, no. 2 (March-April 1983): 2-20.

Stanard, Matthew G. *Selling the Congo: A History of European Pro-Empire Propaganda and the Making of Belgian Imperialism.* Lincoln, 2011.

Stevenson, Rex. "Cinemas and Censorship in Colonial Malaya." *Journal of Southeast Asian Studies* 5, no. 2 (September 1974): 209-224.

Stokes, Melvyn, and Richard Maltby, eds. *Hollywood Abroad: Audiences and Cultural Exchange* London, 2007.

Taylor, Clyde. "Africa: The Last Cinema." In *World Cinema Since 1945*, ed. William Luhr. New York, 1987.

Taylor, C.T.C. *A History of Rhodesian Entertainment, 1890-1930.* Salisbury, 1968.

Thackway, Melissa. *Africa Shoots Back: Alternative Perspectives in Sub-Saharan Francophone Film.* Bloomington, 2003.

Tomaselli, Keyan. *The Cinema of Apartheid: Race and Class in South African Film.* New York, 1987.

———. *The Cinema of Apartheid: Race and Class in South Africa Film.* New York, 1988.

———. *Myth, Race and Power: South Africans Imaged on Film and TV.* South Africa, 1986.

Ukadike, Nwachukwu Frank. "African Films: A Retrospective and a Vision for the Future." *Critical Arts* 7, no. 1-2 (1993): 43-60.

———. *Black African Cinema.* Berkeley, 1994.

———. *Questioning African Cinema.* Minneapolis, 2002.

UNESCO. *Films ethnographiques sur l'Afrique noire.* Paris, 1967.

Vaughan, Megan. *Curing Their Ills: Colonial Power and African Illness.* Stanford, 1991.

Vieyra, Paulin Soumanou. *Le Cinéma Africain: des origines à 1973.* Paris, 1975.

Willan, Brian. *Sol Plaatje: South African Nationalist 1876-1932.* Berkeley, 1984.

Index

Abyssinia (1930) 50, 71
Acres, Birt 18
Adams, Arthur 104–105
Addams, Jane 89
Adventures in Africa (1931) 66
Adventures on the Upper Nile (1931) 51
Africa (1898) 59
Africa Joins the World (1936) 82
Africa Motion Picture Project (AMPP) 82
Africa Speaks (1931) 83
Africa To-day (1927) 82, 176
African Film Center 80
African Film Productions (AFP) 143, 1449
African Films Trust 95
The African in Transition (1924) 114
African Jim (aka *Jim Comes to Joburg*, 1949) 150, 199
African Mirror 93
African Odyssey (1967) 59
African Vernacular Cinema Experiment 195
African Wild Life (1939?) 50
The African Witch-Doctor and the Way Out 107, 110–114
Afrique 50 (*Africa 50*) 5
Afrique-sur-Seine (*Africa on the Seine*, 1955) 4
Agricultural Education at Bukalasa (1936) 190
Akeley, Carl 51, 60, 62, 66, 69–71
Akeley, Delia 76–77
Akeley, Mary Jobe 60
Akeley camera 36, 64
Alarming the Queen's Company of Grenadier Guards at Omdurman (1898) 47
Alassane, Moustapha 6
Alexandria (1921) 50
L'Algérie en flammes (*Algeria in Flames*, 1958) 5
Allégret, Marc 42
Ambler, Charles 9–10
Ambushed (1925) 107, 116
American Board of Commissioners for Foreign Missions (ABCFM) 86–87, 114
American Ninja 2: The Confrontation (1987) 1

Amery, Leopold 154–155
Anglo-African Cinema Company 24
Anschutz, Ottomar 18
Anti-Plague Operations in Lagos (1929?) 162
Armand Denis Belgian Congo Expedition 53–55
Armat, Thomas 18
Arora, Poonam 103
L'Arrivée d'un Train en gare de La Ciotat (*The Arrival of a train at La Ciotat*, 1896) 18
L'Arroseur arrosé (*The Sprinkler Sprinkled*, 1895) 18
L'Art Nègre (*Black Art*, 1938?) 44
Art of Alpine Mountain Climbing 93
L'Atlantide (1921) 56
Au pays des colosses et des pygmées (*In the Land of Giants and Pygmies*, 1925) 76
Au pays du Dogon (*In Dogon Country*, 1938) 76
Audouin-Dubreuil, Louis 56
Auf Tierfang in Abessinien (*Animal Trapping in Abyssinia*, 1926) 62
Auf Tierfang in Afrika (*Animal Trapping in Africa*, 1926) 62
Austrian Motorcycle Expedition Capetown to Cairo, 1935–36 58
Azioni su Sidi Barrani (*Operations in Sidi Barrani*, 1940) 49

Ba, Hampaté 26
Baba Tunde Goes to School (1955) 198
Baboona (1934) 61
Bad Girl (1931) 103
Baker, Aloha 20, 53
Balboa and Company 29
Ballinger, William 98
Banana (1909) 44
Bantu Educational Kinema Experiment (BEKE) 46, 83, 102, 154, 161–162, 165, 169–170, Ch. 7 passim
Bantu Men's Social Centre (BMSC) 87–88, 98, 137, 173
Barsoum Looks for Employment (1923) 34

Basutoland (1935) 143
Baxter, T.H. 82, 176–177, 178
Bayoumi, Mohamed 37–38
Bazaars of Cairo (1921) 50
Beinart, William 133
Bell, Hesketh 159
Ben-Ghiat, Ruth 26
Benett-Stanford, John Montague 47
Benjamin, Walter 112, 120
Better Hides and Skins 198
Bhabha, Homi 115
Bilder aus unseren deutschen Kolonien (*Images from Our German Colonies*, 1913) 41
Bioscope 19
The Birth of Krishna 157
Black Cotton (aka *Cotton-Growing in Nigeria*, 1927) 153
Blazing the Trail (1929) 153
Blonde Venus (1932) 103
Bloom, Peter 56
The Blue Nile (1925) 68
Bogart, Humphrey 124–125
Boggio, Cecilia 42
Bongolo (1952) 45
Borom Sarret (*The Wagoner*, 1963) 6
The Boy Kumasenu (1952) 31
Boyce, William (African Balloonograph Expedition) 29, 61
Braun, Marta 73
Brelsford, William Vernon 151–152
Brennan, James 22
Bridgman, Frederick Ch. 3 passim, 173
The British Army 198
British Egypt (1916) 50
British Film Institute 166–167, 176, 178–179
British Instructional Films 153
British Mutoscope and Biograph 47–48
British South Africa Company (BSAC) 172
Brocklehurst, Sir Philip Lancaster 59
Brom, John 26, 34, 57–58, 75, 77, 79
Buchanan, Capt. Angus 52–53
Buck, Frank 54

231

Bugniet, R. 75–76
Bunche, Ralph 67
Burke, Timothy 163
Burns, James 9, 25
Burton, Andrew 10
The Bushman (1926) 74
Bushmen of the Kalahari (1908) 74
Bwana Devil (1952) 80
Bwana Kitoko (1955) 45

Cabin in the Sky (1943) 199
Cabiria (1914) 41
Cactus Trails (1927) 107, 116
Cadle, C. Ernest 74
Calling on the Sphinx (1921) 50
Cameraing Through Africa I (1919) 50
Cameraing Through Africa II (1919) 50
Cameron-Cadle Expedition (1928) 74
Cameroun (1930s) 76
Canada's Evergreen Playground 106
Candida (1953) 80
Cape to Cairo (1926) 53, 84, 109
Car and Camera around the World (1929) 53
Carmencita's Skirt Dance (1894) 18
Carnegie Corporation 174–178, 184
Carney, Mabel 159
The Catechist (1953) 80
Cattle and Disease (1936) 185
Cattle Breeding in Brazil 94
Cauvin, Andre 45
Central African Film Unit (CAFU) 119, 200
A Century of Progress: Darkest Africa (1933) 50
Century Productions 84
Chamber of Mines 87, Ch. 5 passim
Champion, Allison W.G. 87
Champion, Arthur 197
The Changing African (1928?) 99–100
The Changing Face of Africa (1969) 59
Chaplin, Charlie 4, 24, 91, 97–98, 107–110, 131, 200
The Charge of the Light Brigade (1936) 158
Charlton, Charles 69
La Chasse à la giraffe en Ouganda (*Hunting Giraffe in Uganda*, 1910) 60
La Chasse à la panthère (*Hunting Panther*, 1909) 60
Chasse à l'hippopotame sur le Nil bleu (*Hippopotamus hunting on the Blue Nile*, 1908) 59–60
Chester, Clarence Lyon 47
The Chief (1935) 182
Chikly, Albert Samama 19
Children of Africa (1939) 83
Chisoko the African (1949) 199
Church Missionary Society (CMS) 25, 82

Cinema Christian Council 176
Cinematograph Exhibitions Ordinance 103
Cinematograph Film Act (1917) 101
Cinématographe 18, 156
Ciskei (1935) 143
Cissé, Souleymane 8
Cities of the Desert (1934) 53
Citroën, André 56–57
Citroën Centrafrique expedition 56
The City of Algiers (1921) 50
Clark, James Lippitt 51, 60
Clément, Pierre 5
Cockcroft, Barry 58
Coffee Marketing (1936) 185, 189
Coffee Under Banana Shade (1936) 185, 189
Collier, William 172
Colonial Cinema 119, 198, 201
Colonial Development Act (1929) 156
Colonial Film Unit (CFU) 149, 152, 171
Colonial Films Committee (1929) 103, 155–156, 165
Colorado African Expedition (1928–29) 75, 83
Come Back Africa (1959) 150
Comité de Propagande Colonial par le Film (1928) 42
Commission on Educational and Cultural Films (1929) 165–166
Congo Pictures 84
Congorilla (1932) 63, 75
La Conquête belge de l'Afrique (*The Belgian Conquest of Africa*, 1919) 44
Convents, Guido 8
Cooper, Frederick 174
Copperbelt 104, Ch. 4 passim, Ch. 7 passim
Copperbelt Commission 172
Cotlow, Lewis N. 58, 67
Cottar, Charles 5
Cotton-Growing in Nigeria (aka *Black Cotton*, 1927) 163
A Countryman's First Sight of the Animated Pictures (1901) 25
Cowboy Sports (1913) 94
La Croisière noire (*The Black Journey*, 1926) 57
Crossing the Great Sahara (1924) 53
Cry the Beloved Country (1951) 4
Cudahy-Massee Expedition (1928–29) 84
Cujis, Cecil 5
Cunliffe-Lister, Sir 154
Cutting, Suydam 71–72

Dakar and the Bay of Gorée (1911) 48
Dakar, principal port de commerce de l'Afrique occidentale française (*Dakar, Principal Commercial Port of French West Africa*, 1914) 48

Damon and Pythias (1914) 107
Dangerous Safari (1944) 54
Davis, Hassoldt 38, 53
Davis, John Merle Ch. 7 passim
Dawodu, S.O. 35
A Day in an African Village (1938) 83
De Boe, Gerard 45–46
Denis, Armand 53–56, 58, 67
Denver African Expedition 74
Department of Economic and Social Research and Counsel (Department of Industrial and Social Research) 173, 190
Deutsche Kolonialgesellschaft (DKG) 41
The Devil Fights Back (1953) 80
Diawara, Manthia 9, 124, 151
Dickson, Alec 197–198, 201
Dickson, William 18
Dionnes (Acrobats) (1912?) 93
Division of Photography and Cinema 153
Dougall, James W.C. 178, 181
The Drum (1938) 159
The Dust That Kills 148

Earls Court Exhibition 46
An East African Army Field Bakery (1944) 49
Eastman, George 66, 69–71
Eastman Teaching Films 72
Edinburgh House Bureau for Visual Aids 118
Edison, Thomas 17
Ekwuazi, Hyginus 8
Emitaï (1971) 6
Empire Marketing Board (EMB) 155, 165
Employment Bureau of Africa, The (TEBA) 134
En Afrique Occidentale (*In West Africa*, 1907) 48
Englehardt, Tom 124
Entertainments (Censorship) Act No. 29 (1931) 101
Entertainments Control and Censorship Bill (1932) 102
Epstein, A.L. 127
L'Équateur Aux Cent Visages (released in the U.S. as *Black Shadows*) 45
Essor Cinégraphique 44
Evenpoel, François 44
Events in the Life of a Zulu Chief 110
Explorers Club 62

Farm Implements (1936) 185
Fathoms of the Deep 163
Feelings Struggle (2005) 7
Feinnes, G.I. 193–194
Felix the Cat 142
Fenwick, Mac 124
Festival Panafricain du Cinéma et de la Télévision de Ouagadougou (FESPACO) 7
Une Fête chez les Chillouks au Bahr al Ghazal (*A Festival of the*

Chilluks, Bahr el Ghazal; 1910) 68, 75
Feyder, Jacques 56
Field, William O. 26, 68–69, 79
Fight Between a Lion and a Tiger 144
Fillis, Frank 20
Film in Colonial Development conference (1948) 118
First-Aid—It's Easy to Learn 148
First Farce (1935) 182, 193
First National Pictures 66
5-Inch Siege Guns Crossing the Vaal River (1900) 48
Flaherty, Robert 73, 75
For the Red Flag (1920) 153
Forbes, Rosita 25–26, 52
Fournier, Father 80
Franklin, Harry 119
Frederick Wulsin's Travel Footage of Africa (1927) 68
French Overseas Ministry 11
Friedrich, Adolf 79
From Cape to Cairo (1908) 47
From Here to Eternity (1953) 104
From Kraal to Mine 138
From Red Blanket to Civilization (1925) 13, 107, Ch. 5 *passim*
From Red Sea to Blue Nile (1926) 52
From Rhodesia via Katanga to Angola, Bulawayo to Elizabethville and Kambove to Lobito Bay (1913) 46
From the Manger to the Cross (1912) 107–108
Fuhrmann, Wolfgang 41
Furkel, Georg 41

Gale, Beresford 167
Gann, L.H. 115
Garner, Ray 82–83
Garner, Virginia 82–83
Gatti, Attilio 47
Gaumont 77, 179
Gaumont *Actualités* 48
Gaumont-British Instructional Films 178, 191
Gay Divorcee (1934) 103
Gehrts, Meg 26
Gemmill, William 110, 135, 139–141
Genova, James 3, 43
Genval, Ernest 44
Gershoni, Yekutiel 115
Gertie the Dinosaur (1914) 19
Getino, Octavio 3
Gide, Andre 42
Gilg, Alan 43, 58
Glimpses of Native Life in Basutoland 139
Glover, T.A. 52–53
Glover Memorial Hall 29–30, 32, 35
Gold (1938) 67
The Golden Stallion (1927) 107, 116, 129
Goldschmidt, Walter 76
Gomes, Flora 6

Gone with the Wind (1939) 30
Goona-Goona (1932) 54
Gordon, Robert 26
The Gorilla Hunt 107
Gramsci, Antonio 15
Graphic 93
The Great Kimberley Diamond Robbery (1911) 45
Griale, Marcel 67–68, 76
Grierson, John 152, 155
Griffith, Alison 5
Grimshaw, H.A. 173
Groupe Farid 4
Gumu (1935) 183
Gunning, Tom 46
Guns in the Desert (aka *Italy Beware*, 1941) 198
Gutsche, Thelma 8, 10

Haddon, Alfred Cort 73, 113
Half Track Heroes: The Crusades of André Citroën (2006) 57
Hall, Mourdant 51
Hall, Stuart 126
Hallendorff, J.E. 106, 108, 118
Hardt, Georges-Marie 56
The Hare and the Leopard (1935) 190
Harmon Foundation 82
Harvard African Expedition of 1934 (1934) 72
Hays Code (1934) 125
Healthy Babies (1936) 185–186, 193
Heart of Africa (aka *Lady Mackenzie's Big Game Pictures*, 1915) 61
Heath, Elizabeth 17
Hell Below Zero (1931) 84
Herskovits, Melville 75
Hertz, Carl 18
Hides (1935) 182
High Yields from Selected Plants (1936) 185, 189
Hobsbawm, Eric 128
Hoefler, Paul 22, 74–75, 83–84
Hoernle, Alfred 178
Hoffman, Carl von 52, 75
Hofmeyr, Jan 87, 102
Holmes, Burton 49–50, 68
Holt, Jack 119
Home Alone 2: Lost in New York (1992) 1
Hondo, Med 6
Hookworm (1936) 186
Hookworm Campaign on the Kenya Coast (aka *Harley Street in the Bush*, 1926) 165, 168–169
Horatio-Jones, Edward 17
Hourdebise, Jean 29
How Accidents Happen 148
How an African Tribe Is Ruled Under Colonial Government (1938) 83
Hoxie, Jack 119
Hubbard, Margaret 36, 64, 67, 77
The Hunters (1957) 76
Hunting Big Game in Africa (1909) 83
Hunting Big Game in Africa with Gun and Camera (1923) 62

Huxley, Julian 163, 201
Hyman, Edward 47

In French Guinea, West Africa (1914) 48
In the Land of the Zulus (1930) 47
India To-day (1925) 82, 106
Indian Cinematograph Committee 157
Industrialization of the African 107, 138
L'Industrie du diamant au Kasaï (*The Diamond Industry in Kasai*, 1919) 44
Infant Malaria (1936) 186
Ingagi (1930) 84
Institut für den Wissenschaftlichen 73
Instituto Nacional de Cinema (INC) 7
Interesting Incidents Here and There (1917) 93
International Committee on Ethnographic Films 73
International Institute of Educational Cinematography 169
International Missionary Council (IMC) 173–174
Into Morocco (1930) 50
Invasion of the Body Snatchers (1956) 120
Isherwood, Albert A.M. 178
Izod, Alan 200

Jamieson, Effie 173
Jeeves, Alan 132, 150
Johnson, Martin 36–37, 62–65, 75, 77
Johnson, Osa 36–37, 62–65, 75, 77
Joint Councils of Europeans and Natives 87
Jones, Col. C.J. Buffalo 59
Jones, Thomas Jesse 160–161, 174
Jungle Gods (1927) 51
Jungle Joy Ride (1918) 93
Jungle Killer (1932) 84
Jungle Terror (1949) 38
Kahlil, S. 35
Kalibala, Ernest 187–189
Kasavubu, Joseph 58
Kasoma 199
Kayamba, Martin 189
Kaye, Alfred 45
Kearton, Cherry 64, 83
Keaton, Buster 97, 107
Keïta! Le Heritage du griot (*Keita! The Heritage of the Griot*, 1995) 8
Keppel, Frederick 177
Ker, Donald 75
Kernel (spliced into 7 mining recruitment films) 142–143
Kid Auto Races at Venice, Ca. 108
Kif Tebbi (1928) 42
Kinetoscope 17–18
Kinna-Uganda (K-U) 7
Kluxen, Guido 72
Kodak 26, 69, 86, 187
Korda, Zoltan 4

Kouyaté, Dani 8
Kumekucha: From Sunup 80
!Kung Bushmen Hunting Equipment (1972) 76

Labour Conditions at Geita Mine (1936) 189
Land of the Moors (1926?) 76
Landau, Paul 9
Landing of Savage South Africa at Southampton (1899) 47
Larkan, Bill 144
Larkin, Brian 25
Larson, Ruth 67
The Last King of Scotland (2006) 7
Latham, Geoffrey Chitty 37, 102, Ch. 7 passim
Laval Decree 5, 34, 42
La Leçon de cinéma (*The Cinema Lesson*, 1951) 4
Leibalala (*Sweetheart*, 1925) 77
Le Lèpre (*Leprosy*, 1938) 44
Letcher, Owen 140–141
Das letzte Paradies (*The Last Paradise*, 1932) 62
L'Herbier, Marcel 4
Lieberenz, Paul 61–62
Lt. Rose and the Royal Visit (1911) 93
The Life of a Plant 163
Life on the Zambezi River (1908?) 48
Little Belgium (1942) 45
Livingstone (1925; re-released as *Stanley*, 1933) 82
Livingstone, David 39–40, 58, 112
Lloyd, Harold 107
London-Cape Town-London Airways Survey 61
London Missionary Committee 176
London Missionary Society (LMS) 81–82
Loram, Charles T. 111, 160
Loutfi, Martine 113
Lowell Thomas' Film of Lawrence of Arabia (1920) 61
The Lower Nile (1916) 50
Lubalu, Emmanuel 4
Luciano Serra, pilota (*Luciano Serra, Pilot*, 1938) 4
Lugard, Frederick 160, 178
Lumière 18, 19, 29, 46, 56
Lumumba, Patrice 58

Macaulay, Herbert 19, 29, 35
Machin, Alfred 59–60, 68, 73, 75
Mackenzie, Lady Grace 61
Macnair, D.A. 86
A Madcap of the Veldt 140
Making a Living (1914) 109
La Maladie du sommeil (*Sleeping Sickness*, 1937) 44
Maltby, Richard 10
Marey, Etienne-Jules 73
Mark of the Renegade (1951) 31
Marshall, John 76
Martin, Phyllis 34
Martin Johnson African Expedition Corporation 63

Maryknoll Society 80–81
Matadi (1909) 44
Mattera, Don 129–130
Mayer, Ruth 25
McCay, Winsor 19
Meanderings in Africa (1922) 62
Méliès, Georges 19
Melville Herskovits' Film Study of West Africa (1931) 75
Mensch und Tier im Urwald (*Man and Animal in the Jungle*, 1924) 62
Mer Island Ceremonial Dance (1898) 118
Mesguich, Felix 46
Mill Hill Fathers Uganda Missionary Film (1920) 79
Mill Hill Missionaries 79
Mines' Compound Cinema Circuit 82–83, 129, 144
Ministry of Information (MOI) 171, 197
Les Miserables (1925) 107
Mission Dakar-Djibouti 67
Missionary Film Committee (MFC) 82
Mr. Tea and Mr. Skokiaan (1939) 149
Mr. Wise and Mr. Foolish Go to Town 149, 151–152
Mitchell and Kenyon 47
Mobile Propaganda Unit 171
Moi, un noir (*I, a Negro*, 1958) 76
Moir, James 172
Molefhi, Kgosi 35
Mongita, Albert 4
Montgomery, H.R. 191
Moorman, Melissa 10
Mortu Nega (*Death Denied*) 6
Mouillot, Frederick 20
Mountains of St. Gothards 93
Mouramani (1953) 4
Msukumu Farmer (1936) 185
Mudalla 36, 67
Mueda, Memória e Massacre (*Mueda, Memory and Massacre*, 1980) 7
Müller, Carl 41
Musée de l'Homme 73
Musser, Charles 20
Mussolini, Benito 41
Mutual Film Company 52
Mwansa, D.C. 201
The Mysterious Rider (1927) 119

Nadiope, William Wilberforce Kajumbula 37
Nanook of the North (1922) 73, 75
Natal (1935) 143
Native Affairs Department (NAD) 104
Native Life in the Cape Province (see also *From Red Blanket to Civilization*) 131, 137
Native Recruiting Corporation (NRC) 92, 132, 139, 143–146
Native Veterinary Assistants (aka *Veterinary Training of African Natives*, 1936) 186

Nell, Louis 119
Neville-Jones, the Reverend 178
The New Adventures of Tarzan (1935) 107
New Cowpuncher (1912) 94
New Zimbabwe (1982) 80
Newsreels 48–49
Ngakane, Lionel 4
Nigerian Film Corporation 7
The Night Watchman's Story 179
Nissen, R.C.E. 45–46
Nixon, Rob 124–125
Nkosi, Lewis 125
Nkrumah, Kwame 123
Nollywood 7
Northern Sports Under Southern Skies (1919) 93
Notcutt, Leslie Alan 37, Ch. 7 passim
Nyerere, Julius 80

Oboler, Arch 80
Oil Palm of Nigeria (1928) 153
Okome, Onookome 123–124, 128
Oldham, Joseph 160–161, 163–164, 173, 178
On the Footsteps of Stanley (1955) 34, 59
The Only Way (Safety First) 93
Onofre, José 22
Optique belge 44
L'Or (*Gold*, 1938) 44
Orde-Brown, Major Granville St. John 178
Orenstein, Alexander 148
Orr, James Russell 165–167
Osman, Maqar 22
Osman, Mohamed 22
Our Gang (1930s shorts) 107
Outposts of Empire: British East African Troops Entraining on an Expedition Against German Territory (1915) 49
Overseas Cinema Commission 43
Les Palabres de Mboloko (*The Palaver of Mboloko*) 142

Pan-African Federation of Filmmakers (FECACI) 4
Pape, Richard 58
Parrish, Fred 74
Pas Op Wena! (*Look Out, You!*) 148
Passfield, Lord (Sidney Webb) 156, 165
Passing of the Third Floor Back (1918) 107
Paterson, Dr. Arthur Rutherford 165, 167–169, 177
Pathé 48–49, 59, 68–69, 154
Patterson, Frederick 85
Paul, Robert W. 18, 25
Paul J. Rainey's African Hunt (1912) 61
Pearse, S.H. 35
Pearson, George 152, 197
Peasant Holdings (aka *African Peasant Farms—The Kingolwira Experiment*, 1936) 186

Index

Pêcheurs Wagenia (*Wagenia Fishermen*, 1952) 45
Peeps into Basutoland 139
Peffer, Nathania 177
Perrings, Charles 190
Peter Pan (1924) 107
Phalke, Dadasaheb 156
Phelps-Stokes Fund 174, 179
Phillips, Ray 13, 82, Ch. 3 *passim*, 116, 118, 121, 144, 160, 173–175, 178
Phimister, Ian 15
Pickaninny's Christmas 107, 110
Pilgrim's Progress (1912) 107, 185
Pim, Howard 87
Pinky (1949) 104
Plaatje, Solomon 35
Place des Consuls, á Alexandrie (1897) 46
Plantations cacaoyères du Mayumbe (*Cocoa Plantations of Mayumbe*, 1919) 44
Les Pneus gonflés (*Inflated Tires*, 1953) 4
Pöch, Rudolph 74
Pond, Alonzo 26, 72, 76
Pondoland (1935) 143
Port Sunlight 179
Post Office Savings Bank (1935) 181, 191–192
Powdermaker, Hortense 126–127
Power, Marcus 11, 23
Prasch, Thomas 18
Pratt, Mary Louise 26
La Première Traverse rapide du desert (329 heures) (*The First Rapid Crossing of the Sahara [329 Hours]*, 1924) 56
Preserving Eggs 185
Prins Albert in het Centrum van Kongo (*Prince Albert in Central Congo*, 1910) 44
Prize Performing Ponies 93
Promenade en AEF (*A Stroll Through French Equatorial Africa*, 1931) 42
Promio, Jean Alexandre 46
Public Relations Media Division 152
Pyramids from the Air (1923) 61

Q Ships 166
Quand le nègre danse (*When the African Dances*, 1938?) 44

Raeburn, Michael 5
Rainey, Paul 60–61
Raja Harischandra (1913) 156
Der Ranger (never produced) 62
Raymond-Millet, J.K. 42
The Real Streets of Cairo (1916) 50
Les Réfugies (*The Refugees*, 1956) 5
Regnault, Felix 73
Reinelt, Léon 44
De Reis van Prins Albert in Kongo (*Prince Albert's Journey to the Congo*, 1910) 44
Reliving the Past (1930) 72, 77
Renault, Louis 56

Rheinallt-Jones, John David 111, 118, 125, 160, 173
Rhodes, Cecil 52, 81, 94
Rhodes of Africa (1936) 77
Rhodesia Countdown (1969) 5
Rhodesia To-Day (1912) 45
The Rink (1916) 109
Road to the Pyramids (1921) 50
Roberts, H.D. 47
Robeson, Eslanda 94, 147, 189
Robeson, Paul 8, 178, 189
Robeson, Stella 8
Robin Hood (1922) 107
Rockefeller Foundation 176
Rodrigues, Manuel 22
Roosevelt, Leila 53–56
Roosevelt, Theodore 59, 61
Roosevelt in Africa (1910) 60
Ross, Emory 82
Rossi, Aurélio 74
Rouch, Jean 6, 73, 75
Roux, Edward 90
Rutherford, Eric 199

Safety-First on the Mines 148
Sakiet Sidi Youssef (1958) 5
Sampson, Anthony 28, 124
Sanders of the River (1935) 8
Savage South Africa—Savage Attack and Repulse (1899) 47
Savage Splendor (1949) 67
Schapera, Isaac 178
Schlesinger, Isodore 135, 149
Schomburgk, Hans 26, 61–62, 79
Die Schwarze Katze (*The Black Cat*) 34
Scott, Clifford 87
Scramble for Africa 41, 51
Selig, William 74–75, 83
Selig Polyscope 83
Sellers, William 28, 139, 162, 165, 198, 200–201
Selous, Frederick 59
Sembène, Ousmane 6
Semon, Larry 97, 107
Seven Brothers of Thibar (1953) 80
Shangase, Hlambisinye 112–114, 121
Shaw, Mabel 174
Shiels, Thomas Drummond 167, 178
Shooting Big Game with a Camera (1927) 85
Short, John 40
Siliva Zulu (1927) 47
Simba, the King of Beasts (1928) 63–64, 110
The Sin Ship (1931) 103
Skladanowsky, Emil 18, 20
Skladanowsky, Max 18, 20
Slessor, Mary 81
Smithsonian-Chrysler Expedition 69
Smyth, Rosaleen 8
A Sneaky Boer (1901) 48
Snow, Professor H.A. 62
Soil Erosion (1935) 183
Soil Erosion at Machakos (1936) 194

Solanas, Fernando 3
Soleil Ô (*Oh, Sun*, 1967) 6
Son of Ingagi (1940) 84
Song After Sorrow (1938) 83
Sons of Bwiregi (1976) 80
Sorceror's Village (1959) 38
Sous les masques noirs (*Under the Black Masks*, 1938) 76
Spearpoint, Cecil F. 116–117
Lo squadrone bianco (*The White Squadron*, 1936) 42
Ssemwogerere, Hajji Ashraf 7
Stage Plays and Cinematograph Exhibition Ordinance 103
Stampede (aka *Africa in Flames*, 1930) 84
Stanley, Henry Morton 39, 58
De Stanleyville à Bukama par la voie des eaux (*A River Journey from Stanleyville to Bukama*, 1929) 44
Stannard, Matthew 4
Staples, Amy 67
Starr, Frederick 74
Stevenson, Rex 8
Stokes, Melvyn 10
The Story of Bamba (1939) 83
Street with No Name (1948) 124
Strong, Richard Pearson 72
Sunset Pass (1929) 119
Swanson, Donald 199
Symons, Humphrey 58

Taberer, Henry 87, 108, 131, 134–135
A Tale of Gurgaon 158
Tallents, Stephen 155
Tanga Travel (1935) 182–183
Tarzan of the Apes (1918) 8
Tarzan the Mighty (1928) 89
Taussig, Michael 25, 120
Tax (1935) 191
Taylor, Clyde 12
Tea (1935) 182–183
The Ten Commandments (1923) 107
Thema, Richard V. Selope 87–88, 100
Thief of Baghdad (1924) 107
This Progress 179
Thomas, Lowell 61
Through Africa Unarmed (1937) 67
The Time of Lagos 32
Tobruk (1941) 49
Tomahawk (1951) 31
La Touque (1953) 80
Touré, Mamadou 4
Trader Horn (1931) 27
Trailing African Wild Animals (1923) 62–63
La Traversée du Sahara (*Crossing the Sahara*, 1923) 56
Treatt, Chaplin 52–53, 84
Treatt, Stella Court 52–53, 84
A Trip on the Rhodesian Railway, Amongst the Central African Natives (1908?) 47
Tropical Hookworm (1936) 165

Tuckett, F. Roy 61
Turn Left—The Riffs Have Risen (1933/1981) 58
The Two Brothers (1939) 149–150

Udadike, Nwachukwu 15
Uganda Boy Scouts (1936) 189
Ujamaa 80
Uncle Josh at the Moving Picture Show (1902) 25
Uncle Sam at Work (1916?) 93
Une Nation, l'Algérie (*One Nation, Algeria*, 1955) 5
Unhooking the Hookworm (1920) 165
Unser Kamerun (*Our Cameroon*, 1937) 62
Untamed Africa (1933) 66
Up the Nile to Central Africa (1928) 26, 68
The Upper Nile (1916) 50
Urban, Charles 47

Van Bever, L. 45
Van Dyke, W.S. 26
Van Haght, P.C. 111
Van Onselen, Charles 15, 96
Varre, Andre de la 51
Vaughan, J. Koyinde 28
Vaughan, Megan 25, 150
Vautier, René 4, 5
Vernon, Roland Venables 165–167, 177–178
Vickers-Haviland, L.A.W. 196
Vieyra, Paulin 4
Vilakazi, Absalom 116, 121
Le Ville de Saint Louis de Sénégal (*The city of Saint Louis, Senegal*, 1914) 48
Visages du Congo Belge (*Faces of the Belgian Congo*, 1950?) 45
Vischer, Hanns 160–161, 167, 178, 195
De Voortrekkers (1916) 140
Voyage au Congo (*Travels in the Congo*, 1927) 42
Le Voyage dans la lune (*A Trip to the Moon*, 1902) 19

Vukani (*Awake*, 1962) 4
Waite, George 72, 77
Wakilindi Saga (1938) 196
Wanderkinos 22
Wanderwell, Captain 53
Warner Bros. 66
Warwick Trading Company 47
Webber, Walter 87
Weber 73
Wechsler, Lazar 50
Der Weg in die Welt (*Stroll Around the World*, 1947) 62
Wells, Carveth 84
Wetherell, Captain 21
Weule, Karl 73
Wexelsen, 22, 30
What Price Hollywood (1932) 103
What to Do in Case of Fire 148
Wheels Across Africa (aka *Dark Rapture*, 1936) 54
White Fathers 79, 81

The White Goddess of the Wangora (1913) 27
White Miners' Rand Revolt (1922) 96–98
White People, Part One (1935?) 183
White People, Part Two (1936?) 183
White People, Part Three (1936?) 183
Why Change Your Husband (aka *Red Hot Sinners*, 1931) 103
Widmark, Richard 124–125
Wild Cargo (1934) 55
Die Wildnis Stirbt (*The Wildlife Is Dying*, 1933) 62
Wilson, Godfrey 184
Wings Over Africa (1934) 61
Wings Over Ethiopia (1935) 50
The W.N.L.A. in Portuguese East Africa (1920) 139
Wonders of the Congo (1931) 63
World Missionary Council 173
Wrong, Margaret 187–188
Wulsin, Frederick 26, 68

Yeelen (*Brightness*, 1987) 8

Zannuck, Daryl F. 49
Zanzabuku: Dangerous Safari (1956) 67
Zanzibar and the Clove Industry (1925) 153
Zululand (1935) 143
A Zulu's Devotion 110
Zulu's Pomp 110

www.ingramcontent.com/pod-product-compliance
Ingram Content Group UK Ltd.
Pitfield, Milton Keynes, MK11 3LW, UK
UKHW050533150426
5217IPUK00026B/1914